NEPAL'S ECONOMY IN DISARRAY: THE POLICIES AND POLITICS OF DEVELOPMENT

NEPAL'S ECONOMY IN DISARRAY: THE POLICIES AND POLITICS OF DEVELOPMENT

Pushkar Bajracharya
Mohan Das Manandhar
Rojan Bajracharya

ADROIT

Adroit Publishers

NEW DELHI

Published by
ADROIT PUBLISHERS
4675/21, Ganpati Bhawan, Ansari Road,
Daryaganj, New Delhi-110 002
Phone : 011-23266030
adroitpublishers@gmail.com

ISBN : 978-81-87393-76-4

Cover Design: Lotus Head Design and Studio

Layout: Dongol Printers, Kathmandu
E-mail: dongolprinters@gmail.com

TABLE OF CONTENTS

LIST OF TABLES

LIST OF FIGURES

FOREWORD

Nepal, the country with long prosperous history, remains in fragility, vulnerability, misery, poverty, deprivation and under-development in recent times both due to internal as well as external reasons. Though we must be bold enough to take the responsibility rather than blaming others. The geographical unification heralded new Nepal in the eighteenth and early nineteenth centuries was derailed by internal squabbles within royal court ultimately resulting the country in the Dark Age of autocratic Rana regime. In the era, the state remained in global isolation with negligible initiatives on taking the state, society and its people out of the primitive stage and conservative orientation. It was only after advent of democracy in 1950, the country initiated development efforts albeit with limited and dichotomous vision under the aegis of ritual and conservative orientation with the focus more on consolidating state power rather than to take it forward meaningfully. The donor support played an instrumental role to take forward this development initiative as the country had severely limited financial and technical resources of its own. Development planning process continued to postulate the changes and reforms under the aegis of autocratic Panchayati regime reinstated after taking over the state power by the King in 1960. The reestablishment of democracy in 1990 raised hopes of speedy economic development but the political parties could not come out with clear and concrete approach of economic development with right vision and common agreement unlike during the people's movement phase to take the country forward with fast and judicious development. Consequently, development planning process remained ritualistic and its visions, goals, objectives and strategies mostly disoriented, directionless and dichotomous. So the country could not achieve what it could have done or what is needed to be done.

The country's contemporary debate, after the establishment of federal democratic republic in 2015, is on attaining prosperity for which ritual and conservative orientation needs to be superseded with innovational and forward looking approach. The economic liberalization started in early nineties have stimulated Nepali market to drive on its own but the conservative mentality of state administration and extreme oppositional politicking decelerated the pace or camouflaged the vision. Hence, neither there is optimal utilization of country's resource nor there are innovations to further industrialize the country. In addition, high political aspirations towards rights based advocacy coupled with limited market promotion approach have invited unfavorable environment. The 10 years long Maoist conflict further enhanced the disorientation though it contributed in bringing fundamental changes in the political and social dimensions of the country. The issue therefore is bringing a balance between the reforms of the early nineties that showed significant inspiration in generating growth and development, initiatives to introduce the social welfare programmes oriented to bring equity and ensuring of promoting inclusive society with adequate rights need to be balanced for realizing prosperity as is envisioned in the Constitution of Nepal, 2015. There is need to rethink on how to tradeoff between institutionalization of basic fundamental rights, inclusive economy and growth. Reiterating fundamental rights alone is not adequate but it should manifest state's commitment with requisite outlay of resources complemented by efforts to promote conducive environment for economic dynamism which will lead the country towards economic prosperity and improvement in the overall quality of life.

Nepal should be mindful of the geo-political reality before embarking on major decisions as is may be the case anywhere in the world but much more for Nepal in view of its location and strategic considerations. Economic reform initiatives of early nineties have been epoch making creating a foundation for development even when the nation is engulfed in serious instability and conflicts and the government was almost totally unable to drive the development being bogged down in political issues. The vision and the evidence based policy formulation is only sporadic rather than systemic resulting in disjointed and diverse efforts and this needs to be seriously attended to through consolidated efforts, common agreements both in the goals and in strategic paths and with a perspective vision. It may be recalled here that the ninth plan is the first plan to be linked with the perspective vision, the right way to plan and it is highly appreciated that the fifteenth plan also has followed this approach.

This book titled "Nepal's Economy in Disarray: The Policies and Politics of Development" explores on development issues of Nepal with in depth research digging out reasons responsible in the historical, economic, political and the geo-political realms of the country. It is authored by Pushkar Bajracharya, prominent economist and management expert of Tribhuvan University, along with his other two colleagues, Mohan Das Manandhar and Rojan Bajracharya, of Organisation Development Centre (ODC). The book is an analytical and evidence based exploration of development pathway of Nepal ever since its initiation. The book has explored on policy envisioning right from the pre-democratic era and the Panchayat regime up to recent times and it has explained on how development policy framework changes along with the political transformation The book has meticulously reviewed the post nineties political parties' manifestos, policies, budgets and development plans to explain the economic development framework of Nepal and its outcomes. The book has explained the evolution of development planning process and various instruments being introduced in the course of time. The sector wise chapters on agriculture, industry and others have dug down on policy instruments, institutional mechanisms, achievements, contemporary issues and gaps. Historical evidences explained in the book are encouraging and it makes readers easy to understand whatever is happing today or put the issues on the right perspective. The book is an important insight to the state which has been reiterating development agenda since last many decades and I fully believe that the book will be very useful to all interested in Nepal's development.

The book has tried its best in explaining what has happened in the economic front up to now. Nevertheless, it hasn't detailed about how the country should move forward. The contemporary context is to unfold Nepal's prosperity and the commitment has been made by all three authors to bring another book in this regard soon. I expect they will bring it soon because it is more necessary and without doubt will be useful. The book has unfolded many aspects of Nepalese development adding value to the development discourse in the country. My warm wishes to the authors in their journey to bring out prominent agenda of Nepal's prosperity and development and sincerely wish success of this book.

PRITHVI RAJ LIGAL
Former Vice Chairman,
National Planning Commission
2019-July-12

ACKNOWLEDGEMENTS

The purpose of this book is to make a comprehensive and in-depth evidence based enquiry on Nepal's economy and development initiatives. Nepal's effort to democracy, citizen's sovereignty and inclusiveness leading to federal republic nation within a short period of democracy have been topsy turvy with varied effects on development. Even Nepali populace seem to be confused about how really to attain development and what is development from our/their own perspective. Have the political leaders/ parties in governance and otherwise, exhibited proper vision and adopted appropriate strategies or not? And, have we really failed as a nation state as is being argued in some quarters? These questions must be answered so that the potential as well as the right perspective may be put forth in a proper way. We have tried to answer all these in this book with a promise to answer the path forward in the forthcoming sequel. Of course, we do realize that there may have been many issues unable to be considered. But our sincere efforts have concentrated to encompass the major aspects and elements of development, as we have defined. We have also tried to unearth explanations hidden in the maze of history supported by our own and others' researches. We believe that this should add value in the area of political economy of the country.

In the process, we have received sincere support from many persons, whom we would like to offer our sincere thanks and express gratitude. Bikram Lama, Shreeya Sigdel, Suraj Kumar Das and Sarita Karki have assisted in reviewing the budgets and plans. Thanks also deserve to Niranjan Dhungel, and Prem Bahadur Singh for helping us to review political parties' manifestos and other political documents. Further, Bashuda Gurung, Prabhas Man Singh and Cynara Manandhar Rana have helped us in review of policies, data and information. In due course of writing this book, we have several round of discussion on political issues with Keshab Man Shakya, former Minister of Science, Technology and Environment. Further, the book also gets lot of insights from discussion with Ajaya Dixit of ISET-Nepal on environmental and climate change issues, Arun Rana of ADB, Nepal Resiclent Mission on Social Protection Issues and Dilli Ghimire, former chairman of NACEUN, on community mobilization issues. Likewise, Suman Aryal of Central Bureau of Statistics and Vikash Satyal of Tribhuvan University have provided us support in data analysis and Krishna Man Pradhan of Nepal Law Society has provided support in explaining laws and regulations. We are also thankful for valuable information provided by Padma Shakya, former Senior Agriculture Extension Officer at Department of Agriculture; Prachanda Man Shrestha, former CEO of Nepal Tourism Board; Rajendra Dahal, former press adviser to President of Nepal; Radhesh Pant, former CEO of Investment Board of Nepal; Bhanu Pokharel, immediate past president of Nepal Hydropower Association; Om B Rajbhandari, Exucutive Committee Member of FNCCI and Shilu Manandhar Bajracharya, Dean, Nepal Open University. Further, Prakriti Shrestha, Satish Bajracharya and Manu Manandhar have assisted us in information collection, tabulation works and other research supports.

We express our sincere and heartfelt thanks to Peter Gill for editing this book, who in many areas, helped to improve by making pertinent comments and we highly appreciate the commendable effort. We duly extend our thanks and express sincere gratitude to Mr. Prithvi Raj Ligal, the former Vice Chairman of National Planning Commission, Government of Nepal for writing the foreword that highlights the book wonderfully.

We like to express our sincere thanks to Madhab for his timely suggestions and expertise to publish this book in present format. Thanks also deserve to Nabindra Dongol of Dongol Printers for all prepress works including layout of the book. At the same time, we also like to thank Akhil Sharma of Adroit Publishers, New Delhi for publishing this book.

PUSHKAR BAJRACHARYA
MOHAN DAS MANANDHAR
ROJAN BAJRACHARYA
2019-July-22

ABBREVIATIONS

ABPMDD	Agri Business Promotion and Marketing Development Directorate
ADB	Asian Development Bank
ADBN	Agriculture Development Bank, Nepal
AIC	Agriculture Inputs Corporation
APO	Asian Productivity Organization
APP	Agriculture Perspective Plan
APROSC	Agricultural Projects Services Centre
ASEAN	Association of Southeast Asian Nations
ATC	Agreement on Textiles and Clothing
BAFIA	Banks and Financial Institutions Act
BIMSTEC	Bay of Bengal Initiative for Multi-Sectoral Technical and Economic Cooperation
BOOT	Build-Own-Operate and Transfer
BOP	Balance of Payment
BP	Bishweshwar Prasad
BRI	Belt and Road Initiative
BRICS	Brazil, Russia, India, China and South Africa
BSc	Bachelor of Science
CA	Constituent Assembly
CAAN	Civil Aviation Authority Nepal
CBS	Central Bureau of Statistics
CCD	Credit to Core Capital plus Deposit
CDO	Chief District Officer
CESRAN	Centre for Strategic Research and Analysis
CIAA	Commission for the Investigation of Abuse of Authority

CPN-Maoist	Communist Party of Nepal-Maoist
CPN-UML	Communist Party of Nepal-Unified Marxist Leninist
CSIDB	Cottage and Small Industry Development Board
CSITC	Cottage and Small Industry Training Center
CTEVT	Council for Technical Education and Vocational Training
DCSI	Department of Cottage and Small Industries
DDC	District Development Committee
DFID	Department for International Department
DFTQC	Department of Food Technology and Quality Control
DOE	Department of Education
DOI	Department of Industry
DOLIDAR	Department of Local Infrastructure Development and Agricultural Roads
EEES	Export Exchange Entitlement Scheme
EFA	Education for All
ESAP	Enhanced Structural Adjustment Program
ESP	Economic Stabilization Program
ETFC	Electricity Tariff Fixation Commission
EU	European Union
FAO	Food and Agriculture Organization
FDI	Foreign Direct Investment
FINNIDA	Finnish International Development Agency
FITTA	Foreign Investment and Technology Transfer Act
FNCCI	Federation of Nepalese Chamber of Commerce and Industries
FY	Fiscal Year
GDP	Gross Domestic Product
GDS	Gross Domestic Saving
GNP	Gross National Product
GNS	Gross National Saving
GON	Government of Nepal

GTZ	Gesellschaft für Technische Zusammenarbeit (German Agency for Technical Cooperation)
H1	East-West Highway
H2	Tribhuvan Highway
H3	Arniko Highway
H4	Prithvi Highway
H7	Mechi Highway
H10	Siddhartha Highway
H13	Karnali Highway
H14	Mahakali Highway
H15	Seti Highway
HDI	Human Development Index
HPI	Human Poverty Index
IBN	Investment Board of Nepal
ICAO	International Civil Aviation Organization
IEA	Industrial Enterprises Act
IEDI	Industrial Enterprises Development Institute
IIDS	Institute for Integrated Development Studies
ILO	International Labor Organization
IMF	International Monetary Fund
INGO	International Non-Government Organization
IPO	Initial Public Offering
IRs	Indian Rupees
IRD	Integrated Rural Development
IT	Information Technology
JICA	Japan International Cooperation Agency
Kcal	Kilocalorie
kg	Kilogram
km	Kilometer
KOICA	Korean International Cooperation Agency
KW	Kilo Watt
KWH	Kilowatt hour
LDC	Least Developed Country
LRMP	Land Resource Mapping Project

LSGA	Local Self Governance Act
MAPs	Medicinal and Aromatic Plants
MDG	Millennium Development Goals
MEDEP	Micro-Enterprise Development Program
MEDPA	Micro-Enterprise Development for Poverty Alleviation
MFA	Multi Fiber Agreement
MNC	Multi-National Company
MOAD	Ministry of Agriculture Development
MOC	Ministry of Commerce
MOCS	Ministry of Commerce and Supplies
MOCTCA	Ministry of Culture, Tourism and Civil Aviation
MOE	Ministry of Education
MOF	Ministry of Finance
MOICS	Ministry of Industry, Commerce and Supplies
MOLE	Ministry of Labor and Employment
MOPA	Ministry of Poverty Alleviation
MOWCT	Ministry of Works, Communication and Transport
MW	Mega Watt
NAC	Nepal Airline Cooperation
NBB	Nepal Bangladesh Bank
NACEUN	National Association of Community Electricity Users-Nepal
NBL	Nepal Bank Limited
NBSM	Nepal Bureau of Standards and Metrology
NC	Nepali Congress
NCP	Nepal Communist Party
NEA	Nepal Electricity Authority
NEPC	National Educational Planning Commission
NEPSE	Nepal Stock Exchange
NESP	National Education System Plan
NFC	Nepal Food Corporation
NFDIN	National Foundation for Development of Indigenous Nationalities
NGO	Non-Government Organization

NIDC	Nepal Industrial Development Corporation
NNDSWO	Nepal National Dalit Social Welfare Organisation
NNRFC	National Natural Resources and Fiscal Commission
NORAD	Norwegian Agency for Development Cooperation
NPA	Non-Performing Assets
NPC	National Planning Commission
NRB	Nepal Rastra Bank
NRs	Nepali Rupees
NSU	Nepal Student Union
NTB	Nepal Tourism Board
NTFP	Non-Timber Forest Products
OAG	Office of Auditor General
OBOR	One Belt One Road
ODC	Organisation Development Centre
PCI	Per Capita Income
PEP	Private Electricity Producer
PPA	Power Purchase Agreement
PPP	Purchasing Power Parity
RBB	Rastriya Banijya Bank
RPP	Rastriya Prajatantra Party
SAFTA	South Asian Free Trade Area
SAP	Structural Adjustment Program
SAP-Nepal	South Asia Partnership Nepal
SAWTEE	South Asia Watch on Trade, Economics and Environment
SBPP	Small Business Promotion Project
SDC	Swiss Agency for Development and Cooperation
SDG	Sustainable Development Goals
SEBON	Securities Board of Nepal
SEC	Securities Exchange Centre
SEE	School Education Examination
SEZ	Special Economic Zone
SLC	School Leaving Certificate
SNV	Stichting Nederlandse Vrijwilligers (Netherlands Development Cooperation)

SPS	Sanitary and Phytosanitary
SRN	Strategic Road Network
TAF	The Asia Foundation
TBT	Technical Barrier to Trade
TEPC	Trade and Export Promotion Center
TFM	Task Force on Migration
TFP	Total Factor Productivity
TIA	Tribhuvan International Airport
TU	Tribhuvan University
UGC	University Grant Commission
UK	United Kingdom
UML	Same as CPN-UML
UMN	United Mission to Nepal
UN	United Nations
UNDP	United Nations Development Program
UNICEF	United Nations Children's Fund
UNESCAP	United Nations Economic and Social Commission for Asia and the Pacific
UNESCO	United Nations Educational, Scientific and Cultural Organization
UNIDO	United Nations Industrial Development Organization
US	Same as USA
USA	United State of America
USAID	United States Agency for International Development
USD	United State Dollar
USSR	Union of Soviet Socialist Republics
VAT	Value Added Tax
VDC	Village Development Committee
VS	Vikram Sambat
WFP	World Food Program
WTO	World Trade Organization

Note: Vikram Sambat (VS) – meaning Vikram calendar – is official calendar of Nepal and it is 57 year and 8 and half months ahead of Gregorian calendar.

NEPAL IN TIMELINE

Political and Other Major Events	Development Initiatives
Early Period	
1744: Initiated Unification of Nepal by King Prithvi Narayan Shah of Gorkha by annexing Nuwakot.	• North South Transit Trade. • Initiative to Develop Rudimentary Market by promoting migration of commercial caste groups. • Limited connectivity and primitive economy.
1775: Death of King Prithvi Narayan Shah.	
1816: Signed Sugauli Treaty with British India, under which Nepal agreed to accept British's quasi surveillance in Nepal's Diplomacy.	
1846: Jung Bahadur Rana took state power through bloody Kot massacre which started autocratic Rana regime, converted King into titular head, got more inclined with British and cut off the country from outer world.	• Introduced Infrastructure, Westernized Education, Industrialization, Commercial Banking, Hydropower and Joint Stock Company with Limited Liability. • Attempted development planning and budgeting. • Economic dependence on India and prevalence of wide circulation of Indian Currency in Nepal's border area. • North South Transit Trade as a main commercial activity.
1923: Signed Treaty with British India which formally introduced Nepal as an Independent Country.	

1934: Nepal-Bihar Earthquake of 8.4 magnitude on 15th January .	
1947: India became Independent.	
1950: Signed Treaty of Peace and Friendship and Treaty of Trade and Commerce with Independent India in July.	
1951: Tripartite Delhi Agreement between King Tribhuvan, Rana and Nepali Congress under the mediation of India which ended Rana Regime and introduced democracy and party politics with the presumption to draft constitution through the constituent assembly.	
Experimental Democracy of 1950s'	
• Country could not draft constitution through constituent assembly as there were squabbles between political parties. • The King kept on consolidating state power through its reinstituted position. • King Tribhuvan died in March, 1955 and his son, Crown Prince Mahendra became the King who had more interest to persist with the power. • First Multi-Party Election of Parliament was announced by King Mahendra in 1959 and, to his surprise, Nepali Congress became the largest party with overwhelming majority.	• Initiation of administrative reform and civil service though there were very limited educated and knowledgeable persons. • Foreign (bilateral) donors support initiated in development. • Introduced the First Five Years Plan in 1956 with prime objective of infrastructure development. • Formally introduced overseas trade. • Established the Supreme Court in 1955. • Established Nepal Rastra Bank as the central bank in 1956. • Increased circulation of Nepali Currency to check use of Indian currency in local transactions.

<table>
<tr><td></td><td>• Controversial Treaties on Koshi and Gandak rivers with India.
• Pegged Nepali Currency with Indian Currency to check exchange rate volatility.
• Pegged Nepali Currency with USD as per global standard.
• Started agro-modernization and commercialization under the support of US.
• Introduced tourism, started formal civil aviation inside and outside of Nepal and established Nepal Airline Cooperation as the national flag carrier in July, 1958.
• India supported to develop first road connectivity from Kathmandu upto the border.
• US and India supported in education and established Tribhuvan University in 1959.
• Started skill based training in mid-fifties under the support of US, Swiss and UMN.
• Introduced industrial development financing with the establishment of Nepal Industrial Development Corporation in 1959.</td></tr>
<tr><td colspan="2">Panchayati Era of King's Direct Rule</td></tr>
<tr><td>1960: The King took over the state power in bloodless coup with the backing of army and suspended the constitution, parliament and party politics.</td><td rowspan="2">1960's Decade:
• Brought the Second Three Years Plan in 1962 with prime objective to improve data management and institute Panchayat Administrative structure.
• US support to strengthen institutional capacity of data management in early sixties.</td></tr>
<tr><td>1961: Nepal was divided into 14 zones and 75 districts.</td></tr>
</table>

1962: Brought new constitution with non-party Panchayat system under which the King took total control over the state. **1968:** Introduced Zonal Commissioner through constitutional amendment. Though the post nominated by the King was instituted as *de jure* administrative unit, its main *de facto* work was to serve as intelligence of the King and watch on power abuse and political activities at local level.	• Initiated land reform in 1964. • Initiated to develop East West Highway (H1) along Terai flat-land in 1962 with commitment of support from India, US, USSR and UK. • Support from China to build Arniko Highway (H3) connecting her border with Kathmandu in 1964. • Brought the Third Five Years Plan in 1965 with prime objective of agriculture development. • Initiated to establish Public Enterprises under the support of USSR and China followed by similar support from Japan, Netherlands and others in seventies and eighties. • Introduced import substitution to increase domestic production and to check external dependency but trade with India was open. • Introduced Export Entitlement Scheme to manage overseas trade. • Established Rastriya Banijya Bank in 1966. • Established Agriculture Development Bank in 1968. • Established Nepal Electricity Cooperation and Department of Electricity and India, USSR and China supported to add hydropower plants. • Initiated to develop industrial district/ estate under the support of US and India.

	• In mid-sixties, Norway missionary stepped in to develop human skills by introducing electro-mechanic and hydro mechanic skills. • Different donors started to explore hydropower in major river basins like Karnali, Seti, Kamala, Bagmati, Rapti and others.
1972: King Mahendra died in January and his son, Crown Prince Birendra, became the King. **1979:** King Birendra tested public opinion on Panchayat system through referendum due to pressure over his regime and the result marginally favored the King.	**1970's Decade:** • Brought the Fourth Five Years Plan in 1970 with prime objective of regional development. • Demarcation of Four Development regions in 1972 and Far-West was added as the fifth in 1982. • Brought the Tourism Master Plan in 1972. • Different agro subsidies were started since early seventies. • Multilateral Donors like the World Bank and ADB stepped in to support Nepal. • Brought the Fifth Five Years Plan in 1975 introducing flexible planning. • The World Bank started to develop Kulekhani I Hydropower in 1977 under consortium financing with Japan and Kuwait Fund and ADB stepped in to develop transmission line in mid-seventies. • Introduced Integrated Rural Development (IRD) approach. • Introduced Strategic Road Network.

<table>
<tr><td></td><td>• Introduced National Education System Plan in 1971 at school level and in 1973 at higher education level.
• Initiated secondary security market with the establishment of Securities Exchange Centre (SEC) in 1976.
• Prepared Land Resource Mapping Project (LRMP) in 1978.
• Dual Exchange Rate replaced Export Entitlement scheme in late seventies to manage trade.
• Established public enterprises relating to paddy and rice export trade.</td></tr>
<tr><td>1980: Amended the constitution which made the National Assembly (Rastriya Panchayat) an apex body of directly-elected representatives but on non-party basis.</td><td rowspan="3">1980's Decade:
• Brought the Sixth and the Seventh Five Years Plans in 1980 and 1985 respectively with focus to fulfill basic needs.
• Introduced Block Production approach in agriculture under the support of US in early eighties.
• Set up Nepal Electricity Authority as the sole authority in mid-eighties by amalgamating Nepal Electricity Cooperation, Department of Electricity and others.
• USD was floated breaking pegging in early eighties.
• Opened banking to joint venture banking in early eighties and NABIL bank was established as the first joint venture bank.</td></tr>
<tr><td>1989: Economic blockade of India due to worsening diplomatic relations with India and inability to renew trade and transit treaty.</td></tr>
<tr><td>1990: Nepali Congress and Leftists led mass democratic movement which toppled King's direct rule in April 1990. Interim government was formed with Nepali Congress leader, Krishna P Bhattari, as Prime Minister in 19th April.</td></tr>
</table>

	• Instituted SEBON in 1984 as the regulator of secondary security market. • Introduced Economic Stabilization Program (ESP) in 1985 under the support of IMF to address deepening economic crisis. • Introduced Structural Adjustment Program (SAP) in 1986 under the initiative of the World Bank. • Established Credit Information Bureau in 1989. • The World Bank stepped into Arun III hydropower project in late eighties. • Duty Drawback and Bonded Ware House introduced in late eighties. • Paddy and rice export trade companies dismantled due to lack of exportable surplus. • Forestry Master Plan prepared in late eighties.
Democratic Era of Post 1990	
1991-1993: General election held in May, 1991 which gave full majority to Nepali Congress in the parliament and the government formed under the leadership of Girija P Koirala.	**1991:** • Nepali Congress Government announced to liberalize economy in FY 1990/91 budget. • Allowed to open bank account in foreign currency. • Established Citizens' Investment Fund in March to mobilize domestic savings and to provide merchant banking. • Brought laws on labor management.

	1992: • Brought the Eighth Five Years Plan with prime focus on economic liberalization, growth and employment generation. • Brought New Industrial Policy, Foreign Investment Policy and Hydropower Policy to facilitate the private sector. • Introduced partial convertibility in current account in March. • Amended Financial Company Act to promote Finance Companies and its new financial instruments like hire purchase, lease finance and housing loans. • Enactment of new Industrial Enterprises Act and Foreign Investment and Technology Transfer Act. • NECON Airways established as the first private sector airliner in September. • Formed National Education Commission to improve higher education. • Initiated Basic and Primary Education Program. **1993:** • Introduced full convertibility in current account in February. • Completely Abolished Licensing System by budget of FY 1993/94. • Established Nepal Stock Exchange (NEPSE) Ltd replacing SEC. • Introduced Value Added Tax. • Formed University Grants Commission.

	• Initiated Secondary Education Development Program. • Signed SAPTA. • FINNIDA Map prepared.
1994: Girija P Koirala dissolved his government and the country headed for another election in which CPN-UML emerged as the largest party but short of majority. CPN-UML formed the first communist government in Nepal with Man Mohan Adhikari as the Prime Minister.	**1994:** • Completion of Karnali Bridge in the border of Bardiya- Kailali districts finally culminating East West connectivity started in 1962. • NEPSE opened security trading on 14th January. • Initiated Privatization of Public Enterprises. • Initiated Social Protection Program of Old Age Allowance. • Initiated Mid-Hill East West Highway whose construction even continues at present. • Initiated "Build Your Village Yourself" program. Later similar types of programs continued at irregular interval with different nomenclature.
1995: CPN-UML government dissolved in nine months after its formation which was followed by Nepali Congress government in coalition with pro-monarch Rastriya Prajatantra Party.	**1995:** • The World Bank pulled out of Arun III hydropower. • Launched Agriculture Perspective Plan. • Started removal of agriculture subsidies.
1996: Maoists launched Peoples' Armed Movement in 13th February with demand of People's Republic and abolition of monarchy and constitutional democracy.	**1996:** • Agreement with India on Mahakali River. • Cover page article titled "Good Bye Shangri la" in Newsweek on environmental degradation in Nepal which made tourism.

	business attentive and announced 1998 as Visit Nepal Year. • Kali Gandaki A hydropower plant started with support from ADB. • Brought laws and regulations relating environment. • Norwegian and American FDI in Khimti and Bhotekoshi Hydropower respectively.
1997: • Coalition Government led by Nepali Congress dissolved due to losing no-confidence motion in the parliament. • New coalition government led by pro-monarch Rastriya Prajatantra Party (RPP) was formed in 12th March with Lokendra B Chandra as the Prime Minister but got dissolved within 7 months. • New coalition government led by pro-monarch Rastriya Prajatantra Party (RPP) was formed in 6th October with Surya B Thapa as the Prime Minister but got dissolved within 7 months.	**1997:** • Brought the Ninth Five Years Plan with prime objective of poverty alleviation with perspective vision. • Established Nepal Tourism Board. • Formed Department of Local Infrastructure Development and Agricultural Roads (DOLIDAR).
1998: Coalition government led by Rastriya Prajatantra Party dissolved and Nepali Congress returned to power by heading coalition government.	**1998:** • Visit Nepal Campaign. • Enacted Local Self Governance Act, 1998.
1999: Election of parliament in which Nepali Congress got majority and formed government under the leadership of Krishna P Bhattarai.	**1999:** • Highest Tourist Arrival of the time as aftermath of Visit Nepal 1998.

	• Hijacking of Indian Airline aircraft from TIA (Nepal). • Enactment of new Financial Procedure Act. • Enactment of Private Contractor Act.
2000: Krishna P Bhattarai Government started indirect talks with Maoists but the Bhattarai government got dissolved due to internal squabbles within Nepali Congress and Girija again became the Prime Minister.	**2000:** • Signed Millennium Development Goals in September.
2001: • King Birendra and his family and kins got killed in Royal Massacre in June and the brother of Birendra, Prince Gyanendra, became the King. • The government led by Girija P Koirala dissolved due to internal conflict in NC and Sher B Deuba of NC became the Prime Minister.	**2001:** New Hydropower Policy.
2002: • Girija P Koirala, as NC president, rejected proposal to extend emergency in response to the Maoists movement. • The Prime Minister Sher B Deuba dissolved the parliament. • The King took over power in October.	**2002:** • Brought Industrial Development Perspective Plan. • Created National Dalit Commission, National Women Commission and National Foundation for Development of Indigenous Nationalities. • Brought Tenth Plan under World Bank's PRSP framework.

	• Initiated new financial sector reform programs. • New central bank Act with greater autonomy. • Established Loan Recovery Tribunal.
2003 to 2004: • Country under King's Rule. • Maoists formed caste and ethnic based autonomous peoples' government in January to February, 2004.	**2003 :** • Launched Secondary Education Support Program. • Announced new FDI policy. **2004:** • VAT rate was increased from 10 to 13 percent. • Accession to WTO. • Signed SAFTA Aggrement. • Signed BIMSTEC Aggrement. • Launched Education for All.
2005: Maoists' Conclave in Chunmang decided to make "Democratic Republic" as the immediate political objective while declaring feudalism and monarchy as the main enemies; Signed twelve points agreement between mainstream political parties and the Maoists under the mediation of the India.	**2005:** • Expiry of ATC/ MFA in January. • Initiated to observe Ashad 15 as "Rice Day"[1].
2006: 19 days Peoples' Movement toppled King's direct rule, Maoists became public, Comprehensive Peace	**2006:** • New banking and financial Act (BAFIA) to harmonize laws and regulations governing the financial market.

1 In the farming society of Nepal, Ashad 15 of Vikram Sambat (Vikram Calendar) which lies in the end of June is considered as the end of rice plantation period. So famers celebrate this day by playing in muddy field and eating delicious foods.

Agreement between mainstream political parties and Maoists and formed all party interim government under Girija P Koirala of NC.	• Enactment of new company Act.
2007: Enactment of Interim Constitution to conduct Constituent Assembly election and uprising of Madheshi Movement.	**2007:** • Brought the Eleventh Three Years Development Plan with focus on reconstruction and rehabilitation. • Enactment of BOOT Act. • Enactment of new public procurement Act. • Enactment of new security exchange Act. • Brought Rural Infrastructure Development Strategic Action Plan.
2008: • Uprising of Second Madheshi Movement. • First Constituent Assembly election held with Maoists emerging as the largest party. • Monarchy abolished, Ram Baran Yadav elected as the first President of the country. • Maoists led coalition government with Prachanda as the Prime Minister.	**2008:** • Created Self-Employment Fund. • Reverted back Fertilizer Subsides. • Enactment of Banking Offence Act.
2009: Prachanda government dissolved and UML coalition government formed with Madhav K Nepal as the Prime Minister.	**2009:** • Start of Liquidity Crisis. • Launched School Sector Reform Program.
2010: First Constituent Assembly extended by 2 years.	**2010:** • Launched Visit Nepal 2011 in February.

	• Finance Minister was blocked by Maoists from delivering budget speech in the house.
2011: UML led coalition government formed with Jhala Nath Khanal as the Prime Minister in February and Maoists led coalition government formed with Dr. Babu Ram Bhattarai as the Prime Minister in August.	**2011:** • Brought the Twelfth Three Years Plan with focus on poverty alleviation and LDC graduation. • Launched Contributory Social Security Scheme. • Nepal Tourism Year 2011. • Established Investment Board of Nepal.
2012: First Constituent Assembly dissolved without enacting the constitution.	**2012:** • Maoists militia merged with Nepal Army. • Road widening initiative started.
2013: Election of the Second Constituent Assembly in which NC became the largest party followed by UML and Maoists lost heavily.	**2013:** Initiation to identify poor.
2014: Coalition Government led by NC with Sushil Koirala as the Prime Minister.	**2014 :** • Power Trading Agreement with India. • Brought Thirteenth Three Year Development Plan with focus on LDC graduation.
2015: • Gorkha Earthquake of 7.8 magnitude. • Enactment of Federal Democratic Republic Constitution. • Madheshi Movement against new Constitution.	**2015:** • Brought Agriculture Development Strategy (2015-2035). • Signed Sustainable Development Goal in September. • Post-Earthquake Reconstruction.

• Coalition Government led by UML with K P Oli as the Prime Minister. • Two further districts have been added by splitting Rukum and Nawalparasi. • Bidya Devi Bhandari became the second President of Nepal. • Demarcation of Provinces.	
2016: Coalition Government led by Maoists with Prachanda as the Prime Minister.	**2016:** • Launched School Sector Development Plan. • NEPSE index reached its peak at 1888 on 27th July. • Dematerialized Security Market. • Enactment of new labor act with exit policy.
2017: Coalition Government led by NC with Sher Bahadur Deuba as the Prime Minister, Demarcation of 753 local governments and election of local government.	**2017:** • Enactment of new financial and banking Act with conflict of interest clauses. • Enactment of Act on all Constitutional Commissions. • Enactment of new industrial enterprises Act. • Signed Memorandum of Understanding with China on One Belt One Road (OBOR) initiative framework in March. • Brought Fourteenth Three Year Development Plan with focus on LDC graduation.
2018: • Unification of UML and Maoists. • Election of Federal and Provincial Parliaments in	**2018:** • Brought law relating to Social Security Pension. • Launched Social Security Scheme for formal sector.

which NCP got full majority and Government of NCP formed with K P Oil as the Prime Minister.	• Launched Visit Nepal 2020.
2019 until July: Dissident Group of Dr. Raut entered mainstream politics.	**2019 until July:** • Enactment of new foreign investment Act. • Brought Approach Paper of the Fifteenth Plan in framework of prosperity. • Drafted Fifteenth plan with perspective vision and growth targeting at 10.5 percent.

chapter 1

THE ENTRY

1.1 The Setting: Brief Historical Context Historical evidences suggest Nepal of having been developed since long being aided by the early civilization of the Indus valley and Gangetic civilization and Hwang Ho, Yangtze and Si-Kiang (Chinese) civilization. This early break, however, doesn't seem to have contributed to usher the country into a stage of development constrained both by internal as well as external circumstances[1]. Nepal, despite engaging in planned development since the fifties that to some extent transformed the traditional agrarian economy to modern economy, hasn't been able to attain desired development in multifarious aspects resulting in the persistence of poverty, deprivation and high under employment. On top of that, the development has not been inclusive fueling the feeling of discrimination creating social political problems. Such problems are not only manifest in the daily lives of the people, but have led to violent conflict and has given rise to numerous challenges (Bajracharya, 2013). The nation state has made a substantial transformation in the political front catapulting the kingdom into a federal republic and an ongoing effort to change the socio-economic status of the country, however, has not attained much success so far.

1. In 1 AD, India (33 percent) and China (27 percent) is estimated to have accounted for 60 percent of the global economy that came down to around 20 percent in 1900 during industrial revolution (eighteenth and nineteenth century) and 6 percent in 1970 (Estimated by Angus Maddison of University of Groningen and quoted in Joshi, 2018) meaning that it is not Nepal alone but both its big neighboring countries lagged significantly behind in the development process. China gained steady development only after 1978 under Deng Tiao Xioping and India ushered in the growth in the early nineties pursuant to economic reforms.

Nepal has engaged in planned development[2] since the 1950s. Since that time, the economy has seen major changes from a traditional agrarian economy to a more modern, globalized one. However, despite these changes, there remain high rates of poverty, deprivation, and under-employment. Natural barriers to development in Nepal include its limited resource endowment,

2. Basically, "Development" is considered as a process of enhancing economic and social conditions, priorities, and choices. The term gained popularity after the Second World War as the West brought new programs to (de)colonized countries. US president Harry Truman initiated development assistance in 1949, and from then onward "Development Practice" became an instrument to organize (post) colonial, so-called "backward" countries and their societies. In the beginning, development was defined in terms of industrialization, economic growth, and modernization (Cowen and Shenton, 1996 and Rapley, 2007). It was argued that economic growth would result from political reform and social engineering, and that modernization involved a rejection of traditions in favor of customs and practices of the West. The USSR propounded the Communist development model as an alternative approach after the October revolution and during the Cold War period after the second world war. The Communist model also stressed the importance of industrialization, urbanization, and modernization, but considered the state the main executive agency for development (Ghosh, 2012). But there were failures in Communist countries to protect human rights and sustain economic growth, contributing to the dissolution of the USSR in 1991, with major implications for global geo-politics. The communist approach of development through command economy focused on durable goods, heavy industry and security but failed to meet consumer demands (CESRAN International, 2015). There is also another alternative approach of Quasi-Statist and Neo-Corporatist Model in which government allows private enterprises but also invest at large scale in certain industries and subsidizes for national economic interest (CESRAN International, 2015). It defends for national control over economy against foreign investment and for retaining strong national capitalist class. It further explains that the emerging economies of BRICS (Brazil, China, Russia formed after collapse of USSR, India and South Africa) are largely guided by this model so do the countries like South Korea, Argentina and others. While, Scandinavian Development Model argues for economic foundation with free market capitalism, universalist welfare state, collective bargaining and high unionization (Moene and Wallerstein, 2006). It is to be noted that all Scandinavian countries are ranked high in Inequality-adjusted HDI, Global Peace Index and Happiness Index. Since 1990s, the western approach to development predominates, and it is heavily influenced by neoliberal economics, which had first gained favor in the 1970s due to Robert Solow, T. W. Swan, Milton Friedman and the Chicago School. Since the 1950s, there has been a shift in the Western development agenda from industrialization to structural adjustment, then to globalization, and to the Millennium Development Goals (MDG) and now to Sustainable Development Goals (SDG).

landlocked location, and rugged terrain. These natural factors are compounded by underdeveloped economic and social infrastructure, which, despite improvements, remain inadequate. Connectivity is limited, severely restricting the economy.

Since the country's first Five-Year Plan for economic development in 1956, Nepal has experienced average annual growth of around four percent. After discounting the population growth rate of about two percent during the same period, this has yielded a per-capita growth rate of about two percent per annum. In other words, economic growth has been slow, particularly when compared to neighboring countries – even small countries like Bangladesh and Bhutan.

Following the transition to a democratic government in 1990, Nepal underwent wide-ranging economic reforms that contributed to the acceleration of the economy and brought about improvements in some key sectors, such as industry, trade, and investment. Foreign exchange policies were also reformed. However, the economic

---

But neoliberal development approach is criticized from various perspectives. Dependency theorists criticized neoliberal development thought for being ahistorical, ignoring the role of imperialist exploitation. Pieterse (2001) argues that development is an organized intervention in collective affairs according to a standard of improvement but overtaking role of international institutions and market forces. Development theories and approaches advocated by sociologists like Comte (1830 and 1848) propounded the theory of positivism; Spencer (1855 and 1873) explained social development as an evolutionary approach following Darwin; Durkheim (1873, 1893, 1895 and 1912) explained organic and mechanical solidarity, the suicide and the effect of religion; Weber (1949) explained authority, capitalism and bureaucracy and Parsons (1964 and 1967) explained social systems in the process of adaptation, integration, goal orientation and latency; have contrasting views to the problem of mankind and development. Discrimination on the basis of class, community, caste, race, gender and inequity have evolved as pertinent issues (Drèze and Sen, 2013, Sen, 2000 and Silver, 1995). Furthermore, development discourse has also been criticized for its lack of attention to growing environmental problems, including global warming. Though these issues are gradually getting mainstreamed with global initiatives like MDGs and SDGs, development debate is getting more prominent. Stiglitz (2007) expresses his discontent on globalization and Piketty (2017) on global inequity evolving due to it. Drèze and Sen (2013) argue on development led growth with social security to poor, discriminated and excluded whereas Bhagwati and Panagariya (2013) argue for market led growth to achieve development.

reforms initiated in the 1990s could not be properly sustained, and even when they were, they did not always yield the desired results. Development was uneven geographically and in terms of gender, caste, and ethnicity. Lack of inclusion in development and planning processes fueled perceptions of discrimination. Contradictions and inconsistencies led to growing political turmoil and the rise of the Maoist insurgency from 1996-2006. Political instability slowed down all development processes. It contributed to politicization of many sectors of the economy and other aspects of life, weakened administrative and institutional capacity, and increased problems related to governance (Bajracharya, 2013).

Since the end of the insurgency in 2006, the nation-state has undergone a substantial transformation on the political front, catapulting from a Hindu kingdom to a secular, federal republic. However, efforts to improve the socio-economic situation of the Nepali people have not been very successful even under the new political setup. Nepal remains one of the poorest countries in the world, with about 18.6% of the population living below the poverty line. Nepal still faces regional imbalances, a deepening social divide, and numerous political, social, economic, and cultural problems that are manifest in the daily lives of the people and could still lead to violent conflict (Bajracharya, 2013 and Pyakuryal, 2013). Hence, serious enquiry is required to identify the real causes of Nepal's development shortcomings and seek remedies.

1.2 Growth Scenario The structure of Nepal's economy has changed dramatically over the past half-century or so. Between 1975 and 2019, agriculture's share of GDP declined continuously from 61.3% to 27% (Table 1.1). Industry's share of GDP increased from 10.3% in 1975 to 19.4% in 1995, but declined to 15.2% in 2019. The service sector is the only part of the economy to have experienced a continuously growing share of GDP, reaching 57.8% in 2019.

Table 1.1: Sectoral Contribution to Gross Domestic Product (in %)

GDP by Sector	1975	1985	1995	2005	2015	2019*
Agriculture	71.6	51.2	41.7	35.2	31.7	27.0
Industry	8.2	15.0	19.4	17.2	14.8	15.2
Services	20.2	33.8	38.9	47.6	53.5	57.8

Source: Economic Survey, MOF
* Estimates

However, the structural transformation in GDP has not been accompanied by proportionate changes in labor markets. Despite its shrinking share of GDP, agriculture remains the largest contributor to employment, with more than 60% of the total population fully or partially engaged in this sector today. Seasonal under-employment is a fundamental characteristic of the agricultural economy in Nepal.

High growth in the industrial and service sectors during the 1990s was due in part to deregulation of industrial licensing, liberalization of the foreign exchange regime, reduction in tariffs, and rationalization of domestic tax rates (Bajracharya and Sharma, 1996 and Khanal and Kanel, 2005). However, the economic reforms had only partial impact due to the rise of the armed conflict between 1996-2006. In addition, failure to build capacity, enhance efficiency, and create market-friendly institutions negatively affected the reform process. Persistent power tussles between labor unions and business owners caused significant disruptions in industrial production and development activities. The political transition, lack of infrastructure facilities, and weak government service delivery have all inhibited growth, particularly given Nepal's abundant natural resources. Nepal has yet to take advantage from its proximity to the People's Republic of China and India, two of the world's largest economies which have both experienced strong growth recently.

1.3 Savings and Investment Growth is normally a function of investment. But unusually, in Nepal, investments have been rising without corresponding growth in the economy. From this, it may be deduced that wastage and the costs of development are both increasing. For example, the capital output ratio has increased from 4.3 in 2002 to 5.98 in 2013 and decline to 4.9 in 2019. The traditional argument of increased investment in the infrastructure that is low return sectors as an explanation to enhanced capital output ratio does not hold much ground as we claim to have developed a fair level of infrastructure in the country. This suggests that mismanagement and corrupt practices may have actually increased.

Investment requires sufficient domestic savings. Unfortunately, Nepal has been consistently consuming more and saving less except since 2018. For much of the decade of the 2000s, the gross domestic savings rate stagnated at around one-tenth of GDP (Table 1.2). This growth in savings would not have been possible without assistance from remittances abroad, which are included in the gross national savings rate that increased from 26.9 percent of GDP in 2000/01 to 52.4 percent of GDP in 2018/19. The growth in GNS is explained by remittances while the increase in GDS after 2016 may be explained by higher growth which surpassed the consumption growth and increase in banking practice consequent to Money Laundering Prevention Act, 2008.

Table 1.2: Gross Domestic Saving/ Investment Ratio as Percentage of GDP

Fiscal year	2000/01	2004/05	2009/10	2014/15	2017/18	2018/19*
Gross Domestic Savings Rate (% of GDP)	11.7	11.6	11.5	9.2	17.8	20.5
Gross National Savings Rate (% of GDP)	26.9	28.4	35.9	44.1	47.1	52.4
Gross Domestic Investment Rate (% of GDP)	19.2	19.9	22.2	28.0	34.7	36.9

Source: Economic Survey, MOF
* Estimate

Domestic private-sector investment and foreign direct investment (FDI) have also not been very encouraging. Total private-sector commitment and FDI commitment remained below

NRs 50 billion and NRs. 10 billion, respectively, until FY 2009/10. Investment commitments began to increase only after 2010 reflecting the improvement in political environment or an aspiration for the same.

Figure 1.1: Investment Committed by Private Sector (in NRs Billion)

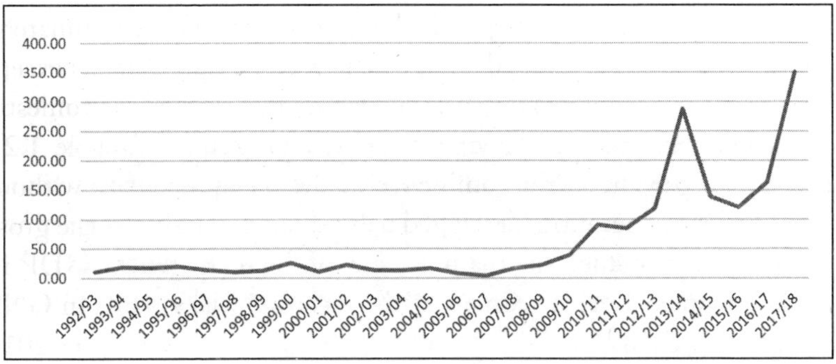

Source: *Industrial Statistics*, Department of Industry

Figure 1.2: FDI Commitment in Nepal (in NRs. Billion)

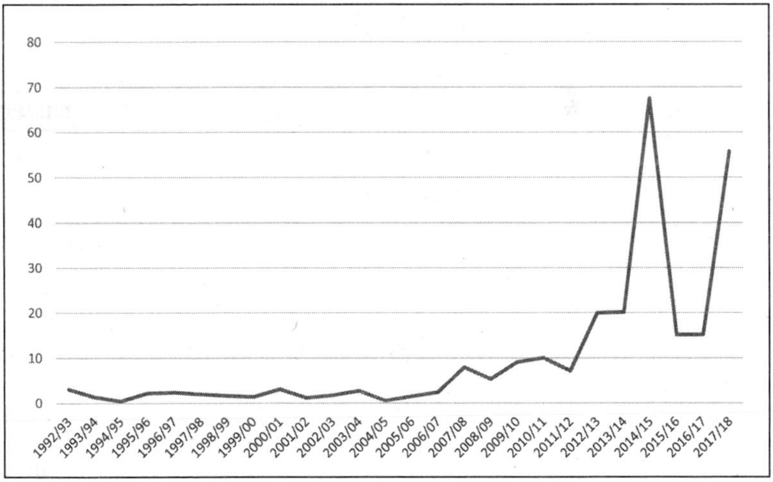

Source: *Industrial Statistics*, Department of Industry

1.4 Employment Situation One of the key indicators of the health of any economic system is its ability to provide a job for anyone who seeks it. The economy must grow to provide jobs for new workers and to provide everyone with a rising standard of living. Income must meet basic needs for food, clothes, shelter, education, medical care, etc. Poverty reduction is directly linked to opportunities for employment, both in the formal and informal sectors.

However, creating full and productive employment opportunities remains a major challenge in Nepal. The government has been allocating annual budgets in sectors that can generate employment for skilled and unskilled labor alike, as well as bringing in new, specifically employment-focused programs.[3] But in the absence of private-sector confidence in the business environment, employment generation has lagged behind targets. Labor migration abroad has become the main source of income generation for many people, but it comes with its own risks and pitfalls (Pyakuryal, 2013).

Table 1.3a: Status of Employment in 2018

Details	Employed	Unemployed	Labor Force
	Number in Thousands		
Nepal	7086	908	7994
Male	4466	511	4977
Female	2640	397	3037
	Percent		
Nepal	88.64%	11.36%	100.00%
Male	89.73%	10.27%	100.00%
Female	86.93%	13.07%	100.00%

Source: CBS, 2019

3. The Government of Nepal (GON) created the Employment Fund in 2008 and the Youth and Small Entrepreneur Self-Employment Fund in 2009 but their contributions in employment generation have been miniscule. Similarly, the GON launched the Prime Minister Employment Program in 2019 with great fanfare, though results have yet to be seen.

Table 1.3b: Working-Age Population in 2018

Details	Not in Labor Force	Labor Force	Working-Age Population
	Number in Thousands		
Nepal	12750	7994	20744
Male	4250	4977	9208
Female	8500	3037	11537
	Percent		
Nepal	61.46%	38.54%	100.00%
Male	46.16%	54.05%	100.00%
Female	73.68%	26.32%	100.00%

Source: CBS, 2019

The unemployment rate is at 11.4 percent in 2018 and 61.46 percent of working age population is not in labor force in 2018 (Table 1.3a and 1.3b).[4] As is often the case in developing countries, Nepal's unemployment rate is not as high as it would be if the country had adequate social protections; the poor simply have to work to survive, even when remuneration is low. Often, the unemployed are educated people from middle-income households who can afford to wait out a period of joblessness. In Nepal's case, unemployment is concentrated among those who have completed secondary education (Campbell, 2010). But, it is worrying that even in the backdrop and introduction of numerous initiatives assisted by exodus of Nepali youth for jobs abroad, the unemployment had started rising with the current rate that may be regarded as very high, a phenomenon that may have serious future implications if not already one.

Challenges to generating employment in Nepal include: low economic growth; a substantial working population involved in low-paying and less-productive agriculture and informal employment; a low skill base associated with the low level of human development;

4. Underemployment is defined as working less than 40 hours a week, while wanting to work more but being unable to do so due to involuntary reasons, or working where skills are mismatched. The working age population is of between 15 and 64 years age.

pervasive vulnerability and uncertainty for businesses; large economic and social disparities; and persistence of conflict, even after the cessation of armed hostilities in 2006. In addition to fighting Nepali labor exploitation abroad, the country must create a more favorable business environment at home in order to attract employment-creating investment. Nepal must also ensure equitable access to employment opportunities from the regional and social perspectives.

1.5 Poverty Situation Many efforts have been made to conceptualize poverty and inequality over the years. Whereas early efforts, such as those by Rowntree, tried to define poverty in absolute terms, later works have also conceptualized poverty in relative terms (Glennerster et al 2004). Absolute poverty is defined as the lack of a basic level of income to achieve a given level of consumption. The ILO's Basic Needs Approach focuses on education, nutrition and health, with reference to the minimum requirements for a decent life. UNDP has produced the Human Poverty Index (HPI) as a measure of deprivation that includes vulnerability to death at a relatively early age, deprivation in knowledge, and lack of decent living standards.

The relative approach produces different definitions for poverty in different societies. As Townsend (1979) observes, "Individuals, families and groups in the population can be said to be in poverty when they lack the resources to obtain the types of diets, participate in the activities and have the living conditions and amenities which are customary, or at least widely accepted and approved, in the societies in which they belong." Others define poverty in terms of deprivation and social exclusion, as a process through which individuals or groups are wholly or partially excluded from full participation in society. According to this definition, the fact of exclusion is forgotten amid the societal tendency to blame the poor for their own poverty. As Bauman (1999) observes, "No society we know of was ever free of a category of people who are seen by the rest as incapable, for whatever reason, of eking out a living by their own effort; of living as the rest do. It is a social decision to classify people in such a way."

Just as there are different definitions of poverty, there are different schools of thought to explain the causes of poverty and inequality. The functional school, propagated by Parsons (1967) and Davis and Moore (1945) emphasizes aspects of harmony, consensus, and functionalism. The conflict school put forward by Marx stresses the importance of conflict, contradictions, and dialectics of power; it does not accept the legitimacy of the prevailing economic order. The cultural school, as explained by Lewis (1966), views the culture of the poor as the reason for their poverty.

Different understandings of the causes of poverty result in different prescriptions to combat it. To the neoclassical economist who believes in the inherent capacity of market mechanisms, poverty and hunger are primarily the result of not allowing markets to function properly. A firm belief in the automatic forces of the market to bring about equilibrium over the long run would mean that these forces must not be tampered with for achieving any short-term objective. Structuralists, on the other hand, tend to point at market failures, market imperfections, and the way a large number of social services resemble public goods meaning that market anyway does not capture public goods and services, the political economy of which is the need for delivering of the services irrespective of economic implications. Vested interests and social-political, structural-legal, tenurial, and economic institutions coalesce and reinforce each other to weaken market mechanisms. Structuralists therefore lay emphasis upon the institutional forces that bias the distribution of products and services to the detriment of the poorest citizens. Neo-Marxists hold a view similar to the structuralists, explaining poverty in terms of the ownership and control of the instruments of production and other productive assets (Foster-Carter, 1973).

The limitations of these three approaches – as far as their ability to explain poverty is concerned – are fairly well known and researched. The neoclassical approach can easily ignore the complex realities that often lead markets to become dysfunctional. The structuralist analysis tends to explain too much in terms of structures and too little in terms of market pressures and the way in which institutions adjust to them, as well as the socio-political causes of such adjustment. The neo-Marxists are long on abstract theory but short on empirical evidence or arguments in support of the theory.

At this point in time, we do not have a theoretical synthesis that waves the three approaches into methodological unity.

Studies show that economic growth reduces poverty (Deininger and Squire, 1996 and Ravallion and Chen 1996). Other studies further demonstrate that the impact of growth on reducing poverty among the poorest appears to be greater than the relationship between growth and income inequality (Bruno et al 1998; Demery et al 1995; Deininger and Squire1996; and Ravallion and Chen 1996). Mehrotra and Delamonica (2007) and Drèze and Sen (2013) argue that economic growth alone will not address poverty rather it will invite inequity and so social security needs to be introduced to protect poor and to lead equitable development. Whereas, Bhagwati and Panagariya (2013) argue that market led growth is indispensable to get poor out of poverty.

However, it is important to note that the impact of growth on poverty reduction depends on the distribution of income: the greater the improvement in income equality over time, the greater the impact of growth on poverty reduction. This clearly indicates that simultaneous efforts are needed to reduce poverty and inequality. Other studies have elucidated the relationship between poverty, inequality, and lack of power. Poverty alleviation, therefore, is not solely an economic issue. It is also a social issue, a cultural issue, and more importantly, a political issue; it requires social transformation and political will.

Many programs to combat poverty do not seem to pay adequate attention to empowering the poor. Enabling the poor to take part in decision-making processes regarding resources can result in sustained poverty alleviation and social transformation. Poverty dehumanizes the poor and strips them of even their basic human dignity. Because poverty is the result of historical marginalization, transformation can be attained only by altering relationships of power and dominance.

Nepal is one of the world's least developed countries, suffering from severe poverty. About 18.6 percent of the population falls below the poverty line, based on income. Though this marks a reduction compared to the past, the absolute number of poor people has been rising in Nepal because the population has grown faster than the economy's capacity to generate additional income and employment. Today, over five million people live below the poverty line. Likewise, with regard to social indicators, Nepal lags behind other South Asian countries despite its relatively good performance in these areas. There are large disparities in social indicators between various geographic regions and socio-economic groups within the country. Many basic services are still undeveloped. Most of Nepal's poor live in rural areas, although poor rural people are increasingly migrating to urban and semi-urban areas in search of economic opportunities. There is no doubt that poverty and employment creation continue to pose serious challenges for Nepal.

Efforts to combat poverty in Nepal must take into account the various causes of poverty. On the one hand, it is necessary to reduce inequality that may be done by creating social safety nets, welfare programs, and redistribution strategies. On the other hand, it is also necessary to enhance productivity and create jobs. Therefore, simultaneous drives to address both, inequality and poverty, are needed. Bajracharya and Bajracharya (1999) argue the need for an integrated approach to address the issues of poverty. These efforts will require not only economic and political measures, but also mass social mobilization for generating awareness about being mindful to reduce wastages, inculcate the habit of sustainable consumption and production[5] and generating awareness in these aspects. It is imperative that efforts to combat poverty focus on poor and excluded groups. Different social groups have different livelihood needs, opportunities, and priorities. Therefore, it is necessary to include the poor and excluded groups' ideas in development planning in order to improve sustainability, good governance, and social inclusion.

Table 1.4: Poverty Trend in Nepal

Year	1995/96	2003/04	2010/11	2018/19*
Poverty Level (%)	42.0	30.8	25.2	18.6
Poverty Criteria (Daily Calorie Intake)	2123	2143	2220	2220

Source: CBS, 2011 and *MOF, 2019b

5. UN's SDGs have rightly captured it in goal 12.

At the same time, the cycle of poverty can be broken only by generating employment opportunities through greater investment and growth. Economic growth must accelerate to provide jobs to the growing population. The business environment must be made attractive for private sector investment, and competing economic political ideologies need to be settled by agreeing at least to some form of minimum approaches so that they are not altered with the change of government. A sense of security regarding the right to private property must be established, and the government must simultaneously improve access to state services among the poor.

1.6 Challenges Nepal faces serious challenges in the forms of poverty, a widening gap in income between the rich and poor, increasing unemployment, and inequality in social indicators between different socio-economic groups. Social indicators show marked inequality between different groups of people. For example, rural people are twice as likely to be illiterate as urban residents, and illiteracy is highest among the lower castes and disadvantaged ethnic groups. Rural regions and disadvantaged groups also lag behind in terms of access to essential services like healthcare, education and safe drinking water. These inequalities are rooted in a historically feudalistic society and institutions that upheld hierarchies based on gender, ethnicity, caste, and religion. The problem is exacerbated when the voice of the rural poor remains muted or virtually excluded from development policy discourse.

It is essential that the poverty reduction programs address such inequalities. There is a need to overhaul approaches and strategies to really focus on the poor and disadvantaged groups. A government that works for the people should be able to develop a policy framework that reflects the people's demands and can allocate and account for resources in accordance with pro-poor policies. Donor agencies and the government have both recognized the importance of integrated and comprehensive strategies for poverty reduction.

Political interference and increasing corruption within the government have undermined development efforts. For example, there is political involvement even in simple procurement decisions, resulting in the misuse and diversion of public funds for unauthorized purposes. Corruption and corrupt practices have actually grown in geometric proportion after the first people's movement (1990) and are eroding the capability of the system. In this environment, project implementation has suffered and desired goals have not been reached. This has clearly heightened the need for good governance. In many quarters, prospect of or already facing the failed state status or paradise lost is being argued and efforts are warranted to put the country in the right perspective and the path.

Given the present context of the country, a growth strategy to improve the opportunities not only for people from the urban areas and those who have access to resource but also to people of the rural, semi-urban and small towns, women, the less skilled and other socially disadvantaged groups is urgently needed. To address this scenario, generating higher growth and creating and promoting productive employment situation become all the more necessary not only for reducing poverty and inequity but also for sustaining and promoting peace, security and indulging in the path of prosperity.

1.7 Scope of the Book Nepal does have potential and ability to come out of the shell, in which we have bogged down for long. We must recognize our own resources and potentials and use them to the fullest extent for the benefit of the humanity in a judicious manner. Of course, it is not surprising that views are aired not to use own resources or the others with diverse arguments.[6] It will be, however, naïve to expect that we can develop relying on resources that we don't have while ignoring the resources that we have. Of course, efficiency, visibility, sustainability and benefit sharing with equity have to be ensured from the very outset. It is equally true that we will have to mobilize rescores not only from within but from our development partners and outside at a much accelerated pace by using forward looking economic diplomacy and convincing them that stronger partnership and cooperation in the next two decades

6. There are many experts, politicians and people who argue against one or the other form of resource that we have. Severe criticism of how hydropower prospect should be utilized is but only one such an illustration. Bogged down in such argument will lead us to nowhere.

or so will realize unprecedented value additions that has not been realized in the sixty years of cooperation and taking Nepal to a lofty situation where international goodwill will be required but financial assistance will no more be required. If we follow the path, we can and have the potential to transform into a middle income country within our life time. Lethargy, hesitation and goaded only by others' interest will only ruin us condemned to live as a citizen of a least developed country for eternity. In the backdrop, the purpose of this book is to lay down the situation of the country in an objective way to the extent possible with evidences and digging deeply into causes so that right and comprehensive remedies could be presented. The book is based on review of development plans, public policies, annual budgets, main political parties' election manifestos and institutional mechanisms which include laws and regulations, state administration and finance. Review of main political parties' manifestos for post 1990 elections is provided in annex C. Likewise, review of policies, programs and activities announced in post 1990 budgets is provided in annex D and review of policies of post 1990 is provided in annex E. As archive of pre-1990 is limited, the information for this time period is collected through secondary literature. The second chapter of book is about policy making in post 1951 more specifically of Panchayat era and the third explains policy making framework of post 1990 democratic regime. The fourth chapter is about innovation and the status in agriculture whereas the fifth explains about industrialization in Nepal. The sixth chapter details about trade, commerce and other service sectors which are also fundamental to make economy dynamic whereas the seventh explains about aspects of human resource development. The eighth chapter is about infrastructure development and this book concludes in the ninth chapter. The answer to the questions including remedies will be put forth in the next book that will be sequel to this.

chapter 2

THE SETTING: PRE 1990's SCENARIO

2.1 Introduction Nepal embarked on its journey towards democracy in 1951, but due to three decades of monarchical rule from 1960 to 1990, democracy became institutionalized only in the 1990s. Nevertheless, the political change of 1951 – when the Rana Regime was ousted[1] – was instrumental in that it raised general public realization and expectation about the state's responsibilities towards citizens. This in turn led to changes in the process, dimension and scope for envisioning policies over the coming decades. This chapter

1. In the mid-eighteenth century, King Prithvi Narayan Shah of Gorkha initiated the unification of Nepal, which had hitherto been ruled by different kingdoms and principalities. King Prithvi justified his unification as a strategy of consolidation against the expanding British colonization in India (Regmi, 1961 and Stiller, 1989). The unification of Nepal continued even after King Prithvi's death in 1775 and it culminated with the signing of an agreement with the British (colloquially known as Sugauli Treaty) in 1816, following a year-long war. In the treaty, Nepal gave up many of its newly-conquered territories and agreed not to establish diplomatic ties with third countries without British consent (Rose, 1971). Thus, despite the fact that Nepal preserved its independence, British India held significant control over Nepal's foreign affairs, trade, and commerce. In 1846, a military official named Jung Bahadur Rana took advantage of conflict among nobles in the King's court to secure the post of Prime Minister through the bloody Kot massacre (Stiller, 1989). The King became a titular head and all executive, judiciary and legislative powers were conferred to the Prime Minister (Shah, 1990). A system of hereditary Prime Ministership continued among the Rana family until 1951. The principle of succession by seniority was applied to depute Rana family members in all executive, administrative, and army posts. Non-Ranas were eligible only for clerical posts, which were filled with Rana loyalists.

discusses political developments and policy frameworks from 1951 to 1990, beginning with the important events of 1951.

2.2 Political Developments Joshi and Rose (1966) and Amatya (2004) argue that the ousting of the autocratic, British-backed Rana Regime in 1951 was brought about by two main political forces, namely: the King, whom the Ranas had hitherto confined to a symbolic role; and liberal political forces like the Nepali Congress (NC) and Praja Parishad, which led the democratic movement against the Ranas. The NC held connections with Indian independence leaders, with whom they had a relationship of mutual esteem. The King, Tribhuvan Bir Bikram Shah, had been a passive supporter of the anti-Rana movement from the palace, but took an active role in late 1950 by seeking political asylum in India, sparking a crisis that challenged the Ranas' legitimacy (Amatya, 2004). Compelled by the King's flight to India and an armed insurrection by the NC, the Rana regime capitulated in a tripartite agreement signed with the King and the NC in early 1951, which declared a democratic system in Nepal with a commitment to draft a new constitution through an elected constituent assembly (Joshi and Rose, 1966).

India mediated the negotiations that led to the tripartite agreement and it was signed in Delhi. India's role in this and Nepali politics more generally would soon become a central issue in Nepali political discourse, helping to shape Nepal's sense of nationalism. Leftists and various other political forces involved in the movement against the Rana Regime considered India's role in the tripartite agreement to be a betrayal of the country's sovereignty and accused the NC of surrendering the country's independence (Joshi and Rose, 1966). On the other hand, Hoftun et al (1999) argue that Delhi agreement was mostly negotiated between India, King and the Ranas and Nepali Congress was called only in the final hour to pen the agreement.

2.2.1 Interim Period of 1950s Following the Delhi agreement, the Interim Constitution of 1951 outlined the institutional setup for a democratic state (Joshi and Rose, 1966). The preamble stated that the government was to serve the Nepali people and to protect their fundamental rights. The constitution created an independent judiciary and envisioned a multiparty democratic system with an independent legislature, elected representatives, and an executive branch accountable to the people. Likewise, freedom of expression and freedom of the press were guaranteed. Furthermore, Nepali people were for the first time granted access to the outside world with the removal of heavy restrictions, imposed by the Rana regime (who had feared the spread of democratic values), on foreigners entering the country and Nepalis traveling abroad. The interim constitution aimed to transform the country's bureaucracy from one that had encouraged nepotism and sycophancy under the aegis of various forms of hereditary rule to one based upon competency and performance, with potentially profound implications for the political economy and policy making. The change was also monumental for the monarch; people admired the King's support of democracy and his commitment to place the monarchy within the framework of the constitution.

However, general elections were continually postponed and the government did not take the agreed-upon route of a constituent assembly election to draft a new constitution; the country remained under the Interim Constitution of 1951 for the next ten years (Joshi and Rose, 1966). The 1950s were characterized by constant inter- and intra-party squabbles; many interim governments came and went. There were splits, new alliances, and assimilations of major political leaders; some formed new parties just to get into the government. The King also played an instrumental role in forming and dissolving interim governments and encouraging political squabbles that made the political environment more fragile, thus helping him to retain temporary powers conferred by the interim constitution. This tendency of interference became more acute under the new King, Mahendra Bir Bikram Shah, who was crowned after the death of his father in March 1955.[2] Meanwhile, India continued to influence in domestic political matters, seeing Nepal as part of its strategic domain. Joshi and Rose (1966) show that

2. A detailed description of the 1950s' political landscape is available in chapters 4-14 of Joshi and Rose (1966).

Nepal added to the problem by pursuing help from India for bureaucratic restructuring, giving Indian diplomats easy access to high-level government officials. Furthermore, bilateral agreements on water use in two major shared river basins[3] raised questions about Nepal's sovereignty. Nepal became increasingly dependent on India, with little room to bargain at the diplomatic level.[4] Among the political parties, leftist forces were most vocal in condemning Indian political interference. Although King Tribhuvan did not take a strong stance against Indian interference, his son King Mahendra, who envisioned a more robust nationalism, did. However, many political actors levelled accusations of cooperation with (or cooptation by) India opportunistically against their opponents (Riaz and Basu, 2007).

In 1959, King Mahendra promulgated a new constitution that provided for a democratic parliament and announced elections. The King did not consult with any political parties before taking this step; Joshi and Rose (1966) argue that the time provided was too short for political parties to adequately prepare for the election. In any case, the elections were held and NC won a clear majority in parliament; most leaders from other parties dominant in the 1950s interim period lost.[5] This opened the door for Bishweshwar Prasad (a.k.a. "BP") Koirala, the prominent NC leader and the King's strongest counterweight, to become the Prime Minister. However, the NC government did not survive long because Mahendra, backed by the army, seized total power through a coup in 1960. Thus, the initiation of democratic innovation in the 1950s was short lived; the

3. Agreements were signed for the Koshi River in 1954 and the Gandak River in 1959. Dixit (2007) and Pun (2009) argue that both agreements accorded first priority to India.

4. This book isn't focused on foreign affairs of Nepal, so detailed analysis of Nepal-India relations is not included; the major events are only mentioned.

5. Joshi and Rose (1966) state that the most prominent leaders to lose in 1959 were Tanka Prasad Acharya and Bhadrakali Mishra of the Praja Parishad and Keshar Jang Rayamajhi and Pushpa Lal Shrestha of the Nepal Communist Party. Likewise, Dilli Raman Regmi of Nepali National Congress and Vedananada Jha of Terai Congress, two parties formed by splitting the Nepali Congress, also lost in the election.

upshot was transfer of state power from the hereditary Rana regime to the hereditary Shah monarchy.

2.2.2 King's Takeover and the Panchayat System King Mahendra justified his 1960 move by arguing that parliamentary democracy was incapable of fulfilling the aspirations of the people and that it had evolved into a threat to the national interest by inviting foreign interference. After the coup, Mahendra dismantled the multiparty parliamentary system, banned political parties, jailed leaders who opposed his move, and curtailed press freedom and freedom of speech (Whelpton, 2005 and Hoftun et al, 1999).

The royal takeover was successful for several reasons. King Mahendra emphasized the monarchy's historical contribution to national unity, promoting himself as the symbol of sovereignty. Moreover, as Bhattachan (2007) and Burghart (1996) argue, the King was traditionally believed to be the reincarnation of lord Vishnu who, in Hindu Mythology, protected the earth from demons and evil-minded people. Many considered King Mahendra to be a benevolent leader, protecting the world's only Hindu kingdom and its people. Likewise, Mahendra's timing for the takeover proved important; India was in the midst of a border dispute with China and Pakistan, and was thus in no mood to jeopardize relations with Nepal by opposing the coup (Riaz and Basu, 2007). Furthermore, within the dynamics of Cold War geopolitics, strategic silence from major world powers prevailed around such takeovers.

Despite his conservative and antidemocratic proclivities, King Mahendra pushed forward modernizing reforms to the state structure and geographical administrative demarcations, beginning with the promulgation of a new Constitution in 1962 (Joshi and Rose, 1966). The Constitution set up four administrative levels of government, including the central government and, underneath it, 14 zones, 75 districts, and several thousand villages/ towns. Each level had an Assembly (Panchayat). Village Panchayats were chosen directly by the people and served as the executive bodies for local development. They chose representatives for District Panchayats, which initiated development at the district level. District Panchayats chose representatives for Zonal Panchayats, which had similar functions covering the zones. The apex national assembly, called the Rastriya Panchayat, was formed with representatives from Zonal Panchayats, class organizations, and members nominated by the King. The King held discretionary power to form a Council of Ministers from the members of the Rastriya Panchayat. This assembly could not introduce budgetary bills or enact legal bills without royal approval. The King was the supreme commander of the army and could appoint or remove members of the judiciary and Public Service Commission; he could even alter court decisions and amend the constitution.

This administrative system was complemented by so-called class organizations, formed at all four administrative levels. These organizations were ostensibly formed to articulate the interests of different sectors of society and to sensitize the government about their interests (Joshi and Rose, 1966 and Baral, 1974). The class organizations nominated some members of the Rastriya Panchayat. Members had to enter class organizations at the local level; higher tiers were selected according to the same principle as the District, Zonal, and National Panchayats. One of the King's hidden interests in forming class organizations was to attract local leaders of the agitating political parties so that their movement against him could be controlled. Joshi and Rose (1966) state that 20% of class organization members were former NC affiliates. However, the class organizations' political character eventually became a threat to the King; they often raised debates at the local, district and zonal levels with an anti-monarchical tone (Joshi and Rose, 1966 and Baral, 1974).[6] In response, the King turned to intelligence and espionage against them, as will be briefly elaborated later.

The NC and leftist forces condemned the King's move from the very first day of the royal takeover.[7] Most dissident leaders were jailed immediately; others were compelled to take political asylum

6. Details on class organizations are available in Baral (1974) and in Joshi and Rose (1966).

7. Many leaders who had lost in the 1959 elections maintained strategic silence, hoping to gain the King's favor. In later years, these leaders' parties became defunct. Examples include the Praja Parishad of Tanka Prasad Acharya and Bhadrakali

in India due to the threat of arrest. Joshi and Rose (1966) argue that the dissidents' movement against the King was not consolidated or vibrant. Dissident leaders tried to gain public support by portraying the Panchayat system as an institution aimed at centralizing power in the palace and among the King's cronies. However, the NC and the leftists acted independently of each other due to an ideological clash (Dhungel, 2007 and Hachhethu, 2006). The NC had long considered itself the sole vanguard of democracy in Nepal, and feared establishment of a communist regime. On the other hand, the leftists perceived themselves as the real representatives of peasants and workers, and accused the NC of being submissive towards the King and India. There were also squabbles within each party. Dhungel (2007) argues that internal rifts were mostly due to the parties' limited institutional capacity leading to inability in consolidating state power. Disagreements also resulted from foreign forces' political infiltration in Nepal and the King's tactical moves to weaken dissident political parties (Riaz and Basu, 2007 and Baral, 1972). Party splits and mergers were especially common among the leftists.

Panchayat-era communist parties espoused the creation of a Peoples' Republic through revolution, but most lacked the institutional strength to become a threat to the state. KC (2003) argues that it was only the Jhapa Armed Movement of 1971 – launched by Nepali leftists trained by Indian Naxalites – that forced the state to become attentive to the leftists' demands.[8] This faction of leftists initiated discourse about accepting parliamentary democracy from the mid-1970s onwards. Following the 1990s democratic change, they consolidated to form the major mainstream

---

Mishra, a leftist party led by Keshar Jang Rayamajhi, the Nepali National Congress of Dilli Raman Regmi, and the Terai Congress led by Vedananda Jha.

8. Certain members of the intelligentsia speculated that King Mahendra secretly supported the leftists as a counterweight to NC and India. However, the Jhapa movement forced the King to review this strategy. There was also evidence that King Mahendra was apprehensive of Communists and uttered it after leftists won election in Kerala, India. However, King Mahendra is alleged to promote anti-India sentiment which later on became a cause of promoting leftism.

party known as the Communist Party of Nepal-Unified Marxist Leninist (CPN-UML)[9].

Change in the international environment, especially in India,[10] played a role in leading Nepal towards democracy. In 1979, King Birendra Bir Bikram Shah, was compelled to test public opinion through a referendum on the Panchayat system, which showed that a substantial minority – 46% of Nepalis – opposed the King's governance system. Dissident political parties accused the King of manipulating the vote by setting the age requirement at 21 years, barring a large number of politically active youth from exercising adult franchise and they also alleged wide scale manipulations in voting to ensure victory of the reformed Panchayat.[11] Following the referendum, the King nonetheless made some reforms to the Panchayat System by forming a Law Commission in 1979 that recommended an amendment to the constitution, which was enacted in 1980. The amendment made the National Panchayat an apex body of directly-elected representatives with the sole right to form the government; the Prime Minister and Council of Ministers needed to have a majority in the National Panchayat. Hence, the King could no longer hand-pick the Prime Minister or other ministers. Following the reform, debates on government policies and programs, as well as criticisms of the King, grew more common. There were public outcries to make the government more transparent. As diplomatic relations between the King and India worsened, India imposed an economic blockade on Nepal in 1989.[12]

---

9. A detailed history of Nepal's communist movement is available in *History of Communist Movement in Nepal* by Surendra KC (2003 and 2008).

10. India's foreign policy was primarily concerned with border disputes with China and Pakistan in the 1960s and early 1970s (Guha 2007). Domestic politics were paramount during the emergency imposed from June 1975 to March 1977. The political paradigm finally shifted after the formation of a non-Congress government headed by the Janata Party in 1977.

11. Twenty-one years was also the age for voting in the Panchayat elections and eligibility for joining officer-level jobs in the government.

12. India was uneasy with Nepal's growing closeness with China, so it did not revive the trade and transit treaty when it expired, resulting in an economic blockade (Panday, 1999). The Indians have argued that the expiry of the trade and transit treaty left no other options, and their actions of reverting to Most Favored Nations

In January 1990, the Nepali Congress finally joined hands with the moderate leftists, who had by this time accepted parliamentary democracy, for a mass movement led by Ganesh Man Singh against the King. Simultaneously, hardline leftists also announced their independent movement against the King with a mission to establish a people's republic. These movements toppled the Panchayat System in April 1990.

2.3 Envisioning Development and Economic Transformation

When the Rana regime handed over state power in 1951, the new government inherited a country plagued by underdevelopment and backwardness; most Nepalis were subsistence farmers who struggled to meet their minimum needs (Joshi and Rose, 1966). There were only a handful of urban settlements, concentrated in Kathmandu Valley and a few parts of the Terai and Hills, which had few modern industries and a rudimentary market system. Domestic capital formation was low, and the national treasury had been left depleted by the Ranas. Infrastructure and connectivity were ill-developed, without public utilities to supply basic necessities like electricity and running water. Only a handful of Nepalis held higher education degrees, and health care was primarily guided by superstitious beliefs. Much needed to be done with limited technical and financial resources and the state faced serious hurdles to progress.

Cognizant of these realities, the political parties decided to focus on the economic development of country. BP Koirala, the NC leader, espoused a pathway to national transformation by addressing village-level backwardness through land reform and other development programs.[13] As a social democrat and follower of Gandhi, B P Koirala advocated supporting self-sufficiency for poor village farmers in NC manifestos and other party documents. Likewise, non-NC leftist politicians espoused anti-feudalism and

treatment should not be misconstrued as a blockade. Others, however, argue that non-revision of the treaty itself exhibited India's intent to effect a blockade.

13. See BP Koirala's one of the last interviews to his journalist friend Bhola Chatterjee published in an Indian daily newspaper "Telegraph, India" dated 23rd July 1982.

anti-imperialism, advocating land and agrarian reform, development of small and cottage industries, and mobilization of cooperatives (Joshi and Rose, 1966). The only significant political party not to back land reform was the Gorkha Parishad,[14] a pro-Rana party, although it was similar to the other parties in its rhetorical emphasis on development.

The political parties argued that village development needed to be complemented by large-scale industrialization, development of cottage industries, and enhancement of trade, commerce, and supply systems. They also advocated for infrastructure development, better connectivity, an improved healthcare system, and training of technically skilled human resources. To achieve these objectives, the NC envisioned a mixed economy with a crucial role for government in increasing domestic production, along with support from foreign donors, foreign investors, and the domestic private sector The NC also advocated devolving more work to the local level. The Gorkha Parishad, though unhappy with the NC's socialist tone regarding agrarian reform, also advocated for a mixed economic system (Joshi and Rose, 1966). Meanwhile, the leftists opposed opening the economy to the private sector. Though they participated in the constitutional democracy, they continued to advocate creating a people's republic with a state-controlled economy. They opposed foreign aid from the USA and other capitalist countries, fearing pseudo-colonization (KC, 2008 and Joshi and Rose, 1966).[15] They contended that opening the economy

14. After losing state power in 1951, the Ranas tried to regain it through several instances of violent armed activity aimed at instigating political instability. Pro-Rana forces later consolidated to form the Gorkha Parishad, which participated in the 1959 general election, becoming the second-largest force in the parliament. This party also condemned the King's 1960 coup and in later years merged with NC.

15. Following the end of World War II in 1945, many colonized countries throughout Asia began the process of decolonization. Brown (2010) argues that, among newly independent countries, there was a common perception that adopting a market-based economic system would allow for pseudo-colonization by the western world. This would occur as international companies took control of poor countries' economies, making them fall prey to Western political and economic interests. It should be noted that previous western colonization in earlier centuries had indeed followed this route, with encroachment by foreign traders gradually

would lead to large-scale foreign encroachment, specifically by India, whose interference and dominance, they claimed, was abetted by the NC. The Praja Parishad and other political forces also presented themselves as passionate defenders of national sovereignty against Indian influence, but they remained mostly silent on economic principles. The political and economic ideologies of parties that were in power at various times during the 1950s were reflected in the development policies and planning documents of the period. Foreign donors – including capitalist, democratic socialist, and communist powers – also played an influential role in designing development policies and plans. King Tribhuvan did not put forward any substantive development agenda, but his son Mahendra did lay out his own vision for taking the country's development forward after he took control in 1960.

King Mahendra initiated a revolutionary land and agrarian reform program and promoted cottage industries as alternative sources of rural livelihoods (Joshi and Rose, 1966, Shrestha, 1981 and Pant, 1982). His "Back to the Village" national campaign, launched in 1967, sent educated youth to villages for a fixed term in order to sensitize them about village realities and gain hands-on experience in local development. Mahendra promoted village- and national-level self-sufficiency to simultaneously overcome poverty and minimize dependence on foreign aid and investment, especially from India (Mahat, 2005). He aimed to protect domestic economic production by imposing various types of licensing, which will be discussed in subsequent chapters. However, cognizant of the need for foreign resources and technology for development, Mahendra's government signed bilateral agreements of support and friendship with both capitalist and socialist donors (Pant, 1982). Donors were thus able to continue to influence development planning and policy making (Riaz and Basu, 2007 and Panday, 2011). Furthermore, some flexibility was provided for small-scale imports when the

---

leading to economic dependence and outright political control. As a result, many independent nations adopted state-led economies to minimize foreign intervention and deliver profits generated through the public sector to the deprived and excluded. In addition, the initial success of socialist countries, particularly the first five-year plan in the USSR, was highly attractive to decolonized nation-states.

country's production could not match demand. Amid a global debt crisis and under pressure from the IMF and World Bank, the Nepali economy underwent gradual restructuring beginning in the early 1980s (Bajracharya and Sharma, 1996 and Acharya et al, 1998). Shrestha (1981) argues that the King envisioned a semi-controlled economy in which the government, public enterprises, the market, and foreign resources and technology complemented each other.

Regarding development planning, King Mahendra envisioned a dual approach of top-down and bottom-up planning and implementation (Joshi and Rose, 1966). Bottom-up planning began with Village/ Town Panchayats, which submitted draft development plans to District Panchayats, which compiled them for submission to Zonal Panchayats, which prepared draft zonal plans. All zonal plans were collated at the center to prepare national development policies and plans. The center finalized guidelines, directives, programs, projects, and budgets, which were disseminated to the Zonal, District, and Village/ Town Panchayats. The planning process also took place according to development regions – delineations created in 1972 on the recommendation of the geographer and then-Vice Chairman of the National Planning Commission, Harka Gurung – of which there were initially four, later increased to five in 1982. The regional demarcations exposed how the mid- and far-western regions, which included extremely remote areas like the Karnali watershed, lagged in socio-economic indicators compared to the eastern and central regions. Despite the realization and increasing the development regions from four to five, linkages and other foundational activities were not initiated for long. The dual planning approach, at best, was also not properly implemented meaning that the centralized system persisted despite the commitment to do otherwise.

2.4 Institutional Framework: Starting immediately after the 1951 political change, steps were taken to set up a new state administrative structure and legal framework for democratic governance: a Law Commission was formed in 1953; an Administration Procedure Regulation Act was enacted in 1956; and a Development Board Act was enacted in the same year to administer development projects and programs. Decentralization was discussed as a means for strengthening local service delivery mechanisms and to make them more people-centric. However, institution-building efforts made little progress due to political uncertainty and frequent changes in government. Line ministries were created immediately after the 1951 revolution through a royal declaration, but being poorly planned, they were frequently restructured (Joshi and Rose, 1966). Other government offices were inherited from the Rana regime and remained unreformed. The Civil Service Commission was formed in 1951 to manage bureaucratic staff, and the first codified Civil Service Act was approved in 1956, but educated human resources for the fledgling bureaucracy was limited (Shrestha, 1975). Joshi and Rose (1966) argue that because the bureaucracy remained largely in the hands of Rana-era staff, the old legacies of conservatism, *chakari* (sycophancy), and *chaplusy* (flattery) remained dominant in the 1950s. Many bureaucrats worried about losing power to the democratically elected NC government, and they played an instrumental role in supporting the King's 1960 coup. Due to the weak institutional setup, the National Planning Commission (NPC), formed in 1956, could not bring any monumental changes.[16] Its first five-year plan took a comprehensive approach to agricultural reform and infrastructure development, but it was not well implemented. Thus, despite the fact that some institutional and regulatory frameworks were established in the 1950s, progress was insubstantial.

Under the Panchayat System, new zonal, district, and local administrative structures were gradually instituted, along with branches and sub-branches of central line ministries. The Home

16. A similar mistake was made by the transitional government of 1990 and the first elected government formed after the 1990 Constitution. Rather than taking a bold initiative to revamp the bureaucracy, Prime Minister Girija Koirala's government introduced poorly designed policies like forced retirement after 30 of service or 58 years of age whichever earlier and also provisioned that the government may terminate services after 20 years of service. It did not lead to desired changes, but actually the initiative boomeranged, becoming one of the causes of the defeat of NC in the mid-term election in 1994 as is reported to be this decision of forced retirement. The mid-term election has to be held due to dissolution of the parliament before completing its full term.

Ministry was converted into the Ministry of Home, Panchayat and National Guidance with an expanded portfolio to look after Zonal, District, and Local Panchayats as well as class organizations. Other line ministries were also restructured, and Nepali was declared the national language for administrative work. A new Law Commission was constituted in early sixties for the purpose of recommending laws and regulations for economic development and social welfare. However, such amendments and revisions were scrutinized through the lens of political risk to the monarchy. Many legal changes were not complemented with changes in practice, and in some cases, there were intentional delays in enacting amendments.

2.4.1 State Administration: Despite the Panchayat System's *de jure* administrative structures, the King, through the Palace Secretariat and his advisors, retained almost total *de facto* control of state operations (Joshi and Rose, 1966 and Dangol, 1999). Ministers and cabinet secretaries needed royal approval for any major plans or policies, and the Palace Secretariat and royal advisors also held sway over the judicial process. The Palace Secretariat gathered intelligence for the King on the activities of ministers, cabinet secretaries, and other important figures with an eye toward stopping any political activities against monarchy; suspects were harshly punished (Dangol, 1999). Bishow Bhandu Thapa, one of the main supporters of the King's 1960 move though erstwhile member of NC, said that he was compelled to resign from a high post in the Panchayat regime because he, at the request of his sister, participated in the Dashain festival's gathering of BP Koirala – an act that the Palace deemed disloyal (Thapa, 2012). All documents submitted by politically suspicious ministers and officials were thoroughly screened by the palace, and their decisions were sometimes made void even without consulting them. Bista (1991) argues that this environment of suspicion and doubt led bureaucrats and officials to focus on pleasing the palace; sycophants and flatterers were preferred over competent personnel. Meanwhile, misdeeds by favored ministers and officers, including embezzlement, were often excused or ignored. The practice of *chugli*, or backstabbing, was common as ministers, royal advisers, and members of the bureaucracy vied to prove their loyalty to the King, feeding the Palace Secretariat information about others' real or rumored treachery (TAF, 2012).

The Civil Service Act, 1956 underwent several amendments to strengthen central command over the bureaucracy. Civil service training institutions were set up and civil servants were sometimes sent abroad for capacity development, but incentives to use new skills were lacking because staff promotions were generally based on personal connections, not performance. Two commissions were created to reform the state bureaucracy – the first in 1968 under the chairmanship of Vedananda Jha, the second in 1975 under Bhekh Bahadur Thapa – but their recommendations were not implemented (Bajracharya and Grace, 2014). Thus, the King's vision for a modernized and streamlined bureaucracy – as well as development more generally – was impeded by his simultaneous efforts to protect the monarchy and its prerogatives.

In 1968, the Constitution was amended to create the post of Zonal Commissioner, to be nominated by the King. The Commissioners wielded significant power in their zones. They were charged with maintaining law and order and therefore commanded all locally stationed armed forces (Joshi and Rose, 1966 and TAF, 2012). Commissioners were also responsible for overall administration – including development activities and liaising with the center and lower tiers – and served as heads of the Zonal Panchayat executive committees. In 1972, the Local Administration Act empowered Chief District Officer (CDO) with responsibilities similar to those of the Commissioners, though in practice the CDOs' work was mostly confined to development activities like disbursing grants to local assemblies. In the political reform of 1980, many of the Zonal Commissioners' powers were deconcentrated to CDOs, but the Commissioners continued to play a prominent role in controlling political activities and maintaining law and order. Though the King created agencies to control the abuse of power – such as the Commission for the Investigation of Abuse of Authority, created in 1977, and the Administrative Court, created in 1988, and the National Vigilance Center – the Zonal Commissioners in fact did most of the intelligence gathering and vigilance to combat abuse.

The efficiency and effectiveness of the Panchayat-era administration was impaired by the government's conservative orientation, as it neither applied new social and economic reforms nor encouraged debate about how best to solve problems. Consequentially, the Kings, Mahendra and Birendra, were not able to effectively institutionalize the dual, bottom-up-and-top-down development planning process as envisioned. Capable human resources were lacking in the lower tiers, and their plans and proposals were not seriously considered by central-level officials. The budgetary mechanism remained highly centralized, resulting in much smaller local budgets than had been originally envisioned. After the 1980 constitutional amendments, a new Ministry of Local Development was created to oversee the Zonal, District, and Village/ Town Panchayats, whose responsibilities became more focused on development activities after their role in forming the National Assembly ended. However, this administrative restructuring was plagued by the same centralized mindset that had previously impeded progress.

2.4.2 Planning and Budgeting Planning and budgeting are important development tools for any nation state. Public budgeting ostensibly began in Nepal under Prime Minister Padma Shumsher Rana in 1947 but in actual institutional practice, it started only after 1951.[17] Public financing was formalized during the brief tenure of the elected NC government with the passage of the Excise Duty Act, 1958, the Income and Tax Justice Management Act, 1959, the Wealth Tax Act, 1960 and the Entertainment Tax Act, 1960. A law was also codified to standardize national debt management. The first budget after the 1951 political change covered the period from March 1951 to February 1952, but from the second budget onward, the fiscal year began and ended in mid-July, a practice that continues to this day (Pant, 1956).

17. Ranas left almost vacant treasury making it difficult for the nascent democratic government to pursue development initiatives. Mahat (2005) quotes the *Nepal Gazette* dated 3rd February 1952, which indicated that the government treasury left behind by the Ranas amounted to NRs 80 million in the form of gold, silver, coins, and foreign currency.

Aside from budgeting, development planning was first attempted by Mohan Shumsher, the last Rana Prime Minister, in an effort to divert populace from the then-ongoing anti-Rana political movement, but he made little progress[18]. The planning process became institutionalized only with the establishment of the National Planning Commission (NPC) in 1956.

Budgets during the 1950s focused on general administration because the government had little time to think about development amid political instability.[19] Furthermore, the small size of the economy provided limited revenue sources beyond land, forests, and customs.[20] Amidst this political fragility and budget crunch, donors like the US, the USSR, China, India, the Ford Foundation, UNDP and the Swiss came forward to support projects in agriculture, infrastructure, industrialization, rural development, health, education and other sectors, beginning in the early 1950s.[21]

---

18. When Mohan Shumsher ascended to power in 1948, the anti-Rana movement had already gained widespread support. He tried to divert popular attention from political activities through a focus on development, declaring that a planning process would start on May 27, 1948 (Jestha 14, 2005 VS). A committee to prepare the development plan was formed, consisting mainly of Rana family members and high-class officials such as Sardar Gunja Man Singh, who later became the first Vice Chair of the National Planning Commission in 1956, and Sardar Bhim Bahadur Panday. The first meeting of the committee was convened on August 26, 1948 (Bhadra 11, 2005 VS). However, as the political movement escalated, this committee remained dormant (Bajracharya and Agrawal, 1980).

19. Pant (1956) states that the total budget for FY 1951/52 was NRs. 52.5 million, of which NRs. 31.2 million (59.43%) was allocated for general civil administration and defense, and the budget deficit stood at NRs. 22 million. Similarly, in FY 1954/55, the total budget was NRs. 59.2 million, of which NRs. 37.8 million (63.85%) was allocated for general civil administration and defense, and the deficit stood at NRs. 16.5 million.

20. Pant (1956) states that total public revenue for FY 1951/52 was NRs. 30.5 million, of which NRs. 7.3 million (23.93%) was collected from customs, NRs 9.4 million (30.81%) from land, and NRs. 3 million (9.83%) from forests. The situation was similar in FY 1954/55, when total public revenue collection was NRs. 43.1 million, of which NRs. 13.6 million (31.55%) was collected from customs, NRs. 12.5 million (29%) from land, and NRs. 3.4 million (7.88%) from forests.

21. During the last days of the Rana Regime, the US signed an agreement to provide technical assistance to Nepal. The first US technical mission began work in 1952, establishing a Village Development Training Centre for community

After its creation in 1956, the NPC began to incorporate foreign aid into the overall development planning of the country. The NPC's first five-year plan, for the period 1956-1961, focused on infrastructure development. This plan allocated 37.5% of its total outlay to infrastructure and communication and 22.5% for agriculture and rural development. Seventy percent of the plan's budget was provided by foreign assistance, with the rest from internal sources. However, foreign aid also served donors' interests, as it created ample opportunity to influence policy. Mihaly (2002) and Riaz and Ali (2007) argue that donors began to interfere in Nepal's domestic politics beginning in the 1950s, starting a pattern that continues to the present day.[22]

After the King's takeover, the government promulgated several new laws to bring different sectors of the economy within the tax net and thus increase revenue. The Acts included: the Hotel Tax Act (1962); the Customs Act (1961); the Sales Tax Act (1967); the Building and Land Tax Act, (1962); and the Contract Tax Act, (1966). Individual incomes were made taxable with the Income Tax Act, (1963) and Revenue Tribunal Act, (1974) was enacted to regulate legal cases related tax and other public revenue. However, most economic activities remained in the informal sector, meaning that the government's revenue base did not increase substantially despite the new laws. For instance, there was no mechanism to collect the sales tax in all commercial activities, so it was levied in production or in import. The national budget continued to depend largely on foreign development aid. From the mid-1970s onwards, multilateral donors like the World Bank and the Asian Development Bank (ADB) began assisting Nepal, adding to the bilateral budgetary support. Borrowing was regulated under the Loan and Guarantee Act, 1968, which entitled the government to raise loans

---

development workers. India began to provide aid in 1953 with the construction of Gaucharan airport (now Tribhuvan International Airport) and the Kathmandu-Raxaul Tribhuvan Highway (H2); the official Indian aid mission was set up in 1954.

22. Mihaly (2002) states that the US hurried to provide technical assistance in order to prevent the spread of communist ideology among poor rural farmers. Foreign aid from the USSR and China, on the other hand, was focused on state-led industrialization.

for approved development projects and to provide guarantees for domestic entities. Likewise, the Amount and Government Contract Management Act, 1963 regulated large-scale government contracts and the Recovery and Settlement of Government Dues Act, 1968 further systematized budgetary processing. However, Seddon (1987) argues that contracting and dues recovery remained challenges in the budget implementation process. Most larger infrastructure development contracts were contracted out at the end of the fiscal year amid a mad rush to avoid any budgetary freeze that could be triggered if the allocated amount was not spent, a practice that continues today. Because of the rush, the government often failed to follow proper procurement methods. Meanwhile, government debt continued to increase and would become one of the reasons for macro-economic instability in the early 1980s.

Immediately after the royal takeover in 1960, an interim development plan was prepared for the period 1962-1965. This second development plan focused on administrative improvement and strengthening institutional capacity for data recording and data analysis. Its total outlay was NRs. 600 million, of which 39% was allocated for transport and communication and 13% for administrative improvement, surveys and statistics. USAID provided major technical assistance for surveys and statistics.

New thematic goals were set in the third through seventh plans. The third plan focused on agriculture, the fourth plan on regional development, the fifth plan on flexible planning (with budgets based on achievement in different sectors), and sixth and seventh plans on meeting basic needs. In the third and fourth plans, transport and communication took the major share of the total outlay and actual expenditure, but these sectors' allocations decreased from the fifth plan onwards (see Table 2.1). The share of the "social service" budget category (consisting of basic education, health and other sectors) increased in each subsequent plan, whereas the budget share of agriculture fluctuated.

Baskota (1989) argues that the Panchayat-era planning process lacked discipline because the central government was not responsive to local-level problems, development projects were diverted to groups and individuals patronized by Panchayat leaders, and

Table 2.1: Planned Public Outlay and Actual Public Expenditure in Different Sectors under the Third to Seventh Five-Year Plans

Plan	Details	Agriculture, Forestry, Irrigation and Land Reform	Industry and Mining**	Transport and Communication	Social Service	Others	Total
Third*	Planned Outlay (NRs. Million)	377.5	125	875	292.5	70	1740
	Share in Total Planned Outlay (in %)	22%	7%	50%	17%	4%	100%
	Actual Public Expenditure (NRs. Million)	349	83	806	228	178	1644
	Share in Total Actual Public Expenditure (in %)	21%	5%	49%	14%	11%	100%
Fourth	Planned Outlay (NRs. Million)	662.8	470	1050	352.5	35	2570.3
	Share in Total Planned Outlay (in %)	26%	18%	41%	14%	1%	100%
	Actual Public Expenditure (NRs. Million)	642	449	1236	600	56	2983
	Share in Total Actual Public Expenditure (in %)	22%	15%	41%	20%	2%	100%
Fifth	Planned Outlay (NRs. Million)	1839.7	1380.7	1432.8	1516.8		6170
	Share in Total Planned Outlay (in %)	30%	22%	23%	25%	0%	100%
	Actual Public Expenditure (NRs. Million)	2349.7	1679.2	2380.6	2460.1		8869.6
	Share in Total Actual Public Expenditure (in %)	26%	19%	27%	28%	0%	100%

Sixth	Planned Outlay (NRs. Million)	6600	5600	4230	5160	160	21750
	Share in Total Planned Outlay (in %)	30%	26%	19%	24%	1%	100%
	Actual Public Expenditure (NRs. Million)	4353	3380	3009	4437	404	15583
	Share in Total Actual Public Expenditure (in %)	28%	22%	19%	28%	3%	100%
Seventh	Planned Outlay (NRs. Million)	8876	7547	5132	7330	115	29000
	Share in Total Planned Outlay (in %)	31%	26%	18%	25%	0%	100%
	Actual Public Expenditure (NRs. Million)	11487	2673	13539	12057	3580	43336
	Share in Total Actual Public Expenditure (in %)	27%	6%	31%	28%	8%	100%

* Figures of Third Plan are in current prices whereas figures in other plans are in constant prices of base year of respective plans so they are not comparable with each other.

** This also includes electricity and power from the Fourth Plan onward. In the Third Plan, electricity and power is included under Transport and Communication.

Source: Mahat (2005)

financial control was weak. Monitoring and evaluation of development programs was also inconsistent. Projects received few assessments and little attention was given to initiatives to make sustained progress on earlier plans (Mahat, 2005). In short, development planning lacked long-term vision. Donors often questioned the effectiveness of Nepal's planning process, but their criticisms were also influenced by their own interests and agendas. In order to improve planning, the fifth plan adopted the approach of flexible planning, defining minimum achievements to be made in each sector. However, institutional mechanisms for implementing flexible planning were not created. Likewise, the government adopted performance-based budgeting, but no institutional mechanisms or processes were created for assessing performance. As the total government expenditure increased without a corresponding increase in revenue, the share of the budget provided by foreign aid rose at an alarming rate (see Table 2.2). Furthermore, the administrative superstructure set up by King Mahendra with a vision of decentralizing development planning and budgeting was largely ineffective, reflecting a lack of coherence and coordination.

Table 2.2 Government Budgets for Selected Years during the Panchayat Period (in NRs. Million)

Details	1975	1980	1985	1989
Total Government Expenditure	1514	3471	8395	18005
Regular Expenditure	499	945	2228	4490
Development Expenditure	1015	2526	6167	13515
Government Revenue	1008	1880	3917	7777
Government's Tax Revenue	842	1539	3151	6287
Government's Non-Tax Revenue	167	351	766	1494
Foreign Aid	387	1341	2678	7347
Foreign Grant	283	806	923	1681
Foreign Loan	104	535	1755	5666
Domestic Loan	100	180	1800	1330
Government Revenue to Total Government Expenditure	66.62%	54.17%	46.66%	43.19%

Continue next page

Foreign Aids to Total Government Expenditure	25.55%	38.62%	31.90%	40.81%
Domestic Loan to Total Government Expenditure	6.61%	5.19%	21.44%	7.39%

Source: Various Issues of *Economic Survey*, Ministry of Finance.

2.5 Growth and Poverty In FY 1964/1965, Nepal's economy was very small, with GDP estimated at NRs. 5,602 million (see Table 2.3). GDP increased to NRs. 8,938 million in FY 1970/71 (see Table 2.3), and due to different development interventions, Nepal achieved a growth rate of 4.28 percent in the decade of the 1970s (see Table 2.3). In the same period, per-capita GDP at current prices increased from NRs 730 to NRs 1,818. The growth rate remained at 4.78 percent in the decade of the 1980s, and per capita GDP in current prices increased from NRs. 1,818 to NRs. 6,510. Nepal's economic growth during the 1980s was much slower than its South Asian neighbors'; the World Bank's World Development Report of 1992 reports that growth in India, Pakistan, and Bhutan during the eighties as 5.3%, 6.3% and 7.5% respectively. Likewise, Nepal had the lowest per-capita GNP at USD 170, compared to USD 210, 350, 380 and 470 for Bangladesh, India, Pakistan and Sri Lanka respectively (World Bank, 1992). Total Factor Productivity (TFP) growth, however, was recorded at 1.54 percent in the period 1985-90 that was slightly higher than in the nineties indicating some what better use of resources (Bajracharya and Bajracharya, 2002).

Despite some economic growth, in 1978, 35.3% of Nepal's population remained under the poverty line, with a higher proportion of poor households in rural (37.33%) compared to urban (27.58%) areas (NPC, 1978). Kansal (1981) shows there was high inequality in income distribution in 1978; the bottom 10% of households received only 1.76% of income, whereas the top 10% of households received over 46.49% of income (see Table 2.4). Likewise, ILO (1980) study on "Poverty and Landlessness in Rural Asia" shows that malnutrition was three times higher in Nepal than in other developing countries.

Table 2.3: Gross Domestic Product of Nepal for Selected Years during the Panchayat Period

Fiscal Year	Nominal GDP (NRs. Million)	Real GDP at Constant FY 2000/01 Price (NRs)	Per Capita GDP in Current Price (NRs)	Economic Growth (%)*
1964/65	5,602	98,566	558	-
1970/71	8,938	112,272	730	2.19% (1964/65 to 1970/71)
1980/81	27,307	170,693	1,818	4.28% (1970/71 to 1980/81)
1990/91	120,370	272,235	6,510	4.78% (1980/81 to 1990/91)

Source: Various Issues of *Statistical Year Book of Nepal,* Central Bureau of Statistics (CBS)
*Source: Calculated by Author using CBS Data
* Time period representing the data is mentioned in parenthesis

Table 2.4: Income Distribution of Nepal in 1978

Cumulative % of Household (Poorest to Richest)	Share in Income (%)	Cumulative Share (%)
10	1.76	1.76
20	2.81	4.57
30	3.40	7.97
40	4.62	12.59
50	5.22	17.81
60	6.47	24.28
70	7.50	31.78
80	8.99	40.77
90	12.74	53.51
100	46.49	100.00

(Source: Kansal, 1981)

2.6 Conclusion Nepal's planning history is beset with underachievement and development failures (Sharma, 2013). There are many reasons for this, but several prominent conclusions emerge. First, the monarchy's interest in protecting its prerogatives led to a lack of focus on real development outcomes. King Mahendra, despite being hailed by some as a visionary, showed a lack of purpose when it came to implementation; his initiatives were limited and exhibited a lack of wholistic perspective. Second, the planning process constantly shifted priorities without realizing goals; government planners' attention was scattered. Constant shifts in priorities and discontinuity of initiatives led to confusion, high costs, wastage and, more importantly, gross underachievement in Nepal's development. Not surprisingly, Nepal, a food-surplus country even up to the 1980s, has since become a net importer of food. By contrast, India, a severely food-deficit country even up until the 1960s, has since become a food-surplus country thanks to the Green Revolution. Nepal's policies and practices have not changed much since the Panchayat era, meaning that these conclusions are valid even today.

chapter 3

THE SETTING: POST 1990's SCENARIO

3.1 Introduction Nepal's development during the period 1951-1990 was affected most by the King's attempts to strengthen the monarchy and by various external development partners' influence, whereas the period from 1990 to the present has been more turbulent, characterized by political instability and uneven development. Amid political pluralism after the democratic opening of 1990, popular expectations about economic growth and prosperity skyrocketed. However, hopes were dashed by nearly two decades of political instability that began with the launch of an armed revolt by the Maoists in 1996 and ended with the promulgation of a new Constitution in 2015. This chapter examines political developments from 1990 onward and discusses the policy frameworks adopted by political parties during the period.

3.2 Political Developments of Post 1990 The political change of 1990 restored multiparty parliamentary democracy along with constitutional monarchy. Unlike in the 1950s, the transition period was short; a new constitution was immediately adopted, followed by elections for parliament and local bodies within one year.[1] The 1990 Constitution's main features were: i) the creation of an independent

1. The long-standing desire – dating from the 1950s – of Nepalis to write their own Constitution was not fulfilled. Instead, the Constitution was drafted by an ad-hoc commission with representatives from the King, the NC and the leftist forces. Hoftun et al (1999) argue that there was strong pressure from the palace and army to preserve royal power while drafting 1990's constitution.

executive, legislature, and judiciary; ii) the requirement of a parliamentary majority to form a government; iii) the obligation of the state to conduct elections for Parliament and local bodies every five years; and iv) the institutionalization of oppositional politics by enshrining rights to criticize the government, its policies and programs (Ellingson, 1991). Furthermore, the Constitution aimed to enhance government accountability by creating constitutional agencies empowered to supervise, monitor and caution the government and making the Council of Ministers accountable to Parliament. The Constitution also guaranteed media freedoms, reinforcing citizens' fundamental rights. It empowered civil society and pressure groups to demand government accountability, creating a freer environment for people to bring forward grievances.

Following the 1990 political change, three mainstream political forces emerged: the centrist[2] Nepali Congress (NC), the country's oldest democratic party; the leftist Communist Party of Nepal-Unified Marxist Leninist (CPN-UML), which launched the Jhapa Revolution in the early 1970s but later renounced violence; and the conservative Rastriya Prajatantra Party (RPP), formed by politicians who had formerly served under the king's Panchayat System (Dhungel, 2007 and Baral, 2004). In the first and the third elections held under the 1990 Constitution, conducted in 1991 and 1999, the NC received the most votes while the CPN-UML led the opposition in the parliament[3]. In the second general election, held in 1994, the CPN-UML was the largest party with NC dropping to second position. Some radical leftists, who considered the 1990 Constitution to be only a partial achievement towards the ultimate goal of a people's republic, also participated in the first parliamentary election, becoming the third-largest force (KC, 2008). However, a large faction of leftist hardliners departed from parliamentary politics after the first general election, weakening their performance in 1994 and 1999. In their place, the RPP, which had performed poorly in 1991, gained third position in parliament after the 1994 and 1999 elections.

2. NC claims itself a socialist party.

3. List of government formed in Nepal in post 1990 is provided in Annex G.

Though the NC and CPN-UML controlled the government in the 1990s, they faced many impediments to nurturing the fledgling democratic governance system. As in the 1950s, parliamentary politics in the 1990s was characterized by frequent inter- and intra-party squabbles, leading to splits and assimilations (Baral, 2004). No government formed during the 1990s served a full term. Even the NC's majority governments were dissolved due to intra-party conflicts, while the hung parliament formed after the 1994 second general election became a battleground, with a series of no-confidence motions attempting to dissolve the government. Foreign forces were reported to take advantage of the fluid political situation to become more active; the country became a fertile land for ideologues of every hue and color. Dhungel (2007) argues that political parties' activities during the 1990s reflected leaders' greed for power; parties became highly centralized institutions, with power concentrated among top leadership. Aditya and Bhatt (2016) argue that local-level party leaders had no role beyond campaigning in elections. Vested interests prevailed amid political fiascos, leading the nascent democracy to falter and leaving development efforts mired.

3.2.1 Maoist Revolution Amidst this political milieu, the Communist Party of Nepal-Maoist[4] – a group of radical leftists who rejected the 1990 Constitution and sought to establish a people's republic – began what would become the country's longest armed movement in 1996, popularly known as the "10 Years' People's war". In his writings, Maoist ideologue Babu Ram Bhattarai (2003)[5] blamed the King, the parliamentary system, and the mainstream political parties for perpetuating feudalism by promoting the government's centralized unitary system, sycophancy, favoritism, corruption, elitism, poverty, social exclusion, caste, and untouchability. The Maoists focused on taking control of rural

4. Hereafter, CPN-Maoist or Maoists refers to the political party headed by Pushpa Kamal Dahal, known by his *nomme de guerre,* Prachanda, not the split away group.

5. Babu Ram Bhattarai later broke away from the Maoist party and formed his own party, Naya Shakti which he again merged recently with identity based Federal Socialist Party.

areas, encircling urban settlements, and ultimately hoping to capture the state (Dahal [Prachanda][6], 2003).

The armed movement helped to bring spectacular changes in Nepal's political discourse; for example, their "Parallel Ethnic-Based Peoples' Government" not only legitimized their movement, but also made them appear compassionate towards the marginalized and excluded (Gellner, 2008).[7,8] The Maoists also highlighted the problems of wealth inequality and youth and labor exploitation. They began a land redistribution program that benefited the poor. Another main cause for the Maoists' popularity was the gap between the socio-economic changes that the political parties had envisioned and their actual achievements. This led to a withering of mainstream political forces and the strengthening of the revolutionaries.

The violence intensified within a few years of the movement's launch, and the Maoists gained partial or full control over large swaths of the country by mid-2000, resulting in a political vacuum.

3.2.2 King's Power Play and its Aftermath King Gyanendra, who became the King after 2001's royal massacre[9], seized central state powers in October 2002, claiming that he could not remain on the sidelines while the government and the country remained threatened by the Maoists movement. However, Gyanendra's period of direct

6. Pushpa Kamal Dahal (Prachanda) is the current co-president of the Nepal Communist Party and led the 10 year-long armed revolution.

7. Please refer to Annex A on social exclusion practices in Nepal.

8. Maoists formed the first ethnic-based autonomous peoples' government of Magarat in 9th January, 2004 which was followed by autonomous peoples' government for Tamangs in 16th January, 2004 and many others in succeeding days (CPN-Maoist, 2006).

9. In 1st June 2001, King Birendra, his entire family members and four other royal relatives were gunned down during royal banquet held in the palace. Several other royal relatives were injured in this incident. The commission formed under the chairmanship of the then Chief Justice solely accused the crown prince Dipendra who also shoot himself during the incident. The memoir of king's then army secretary, Vivek K Shah, explains the incident as a result of palace's indecisiveness (Shah, 2018). The incident has been explained through different lens of conspiracy theory. But, for the general Nepali public, this incident is the most shocking one and they lost their faith towards the monarchy.

rule was perhaps doomed to fail; he essentially tried to reinstate the old Panchayat governance structure that had been rejected by citizens over a decade earlier. The King's autocratic tendencies and brutal prosecution of the counter-Maoist movement drove the mainstream political parties and the revolutionary Maoists – who had previously been enemies – into an alliance in 2005, for which India, as in 1951, acted as mediator. The Maoists and the political parties made a 12-point agreement to overthrow the King and draft a new constitution through an elected Constituent Assembly (CA)[10]. All political parties except a small faction of the conservative RPP agreed that the time had come to end the monarchy. Following massive street protests in the spring of 2006, Gyanendra relinquished his direct powers and, in 2007, an Interim Constitution was enacted, empowering a Constituent Assembly to draft a new constitution. Following several amendments brought about by the Madhesh Movement,[11] the Interim Constitution reaffirmed that Nepal was to be a republic, incorporating federalism, proportional representation in Parliament, and due recognition for the Maoist Revolution and the Madhesh Movement for playing instrumental roles in the political change.

3.2.3 Constituent Assembly and the Federal Republic The Constituent Assembly (CA) – the constitution-drafting body that had been the goal of multiple post-1990 democratic and nondemocratic movements – was finally elected in 2008. It was made up of five main political forces. Two of them – the Nepali Congress and CPN-UML – had existed underground during the

---

10. Ever since the start of Maoist revolution, there were series of formal and informal talks between Maoists and government/ mainstream political parties on ending the deadlock but none were conclusive. The rapprochement was only made after the initiation of India in 2006 resulting in to the culmination of Comprehensive Peace Agreement.

11. The Madhesh Movement was started by Madheshi – a term for historically marginalized castes in Nepal's Terai region who share language and culture with Indian groups across the border – after the initial version of the Interim Constitution failed to ensure federalism and provision for inclusion of marginalized groups. The Movement pushed for greater autonomy of provinces and the creation of an ethnicity-based province in the Terai.

Panchayat era but joined parliamentary politics after 1990. The third, the Maoists, ended their 10 years' revolutionary movement and adopted parliamentary politics after signing the Comprehensive Peace Accord in 2006. The fourth political force in the CA were identity-based political groups – including those who led the Madhesh Movement – who had challenged what they saw as the discriminatory nature of the hill- and high-caste-dominated Nepali state. Finally, the fifth political force in the CA was the RPP, the conservative party made up of supporters of the monarchy and Hindu state. Due to intense rivalries and lack of consensus among these five political forces,[12] the first CA, was unable to promulgate a constitution.[13] A second CA was elected in 2013[14] and promulgated a new constitution in 2015 that declared Nepal a secular federal democratic republic and restructured the state into three tiers, envisioning the devolution of power.

In 2017, elections were held for all three tiers of government – federal, provincial, and local – and governments were subsequently formed. Almost all political parties participated in 2017, demonstrating their commitment to institutionalize federal democracy. Nevertheless, a splinter Maoist group led by Netra Bikram Chand (known by his *nomme de guerre* "Biplav") has not accepted the political framework provided by the Constitution of Nepal. The group did not participate in the elections and is leading an underground violent movement against the government. Similarly, a protest movement led by Dr. CK Raut presented a challenge to the federal democratic transition by advocating for secession of the Terai/ Madhesh. However, in early 2019, Dr. Raut entered an agreement with the government to accept the Constitution and he appears set to enter mainstream politics. Not

---

12. The detailed proceedings of the first Constituent Assembly were compiled in a book published by the Parliament Secretariat titled *Sambhidhan Shaba Darpan*, meaning "Reflection of the Constituent Assembly." See: Parliament Secretariat (2013).

13. The first Constituent Assembly was elected on 10th April, 2008 and served from 28th May, 2008 to 28th May, 2012.

14. The second Constituent Assembly was elected on 19th November, 2013 and it promulgated the new Constitution on 20th September, 2015.

surprisingly, the government has also been challenged by inter- and intra-party squabbles in due course. Notably, however, the CPN-UML and CPN-Maoist merged in 2018 to form the Nepal Communist Party (NCP), which commands a two-thirds majority in federal Parliament as well as control of 6 out of 7 provincial legislatures. The NC, as the second largest party, is currently the main opposition.

Ministry of Law Justice and Parliamentary Affairs (2016) state that 315 acts and 270 regulations of Nepal need to be revised and amended as per federal constitution's principle and new federal laws need be formulated in 110 issues; state laws on 22 issues and local level laws on 6 issues. The government is currently carrying out legal revisions and many new laws and regulations have been brought in recent one and half year since the formation of federal parliament through 2017 election. However, there are time and again news of legal revision not following federal principles and these legal revisions have not been able to fairly unbundle jurisdiction between federal, provincial and local governments. Further, institutional capacities of province and local governments are still weak to function on their own hence it is going to take some time to effectively institutionalize federalism in Nepal.

3.3 Policy Envisioning by Political Parties During the 1990s, mainstream political parties focused on policies aimed at reforming autocratic monarchical governance institutions and establishing democratic norms in an accountable and transparent manner. The manifestos of the liberal NC and leftists like the CPN-UML advocated for addressing poverty and underdevelopment through large-scale land and agrarian reform, upliftment of farmers and the poor, reservations for historically marginalized groups, infrastructure development, and industrialization, among other things. Another prime political agenda, popularized by the erstwhile rebel Maoists, was to make the state more inclusive and decentralize government structures to improve access to services like education, healthcare, and drinking water. Various parties also made commitments to improve the quality of government services, and they proposed roles for the private sector, pressure-group organizations, the media, the international community, and donors as partners for actualizing reforms in the country.[15]

However, despite their rhetoric, mainstream parties were unable to realize major policy commitments during the 1990s and early 2000s. This was both a cause for and a result of the decade-long Maoist conflict, which created severe political instability beginning in 1996 (Bhattarai, 2003). The rebel movement sought to establish a people's republic, but many of their other goals were the same as those espoused by the mainstream parties in the 1990s, including greater social inclusion, power devolution, and reducing poverty. Thus, there was a great deal of continuity in the post-1990 policy discourse, leading all the way to the promulgation of the 2015 Constitution and the establishment of the federal republic. Policy discourse was shaped not only by contestations between mainstream and dissident political forces, but also by foreign powers as donors used aid as an avenue to impose their interests (Riaz and Basu, 2007 and Panday, 2011).[16] The focus since 2015 has been to institutionalize changes and address poverty and underdevelopment. However, apprehension remains that bold rhetorical goals will not be supported by policy and action.

3.3.1 Defining the Route for Growth Economic progress during the Panchayat era was limited and inadequate. Visible changes did take place in infrastructure development, the agrarian economy, small-scale industries, and the services sector. However, despite King Mahendra's grand visions, the scale of change was limited due to a lack of effective policies and sustained implementation, as discussed in the earlier section. Many potentially cost-effective and easy development opportunities were missed during the 1960s and

15. See the manifestos of NC and UML for the elections held in 1991, 1994 and 1999. Review of manifestos of major political parties (NC, CPN-UML, CPN-Maoist and NCP) for post 1990's general and CA elections is provided in Annex C.

16. There was alleged interference by various foreign forces in favor of secularism, the proportional election system, inclusion, and other issues. These forces were alleged to have used NGOs, INGOs, influential persons and even parliamentarians/members of the Constituent Assembly for the purpose.

70s.[17] International donors like UNDP and the World Bank categorized Nepal as a "least developed country," and the government courted foreign support. After 1990, newly-empowered political parties were finally given a role in defining the country's route for growth and prosperity.

The pathway envisioned by the NC during the 1990s was to use a liberal approach to position the country as a mixed economy with a focus on growth and creating employment; this approach continues to predominate today. The NC argued for continuity of the market liberalization reforms initiated by the IMF and the World Bank during the Panchayat period under the Economic Stabilization Program (ESP, begun in 1985), the Structural Adjustment Program (SAP, begun in 1986) and Enhanced Structural Adjustment Program, (ESAP, begun in 1989) to address economic vulnerabilities like debt traps, foreign exchange crises, and inflation (Mahat, 2005). The first elected government under the NC brought about a package of policy measures, beginning in 1992, to deregulate the economy and liberalize the market. These polices sought to increase the role of the private sector in the economy by encouraging both domestic and foreign investment as well as technology transfer. The package included removing licensing regimes from almost all sectors, introducing partial convertibility (ultimatcly reaching full convertibility) in current

17. Supporters of the monarchy argue that King Mahendra was a visionary leader dedicated to national transformation. It is true that he initiated a number of development initiatives, including: creating a full-fledged judiciary; conferring limited powers to elected local governments under the Panchayat System; enacting a new National Code (Muluki Ain); initiating development planning; developing transportation, energy, and communications infrastructure; developing the education and health sectors; and initiating resettlements and population management. However, the slow growth of the economy failed to lead to the total transformation envisioned by the King. Mahendra remained bogged down in efforts to consolidate his political power, leaving less emphasis on development. King Birendra, who was said to be more politically liberal, transferred power to an elected parliament and operated as a constitutional monarch after 1990, but for him too, concerns about maintaining power got in the way of development progress. For example, the Back to the Village campaign during the early part of his rule was cancelled when it appeared to threaten the monarchy's power.

accounts, and privatization of public enterprises[18] in order to create a better environment for private investment. The NC argued that the government's role should be confined to building a conducive environment for market expansion and effective functioning, enabling dynamism in the economy for job creation, production increases, and improvements in service delivery mechanisms, ultimately leading to higher growth.[19]

On the other hand, leftists remained suspicious of economic liberalization and market deregulation. As global changes in the 1990s began to reorient the economies of China, Russia, former Soviet bloc countries, and other erstwhile communist states, leftist parties in Nepal also gradually changed their anti-capitalist approach. However, leftists' party resolutions reveal a continuing suspicion of capitalism and the market-based economy as symbols of exploitation, and neo-colonization by inviting threats to the country's sovereignty. They feared that foreign investors – especially from India and other capitalist countries – would exploit Nepal's national resources and impoverish the nation and its people. So, while accepting foreign aid, the leftist parties pushed back against encroachment by foreign and multinational companies.

Instead, the leftists argued Nepal should become self-sufficient[20] by keeping the country's economy in the hands of Nepali entrepreneurs. The CPN-UML, in particular, was active in mobilizing community organizations and cooperatives, believing

18. The privatization that was necessitated by the IMF and the World Bank's SAP and ESAP became the center of criticism from many quarters, including from dissidents within the NC. Critics pointed out that national assets were sold off for peanuts, and this became one of the causes of defeat for the NC in 1994. However, what many critics failed to see was that after the restoration of multi-party democracy in 1990, appointments in public enterprises had become more overtly political, the practice also promoted by the Panchayat regime, with negative implications on performance. Indeed, a number of them had to be closed. Examples included the Himal Cement Company, the Birgunj Sugar Factory, and the Janakpur Cigarette Factory.

19. Refer to manifestos of NC for the elections held in 1991, 1994 and 1999.

20. The notion of total self-sufficiency has become widely discredited. Even leftists like Babu Ram Bhattarai have acknowledged that total liberalization and total state control are both unfeasible (Nepal, 2019).

these types of organizations were ideal conduits for enlisting the rural poor in development work.[21]. The NC[22] also took this approach, but not as aggressively as the CPN-UML. In 1994, the minority government of the CPN-UML announced a plan to set up a new government-owned commercial bank, but the plan was never realized. In many cases, hardline leftist parties' strong-worded propaganda became tempered over time. For instance, after launching their movement, the Maoists stated in their party resolutions that they would confiscate land from all landlords and redistribute it to the poor.[23] But after joining mainstream politics, the Maoists dropped this hardline agenda. Today, the NCP has adopted the slogan "prosperity and development," reflecting a move towards a more centrist economic agenda. Nevertheless, leftists sometimes express anti-capitalist sentiments when they are in government.

Over time, the NC's and leftist parties' economic agendas have each adapted in response to each other. Though the leftists do not want to make foreign capital the linchpin of the economy, they have accepted the semi-liberal growth model initially propounded by the NC. Cognizant of the need for foreign money and technology – either from aid or investment – the parties gradually toned down their rhetoric about the threat of foreign economic encroachment. Instead, leftists called for social protection measures to address poverty and underdevelopment. Most of the social protection programs in Nepal have been introduced by leftist governments, including the old age pension initiated by the UML in 1994 and the inclusive prosperity strategy adopted by the Maoists in 2006 to promote its welfare programs. Leftist parties attempted to utilize grants and soft loans to create self-employment opportunities for youth and the unemployed. The NC also brought similar programs, such as the 'Bishweshwar for Poor'. Available evidence, however, indicates that many of these programs were unsuccessful or less

21. Refer to manifestos of UML for the elections held in 1991, 1994 and 1999.

22. NC claims to be a democratic-socialist party following the ideals of BP Koirala, but there is continuing debate about its economic policy orientation. Many people consider it a centrist party.

23. Refer to Maoists statements and documents in Karki and Seddon (2003).

successful in alleviating poverty, although they were used instrumentally for political patronage.

In sum, most mainstream political parties since 1990 have called for adoption of a mixed economy through large-scale mobilization of the market in order to achieve economic growth, development, and poverty alleviation. In support of these goals, various parties have advocated decentralized government structures, an inclusive state, and social welfare through community mobilization. Interestingly, one prominent issue on which parties have not expressed clear policy commitments is skill development.

3.4 Institutional Framework After 1990, the Palace Secretariat, which had played an important role under the King's direct rule, was converted into the King's private secretariat and given only a limited role in state administration; virtually all of its power was transferred to the Prime Minister's Office. The Zonal Commissioners, which the King had used to control oppositional political activity, were removed. An Administration Reform Commission was created to reform the civil service under the chairmanship of Prime Minister Girija Prasad Koirala in 1991, and civil servants sympathetic to the King were sacked. However, a negative consequence of the post-1990 administrative restructuring was that despite being confused at the beginning, the state administration gradually gained leverage by being associated with the political parties. Agencies like the CIAA, the National Vigilance Center, and Administrative Courts were not always able to fill in as watchdogs, a role shouldered by erstwhile Zonal Commissioners,[24] leaving ample opportunity for the state administration and political parties to collude in corruption.

Donor agencies and other pressure groups began to emphasize the importance of good governance and accountability in post-1990 public discourse. Though a Good Governance Management and

24. The CIAA has become a little more active since the mid-2000s, following global outcries against terrorism and terrorist financing after attacks in the US, Europe, India, and other parts of the world. As a result, the CIAA began to wield more power in Nepal.

Operations Act was passed in 2008 and its regulations were enacted in 2009, there were no substantial changes in administrative practice[25]. Likewise, different Administrative Reform Commissions were formed after the promulgation of the Interim Constitution in 2007. These commissions, formed in 2008 and 2014, were charged with recommending how to transform the state administration to accommodate federalism, but their recommendations were not implemented (Bajracharya and Grace, 2014).

3.4.1 The Story of Decentralization After 1990, Nepal embarked on a course toward decentralization by gradually devolving more and more power to the lower levels of government. All Village, Urban, and District Panchayats were converted into local bodies as Village Development Committees (VDCs), Municipalities and the District Development Committees (DDCs). VDCs and municipalities were directly elected and DDCs were elected by the electorate formed from the elected members of VDCs and municipalities. The erstwhile Ministry of Local Development remained the line ministry to oversee these local bodies. The Village Development Committee (VDC) Act, the Municipality Act, and the District Development Committee (DDC) Act were passed in 1991, which provided more *de jure* power to the local bodies, charging them with responsibilities related to agriculture, basic health, basic education, local infrastructure, vital registration, local tax collection, and other local affairs. However, in actual practice, local bodies' functions were limited to local infrastructure development, vital registration, and local development affairs because other laws were not revised in line with decentralization principles (Sapkota et al, 2009). Programs like the "*Aphno Gaun Aphai Banaun*" ("Build Your Village Yourself") Campaign[26] in which Members of Parliament were allocated funds to develop local infrastructure, contributed to decentralization. The CPN-UML

25. List of prevailing acts referred in this book and their regulation are provided in annex F.

26. This program had a great impact; most of the roads developed in rural areas can be attributed to this program.

liked to call itself the "initiator of decentralization" because it announced this program in FY 1994-95.[27] However, these programs lacked a strong institutional base, especially regarding their ability to plan and monitor.

In 1998, the Local Self Governance Act (LSGA) was passed, repealing all earlier laws pertaining to local bodies. The LSGA was accompanied by the Local Self Governance Regulations, 1999. The LSGA and its Regulations were the strongest-yet attempt to give real power to DDCs and other local bodies. They gave local bodies a prominent role in local planning, enabling them to actively mobilize community organizations and also providing them with unconditional grants (Sapkota et al, 2009). Furthermore, they reiterated the decision to give functions relating to agriculture, health, education and other affairs to local bodies by devolving them from the district-level offices run by the central government. Again, however, actual empowerment of local bodies was limited because of a lack of revisions in other relevant laws.[28] On the other hand, the LSGA resulted in significant improvements in local infrastructure development through community organizations. However, most of these "community organizations" did not work using a community-mobilization model; rather, they took work from local bodies and sub-contracted it out to other firms. Because there was no regulating agency to control the community organizations, many of their leaders became successful businessmen by acting as middlemen.

With the promulgation of the 2015 Constitution, all local bodies were converted into local governments, with autonomous

27. The UML's claim is weakened by the fact that there had been previous direct allocation of resources to local bodies. For example, the 1993 budget of the erstwhile Kathmandu Municipality (now a Metropolitan City) allocated funds to wards to use at their discretion, following the premise that real decentralization lies in financial empowerment.

28. Dhungel (2004) notes that district-level offices run by the central government continued to handle most functions conferred to local bodies, resulting in duplication. For instance, though many schools were officially handed over to communities, local governments lacked a role in their budgeting and planning processes. The situation was similar in the health sector.

powers described in the Constitution's Annex 8, along with other concurrent powers shared between the local, provincial, and federal governments. Local Government Operation Act, 2017 and its regulation have been brought to carry out independent function conferred to local governments. However, state administrative restructuring remains in limbo as the government is still in the process of making revisions to bring existing laws into compliance with the 2015 Constitution. In many cases, the federal government appears reluctant to devolve powers to the provinces and local bodies. Recently, there have been stories in national dallies about new bills on education, disaster management, and other topics that contravene the principles of federal governance. The big question is how policies envisioning decentralization, an inclusive state, and social welfare will be implemented amid an atmosphere of confusion.

3.4.2 Social Security Social security programs in Nepal have focused on providing cash and non-cash grants and soft loans to uplift the socio-economic status of farmers, unemployed youth, women, the poor, and historically marginalized groups. The programs address livelihoods, poverty, unemployment and basic services like health and education. Generally, social security programs are announced in the government's annual budget. Following the budget announcement, the concerned line ministry or office must prepare its working guidelines and implement the program. Most line ministries operate these programs through their district offices, although social allowance programs like Old Age Allowance, Single Woman Allowance are handled by local governments.

Social security programs in Nepal have numerous shortcomings. Most are managed by line ministries or offices that lack sufficient staff to manage them effectively. For instance, under the Self-Employment Fund announced by the 2008's Maoist government and the Bishweshwar for Poor Program announced by the1999's NC government, administrative staffs were able to handle only the application process, not the other necessary tasks.

Monitoring and evaluation is missing from most government-supported projects, and some do not even have training or capacity-building components. In addition, lack of regulatory oversight has led to frequent misconduct in the distribution of resources through social security programs, which are used for political patronage or personal gain. Another problem is a lack of coordination between different social security programs run by different agencies. For example, the Ministry of Poverty Alleviation (MOPA)[29] was created in 2011, but it is responsible only for some of the social security programs and projects; other programs are administered by separate ministries such as those for Agriculture, Industry, and Women, Children and Social Welfare, among others.

There is also no consistent benchmark for identifying the poor, despite the fact that the government has been implementing poor-focused programs since the 1990s. After MOPA was set up, an attempt was made in 2013 to identify the poor in 25 districts. However, it faced substantial criticism regarding its methodology and it did not continue. Recently, however, substantial progress has been reported in the identification of the criteria and identification of the poor people based on the criteria.

Though social security programs have had some positive impacts for Nepal's poor and marginalized groups, especially in the fields of health and education, many problems remain. The instrumental use of social security distributions for personal or political gain is a serious problem. In general, political parties have used such programs to gain popularity for themselves. Government has very recently enacted Social Security Act (2018) to effectively regulate social security allowance though its distribution has started two decades ago. But, as discussed above, different social security programs related to poverty, employment, livelihood and others are still not coordinated with each other, meaning that the requisite institutional base and processes (basic requirements for any successful policy implementation) have not been established. Contributory social security scheme was introduced only in 2011 with the establishment of Social Security Fund though the country

29. After 2015, this ministry was combined with the Ministry of Land Management and Cooperatives and is now called the Ministry of Land Management, Cooperatives and Poverty Alleviation.

started provident fund and citizens fund quite early. But, the Social Security Fund almost remained dormant as Contribution Based Social Security Act was enacted only in 2017 and its regulation in 2018. It is only after recently announced contributory social security scheme of NCP government in late 2018, the fund has formalized social security system for employed workers. At present, the fund is preparing to initiate medical, health, maternity, accidental, disability, dependent and old-age benefits for employed workers. Government has also targeted to include informal sector soon[30]. It is expected that contributory social security scheme will be carried out effectively and it will contribute to growth of the country by increasing productivity.

3.4.3 Inclusive State Attempts to counteract centuries of exploitation and marginalization of certain caste and ethnic groups began in the 1950s. In 1951, NC leader BP Koirala lifted restrictions against Dalits (so-called "untouchable" castes) from receiving an education (Joshi and Rose, 1966). In 1963, King Mahendra officially abolished caste-based discrimination by revising exclusionary clauses in the National Code, 1963. The Constitution of 1990 included provisions abolishing discrimination and untouchability. In order to address the persistent nature and multiple dimensions of social exclusion, the National Inclusion Commission was set up in mid-2000, while the National Dalit Commission and the National Women Commission were both created in 2002. Furthermore, an autonomous National Foundation for Development of Indigenous Nationalities was created in 2002 under the erstwhile Ministry of Local Development to ensure the overall welfare of different indigenous groups, although they were not given any substantive role in policy making or planning.

The issue of social inclusion gained attraction in public discourse during the 2000s. As it was one of the major agendas

30. Social Security Fund has not included informal sector so there is a big apprehension on whether the initiative of the fund is pervasive because ILO (2015) indicates that 58% of youth aged 15-29 are self-employed and Rajbhandari (2018) reports that 4 out of every 5 workers are in self-employment or the informal sector with no social security insurance.

raised by Maoists. NGOs, INGOs and international donor agencies played an instrumental role in emphasizing the importance of inclusion. For instance, a joint 2006 report by the World Bank and DFID, *Unequal Citizens,* highlighted the persistent nature of inequality in socio-economic development indicators between different caste and ethnic groups. Likewise, the Social Inclusion Research Fund, created with funding from the Norwegian Embassy in 2005, discussed the complexities of social inclusion practices in Nepal (Gurung, 2006 and Stokke and Manandhar, 2010). The grievances of excluded groups were also reflected in their large-scale mobilization in support of the Maoists during the armed insurgency. Further concerns about discrimination motivated the Madhesh Movement of 2007 and 2008.

As a result of the discourse on inclusion, the Interim Constitution, 2007 created a system for proportional representation of specific social groupings in Parliament. In the same year, the Civil Service Act was amended to reserve 45% of civil service job openings for new recruits from designated social groups. Of these, 33% are reserved for women, 27% for Ethnic Nationalities (i.e. Janajati groups), 22% for Madheshi/ Terai Indigenous groups, 9% for Dalits, 5% for disabled persons, and 4% for people from "backward" (i.e. remote) areas. The 2015 Constitution has kept the proportional representation system, with some adjustments. Part 27 of the 2015 Constitution has also created new Constitutional Commissions to address discrimination issues, such as the National Madheshi Commission, the National Tharu Commission and many others and the government has also brought acts relating to these commissions in 2017.

Though these initiatives established representation of excluded groups in the public domain, their weak and fragmented institutional setup hampered their ability to effect policy reforms and changes in practice. The ongoing delay in federal restructuring reflects a similar inertia in terms of making changes to the *status quo* balance of power in Nepal. In addition, the question of how inclusion policies affect the mixed economic model supported by political parties remains unanswered. In sum, many discrimination-related grievances and injustices remain unaddressed.

3.4.4 Planning and Budgeting The political change of 1990 did not bring any immediate changes to the planning process. Rather, the country's Eighth Five-Year Plan, for the period 1992-97, captured holistic economic liberalization but continued the process of Panchayati planning process. The Eighth Plan focused on market reforms for economic growth and employment generation. It set targets for privatization, market deregulation, and restructuring financial institutions.

The Ninth Plan, for the period 1997-2002, established poverty alleviation as its main mission, setting a precedent that would be followed by all subsequent plans. The departure of the plan was the inclusion of the perspective vision for the first time in the annals of Nepali planning. The Tenth Plan, for 2002-2007, was designed under the framework of the World Bank's Poverty Reduction Strategy Paper. It also introduced a log framework, facilitating implementation, and a Mid-Term Expenditure Framework, enabling multi-year contracting under government budgets. Poverty reduction remained the cornerstones of the Eleventh[31] through Fourteenth Plans. The Fifteenth Plan, which is currently being drafted, also makes poverty reduction a core focus while emphasizing on prosperity

However, the government's focus on poverty reduction relied on generic development programs without a clear poverty focus. For example, the Ministry of Finance's 2008 budget directive considered all allocations made in rural areas, as well as social security and local grants, as "poverty focused" budget allocations (MOF, 2008b)[32]. This broad categorization of "poverty-focused" budgets can be critiqued in several ways. First, not all social security money is delivered to the poor (CBS et al, 2006[33], Rajbhandari,

31. Each Plan since the Eleventh Plan has covered a period of three years, in contrast to the previous plans of five years. However, the fifteenth plan has again been reverted back to the five years.

32. Subsequent Budget Preparation Directive of Ministry of Finance has not made any substantial changes in this regard (MOF, 2019a).

33. CBS et al (2006) report that education stipends were received by 384,000 Dalit students out of 527,000 eligible Dalits. Half of the stipends provided to non-Dalits were allocated to males, and 60% of recipients were students from non-poor families.

2018 and NPC, 2012). Second, it may not be correct to assume a multidimensional trickle-down effect of generic projects. For instance, budgets allocated for infrastructure and local bodies will not necessarily increase the incomes of poor households. The issue of which types of roads best address poverty is still being debated.[34] Targets for inclusion, human capacity development, and gender rights have been addressed in a similarly problematic way by the plans and the budgets. For instance, gender empowerment projects are set with multidimensional objectives of skill development, market intervention, gender equality, product diversification, income generation and many others but they were allocated minimum resources affecting accomplishment of goals. Though there have been initiatives to gradually sensitize the budgeting process with gender issues, environmental protection, and climate change adaptation, the approach is still not holistic. A lack of exclusively poverty-focused development projects makes it difficult to achieve poverty reduction and other goals. Sector-wise budget allocations made by the Plans are shown in Table 3.1a and Table 3.1b which explains government's concerns for developing all sector. But the programs and projects are not concrete and analysis of the specific effects of each project on the defined broader goals is lacking.

Another problem with the Plans is that despite the overall focus on poverty alleviation, other priorities were changed from plan to plan. This constant shifting has resulted in a lack of substantial progress on any individual priority. For example, the Eleventh Plan focused on reconstruction and rehabilitation in the aftermath of the Maoist insurgency, while the Twelfth Plan made a target of graduating from Least Developed Country status by 2030. The Thirteenth plan moved the deadline up to 2022 without analyzing the feasibility or benefit of this change.

Over the years, there have been legal reforms in the planning and budgeting process under the initiation of donors. In FY 1996/97, a budget preparation directive was issued jointly by National

34. Sapkota (2009) explains that most of the money allocated for local development has been used for infrastructure.

Planning Commission and Ministry of Finance to make the budgeting process more systematic (MOF, 2008b). The Financial Procedure Act, 1999 has been enacted repealing all earlier laws pertaining to public finance administration. This Act and regulation has been brought to operationalize financial procedures in a regulated and systematic manner. The Public Procurement Act, 2007 has been enacted to make the government procurement process more systematic and transparent. Likewise, the LSGA, 1999 opened the door for providing unconditional grants to local bodies.

Despite these initiatives, due diligence for government contractors and transparency in financial transactions remain insufficient. Assessments on public expenditure and financial accountability under the assistance of the World Bank and other donors report that though there are some improvements in budget formulation process, there remains many constraints in implementation of competitive bidding[35], procurement process and financial transparency, (MOF, 2008a and 2015). The studies add that most of the government organizations don't prepare their procurement plan, there is routine delays in development aid disbursement which consequently decreases development/ capital expenditure and there isn't effective internal auditing system. Further, excessive support to public enterprise could invite financial threat though the country's present debt sustainability condition isn't so bad. These public enterprises along with local government should follow prudent norms of financial management and regularly carry out standard auditing practices. Likewise, annual reports of the Office of Auditor General (OAG) also shows slow recovery of advance payments[36] and slicing of procurement into smaller packages to avoid open bidding thresholds (OAG, 2014 and 2017). Further, OAG also reports that most of the ministries/departments

---

35. OAG (2014) reports that only 8.46 percent procurements were carried out through less competitive methods in FY 2012/13 and the rest on a competitive basis.

36. The OAG (2017) report notes that national dues and arrears amounted to NRs. 328,520 million in FY 2013/14, increasing by 20% to NRs. 396,250 million in FY 2014/15. Given that the size of Nepal's economy is only around NRs. 3,000 billion during the period, the amount of dues and arrears is very high.

have not followed Financial Procedure Act, 1999 as they haven't prepared and implemented internal control systems; there is no regular inspection and monitoring, there is not effective internal audit and the salary reports and procurement plans are not properly prepared. So, even after the institutionalization of democracy in 1990, the budgeting and planning follows ritual administrative process, as during the Panchayat period. There is little innovation besides continuity of generic programs guided by macro approach. The brief review of the policies and programs announced in post 1990's budget shows similar pattern[37]. On top of that, Maoist insurgency deviated focus of government as security expenses needed to increase with commensurate decrease in capital expenditure since mid-nineties which countervailing effected economic growth (Ra and Rhee, 2005; Khanal and Kanel, 2005 and Ra and Singh, 2005). Interestingly, there is no reverting in expenditure pattern even after political settlement with Maoists in mid-2006 because Public Procurement Act and its regulation brought in 2007 require more transparency in contracting large scale development works and the state administration as well as other stakeholders have hesitation to do so leading to stagnancy in capital expenditure. This portrays limited change in overall development and planning process of Nepal.

Planning is a macro process and in Nepal too similar approaches were followed. But such approaches did not help to realize certain goals for example the current employment elasticity is 0.4 that would mean that total budget allocation for 2019/20 is expected to generate 500,000 jobs which generally is never realized. So calculations have to be done from the micro perspective as well that is how many jobs will be created in each activity and how does it match with the macro estimations. In Nepal, therefore, both, micro and macro approaches need to be adopted in the planning process.

37. Review of policies, programs and activities announced in post 1990 budgets is provided in annex D.

Table 3.1a: Sector-Wise Allocation of Planned Development Outlay for the Eighth to Tenth Plans (in NRs. Million)*

Sectors	Eighth		Ninth		Tenth	
	Planned Development Outlay	Share in Total (in %)	Planned Development Outlay	Share in Total (in %)	Planned Development Outlay	Share in Total (in %)
Agriculture, Irrigation and Forestry	29,193	25.73%	51,284	27.05%	56,210	24.4%
Industry and Mining	2,245	1.98%	1,588	0.84%	2,271	1.0%
Electricity, Gas and Water	23,719	20.90%	35,461	18.71%	36,004	15.7%
Trade, Hotels and Restaurants	1,481	1.31%	2,917	1.54%	3,511	1.5%
Transport, Communication and Other Infrastructure	20,030	17.65%	33,340	17.59%	36,428	15.8%
Social Services	35,808	31.55%	63,138	33.30%	90,386	39.3%
Miscellaneous**	1,003	0.88%	1,852	0.98%	5,219	2.3%
Total	113,479	100.00%	189,580	100.00%	230,029	100.0%

* Figures from each Plan are in constant prices of the base year of the respective plan, so they are not comparable with each other. ** Miscellaneous includes finance and real estate.

Source: Various *Development Plans*, National Planning Commission

Table 3.1b: Sector-Wise Allocation of Planned Development Outlay for the Eleventh to Fourteenth Plans (in NRs. Million)*

Sectors	Eleventh		Twelfth		Thirteen**		Fourteen**	
	Planned Development Outlay	Share in Total (in %)	Planned Development Outlay	Share in Total (in %)	Planned Fixed Capital Investment	Share in Total (in %)	Planned Fixed Capital Investment	Share in Total (in %)
Agriculture, Irrigation and Forestry	36,018	12.85%	72,280	12.79%	70,176	15.12%	140,240	14.69%
Industry and Mining	1,676	0.60%	6,270	1.11%	2,840	0.61%	10,500	1.10%
Electricity, Gas and Water	54,602	19.48%	85,110	15.06%	69,076	14.89%	200,020	20.96%
Wholesale and Retail Trading	3,239	1.16%	4,150	0.73%	1,487	0.32%	12,670	1.33%
Hotels and Restaurants	1,970	0.70%	7,700	1.36%	5,656	1.22%	8,340	0.87%
Transport, Communication, Storage and Other Infrastructure	50,195	17.91%	110,920	19.63%	102,224	22.03%	256,160	26.84%
General Administration and Defense	8,639	3.08%	27,900	4.94%	24,050	5.18%	36,010	3.77%
Social Services	116,348	41.51%	219,580	38.85%	179,150	38.61%	182,620	19.13%
Miscellaneous***	7,595	2.71%	31,230	5.53%	9,352	2.02%	107,860	11.30%
Total	280,282	100.00%	565,140	100.00%	464,011	100.00%	954,420	100.00%

* Figures from each Plan are in constant prices of the base year of the respective plan, so they are not comparable with each other. ** Sector-wise Fixed Capital Investment of Public Sector because development outlays were not published in these plan documents. ***Miscellaneous means Financial Intermediary.

Source: Various *Development Plans*, National Planning Commission

3.4.5 Taxation and Revenue The government introduced the Value Added Tax (VAT) in 1993, replacing all commercial taxes like the Sales Tax, Entertainment Tax, Hotel Tax, and Contract Tax. VAT is levied at each stage of value addition and commercial activity. It has increased public revenue substantially, enabling the government to mobilize more resources and to enter a new phase of development. The VAT rate was uniformly set at 10% during the period 1993-2003, and was increased in 2004 to 13%, the rate at which it remains today. In the 2000s, customs administration underwent major reforms aimed at discouraging embezzlement and fulfilling World Trade Organization (WTO) commitments. A new Customs Act in 2007 has simplified customs clearance procedures, and customs rates were also cut to bring them in line with WTO commitments. However, the Excise Duty Act, 2002 has brought imported goods under its bracket. Likewise, the Income Tax Act, 2002 has increased the domain of taxable income for individuals and corporate bodies.

As government revenue has increased specifically due to VAT, the government's contribution to public expenditure has also increased, while the share of foreign aid has dropped (Table 3.2). Government revenues contributed 47% of public expenditure in FY 1989/90 but increased to 78% in FY 2009/10 and reached 94% in 2014/15, as seen in Table 3.2. Government expenditure rose steeply after 2015 due to post earthquake construction work so government revenue to expenditure remained at 75 percent in 2017/18. However, the ability of the government to raise taxes is still questioned (Bajracharya, et.al, 2014). OAG (2017) report argues that Nepal's tax arrears is mounting as it has reached NRs. 132 billion in FY 2015/16 from NRs. 73 billion in FY 2011/12. Beside Inland Revenue Department and Customs Department, there are also institutions like Revenue Tribunal and Department of Revenue Investigation to facilitate revenue collection but tax arrears remain high and it is increasing. Routine Tax Clearance Commission is generally formed to recover such unpaid taxes but the inherent interest behind forming these commissions is eroded because of the actions of some deliberate defaulters with connection to powerful people, leading to cancellation of dues. OAG (2017) reports that tax clearance commission formed in FY 2012/13 provided huge

Table 3.2 Government Budgets for Selected Years of Post 1990 (in NRs. Million)*

Details	1989/90	1994/95	1999/2000	2004/05	2009/10	2014/15	2017/18
Total Government Expenditure**	19,669	39,060	66,273	102,560	227,107	428,252	967,133
Recurrent Expenditure	5,195	13,182	35,579	61,686	186,598	339,408	696,920
Capital Expenditure	14,474	25,878	25,481	27,341	40,510	88,844	270,213
Government Principal Payment (Amortization)			5,213	13,533	18,432	64,472	55,674
Net Loan Investment					7,479	26,257	15,960
Net Share Investment					4,716	10,510	44,777
Government Revenue	9,313	24,605	42,894	70,123	177,992	405,867	726,717
Government's Tax Revenue	7,284	19,660	33,152	54,105	159,785	355,956	659,491
Government's Non-Tax Revenue	2,029	4,945	9,742	16,018	18,206	49,911	67,226
Foreign Aids	7,935	11,249	17,524	23,657	49,769	65,638	133619
Foreign Grant	1,975	3,937	5,712	14,391	38,546	36,374	34,715
Foreign Loan	5,960	7,312	11,812	9,266	11,223	29,264	98,904

Domestic Loan	2,150	1,900	5,500	8,938	29,914	42,423	144751
Government Revenue to Total Government Expenditure***	47.35%	62.99%	64.72%	68.37%	78.37%	94.77%	75.14%
Foreign Aids to Total Government Expenditure***	40.34%	28.80%	26.44%	23.07%	21.91%	15.33%	13.82%
Domestic Loan to Total Government Expenditure***	10.93%	4.86%	8.30%	8.71%	13.17%	9.91%	14.97%

Economic Survey, Ministry of Finance

* The public finance recording format changed in FY 1999/2000 and in FY 2011/12 as per IMF's Government Finance Statistics, 2001. As a result, figures may not be comparable with each other. Recurrent Expenditure and Capital Expenditure represent Regular Expenditure and Development Expenditure, respectively for FY 1989/90 and 1994/95.

** For FY 1999/2000 and FY 2004/05, Total Government Expenditure is the sum of Recurrent Expenditure, Capital Expenditure and Government Principal Payment. For the rest, it is the sum of Recurrent Expenditure and Capital Expenditure.

*** While calculating ratios between FY 2009/10 and 2017/18, Total Government Expenditure also includes Government Principal Payment, Net Loan Investment and Net Share Investment so that figures could be compared for different fiscal years.

concession of NRs 400 million to one distillery and NRs. 180 million to one hotel and some of the private companies are also provided concessions of above 90 percent.

As part of the transition to a federal governance structure, the country is currently in the process of institutionalizing financial federalism. The National Natural Resources and Fiscal Commission (NNRFC) has been created as an independent body to distribute resources between the three tiers of the government. National Natural Resources and Fiscal Commission Act, 2017 and Inter-governmental Fiscal Arrangement Act, 2017 have been enacted to strengthen institutional capacity of NNRFC on expediting fiscal federalization. Provincial governments each have their own planning commission and an Economic Affairs Ministry to prepare provincial plans and budgets; local governments have departments to do the same. However, the delayed process for institutionalizing the inter-government financial mechanism has raised suspicions among the general public about the government's commitment to federalism.

3.5 Growth and Poverty The size of Nepal's economy in FY 1990/91 was around NRs. 120,370 million (Table 3.3). During the decade of nineties, economic growth was at 4.95% (Table 3.3), with per-capita GDP at current prices increasing from NRs. 6,510 to NRs. 19,071. For three years in the mid-1990s, growth crossed five percent (Figure 3.1). However, economic growth slowed at 3.78% in the decade of 2000s and the growth rate of fiscal year 2001/02 reached record low of 0.12 percent. This can be attributed to the Maoists' armed revolution, which reached its peak in the first half of the 2000s. Political instability continued even after the Maoists joined mainstream politics due to emergence of Terai conflict and frequent change in governments. The return to stability extended hope to investors in encouraging investments resulting in higher growth. Per-capita GDP at current prices reached NRs. 51,594 in FY 2010/11 and the economic growth dropped to 0.59 percent in FY 2015/16 due to earthquake. However, it should be noted that Nepal has achieved unprecedented growth during the last three years, at 8.22% in 2016/17, 6.66% in 2017/18, and just under 7.05% in 2018/19. The growth can largely be attributed to political stability

Figure 3.1: Annual Economic Growth in Post 1990 (in %)

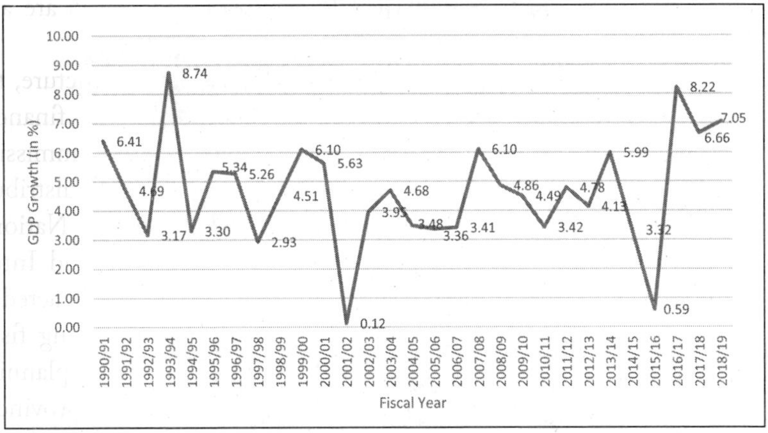

Source: Various Issues of *Statistical Year Book of Nepal,* Central Bureau of Statistics

rather than any specific government effort. The main drivers of growth during the last three years were reconstruction as well as new construction, expansion of trade, increase in electricity production and consumption and increase in remittances besides the favorable monsoon in 2017-18 and 2018-19. It also suggests that properly planned efforts still have the potential to unleash development. But, IMF (2018) argues that Nepal's growth failed to match that of other South Asian nations. TFP grew by 0.69 percent during the period 1975 to 2001 explaining about 31 percent of economic growth during the period meaning that the rest of the growth was generated through additional investment (Bajracharya and Bajracharya, 2002). This signifies that Nepal's economy lacks dynamism which is explained in greater detail in subsequent chapters.

The poverty rate has decreased significantly over the last two decades according to both the national and UN definitions.[38] The National Living Standards Survey shows that poverty declined from 41.8% to 30.9% between 1996 and 2004, and further decreased

38. The national definition of poverty defined in 2011 is 2220 Kcal per person, which comes to approximately PPP $1.29 and the UN definition is PPP $ 1.25 (For the MDG it defined at PPP $ 1.00. The UN has defined PPP $ 1.90 for SDG for 2030).

Table 3.3: Gross Domestic Production of Nepal for Selected Years of Post 1990 (in NRs Million)

Fiscal Years	Nominal GDP	Real GDP (at Constant Price of FY 2000/01	Per Capita GDP in Current Price (NRs)	Economic Growth (%)*
1990/91	120,370	272,235	6,510	4.78% (1980/81 to 1990/91)
2000/01	441,519	441,519	19,071	4.95% (1990/91 to 2000/01)
2010/11	1,366,954	639,694	51,594	3.78%(2000/01 to 1980/81)
2015/16	2,253,163	768,835	79,528	0.59%
2016/17	2,674,493	832,060	92,031	8.22%
2017/18	3,031,034	887,455	104,159	6.66%
2018/19**	3,464,319	950,033	117,474	7.05%

Source: Various Issues of *Statistical Year Book of Nepal,* CBS
*Source: Calculated by Author using CBS Data
* Time period representing the data is mentioned in parenthesis
**Preliminary Estimate

to 25.2% in 2011 (CBS, 2011). It is estimated at 18.6 percent in 2018 (MOF, 2019b). The trend is similar in rural and urban areas. However, inequality persists. The poorest 30% of the population earn only 7.5% of total income, whereas the richest 10% earn 39.5% of total income (Table 3.4). Furthermore, Nepal is far behind other South Asian countries in education, competency, health, and other social indicators; the nation has yet to break the shackles of underdevelopment (World Bank, 2017a).

3.6 Conclusion As the above discussion makes its clear, despite important political changes over the past three decades, Nepal's pace of development lags far behind its neighbors and much of the world. The official planning process continues to set new goals without attaining substantial success on any of them. Despite the fact that each political party emphasizes how it differs from the others, all mainstream political parties have accepted a mixed economic model, incorporating liberal openness and a welfare system. The continuity in overall economic strategy should have

Table 3.4: Income Distribution of Nepal in 2010/11

Income Percentile Range (Poorest to Richest)	Share in Income (in %)	Cumulative Share (in %)
10%	1.5	1.5
20%	2.6	4.1
30%	3.4	7.5
40%	4.4	11.9
50%	5.4	17.3
60%	6.8	24.1
70%	8.5	32.6
80%	11.2	43.8
90%	16.8	60.6
100%	39.4	100

Source: CBS, 2011

been a great asset in attracting investment. Unfortunately, however, conflicting and contradictory policies and the corruption induced environment have discouraged investment. It seems political parties have lost their vision, purpose and focus. Discourses on economic policies are dichotomous, inconsistent and non-continuous. The current government, with its two-thirds majority in parliament, has called for national and individual prosperity as the ultimate mission of governance and transformation. However, the dimensions of prosperity have yet to be defined despite some effort to do so in the fifteenth plan, and policies and strategies to attain prosperity are unclear. The time has come to set a clear path to prosperity, and to remain focused on this goal – making adjustments as necessary, and including all social groups – until it is attained.

chapter 4

ECONOMIC SECTORS: AGRICULTURE

4.1 Introduction As Nepal entered a new, post-Rana era in 1951, the country's agriculture sector remained both technologically and socially backward. Agriculture dominated the Nepali economy, contributing two third of the GDP and providing jobs to 93% of the economically active population in mid-sixties. Land ownership was highly unequal, with a small minority of landlords owning vast tracts of land while many others remained landless. Different feudalistic tenancy systems prevailed in different areas of the country. Labor exploitation was routine: under practices like *Haruwa-Charuwa* in the eastern Terai and *Haliya* in the far-western hills and low-caste Dalits were in effect enslaved by their landlords (KC et. al., 2013). Most smallholders and landless farmers paid high rents – often over 50% of their crops' yield – to landlords. With their share of the harvest, tenant farmers had to feed themselves and save seed for the next year's cultivation. Because irrigation was limited and cultivation methods remained traditional, agriculture was highly dependent on weather, that has still persisted, and farmers remained vulnerable to climatic changes and extreme weather events like droughts and floods. In order to supplement their livelihoods during lean periods, most farmers depended on high-interest loans from landlords, perpetuating vicious cycles of poverty. The Rana Regime had set up a Department of Agriculture in 1924, but its work did little to transform the feudalistic agricultural sector.[1]

1. The Ranas established one demonstration farm and one nursery farm in

4.2 Initiation of Reforms During the 1950s, all political parties expressed commitments to address the backwardness of the agriculture sector by modernizing farms and implementing land reforms. Joshi and Rose (1966) note that land reform was central to the democratic-socialist ideology of the Nepali Congress (NC), the most popular political party at the time. In the 1959 general election, NC introduced the slogan "*Jamin Jotneko*" meaning "Land to the Tiller." Similarly, the first convention of leftists, held in January 1954, passed a resolution demanding confiscation of land from "feudal landlords" and redistribution in favor of peasants and the landless (Karki, 2004). These political commitments were reflected in the government's first Five-Year Plan, for the period 1956-61, which set a goal of bringing about major land reform policies. This Plan also emphasized the need for agricultural modernization by setting up large-scale irrigation projects and initiating the use of improved seeds, fertilizers, and equipment. Likewise, it aimed to develop market mechanisms in order to expand commercial agriculture. However, progress in bringing about land reform and other agricultural changes was slow. The government formed a Land Reform Commission in 1953 and passed different laws[2] aiming to ensure security of tenancy for farmers, but the Acts were not implemented successfully.

Donors also supported the initiation of some agricultural modernization and commercialization projects during the 1950s. For instance, the US brought improved maize seeds to Nepal in the mid-1950s, while the Swiss began to provide technical support for milk processing and cheese production in 1955. A conference was organized in November, 1958 to explore possibilities for creating an institutional framework to support agriculture development. However, despite these efforts, no major changes in Nepal's agricultural sector were observed at the time due to a lack of

---

Kathmandu. During their regime's last days, the Ranas also signed an agreement with the US government to establish a Village Development Training Center in order to prepare community development workers.

2. Land-related Acts brought by the government in the 1950s included the Nepal Rights and Security Act of 1951, the Tenancy Rights Acquisition Act of 1952, and the Land and Cultivators' Records Act of 1954.

institutional mechanism, technical capacity, political stability, and resources.

4.3 Agrarian Reforms under the King Following the 1960 royal coup, King Mahendra also expressed his commitment to agrarian reforms and assured the public that good policies initiated by the political parties would be continued. In periodic planning documents, the Panchayat government reiterated the need to maximize agricultural production through optimal land utilization, crop diversification, and modern technology. In 1964, King Mahendra took a major step toward addressing land inequality when he signed into law the Land Reform Act. The Act established ceilings for the amount of land any individual could own, specified tenant farmers' rights for example, by fixing rent prices, regulated land surveys and land categorization, and established other land administrative procedures. Furthermore, the King also formed a farmer's association – one of the so-called "class organizations" overseen by the government – which was mandated for advising leaders on agricultural development policy and nominating two members to the National Panchayat.

Various foreign donors including Ford Foundation (Gill, 2009) supported different technological advancement projects that complemented land reform efforts. METCON's (1994) assessment of technical assistance to Nepal in the agriculture and irrigation sectors between 1950 to 1990 shows that donor assistance focused primarily on: i) providing improved seeds and fertilizers and increasing their use; ii) diversifying production and cultivation processes; iii) providing soft agricultural credit and seed money for investments; iv) providing scholarships and capacity-building trainings for Nepali farmers/people; and v) institutionalizing agricultural research and market mechanisms.

The government established the Agriculture Development Bank, Nepal (ADBN) in 1968 to provide soft loans to cottage industries and to farmers' cooperatives using a group liability scheme. Beginning in the mid-1970s, different credit programs through ADBN and other commercial banks were designed and supported by various donors. Two major programs were the Small

Farmer's Development Program, which began in 1974 with support from the UN's Food and Agriculture Organization (FAO), and the Production Credit for Rural Women, begun in 1982 by UNICEF. These soft credit schemes were instrumental in introducing small farmers to the cooperative and collective farming approaches.

Agriculture was central to the Integrated Rural Development (IRD) approach that became popular in the 1970s. The basic focus of IRD was to improve agricultural production and rural living standards by improving the supply of inputs, institutionalizing extension services, and developing infrastructure (Adhikari, 1982). Agriculture Service Centers were set up at important points in a district to provide technical support to needy farmers, while small irrigation systems and rural roads were constructed to improve their productivity and link them with nearby markets. The government declared FY 1974/75 as the "Agro Year," launching a nationwide campaign to promote modern agricultural practices and technologies (Pyakuryal, 1980). Likewise, USAID initiated the Integrated Cereals Project using the "block production" approach in 1982. Under this approach, small parcels of land were integrated into contiguous plots for planting particular cereals, so that small farmers could benefit from economies of scale, consequentially increasing productivity. Donor support also aimed to diversify cropping patterns. Examples included the UNDP's support for livestock and cotton production as well as fruit horticulture in the hills region, FAO's support for vegetable seed production and fisheries, Swiss support for potato production, and Dutch support for beekeeping (METCON, 1994). In 1979, the Department of Livestock was created within the Ministry of Agriculture with the support of the Asian Development Bank. The National Commodity Development Program was launched in 1972 to research and develop new varieties of rice, wheat, maize, potato, citrus, and sugarcane.

The government also provided agricultural subsidies to increase production and productivity. (Awasthi and Adhikary, 2004). Fertilizer prices were kept uniform throughout the country beginning in 1973 by subsidizing their transport to remote regions.[3]

3. Because the global price of fertilizer increased in 1972, the government initiated a subsidy to facilitate the farmers (Sharma and Anderson, 1985).

Major surface water irrigation systems were also constructed, financed by the government and donors. Awasthi and Adhikary (2004) report that revenue received from irrigation system users was only 1.3% of total operation and management costs, meaning that 98.7% of these costs were subsidized. The government also subsidized installation costs for shallow tube wells used in irrigation.

Several agricultural public enterprises and research institutions were established during the Panchayat era. The Agriculture Inputs Corporation (AIC) was created to supply the nation with inputs like fertilizers, and the Agriculture Tools Factory was established in Birgunj to make the country self-sufficient in basic agricultural tools. The Food Act of 1966 aimed to ensure food security by creating The Nepal Food Corporation (NFC) to store basic food requirements and distribute food at reasonable prices. In FY 1976/77, the NFC assured farmers a minimum farm-gate price for paddy and wheat. Meanwhile, the Janakpur Cigarette Company and the Birgunj Sugar Mills were established to process raw agricultural outputs. New departments and divisions were also created in various line ministries to look after agricultural research, market promotion, and quality control. The APROSC also played an instrumental role in strengthening the government's institutional capacity in the agriculture sector through research support.

4.3.1 Assessment of the King's Reforms Use of improved seeds and chemical fertilizers started in the early 1960s and expanded significantly during the period of the Third Plan (1965-1970), which gave special priority to modernizing Nepal's agricultural sector. By 1990, the Agriculture Inputs Cooperation (AIC) was selling 67,000 metric tons of chemical fertilizers and 2,000 metric tons of improved seeds per year (Economic Survey 1990/91, MOF). Dhital (2017) notes that there were significant improvements in livelihoods due to cultivation of vegetable and cash crops in districts like Jhapa, Bhaktapur, Kailali, and other areas during the Panchayat period. In the Terai region, the creation of new private-sector agricultural processing mills created employment opportunities.

However, chemical input use in Nepal was still low compared to other South Asian countries (Figure 4.1). Most fertilizer came to the country in the form of foreign aid (Sharma and Anderson, 1985). The AIC, which was the main distributor, was unable to provide fertilizer in a timely manner to farmers, especially those in remote areas (Seddon, 1987 and ADB, 1982). Difficulty in accessing fertilizers hindered farmers' productivity (Table 4.1).

At the same time, irrigation systems remained under-developed, with most farmers depending on rainfall. Sharma and Anderson (1985) report that in the early 1980s, only three percent of arable land was irrigated. The basic flaw of Nepali development has been inability to provide irrigation despite various efforts. The economic benefits of providing such facilities would have been enormous particularly if all low land areas that would have required relatively less investment have been fully irrigated.

Agricultural research and expertise were also lacking. A study by APROSC (1981) showed that the number of agricultural experts in Nepal more than doubled between 1971 and 1980, but the total was still not enough to meet needs.[4] The government devoted insufficient resources to agricultural research (Sharma and Anderson, 1985),[5] and data in the agriculture sector remained limited (Gill et al, 1990).

Likewise, technological improvements in agriculture failed to gain full momentum because agricultural development was not complemented by parallel development in other sectors like industry, transport, and infrastructure. A METCON (1994) assessment on technical assistance in Nepal's agriculture sector found that most foreign assistance was concentrated in areas easily accessible by motorable roads, such as in the Terai and villages near urban settlements in the eastern and western hills. Support was lacking in the Far and Mid-Western regions, where road access was negligible. Furthermore, support to develop market mechanisms

4. The number of nationwide trained staff with educational qualification of BSc or above increased from 352 in 1971 to 873 in 1980 (APROSC, 1981). Likewise, the number of staff with vocational training in agriculture increased from 1,045 to 2,510 during the same period.

5. Sharma and Anderson (1985) report that investment in agriculture research was 0.14% of GDP and 0.22% of agricultural GDP in seventies and eighties, which is lower than many other countries.

was limited and ineffective, hampered by limited connectivity and a lack of proper storage facilities.

Government regulation in the agriculture sector was often ineffective. The Food Act, 1966 aimed to prevent adulteration, while certain clauses in the Civil Code of 1962 prohibited harmful chemical use, and the Infectious Disease Act, 1964 promoted animal health. Technical infrastructure like laboratories and veterinary centers were created in accordance with these laws. However, these pieces of legislation were not well-harmonized with one another, the laboratories had minimum modern equipment and procedures to charge violators for misconduct were cumbersome with many loopholes.

Figure 4.1: Fertilizer Consumption in South Asia, 1980-90 (kg per hectare)

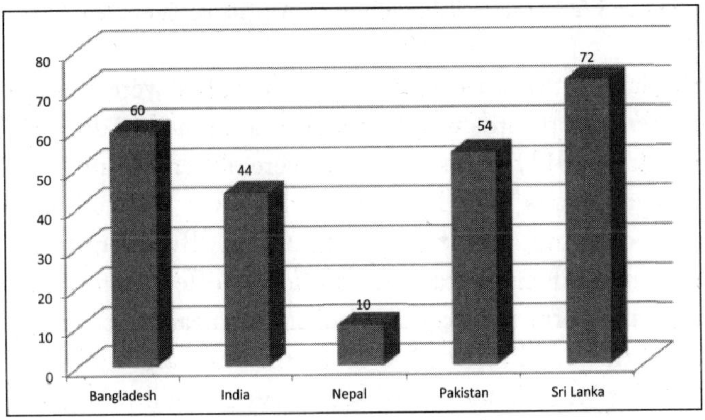

Source: Piya et. al. 2011

Though Mahendra's land reform program held great potential, it lacked effective implementation (Joshi and Rose, 1966). Despite the land ceilings imposed by the Land Reform Act (1964), most landlords were able to keep their landholdings under the threshold by transferring excess land to family members and other allies. In the end, only about 23,000 Bigha (about 14,950 hectares)[6] of land

6. One Bigha is approximately 0.65 hectares.

was seized, representing only 0.7% of the country's cultivated land. Despite this failure, the initiative was popularly appreciated and helped set an expectation that the government would not tolerate unlimited holdings and exploitative agricultural labor practices. Overall, however, the land distribution pattern remained unchanged during the King's rule and land redistribution did not take place.

Table 4.1: Cereal Crop Yields in South Asia (kg per hectare)

Countries	1981	1991
Bangladesh	1938	2586
India	1399	1926
Nepal	1701	1848
Pakistan	1670	1806
Sri Lanka	2548	2926

Source: FAO Data available at http://www.fao.org/faostat/en/#data

Similarly, efforts to ensure tenancy rights were unsuccessful because tenancy records were not well-maintained (Adhikari, 2010 and Dhakal, 2011). Most tenants were illiterate and relied on spoken agreements with landlords, who often took advantage of them by cheating and embezzling funds. By submitting false administrative documentation, landlords often benefited from agricultural reform projects and subsidies meant for tenants and landless farmers,[7] diverting aid from the real target groups. As a result of this weak institutional setup, agricultural reform projects and subsidies were unable to achieve their dual goals of agricultural development and poverty alleviation.

Although the ADBN had been set up to promote agricultural development, its work was hindered by a shortage of loanable funds (Acharya et al., 1998).[8] To address this problem, the bank was permitted to conduct commercial banking and collect deposits from

7. Many landlords registered their own relatives as peasants.

8. ADBN used to take soft loans from donor agencies under different agricultural development programs and supplied credit to farmers at low interest rates. The bank also used to borrow from the central bank.

the public beginning in July 1984. However, the institutional setup for agricultural reform projects was weak, and subsidies provided by government did not give proper returns (ADB, 1982).

Small-scale farmers had little recourse to voice their dissatisfaction with ineffective agricultural policies during the Panchayat era. The farmers' class organization failed to play a pivotal role in raising issues in development discourse because it was dominated by landlords and puppets of the Panchayat regime. Instead, its role was limited to nominating members to the National Panchayat.[9]

Table 4.2: Agriculture Sector of Nepal in Selected Years of the Panchayat Period (in NRs. million)

Fiscal Years	Agro GDP (Current Price)	Agro GDP (at Constant Price of FY 2000/01)	Share of Agriculture Contribution in GDP (in %)	Percent of Economically Active Population in Agriculture	Agriculture Growth (%)*
1964/65	3,654	64,292	65.23%		
1970/71	6,034	75,794	67.51%	94.37%	2.78% (1964/65 to 1970/71)
1980/81	15,510	82,140	65.47%	91.15%	0.81% (1970/71 to 1980/81)
1990/91	55,368	118,715	47.68%	81.23%	2.27% (1980/81 to 1990/91)

Source: Various Issues of *Statistical Year Book of Nepal*, CBS
*Source: Calculated by Author using CBS Data
* Time period representing the data is mentioned in parenthesis

At the end of the Panchayat era in 1990, agriculture remained backward in many respects (Seddon, 1987). The sector was still the main contributor to GDP, making up 47% of the economy in 1990/91 (Table 4.2), this represented a significant decrease from

9. The political parties agitating against the King at the time criticized these agricultural reform programs for their failures. They reportedly launched campaigns in favor of poor farmers, like looting food grains from landlords and redistributing them, albeit on a small scale.

ten years before, due mainly to the expansion of the service sector. Nonetheless, the majority of the population – 81% – was still engaged in agriculture. It is interesting to note that Nepal established a number of Paddy and Rice exporting companies in the public sector in the seventies to sell its surplus paddy but had to be closed by the late eighties due to evaporation of the surplus meaning that the reforms did not contribute in developing agriculture sector.

4.4 Reforms during the Democratic Regime In 1990, the newly empowered political parties inherited a backward agricultural sector that had changed little over the course of the Panchayat era. The Eighth Five-Year Plan, for the period 1992-97, reported that agriculture remained dominated by traditional subsistence farming of cereal crops. Initiatives for change were visible, but the scale of production and commercialization was limited. Furthermore, the Plan noted that there was limited irrigation and minimal use of improved seeds, fertilizers, or equipment, despite the fact that donors had been providing technical support in these areas for some time.

As in the 1950s, political parties again expressed their commitment to modernize agriculture and bring about land reform in their post-1990 manifestos, general convention resolutions, and other documents.[10] All major political parties shared a common voice in committing to continue positive policies begun under the King.

The government set out a pathway to accelerate economic growth, generate employment, and reduce poverty through the Agriculture Perspective Plan (APP) in June 1995 (APROSC and Mellor, 1995). The APP envisioned transformation from subsistence-based agriculture to commercial farming, with special focus on crops for which Nepal had a comparative advantage. It also urged better coordination between short- and long-term strategies for agriculture planning. Many of these points were reiterated in the National Agriculture Policy, which was produced

10. Review of manifestos of NC, CPN-UML, CPN-Maoist and NCP for post 1990 elections is provided in annex C. Refer manifestos of mainstream political parties for post 1990 elections for details.

in 2002[11]. Likewise, the government's Agriculture Development Strategy for the period 2015-2035 envisioned making the country self-reliant and internationally competitive in agriculture, whilst improving livelihoods, nutrition, and social inclusion (MOAD, 2015). In addition to these plans, post-1990 governments brought out 20 other policies that directly or indirectly sought to reform the agricultural sector (MOAD, 2013). The remaining sections of this chapter discuss agricultural reforms since 1990.

4.4.1 Agricultural Modernization and Diversification After 1990, new projects aimed to continue the modernization process set in motion under the Panchayat regime. Bilateral and multilateral donors like the ADB and the World Bank came forward to support agricultural development. In addition, the government started to design a few projects using its own financing. Policies on fertilizer and seeds aimed to ensure an uninterrupted supply of agricultural inputs. Likewise, sub-sector policies on tea, coffee, dairy development, floriculture, medicinal plants, and livestock aimed to increase production and develop market linkages for domestic consumption as well as export. Furthermore, irrigation policy aimed to ensure easy access to water. The Nepal Agriculture Research Council was formed in 1991 to conduct research on farming and allied sectors, and financial institutions were ordered to prioritize financing for agriculture. There were also changes to projects' implementation modalities. Whereas most donor-funded projects had previously been managed by foreign consultants due to limited domestic human resources, after 1990 the spread of technical education enabled more Nepali people to manage and implement projects themselves, helping to "localize" development work (METCON, 1994).

With economic liberalization and decentralization measures in the 1990s, more actors became engaged in the agricultural modernization process (WFP and FAO, 2007). Specifically, decentralization brought large-scale construction of rural agri-

11. Review of policies for selected sectors brought in post 1990 is provided in Annex E.

cultural roads by local bodies. The Department of Local Infrastructure Development and Agricultural Roads (DOLIDAR), formed under the Ministry of Local Development in the mid-1990s, was instrumental in improving rural access. Due to these improvements, even the Mid- and Far-Western Regions, which had lagged far behind the rest of the country in terms of development, began to receive foreign assistance. Donors like SNV, FAO and other came forward to serve these regions with agricultural projects. Road access facilitated agricultural projects in other parts of the country as well by increasing the supply of inputs and connecting farmers to outside markets.

Table 4.3: Agriculture Sector of Nepal in Selected Years of Post-1990 (in NRs. Million)

Fiscal Years	Agro GDP (Current Price)	Agro GDP (at Constant Price of FY 2000/01)	Share of Agriculture in GDP (in %)	Percent of Economically Active Population in Agriculture	Agriculture Growth (%)*
1990/91	55,368	118,715	47.68%	81.23%	2.27% (1980/81 to 1990/91
2000/01	155,625	155,625	36.58%	65.70%	2.74% (1990/91 to 2000/01)
2010/11	478,149	214,786	37.06%	64.01%	3.27%(2000/01 to 2010/11)
2015/16	656,779	240,681	31.61%		0.23%
2016/17	724,283	253,197	29.65%		5.20%
2017/18	766,620	260,255	28.06%		2.79%
2018/19**	826,007	273,353	26.98%		5.03%

Source: Various Issues of *Statistical Year Book of Nepal*, CBS
*Source: Calculated by Author using CBS Data.
* Time period representing the data is mentioned in parenthesis
**Preliminary Estimate

Due to these efforts, annual growth in the agricultural sector averaged 2.7% during the 1990s and 3.2% during the 2000s, reaching the contribution NRs 766,620 million in FY 2017/18 (Tables 4.3). At the same time, however, agriculture's share of GDP dropped from 47.68% in 1990/91 to 28.06% in 2017/18 (Table 4.3). The number of people engaged in agriculture also dropped after 1990 – reaching 64.01% in 2011 – as more people found work in the service sector.

Agricultural modernization also led to crop diversification. By 2000, cereals accounted for only 34.9% of the total agricultural output, while cash crops accounted for 8.5%, fruits and vegetables for 13.6%, and livestock and fisheries for 31.1%. This showed shift from heavy reliance on cereal production to a more diversified production mix that can be attributed to commercialization and trade.

Figure 4.2: Contribution of Various Sub-Sectors to Nepal's Total Agricultural Output in 2010

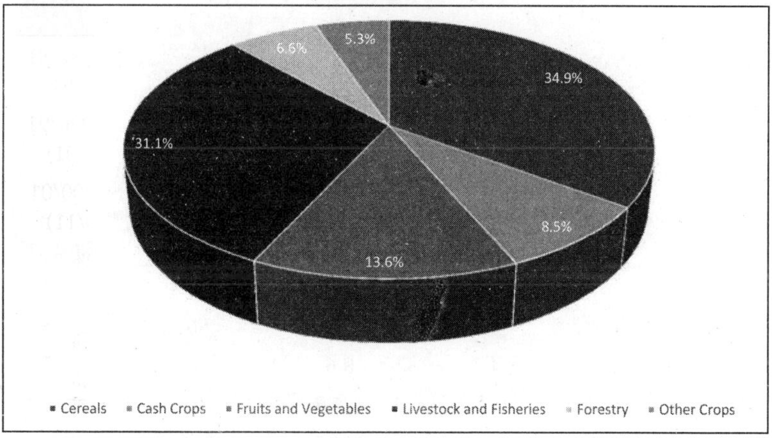

Source: CBS quoted in ABPMDD[12], 2010

However, despite these changes, agricultural productivity remained low (Table 4.4) due to limited access to irrigation and inputs (Table 4.5). Of 2.522 million hectares of land used for

12. Agri Business Promotion and Marketing Development Directorate, 2010; pp 255

agriculture, only 1.313 million hectares were irrigated in 2012 (CBS, 2013)[13]. The government's agricultural research expenditure remained at around 2.5% to 5.5% of total agricultural output (Awasthi and Adhikari, 2004). Many households continued to use traditional seed varieties rather than improved seeds (Table 4.5). Per-capita fertilizer consumption (Table 4.6) and tractor utilization (Figure 4.3) also remained low.

Table 4.4: Yield of Cereal Crops in South Asia (kg per Hectare)

Countries	2001	2011	2017
Bangladesh	3311	4353	4411
India	2423	2861	3161
Nepal	2177	2477	2796
Pakistan	2231	2953	3171
Sri Lanka	3425	3521	2147

Source: FAO Data Available at http://www.fao.org/faostat/en/#data

Table 4.5: Agricultural Households Using Improved Seeds and Fertilizer

Commodities	Percent of Agricultural Households Using Improved Seeds		Percent of Agricultural Households Using Fertilizer	
	2003/04	2010/11	2003/04	2010/11
Paddy	5.4	15	66.4	70.1
Wheat	5.6	13.3	56	52.5
Maize	4.3	8.6	30	36.5
Summer Vegetables	11.9	26.3	3.7	8
Winter Vegetables	20.7	16.5	8.1	4

Source: CBS, 2004 and 2011b

13. This is total irrigation but year round irrigation coverage is significantly lower.

Table 4.6: Fertilizer Consumption in South Asia, Post-1990 (kg per Hectare)

Countries	1991-97	2011	2016
Bangladesh	141	256	289
India	91	181	166
Nepal	19	36	74
Pakistan	103	129	144
Sri Lanka	102	257	132

Source: FAO Data Available at http://www.fao.org/faostat/en/#data

Figure 4.3: Tractor Utilization in South Asian Agriculture (Number per Thousand Hectares)

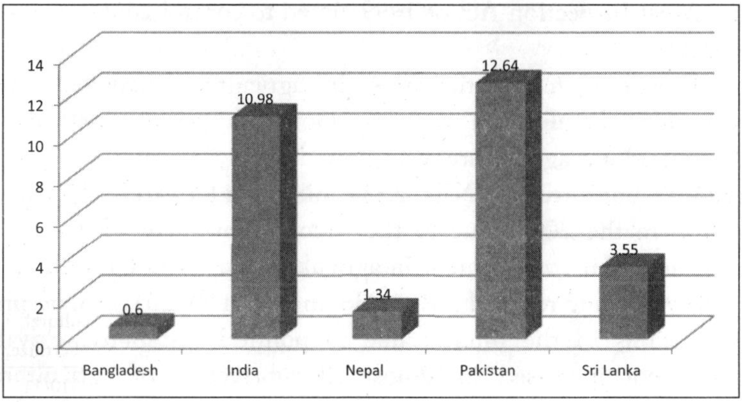

Source: Piya et. al. 2011

4.4.2 Agriculture Liberalization Economic liberalization measures during the 1990s represented a forward step for agricultural commercialization, which has been a goal reiterated in various policy and planning documents over the last five decades. The openness of the economy brought market dynamism with multiplier effects in agriculture's forward and backward linkages, but there were also many challenges.

The Industrial Enterprises Act (IEA) passed by the NC in 1992 and the Foreign Investment and Technology Transfer Act, passed in 1992, opened the economy for private and foreign investment in agriculture. The IEA also allowed for domestic entrepreneurs to start agribusiness-related cottage and small industries. In 1996, the government allowed the private sector to import and distribute fertilizer, removing the monopoly once held by the AIC[14] (NARMA, 2006). The government also set up institutions to monitor and regulate the agricultural private sector. It began to improve market information collection and agricultural statistics by collaborating with private association bodies like the FNCCI. Likewise, it set up the Department of Food Technology and Quality Control as a regulatory body. The Food Act of 1966 was amended and the Pesticide Act of 1994 was passed to control the use of harmful agricultural chemicals. Similarly, the Animal Health and Livestock Act of 1999 and the Animal Slaughterhouse and Meat Inspection Act of 1999 aimed to control contamination in meat.

Private sector participation in agriculture increased with economic liberalization policies. Domestic private investment committed in agriculture was only NRs 1,832 million in FY 1994/95, but it reached NRs. 2,517 million in FY 2017/18, despite a drop in the 2000s due to the Maoist movement (Table 4.7). Likewise, FDI commitment in agriculture was NRs 65 million in FY 1994/95 and reached NRs 1,936 million in FY 2017/18, despite fluctuations in the interim due to political instability. Private investment increased in almost all sub-sectors of agriculture, including input supply, product trading, and cultivation. Likewise, the number of registered agribusiness-related small and cottage industries reached more than 26,000 in FY 2016/17, most of them related to plant propagation, tea, mushrooms, bee-keeping, and livestock.[15]

14. As a part of liberalization measures, in May 2002, AIC was converted into government owned private companies with the names of Agriculture Inputs Company Ltd. (AICL) and National Seed Company Ltd. Both of these companies are registered under Company Act.

15. Department of Cottage and Small Industries (2017)

Table 4.7: Private and Foreign Investment Committed in Nepal's Agricultural Sector (in NRs Million)

Fiscal Year	Total Private Investment Committed	Total FDI Committed
1994/95	1,832	65
2000/01	684	31
2010/11	536	434
2013/14	1,566	1,013
2014/15	1,348	735
2015/16	987	297
2016/17	3,261	256
2017/18	2,517	1,936

Source: Various Issues of *Industrial Statistics,* Department of Industry

Economic liberalization lessened the dominance of the government-owned AIC in inputs supply and of the NFC in food supply. The functions of NFC were revised and its role was limited to food distribution in scarcity-affected mountain districts (Acharya et al, 1998). Reforms also led to a gradual reduction in agricultural subsidies. Fertilizer subsidies had begun in 1973, and later subsidies for irrigation and different types of soft loans were also introduced (Sharma and Anderson, 1985). By FY 1994/95, fertilizer subsidies amounted to NRs 655 million, or 12% of the government's agricultural budget (Awasthi and Adhikary, 2004). Beginning from 1995 onward, fertilizer and irrigation subsidies were gradually phased out as part of the reforms, though these were later reintroduced after 2008, although agricultural soft loans were continued.

Political parties have debated whether the effects of agricultural liberalization have been positive or negative. The NC, which initiated many of the policies allowing the participation of big as well as small businessmen, cooperatives, and others in agricultural markets, insist that these reforms resulted in smooth value chains with fair prices for farmers, traders, wholesalers, commission agents, and consumers. By contrast, the UML call for promoting national capital and controlling foreign investment in agriculture.[16] The leftists criticize liberalization for failing to benefit poor farmers and inviting exploitation by big businessmen who manipulated prices. The UML argue that only small and medium-sized businessmen should be allowed to participate in the agricultural trade, using a cooperative model. Under this model, farmers' cooperatives collect products from their members to sell to consumers, thus curtailing the role of middlemen and ensuring fair distribution of returns to all participating stakeholders. The Maoists, on the other hand, held extreme views, espousing total state control over the supply of agricultural products and food. They claim all middlemen – including big businessmen and cooperatives – are exploiting farmers and consumers. However, despite the UML's and the Maoists' objections to agricultural liberalization, they never made serious efforts to reverse the trend during their periods of tenure in government over the years except reintroduction of subsidies to a limited extent.

Since the initiation of economic liberalization, various donors have played roles in developing agricultural markets. The UNDP and FAO played an instrumental role in setting up agricultural collection centers, while SNV, GTZ and DFID were focused on developing value chains for high-value products like fruits, spices, pulses, and dairy products. The World Bank initiated a project on agricultural commercialization and trade, among other agriculture-related projects. ADB also introduced various agriculture commercialization projects. These activities contributed to crop diversification and also helped expand the reach of farmers' cooperatives. In addition, certain Nepali agricultural exports have found significant markets abroad, including pulses, ginger, cardamom, and pashmina (made from Changra Wool) (MOC, 2016).

---

16. See, for example, the resolution of the Fifth General Convention of UML, which was held from 27th January 1993 to 2nd February 1993. The resolution was drafted by then-secretary Madan Bhandari, and remained the guiding document for the UML until united with CPN-Maoist in May 2018 to form the Nepal Communist Party.

However, challenges remain for successful agricultural commercialization in Nepal. Timely access to fertilizers remains a problem for many farmers. The private sector delivers these materials only up to market towns that are accessible by road (Shrestha, 2010). Many rural farmers remain unaware of commercial opportunities or are skeptical about engaging in trade with middlemen, from whom they fear exploitation. Such fears gained intensity during the Maoists' armed revolution, and have spread in the years since due to weak regulation of the agricultural sector. There is a profound lack of regulatory bodies and monitoring mechanisms to oversee cooperatives and private firms active in agricultural trading (ADB, 2013). Though the Cooperative Act of 2017 and its earlier iteration in 1992 designated the Department of Cooperatives as the main regulatory body, in practice its work has been limited to registration and renewal of certificates for cooperatives. It lacks district line offices or sufficient staff to monitor and evaluate the thousands of cooperatives spread all over Nepal. Similarly, relevant line ministries and departments for regulating the private sector like DFTQC, ABPMDD and others are understaffed and lack the hardware capacity (like laboratories and automated price monitoring systems) to properly monitor; some do not even have district offices.

After Nepal's accession to the WTO in 2004, there was intense debate about the implications of the WTO's SPS and TBT clauses for Nepali agriculture (Sharma et al 2002). Furthermore, quarantine offices at border points are ill-equipped, limiting their capacity to check agro imports and exports like Pashmina and carpets, leading to quality-control problems (MOC, 2016). The weak regulatory system is riddled with loopholes allowing for corruption.

4.4.3 Land Reform and Its Unmet Goal During the 1990s, both major political parties – the NC and the UML – reiterated their commitment to major land reform in their party manifestos and they formed various commissions on the subject when they were in the government. For instance, the NC government formed after the 1991 general election created a high-level commission on land under the chairmanship of the erstwhile Minister of Land Reform,

Table 4.8: Landholding Pattern of Nepal (in Percent)

Size of Holding (In Hectares)	1961/62		1971/72		1981/82		1991/92		2001/02		2011/12	
	Holdings	Area	Holdings	Area	Holdings	Area	Holdings	Area	Holdings	Area	Holdings	Area
Under 0.5	56.2	11.9	62.7	13.8	50.3	6.6	43.2	11.3	47.3	14.7	53.5	19.2
0.5-1.0	18.8	12.2	14.9	12.1	16.3	10.8	26.3	19.2	27.4	24.2	26.5	27.6
1.0-2.0	11.9	15.4	11.1	17.4	17.3	19.9	19.6	27.6	17.6	29.8	14.8	29.7
2.0-3.0	5.2	11.7	5.0	13.4	7.2	15.4	6.2	15.4	4.7	14.0	3.5	12.2
3.0-4.0	2.7	8.6	2.3	8.6	3.5	10.8	2.2	7.8	1.5	6.6	1.1	5.3
4.0-5.0	1.5	6.2	1.2	5.7	1.9	7.7	1.1	4.8	0.6	3.4	0.4	2.6
5.0-10.0	2.6	16.4	2.1	15.5	2.7	15.8	1.2	8.1	0.6	5.3	0.3	2.7
10 and Above	1.0	17.4	0.7	13.7	0.7	13.1	0.3	5.8	0.1	2.0	0.0	0.6
Total	100	100	100	100	100	100	100	100	100	100	100	100

Source: CBS, 2006 and 2013

Shailaja Acharya. Likewise, the UML-led minority government in 1994 formed a High-Level Land Commission under one of its Central Committee members, Keshav Prasad Badal. However, neither Commission's recommendations were implemented (Adhikari, 2010 and Dhakal, 2011). Meanwhile, no initiatives were taken to document who the true tillers and farmers really were. A small amount of land was distributed to the landless (squatters) on an ad-hoc basis, as in the Panchayat era, but there were no major changes in land distribution.

The UNDP's Human Development Report for 2004 shows that almost 29% of rural households did not own farmland and 10% of Nepali people were completely landless. Table 4.8 shows that between 1961/62 and 2011/12, the proportion of landholders who own between 0.5 and two hectares has increased from 30.7% to 41.3%. This increase is primarily due to sub-division within families of larger landholdings above two hectares in size. The proportion of small landholders owning less than 0.5 hectares decreased, because there was no significant redistribution of small plots of land to the landless.

During their decade-long armed movement, the Maoists challenged landlords and claimed to oppose land inequality. They formed a parallel government that captured barren agricultural land. This helped popularize their movement in rural areas, but the Maoists did not use the captured land for any productive purpose. After entering mainstream politics, they continued to demand "revolutionary land reform" by confiscating land from landlords and distributing it to smallholding peasants and the landless. However, the Maoists faced difficulties in legitimizing this demand because they could not show that the land they had captured during the armed revolution had been put to proper use. When the Maoists controlled government during 2008-09, 2011-13, and 2016-17, they failed to take any meaningful step towards land reform. The new federal constitution of Nepal, 2015 has guaranteed property right and declare scientific land reform as the state policy as per Article 51-e.

4.4.4 Effects of Agricultural Reform on Poverty The government's and donors' agricultural and land reform policies and programs have aimed to improve the livelihoods, incomes, and the overall human development status of poor farmers. The first National Living Standards Survey (NLSS), which was conducted in 1995/96, revealed that 76.4% of the poor were self-employed farmers and/or agriculture wage earners, while 67% of the rural poor owned less than one hectare of land (CBS et. al. 2006). During the 1990s, donor agencies like the World Bank questioned the effectiveness of government agricultural subsidies, arguing that these programs primarily benefitted large landholders and landlords, with minimal benefits for poor farmers and the landless (Picclotto and Anderson, 1997; Panagariya, 2004; and World Bank, 2005).[17] The World Bank (2005) also pointed out that a lack of documentation of land rental agreements led to confusion in identifying landlords versus actual farmers. This ambiguity allowed landlords to claim benefits from subsidies for themselves, while smallholders, the landless, and agricultural wage earners received only marginal benefits. In response, the government under the NC gradually removed various agricultural subsidies from 1995 onward, and instead espoused alternative approaches aimed at directly supporting small landholders and the landless.

However, mainstream leftists such as the UML challenged the policy of removing subsidies, claiming it hurt farmers and the poor whilst encouraging dominance of imported Indian agricultural products in Nepal, since India maintained heavy agricultural subsidies.[18] The Maoists included opposition to subsidy removal in their political agenda to attract farmers and the poor during their armed movement. Similarly, pressure groups like Action Aid also

17. The highest agro-subsidy in India is provided in the state of Punjab, where a farmer with more than six hectares of land receives a 52.2% fertilizer subsidy and a 55% canal water subsidy (World Bank, 2005). By contrast, a poor farmer with less than one hectare of land receives a 2.5% fertilizer subsidy and a 1.4% canal water subsidy.

18. India gave a wide range of subsidies in agriculture, so their cost of production was low (Awasthi and Adhikary, 2004).

protested the removal of subsidies, emphasizing farmer's rights (Dasgupta and Pieterse, 2009).[19]

Removal of subsidies indeed had unintended consequences, especially by contributing to changes in land use in the Terai region and emerging urban areas of the hills. The Terai is naturally well-suited for industrialization and urbanization because of its flat land and proximity to India, enabling international trade. By increasing the operational costs of agriculture, subsidy removals provided further incentives for large landholders to utilize their land in other alternative ways. Many invested in constructing housing settlements, resulting in a great increase in land prices. Foreign remittance inflows also increased with large-scale rural out-migration caused by the Maoist insurgency, further accelerating the urbanization trend. The high inflow of remittance has contributed to increase real estate sector in last few years (World Bank, 2011 and Tuladhar et al, 2014). The trend of converting agricultural land to urban land was especially high in the Terai districts of Morang, Banke, Kailali, Rupandehi, Chitwan, Jhapa, and others. In the hills, urbanization has been most accentuated in Kathmandu, Pokhara, Kavre, and Surkhet. Tuladhar et al (2014) argue that there is no increase in agriculture yield of remittance receiving households which signifies that these households are not using the remittance money in agriculture and any productive area. During the Maoists' first term in government, the Council of Ministers greenlighted the reintroduction of the fertilizer subsidy in November 2008, and the Ministries of Agriculture and Finance prepared an operational guideline to distribute the subsidies in March 2009.

Between 1990 and 2010, there was a rise in the number of food-deficit districts in Nepal.[20] Food scarcity has worsened due to

---

19. As discussed in the previous chapter, development programs in Nepal tend to follow a generic model, resulting in unfair distribution of support. For support distribution pattern of Nepal, refer to NPC (2012) and CBS et al. (2006).

20. ABPMDD (2010) reports that total national cereal production was 3,549,587 metric tons in 1989/90, while consumption was 3,559,011 metric tons, resulting in a deficit of 9,424 metric tons. By 2009/10, total national cereal production reached 4,967,469 metric tons, while consumption was 5,297,444 metric tons, resulting in a deficit of 329,972 metric tons. Deficit in 2018 is estimated at 600,000 metric tons

limited institutional capacity to address this issue. For example, since liberalization, the NFC's role has been limited to food distribution in food-scarce mountain districts that too in limited quantities. No other government organizations oversee food storage for emergency purposes.

A number of new programs to provide financial and technical support for poor farmers, many of them developed with donor aid, were introduced after 1990. Such initiatives included the World Bank's Poverty Alleviation Fund and the ADB's Livestock Development Program. Beginning in the mid-2000s, the government also started to design and implement programs targeting poor farmers, such as the Prime Minister's Agriculture Modernization Project, initiated in 2016. Likewise, beginning in the mid-1990s, the National Living Standard Surveys collected data that helped create a better understanding of the relationships between farmers, landlords, and poverty. These various projects targeting the rural poor have contributed to the decline in poverty during the last two decades. However, they were impeded by institutional faults. The projects were administered by guidelines which generally do not continue after the completion of the project period. Likewise, there was a lack of long-term monitoring and evaluation after the projects' completion. Many beneficiaries who exhibited good performance during the project period were inactive afterwards, calling into question the projects' long-term impacts. Sustainability is a common problem in poverty alleviation projects, and donor activities frequently run into trouble once handed over to the Government of Nepal.[21]

---

cereal, 300,000 metric tons milk and more than 500,000 metric ton meat (Pant and Bajracharya, 2019). Vegetables and fruits also are met sizable through imports

21. One example is the Industrial Enterprise Development Institute (IEDI), established after the termination of the successful Small Business Promotion Project assisted by the German aid organization GTZ. A recent Auditor General's 2017 report has recommended closing down the Institute because it has become defunct.

4.5 Conclusion Overall, agricultural reforms in Nepal have focused on increasing production, diversifying products, liberalizing the sector, ensuring quality control, and alleviating poverty. During the Panchayat era, the initiatives were more focused on increasing production using improved seeds and fertilizers, while after 1990, priority was placed on liberalizing the sector and developing regulatory capacities. For the most part, the political parties have yet to initiate meaningful efforts to improve farmers' productivity; contrastingly it is only donors who are pushing this issue.

Political parties and the government have done little to address labor scarcity in rural areas, which is associated with labor migration to foreign countries. Many people, especially men, appear demotivated to work in the agriculture sector; a large number of youth are willing to work in harsh conditions abroad but are not interested in working on farms at home. Labor migration has contributed to the feminization of agriculture in Nepal (Tamang et al, 2014), and also to the decline of productivity and an increase in fallow land. In the last few years, the government has introduced some programs to attract youth and foreign returnees to agriculture, but, with the continuation of the labor outflow, agriculture is expected to face continued labor scarcity. For the most part, government policies lack appropriate vision, which creates confusion and makes the agriculture sector unattractive for private investment.

chapter 5

ECONOMIC SECTORS: INDUSTRY

5.1 Introduction Nepali peasants, since early period, have engaged in small-scale handicraft production or home-based manufacturing, using raw materials from farms and forests during the agricultural off-season (Regmi 1984). In addition, certain commodities have for centuries been produced by socially excluded, low-caste occupational groups such as the Teli (oil pressers), Kumha (potters), Kami (blacksmiths), and Sarki (leather workers). Production techniques were primitive and required little capital investment, while the products typically fulfilled only local needs. Domestic and international trade in such products was limited due to poor infrastructural connectivity compounded by harsh terrain.[1]

Partly in response to the devastation wrought by a major earthquake in 1934, the government under Juddha Shumsher Rana began to envision industrializing the country in the mid-1930s.[2] An industrial board, the Udhyog Parishad, was created in 1935 and a Company Act was passed in 1936. The latter provided a framework for incorporating industrial and commercial enterprises under the

1. Timilsina (1989) notes that for many decades, the Rana regime did not see development of local industries as a priority. Rather, they encouraged the import of manufactured goods in order to increase their customs revenue. Furthermore, because occupational castes were considered lowly in the Hindu caste system – indeed, some of these groups were considered impure and untouchable (Bista, 1991) – the regime was not much concerned about increasing their skills or capacities.

2. Juddha Shumsher sent Bijaya Shumsher and Sardar Gunja Man Singh, the first vice chair of NPC formed in 1956, to Britain in 1934-35 to explore the reasons behind Britain's development. Based on their suggestions, the government undertook efforts to begin industrialization (Bajracharya and Agrawal, 1980).

joint-stock and limited-liability principle.[3] In order to finance industrial development, the government established a financial institution, Nepal Bank Limited, in which it held the majority (51%) of shares.

In 1936, the Biratnagar Jute Mill became the first industry to officially register with the government.[4] A collaboration between Indian and Nepali entrepreneurs, it had an initial capital investment of IRs 160,000 (Savada, 1991). Medium- and large-scale industries related to mining, cigarettes, cotton textiles, food oil, paper, and soap were gradually established in response to shortages of consumer goods in Nepal and India during World War II (Timilsina, 1989). A total of 64 industries were eventually established during the Rana period (Bajracharya and Agrawal, 1980). Most emerged as joint ventures between Nepali and Indian entrepreneurs and were located in towns along the border like Janakpur, Birgunj, Biratnagar and Nepalgunj. In 1940, the government established the Cottage Skill Promotion Office (Gharelu Ilam Prachar Adda) to promote and develop small and cottage industries. Likewise, a Canal and Geology Office (Nahar Tatha Geology Adda) was established in 1929, which was later converted into the Mining Office (Khanni Adda) in 1942.

However, due to limited connectivity, industries developed only slowly and were concentrated in the Kathmandu Valley and some Terai towns nearby Indian railheads. At the same time, the government offices created to promote industrialization lacked trained manpower in the fields of industrial, geological, and chemical engineering,[5] circumscribing their capacities to plan and

3. In March 1930, the first technical school was established in Kathmandu to promote technical education in Nepal.

4. The Biratnagar Jute Mill was established somewhat by chance as Layalka, a jute merchant and industrialist of Katihar, Bihar, fled with his workers and resources to Nepal to escape a British crackdown on his support of the Indian independence movement (Bajracharya and Agrawal, 1980).

5. In 1902, eight Nepali students were sent to Japan for engineering education. Among them, two specialized in arms technology, two in mining, one in agricultural engineering, one in mechanical engineering, one in chemistry, and one in sericulture (Embassy of Japan in Nepal, Online Available at https://www.np.emb-japan.go.jp/history/student.html).

design the industrialization process. Instead, these offices concentrated on general administrative work.

While Juddha Shumsher did exhibit vision and commitment for industrializing the country, the object of this industrialization was to further enrich himself and the other members of the autocratic ruling family. Ultimately, only a small amount of industrialization occurred under the Ranas.

5.2 Era of State-Controlled Industrialization As Nepal became exposed to the outside world after the 1951 political change, the need for industrialization – seen as a way to "catch up" with other countries – became popular in development discourse. Major political parties called for industrialization in order to generate employment, address poverty, meet the country's basic requirements, and enhance trade (Joshi and Rose, 1966). During the 1950s the nascent industrial sector did not take meaningful initiatives on its own, and so the government stepped in to directly participate in the industrialization process. The state considered private businessmen and industrialists as inseparable partners in this process.

In the first fiscal budget after the 1951 political change, erstwhile Finance Minister and influential Nepali Congress (NC) leader Subarna Shumsher Rana announced that the country would adopt a mixed economic approach, giving an equal role to the state and the private sector in economic affairs (Joshi and Rose, 1966). Subarna Shumsher played an influential role in designing much of the economic policy framework during the 1950s, including creating various legal and institutional mechanisms.

The New Company Act, 1951 allowed for the opening of private limited companies, while incentives were announced to attract private and foreign investors. The Industrial Policy of 1958 and the First Five-Year Plan (1956-61) recognized the government's prime responsibility in industrial development and also committed to strengthening private sector involvement in the industrialization process.[6] The Factory and Factory Workers Act, 1959 fixed

6. Shrestha (1989) argues that the First Plan intended to establish state monopolies in the fields of transportation, telecommunication, hydro-electric power generation,

minimum wages for skilled, semi-skilled, and un-skilled labor, and stipulated standards for labor safety and healthy working conditions. New administrative institutions were set up to support industrialization. The Ministry of Industry and Commerce was empowered with overall responsibilities related to the country's industrialization process. All existing government offices relating to industry – such as the Udhyog Parishad and Gharelu Ilam Prachar Adda – were positioned under it. The Nepal Industrial Development Corporation (NIDC) was established in 1959 to provide financial assistance to public as well as private-sector industries. Different donors came forward to support industrialization. Aid from the Soviet Union and China became instrumental in establishing many public enterprises. In the period 1952-64, 92 private joint stock companies were registered.

However, political instability during the 1950s hindered effective implementation of laws, policies, and plans related to industrialization. Many of the offices that were supposed to operate under the Ministry of Industry and Commerce were never effectively set up (Joshi and Rose, 1966).

After the royal coup in 1960, King Mahendra continued the state-led industrialization process with a tougher, inward-looking approach that emphasized import substitution. With this strategy, Mahendra aimed to promote nationalism and safety from foreign encroachment. A new industrial policy brought in 1960 called for the establishment of large-scale public enterprises in order to achieve national self-sufficiency in basic industrial outputs such as consumable and construction items. The policy discouraged the free flow of imported goods. It was complemented by the Industrial Enterprises Act, 1962, which controlled private investment through licensing. Likewise, the Company Act, 1964 required businesses in all industries to obtain licenses to establish new undertakings as well as to expand their capacities. The government set industrial priorities and used the licensing mechanism to channel investments in desired directions (Regmi, 1994). As a result, domestic and

---

and irrigation, and to run some large industries like cement, sugar, cigarettes, textiles, and steel.

foreign private investors had limited options in choosing where to invest their money.

In sixties, the Udhyog Parishad was converted into the Investment Promotion Board, which was put in charge of providing recommendations to large and medium-scale industries to get licenses from the Department of Industry (DOI). Likewise, in 1970, the Gharelu Ilam Prachar Adda was converted into the Department of Cottage and Small Industries (DCSI), charged with regulating small-scale industries across the country.[7] Similarly, mining was regulated under the Mining Act of 1965 (later in 1985 replaced by new Mines and Minerals Act) which set up the Department of Geological Survey in 1967. The Nepal Standard (Certification Mark) Act, 1980 created the Nepal Bureau of Standards, which was set up in 1981 and charged with overseeing industrial quality control. In 1988, this office was merged with the Department of Weight and Measures to form the Nepal Bureau of Standards and Metrology (NBSM). Likewise, the Corporation Act, 1964 was enacted to manage the Public Enterprises and Division of Public Corporation under the Ministry of Finance was designated as the financial custodian of public enterprises

Though government control over the economy was attractive from a nationalistic perspective, Nepal had neither the financial nor the technical capacity for large-scale industrialization on its own. Foreign support – in the form of aid or investment – was required. In reality, most of the public enterprises established during the Panchayat era were set up with foreign assistance. Specifically, the Soviet Union and China[8] played an important role in the

7. DCSI also contained a Technical Training Section, which ran different technical trainings during the 1970s under various donor-funded projects. These included tailoring and handmade paper trainings funded by JICA, ceramic trainings funded by GTZ, and leather processing and leather goods trainings funded by the World Bank. Because these initiatives operated under the project model, they lacked sustainability – a common drawback of Nepal's human development approach.

8. Just as India and the US came forward to assist Nepal immediately after the establishment of democracy in 1951, the USSR and China came to the rescue of King Mahendra after the royal takeover. The USSR constructed the Pathlaiya-Dhalkebar section of East-West (H1) Highway, the 2400 KW Panauti Hydropower project, the Birgunj Sugar Factory, the Janakpur Cigarette Factory, and the Agriculture

establishment of many public enterprises. Later, countries like Japan, the Netherlands and others also supported a few public enterprises (Savada, 1991). Likewise, Nepal's first industrial district was developed in 1960 in Balaju, Kathmandu with US assistance to encourage private as well as public industries by availing standard low cost facilities[9]. The NIDC and DOI managed this and other industrial districts that gradually developed in other parts of the country. As the number of industrial districts grew, the Industrial Services Center was formed in 1975 to envisage new development, develop business plans, and extend other support services. This Center was converted into Industrial Districts Management Limited in 1988. Efforts were also undertaken to increase the skilled and technical manpower needed for industries with support from donors like USAID, the Swiss, UMN, Helvetas, and others.[10]

5.3 Assessment of State-Controlled Industrialization Between 1951 and the mid-1980s, 10 industrial districts were set up in Nepal. Industrial production, which was NRs 576 million in FY 1964/65, grew by an annual average of 3.19% over the six years until FY 1970/71 and then grew by 3.47% during the 1970s and increased dramatically to 8.14% in the 1980s (Table 5.1).

The industrial sector employed 1.21% of Nepal's population in 1971, increasing to 2.27% in 1991. Altogether, 64 public enterprises were established by the early 1980s (Bajracharya and Shrestha, 1983). Most were large-scale industries, which contributed 35% of industrial value addition in 1986/87 (Regmi, 1994). For example,

Tools Factory. China constructed the Arniko (H3) and Prithvi (H4) Highways, the 10,000 KW Sunkoshi Hydropower Project, the Bansbari Leather and Shoe Factory, the Harisiddhi Brick Tile Factory, the Bhaktapur Brick Tile Factory, and the Hetauda Textile Factory. Factories established with donor assistance were incorporated as public enterprises. National Trading Limited was established to sell goods donated by the USSR and China in lieu of cash needed for local expenses while executing the development projects. Nepal Timber Corporation was established with the assistance of USA and also became public enterprises.

9. International soft drink, Coca Cola, started production in Nepal in 1979 with two plants – one in Balaju Industrial District and another in Bharatpur of Chitwan.

10. More elaboration in Chapter 7 on Education and Human Resource Development.

the Janakpur Cigarette Factory alone contributed some 10% of government revenue (Bajracharya and Shrestha, 1983). The development of public enterprises was important in the sense that it helped to create a conducive foundation for private sector development. Concurrently, the private sector owned 96.8% of industrial firms in the country, most of which were small in scale but which collectively contributed 65% of industrial value addition (Regmi, 1994). In other words, state-led industrialization has been conducive for industrial growth in the country at least during the beginning when private sector did not come forward particularly during the fifties and the early sixties. But it is argued that the public enterprises remained longer than needed even when the private sector has developed and shouldered most of the business sector. An example is National Trading Limited that was closed only in 2018 after incurring huge losses being unable to compete in the market.

Table 5.1: Industrial Sector of Nepal in Selected Years of the Panchayat Period (in NRs Million)

Fiscal Years	Industrial GDP (Current Price)	Industrial GDP (at Constant Price of FY 2000/01)	Share of Industrial Contribution in GDP (in %)	Percent of Economically Active Population in Industry	Industrial Growth (in %)*
1964/65	576	10,135	10.28%		
1970/71	974	12,235	10.90%	1.21%	3.19% (1964/65 to 1970/71)
1980/81	1,371	17,202	5.79%	0.56%	3.47% (1970/71 to 1980/81)
1990/91	20,362	37,607	17.53%	2.72%	8.14% (1980/81 to 1990/91)

Source: Various Issues of *Statistical Year Book of Nepal,* CBS
* Source: Calculated by Author using CBS Data
* Time period representing the data is mentioned in parenthesis

Consumer goods dominated industrial production in the 1970s and 80s, but their share of overall industrial production dropped between 1972/73 and 1986/87 due to growth in other areas, especially exportable products for example carpet, garment and technical and construction goods (Table 5.2). At the same time, within the consumer goods sub-sector, cotton and textiles production increased significantly due to expansion of the ready-made garments industry, which was spurred by preferential trade status provided by the USA and EU to Nepal and other developing nations.[11] There was also a slight increase in the production share of intermediate goods like jute, paper, rubber, and plastics, and a major increase in technical and construction goods like iron, steel, cement, lime, and other metallic and nonmetallic goods. Road and hydropower infrastructure construction, built with foreign assistance, also contributed to the development of industries in the Terai Belt and the Eastern and Central Regions (MOICS and UNIDO, 2002) providing better access to industries.[12] The share of food industries, that dominated early industrialization began to gradually decline with the growth of other sectors.

11. The Multi-Fiber Agreement (MFA) was a global agreement on textiles and clothing, signed in 1974. Under the MFA, developed countries like the USA and EU nations created quotas for developing countries to export textiles and garments under preferential conditions. Due to the exhaustion of the quota for India, Indian industrialists invested in Nepal in the early 1980s, often using Indian labor and management, helping to kick-start the garment industry in Nepal. MFA was succeeded by the Agreement on Textiles and Clothing (ATC) in 1994, which continued preferential treatment for developing countries. This quasi-guaranteed market access increased exports of readymade garments from Nepal in the 1980s and 90s (Shakya, 2005). However, Panday (1989) argues that the government failed to fully utilize the MFA and ATC to mobilize national capital and create an environment to develop an industrial labor force. Rather, he says, the government was narrowly focused on accumulating foreign currency.

12. In 1986/87, 63% of manufacturing industries were in the Terai, while the remaining 37% were in the Hill and Mountain Regions (Regmi, 1994). Likewise, the Central Region (encompassing parts of the Terai, hills, and mountains) had 47% of manufacturing industries, while the Mid-Western and Far-Western Regions had 6% and 5%, respectively. There is less industries in Mid and Far Western Region due to less development in infrastructure like road, electricity and others.

Table 5.2: Share of Various Industrial Groups in Gross Output in Panchayat Period (in Percent)

Industrial Groups	1972/73	1976/77	1986/87
Consumer Goods	90.89	98.04	79.18
Food Manufacturing	78.41	48.09	52.99
Beverage and Tobacco	1.56	1,49	2.55
Cotton and Textile	0.63	1,69	13.50
Intermediate Goods*	5.15	0.38	5.69
Technical and Construction Goods**	3.96	1.58	15.13
Total	100	100	100

Source: Regmi (1994; pp 36-37)
* Intermediate Goods consist of jute, textiles, paper, printing, rubber, plastics, and others.
** Technical and Construction Goods consist of metallic and non-metallic goods, cement, lime, electrical machinery, and others.

The industrial sector's share of GDP grew from 11% to 18% between 1970/71 and 1990/91 (Table 5.1). While this represented a significant shift in the economy, the change was not as dramatic as in other South Asian countries.[13] Furthermore, Nepal's labor productivity remained low (Figure 5.1) despite efforts to strengthen technical and vocational education. There was no initiative to establish a research center for industrial development as such initiatives were not coming from the private or the educational sectors[14]. Critics of the monarchy have argued that the Panchayat-era government was driven by a rent-seeking mentality and was uninterested in really developing the country's production base. For

13. The ADB (2017) reports that industry's contribution to GDP was 20.6% in Bangladesh, 24.3% in India, and 29.6% in Sri Lanka in 1980.

14. The government formed the Royal Nepal Academy of Science and Technology in 1982 as an autonomous body for the advancement of science and technology. However, this institution did not primarily focus on industrial development. The government invested only 0.22 percent of GNP in science and technology research – a very low amount compared to developed countries (MOICS and UNIDO, 2002; pp 126). Due to limited government investment in industrial research, the country hasn't carried out mineral resource mapping which is essential to industrialize the country.

instance, Panday (1989) argues that government preferred to collect royalties from exports of un-milled wood than to provide subsidies for machinery imports so that a domestic milling industry could begin. Panday further argues that the King could not have been expected to encourage too much growth in the industrial sector because this would have given rise to an independent capitalist class who could challenge his power.

Figure 5.1 Per-Worker Labor Productivity of South Asia in 1980*

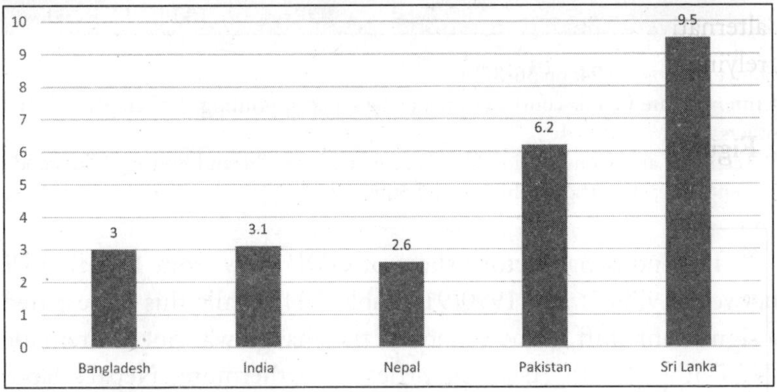

Source: APO (2017; PP. 59)
* GDP at constant basic price per worker using 2011 PPP, (in Thousand USD with reference year 2015)

Due to the limited extent of industrialization, natural resources with which Nepal is well-endowed like timber, non-timber forest products, limestone, and iron ore remained untouched. Public enterprises often failed to meet production expectations. A World Bank (1979) study[15] found that the average capacity utilization rate of public enterprises was below 60%. Meanwhile, Bajracharya and Shrestha (1983) shows that performance – as measured by capacity utilization, profitability, and market performance – was weak. Similarly, KC (2003) finds that the gross profit-to-capital ratio and labor-output ratio of industrial public enterprises were

15. World Bank, 1979; pp 25

very low.[16] The contribution of manufacturing public enterprises to GDP in Nepal remained low in comparison to other Asian countries (Figure 5.2; Balassa, 1987).

Thus, the controlled economy of the Panchayat Era led to a surge in public expenditure but did not lead to economic growth. Rather, the injection of more money in the market resulted in a rise in demand, leading to a sharp increase in imports that resulted in balance of payments problems, particularly in the early 1980s.[17] Public enterprises in Nepal suffered from poor management and had outlived their usefulness. The country needed to adopt an alternative approach based on private investment, rather than relying on public enterprises.

Figure 5.2: Contribution of Manufacturing Public Enterprises in GDP of Selected Countries (in Percent)

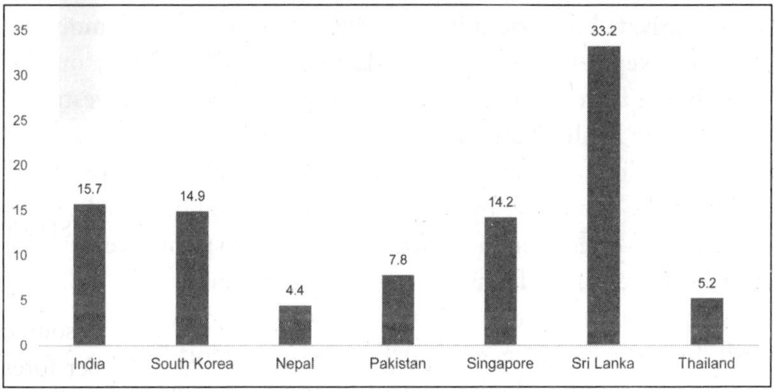

Source: Balassa (1987; pp 4)

16. KC (2003) reported that the gross profit-to-capital ratio of public enterprises was -0.23% in FY 1988/89, decreasing to -5.22% in 1990/91. Value added per employee in public enterprises dropped from NRs. 12,739 in FY 1974/75 to NRs. 12,204 in FY 1984/85.

17. Nepal's foreign exchange reserves dropped to a level sufficient to buy only 18 days' worth of imports in 1984. This coincided with a global balance of payments crisis.

Beginning in the mid-1980s, revisions were gradually made to the industrial licensing regime and foreign investment procedures in accordance with the IMF's Economic Stabilization Program in 1985 and World Bank's Structural Adjustment Program (SAP), initiated in 1986, and Enhanced Structural Adjustment Program (ESAP), initiated in 1989. These changes laid the foundation for the country to initiate major reforms in the industrial sector after the restoration of democracy in 1990.

5.4 Reforms in the Industrial Sector Following the political change in 1990, three competing political forces put forward diverse visions regarding the proper role of government in Nepal's industrialization process. On one side of the spectrum, the economically liberal NC and the culturally conservative RPP sought to initiate reforms and open the economy to more private investment.[18] They argued for removing all licensing provisions and attracting foreign private investment in the industrial sector. The Communist Party of Nepal-Unified Marxist Leninist (CPN-UML), on the other hand, feared that opening the country to foreign investment would allow Multi-National Companies (MNCs), especially those based in India, to overexploit Nepal's natural and human resources and hurt the economy. Instead, the UML argued, national capital should be invested in industrialization in order to minimize imports, address poverty, and ensure fair wages.[19] Finally, the Maoists considered any economic liberalization as a threat that would allow both domestic and foreign capitalists to overexploit Nepal's people and resources. The Maoists waged their armed movement against parliamentary democracy, monarchy, and capitalism in order to establish a "People's Republic."

While it led a majority government after the 1991 elections, the NC under Girija Prasad Koirala initiated liberal reforms aimed at more extensively opening the economy to the private sector and foreign investors. In line with ESP, SAP and ESAP, it gradually initiated the privatization of public enterprises that were

18. Election manifesto of the NC for the 1991 election.

19. Resolution of Fifth General Convention of UML.

running at losses. The UML, as the main opposition party, voiced its concerns with these policies, initiating activities with labor rights organizations and trade unions. However, when the UML and RPP led governments later in the 1990s and 2000s, they did not revert back from these policy reforms initiated by the NC. Various large and small-scale industrial development programs and projects funded by donors continued to be designed and implemented in line with the liberal approach.

Likewise, despite their radical rhetoric during the armed movement, the Maoists did not take any major steps against economic liberalization after joining mainstream politics in 2006. Rather, the Maoists actually tried to further encourage foreign investment, as will be discussed below. The remainder of this chapter discusses economic policy reforms from 1990 to the present.

5.4.1 Policy Reforms and Changes Following its victory in the 1991 general elections, the NC introduced economic liberalization in the industrial sector through a package of reform-oriented policies. It initiated partial convertibility of Nepali currency – ultimately leading to full convertibility – in current accounts in the early 1990s. This led to enabling of the determination of currency exchange rates thus reducing the prospects of over-rating or under-rating. The Industrial Enterprises Act (IEA), 1992 and Trade Policy, 1992 scrapped all licensing provisions and allowed unrestricted private and foreign investment in all sectors except those listed as "sensitive."[20] Likewise, the Foreign Investment and Technology Transfer Act (FITTA), 1992 facilitated foreign direct investment (FDI) in Nepal. Together, IEA and FITTA charged the DOI with oversight of FDI. A new Foreign Investment and One Window Policy, 1992 stipulated procedures for FDI to easily enter Nepal. These acts provided different incentives for FDI, including special incentives for businesses in rural and underdeveloped areas. A Company Registrar's Office was created in 1993 to harmonize the administration of company affairs.[21] In

20. They included items like drugs, arms etc.

21. Prior to 1993, companies were registered in various offices depending on the

addition, the Industrial Enterprises Development Institute (IEDI) was established in 1996 to develop knowledge resources for entrepreneurship and business promotion. Complementing the new investment regime, the NC government also lowered tariffs and introduced a bonded warehouse scheme and a duty-drawback scheme to encourage exports and support trade development.[22]

In part due to these policy changes, about 800 new manufacturing companies were established in the five years between 1993 to 1997, among which about 100 were established with FDI. FDI commitment in the manufacturing sector amounted to NRs. 411 million in FY 1994/95 (Table 5.3). The major industries from the 1990s to the present have been food processing, textiles, readymade garments, cement, iron and steel, carpets, footwear, electronics, and furniture (Table 5.4). Textiles dominated industrial value addition in the 1990s, making up 25.9% of total value addition in 1996, followed by food and beverages, with 22.8%. Nepal's textile industry benefitted from preferential trade status granted by the USA and the EU under the Multi Fiber Agreement (MFA) of 1974 and the Agreement on Textiles and Clothing (ATC) of 1994 (see footnote 11 of chapter 5). However, large-scale investment by MNCs failed to materialize the way it did in other recently liberalized South Asian countries like Bangladesh and Sri Lanka. Industrial expansion also followed the expansion of roads in Nepal; the Far and Mid-Western Regions largely failed to develop industries due to their lack of basic infrastructure besides the geography, sparse population distribution and distance from the market.

In the 1990s and early 2000s, private sector and FDI commitments in the industrial sector fluctuated greatly due to a variety of problems (Table 5.3). The Maoist movement was a major stumbling block for industrial development. The armed struggle

---

nature of their business. For example, companies relating to wholesale and retail trading were registered at the Department of Commerce, while companies relating to agricultural processing were registered at the Department of Agriculture.

22. Under the bonded warehouse system, exporters can store imported raw materials in government-managed warehouses under a bond, deposit payable duties, and release the deposit upon successful completion of export. Likewise, duty drawback allows exporters to get reimbursed for tax paid on imported inputs.

Table 5.3: Private and Foreign Investment Committed in the Industrial Sector of Nepal (in NRs million)*

Fiscal Year	Total Private Investment Committed	Total FDI Committed
1994/95	9,455	411
2000/01	5,850	1,816
2010/11	75,77	197
2013/14	53,187	2,133
2014/15	18,867	2,443
2015/16	58,700	3,178
2016/17	45,736	3,781
2017/18	84,418	10,646

Source: *Industrial Statistics,* Department of Industry
*Industrial Sector Includes Manufacturing, Mining and Construction

drove the country towards chaos and instability. Political instability was frequently accompanied by labor disputes, which were often more influenced by political motives than the true interests of workers. Furthermore, load shedding – caused by electricity shortage but compounded by corruption within the Nepal Electricity Authority – made private investment in Nepal even less attractive.

Furthermore, new policies in the 2000s – driven by the government's desire to increase its revenue – curtailed or eliminated most of the reforms initiated by IEA and FITTA in 1992. New laws such as the Income Tax Act 2001, Company Act 2006, Excise Duty, 2002 and other contemporary legal amendments seemed driven by a rent-seeking mentality than promoting industrialization. Likewise, continued administrative bottlenecks and corruption hindered private investment. Despite the Foreign Investment and One Window Policy, 1992,[23] the process for registering and renewing companies remained lengthy. The World Bank (2019) reported that it took 16.5 days to register a company in Nepal,

23. The Member-Secretary of the Industrial Promotion Board, Director General of DOI was often reported to have been unable to operate the One Window system. Critics disparaged the system as "One Window, Many Doors" because of the many steps entailed.

compared to the South Asian average of 13.7 days; likewise, Nepal ranked 107th in the world for ease of starting a business. In 2018, Transparency International ranked Nepal 124th in the world for controlling corruption; bribery is considered a discretionary right affecting all facets of business.

All these factors resulted in a sharp decline in FDI in the decade of the 2000s. In particular, the textile industry shrunk dramatically. Textiles' share of industrial value addition declined from 10.2% in 2006 to 3.8% in 2011 (Table 5.4) due to the expiry of the ATC and Nepal's limited institutional capacity to carry on after entering the globally competitive market (Shakya, 2005).[24] As a result, Nepal's food and beverage industry reverted back to holding the highest share of industrial value addition. Likewise, the shares of metallic products and non-metallic mineral products also increased due to increase in production of construction materials like cement, iron and others.

Amidst this difficult investment climate, insufficient efforts were undertaken to improve quality control. The NBSM had limited technical capacity and few branches outside of the Kathmandu Valley. Likewise, the IEDI failed to play an instrumental role in developing entrepreneurship skills within Nepali industries, as originally envisioned.[25] The bonded warehouse and duty drawback schemes were quite successful in supporting the readymade garment industry in the early 1990s, but these policies

24. After the ATC expired in January 2005, the US provided no special treatment for developing countries' exports of textiles and garments. As Shakya (2005) argues, Nepali garment prices became higher than those produced in China due to Nepal's lower labor productivity, poor international market information system, and limited backward linkages. By contrast, in Bangladesh, the expiry of ATC was not as detrimental because of Bangladesh's institutional mechanisms to make itself competitive. In 2002, the US eased garment imports from Africa. It was only a decade later that the US passed the Trade Facilitation and Trade Enforcement Act in February 2016, which provided duty-free access for certain items, including textiles from developing countries. Nepal's garment export has mainly concentrated at the USA and has been able to make only limited entry in EU and Japanese market.

25. The IEDI, established to institutionalize GTZ's successful SBPP, has been so inactive that a recent Auditor General's report recommended closing it down.

on their own were not sufficient to promote large-scale industrialization (MOICS and UNIDO, 2002).[26] Furthermore, as Bajracharya and Sharma (1996) point out, there was no proper institutional mechanism to sensitize traders about foreign markets.

In 2011, the Maoist-led government under Babu Ram Bhattarai established the autonomous Investment Board of Nepal (IBN) to attract large-scale FDI. The IBN was initially portrayed as an entry point and one-window mechanism for administering investments above NRs 20 billion. However, the legislation that established the IBN gave it only limited powers for initial approvals; investors going through the IBN still needed to follow many of the same procedures as other small-scale foreign investors. Although several MNCs, including India's GMR Group, China's Three Gorges Corporation, and Nigeria's Dangote Cement have liaised with the IBN, only one – Hongshi Cement – has invested in Nepal through it.

After the promulgation of the new federal Constitution in 2015, there has been relative political stability in the country. Likewise, a new energy agreement with India has minimized load shedding. The Government has also brought new Industrial Enterprises Act (2016) and Foreign Investment and Technology Transfer Act (2019) with the provision of 20 percent income tax for productive industries against 25 percent corporate income tax rate and providing many other (non) financial incentives. These acts also have provision of one window system and of detailed industrial classification. As with other federal legal revisions, these acts also have confusion over jurisdiction of federal and provincial governments. FITTA (2019) has streamlined IBN's role. The ongoing federal restructuring process is becoming lengthy, creating doubts and apprehension in the market. Additionally, continued hikes in minimum wages without a commensurate rise in

26. MOICS and UNIDO (2002) argue that although the readymade garment industry made use of the bonded warehouse system in the early 1990s, administrative bottlenecks and unclear procedures remained. Duty drawbacks from customs, excise, and VAT taxes had to be collected from different offices with little coordination between them, making the process cumbersome.

Table 5.4: Gross Value Added in Various Industrial Sub-Sectors in Post 1990 (in NRs. million)

Details	1996		2006		2011	
	Value Added	% Share	Value Added	% Share	Value Added	% Share
Food and Beverages	4,996	22.8	12,907	27.0	30,865	34.0
Tobacco Products	2,624	12.0	8,164	17.1	11,921	13.1
Textiles	5,673	25.9	4,873	10.2	3,425	3.8
Wearing Apparel	1,376	6.3	668	1.4	486	0.5
Leather, Leather Products and Footwear	288	1.3	293	0.6	771	0.8
Wood Products (excluding Furniture)	309	1.4	615	1.3	1,798	2.0
Paper and Paper Products	370	1.7	2,007	4.2	904	1.0
Printing and Publishing	316	1.4	541	1.1	571	0.6
Coke, Refined Petroleum Products and Nuclear Fuel	33	0.2	942	2.0	366	0.4
Chemicals and Chemical Products	1,318	6.0	3,897	8.1	6,976	7.7
Rubber and Plastics Products	649	3.0	2,004	4.2	4,225	4.7
Non-Metallic Mineral Products	1,584	7.2	3,758	7.9	12,716	14.0
Basic Metals	386	1.8	2,418	5.1	4,903	5.4
Fabricated Metal Products	1,095	5.0	3,409	7.1	8,117	8.9
Machinery and Equipment (Nothing Elsewhere Classified)	18	0.1	132	0.3	270	0.3
Electrical Machinery and Apparatus	483	2.2	547	1.1	772	0.8
Radio, Television and Communication Equipment	59	0.3	188	0.4	492	0.5
Motor Vehicles, Trailers and Semi-Trailers	5	0.0	23	0.0	82	0.1
Furniture and Manufacturing ((Nothing Elsewhere Classified)	292	1.3	449	0.9	1,169	1.3
Total	**21,874**	**100**	**47,835**	**100**	**90,829**	**100**

Source: CBS and UNIDO (2014; pp 15)

productivity has made Nepal an increasingly high-cost economy.[27] As a consequence, investment in industries remains at a standstill.

Average annual industrial sector growth between 1990/91 and 2000/01 was 6.94%, but it dropped to 2.62% between 2000/01 and 2010/11 (Table 5.5) due to Maoists and Madheshi movement in particular and political instability in general. The industrial sector employed 2.72% of the economically active population in 1991, a figure that grew to 13.35% in 2001, but shrunk to 9.52% in 2011 (Table 5.5). Industrialization did not significantly change Nepal's trade orientation. The country's economic transformation has lagged behind that of other South Asian countries,[28] with industry's contribution to GDP remaining roughly stagnant over the last three decades (Table 5.5). Global competitiveness remains a challenge – a topic that will be discussed further below.

5.4.2 Privatization and its Impact With loss-making public enterprises burdening the national exchequer and goaded by the IMF, the NC government adopted privatization as a key component of its economic liberalization policy in the early 1990s.[29] This policy was complemented by the Privatization Act, 1994, which detailed the process of privatizing public enterprises (MOICS and UNIDO, 2002). Between 1992 and 1997, 16 public enterprises were privatized under different modalities, and three were liquidated (KC, 2003). The Ninth Plan, for the period 1997-2002, focused on privatization, providing detailed plans for different phases of privatization and setting targets. The Privatization Cell in the Ministry of Finance

---

27. Bangladesh has been a more attractive destination for FDI because of low wages and high productivity. Even after the recent doubling of the wage rate in Bangladesh – at the initiative of importers, activists and others – to 8,000 Taka, wages are well below those in Nepal. Additionally, productivity is higher in Bangladesh (the average time for producing one male shirt in Bangladesh is 11 minutes, compared to about 23 minutes in Nepal) and its PCI is about 40% higher than in Nepal. Hence, there is a need to link wages with productivity, at least to some degree, while ensuring labor rights.

28. Industry's share of gross output was 27.6% in Bangladesh, 24.8% in India and 32.5% in Sri Lanka in 2013 (ADB 2017).

29. The first privatization policy was drafted in 1990 by a committee that was constituted in 1989. This policy set the stage for future privatization policies.

Table 5.5: Industrial Sector of Nepal in Selected Years of Post 1990 (in NRs Million)

Fiscal Years	Industrial GDP (Current Price)	Industrial GDP (at Constant Price of FY 2000/01)	Share of Industrial Contribution in GDP (in %)	Percent of Economically Active Population in Industry	Industrial Growth (in %)*
1990/91	20,362	37,607	17.53%	2.72%	8.14% (1980/81 to 1990/91)
2000/01	73,561	73,561	17.29%	13.35%	6.94% (1990/91 to 2000/01)
2010/11	192,848	95,250	11.39%	9.52%	2.62% (2000/01 to 2010/11)
2015/16	295,095	102,437	14.20%		-6.36%
2016/17	354,003	115,140	13.79%		12.40%
2017/18	407,713	126,185	14.33%		9.59%
2018/19**	465,580	136,464	15.21%		8.15%

Source: Various Issues of *Statistical Year Book of Nepal,* Central Bureau of Statistics
*Source: Calculated by Author using CBS Data
* Time period representing the data is mentioned in parenthesis
**Preliminary Estimate

was given responsibility for these efforts.[30] However, the privatization process did not proceed as per the plan due to organized opposition from leftists. Furthermore, readjustment of government staff employed by public enterprises proved to be a major stumbling block. After 1997, the privatization process remained almost stagnant: between 1997 and 2002, only one public enterprise was handed over to the private sector. Nonetheless, an attempt was made to better systematize the bidding process for buying public enterprises with the passage of the Financial Procedures Act, 1999 and the Financial Administration Regulation, 1999.

At present, there are 40 public enterprises, of which only 37 are in operation (MOF, 2018).[31] Among these, 26 are making profits and 11 are running at a loss. Only 10 public enterprises conduct timely audits; audits for the rest have been delayed by one or more years. In FY 2016/17, Nepal's public enterprises held a total capital investment of NRs. 445,902 million and earned a net profit of NRs 41,427 million, which amounts to 9.29 percent of net capital. However, 19 public enterprises have accumulated losses. As a result, dividends received by the government from public enterprises amount to a mere 4.87%. OAG (2017) reports that these public enterprises have 81 percent tax arrears in FY 2017/18. Public enterprises lack operational efficiency due to lack of commercial

30. The Privatization Cell was created in the Corporation Coordination Division at the Ministry of Finance. This Cell initiates the privatization process for any public enterprise on the basis of its own studies, on the recommendation of the concerned line ministry, or as per the request of the management of the concerned public enterprise. The bid notice is then published in national and international media, as required. The bidding process is opened in front of representatives of all the bidders. Two-tier negotiation teams are constituted to negotiate with the bidders. The primary negotiation team is created under the chairmanship of the secretary of the concerned line ministry and it discusses each and every aspect of the bid, except price, with the concerned bidders. The primary team submits its report to the higher-level negotiation team, which is headed by the concerned line minister and also includes the Finance Minister. The higher-level team discusses all the aspects of the bids and submits its final findings to the Privatization Cell, which recommends the proposal to the cabinet. The cabinet makes the final decision on privatization.

31. It has been decided to dissolve Janakpur Cigarette Factory, the National Construction Company, and the National Engineering Consultancy Service Center, but the process for doing so has not yet been completed.

orientation, poor management, inefficient use of resources, poor accounting, overstaffing, frequent political interference in management, low levels of technology, and lack of competent managers and staff.[32]

5.4.3 Small Manufacturing Industries and Rural Development

Over the last few decades, small manufacturing and cottage industries have been portrayed in Nepal's development discourse as effective means to address poverty and rural development. Small industries can be established in rural places where big manufacturing industries will not invest due to minimal road access and other infrastructure, or so the thinking goes. In such circumstances, small manufacturing industries operated by villagers can provide alternative sources of livelihood (MOICS and UNIDO, 2002). In order to help create such opportunities, the Department of Cottage and Small Industries (DCSI) has established offices in 27 district headquarters. In the rest 48 districts, there are Cottage and Small Industries Development Board (CSIDB). These district offices administer various small manufacturing promotion projects funded by donors and the Government of Nepal. Since FY 1992/93, DCSI has also been instituted with Cottage and Small Industry Training Center (CSITC) to provide skill development training.[33]

The DCSI and CSIDB have provided soft loans as well as cash and non-cash grants to villagers as seed money to start small-scale manufacturing industries. In many cases, the DCSI and CSIDB help projects to develop forward and backward linkages, such as by

32. These problems have persisted for decades, despite early studies such as Bajracharya and Shrestha's 1983 study that called the government's attention to them. In fact, the status of many public enterprises has deteriorated in the democratic era, with political appointments of CEOs and board members on the rise. A number of public enterprises, for example Birgunj Sugar factory, Janakpur Cigarette Factory, Hetauda Textile Factory, Gorakhkali Rubber Udhyog, Butwal Dhago Udhyog, Himal Cement Company, Nepal Transport Company, National Trading Limited, Jute Trading Corporation and Tobacco Trading Corporation etc were closed.

33. CSITC replaced the Technical Training Section of DCSI, which previously looked after skill training.

promoting the use of locally available raw materials.[34] Most small manufacturing industries found in rural areas have received support from these initiatives.[35]

Donor-funded projects provide budgets for skill development and entrepreneurship trainings for beneficiaries, as well as separate capacity development activities for project staff. However, a common problem is that there is nobody to follow up with beneficiaries after the project is over and all the project staff are gone. Government-funded initiatives, on the other hand, usually lack a training component and provide no extra staff to look after the project. In these projects, there is also a lack of follow-up with beneficiaries after they have taken the monetary or non-cash support from the government.[36] Though DCSI and CSIDB run different types of trainings with support from the government or foreign donors, their activities are still guided by a "project approach" that is bereft of long-term sustainable goals or plans. As a result, these initiatives have largely failed to achieve long-term impacts in sensitizing rural people about market mechanisms, value chains, and other commercial and management issues.

34. Some major donor-funded microenterprise programs are UNDP's Micro-Enterprise Development Program (MEDEP), the Australian-supported Micro-Enterprise Development for Poverty Alleviation (MEDPA) program, and the World Bank's Poverty Alleviation Fund. MEDEP's support package included identification of entrepreneurs, entrepreneurship training, skill training, and market, technical, financial and business development services. UNDP had also initiated the Training for Rural Employment (TRE) and Training for Rural Gainful Activities (TRUGA) projects before MEDEP. HELVETAS has also conducted the ELAM and ELAM+ projects. Likewise, DFID supported the Community Support Program (CSP), while the Swiss supported the SE project, and the ADB the SFE project.

35. DCSI (2017) reports that there were 290,459 registered cottage and small industries in Nepal by the end of FY 2016/17. Among them, 103,432 were related to manufacturing, 110,295 were related to the service sector (wholesale and retail), 10,020 were related to construction, 33,819 were related to agriculture or forestry, 30,225 were related to tourism, 1,412 were related to mini- and micro-power development, 1,231 were related to mining, and 25 were related to communication.

36. Some government-funded micro-enterprise development programs include the Youth Employment Fund, the Karnali Employment Fund, and others.

Limited government support has meant that village entrepreneurs have missed opportunities to develop their skills and become more productive. Beyond a few isolated success stories, rural micro-enterprise projects have not been very fruitful. More commonly, the resources they provide are exploited by a few clever people who tend to get support from multiple projects repeatedly. Thus, persistent challenges remain for rural industrialization; there is a need for long-term vision to drive the process forward in a sustainable manner.

The 2015's Constitution and recently enacted Local Government Operation Act, 2017 have conferred the responsibility of looking after small and cottage industries to local governments. But the technical, financial and human resource capacities of these local governments are limited to look after small and cottage industries independently. These acts don't have clarity on how the local governments will coordinate with federal government on developing small and cottage industries and how DCSI and CSIDB work with local governments.

5.4.4 Employment, Labor and Migration Nepal's industrial sector engages only a small portion of the population, although the multiplier effect is noteworthy meaning the effect on diverse sectors e.g. transportation, trade, education and the health sectors are prominent. The manufacturing sector's share of employment rose from 2.72% in 1991 to 9.52% in 2011.

The government has taken different measures to manage and protect labor in the post-1990 era. The New Labor Act, 1991 regulates overall labor management and designates the Labor Department, which has branches in each Zone, as the officiating regulatory body. There is also a Labor Court, which is a special tribunal for settling labor disputes. The Trade Union Act, 1992 grants workers the right to form labor unions[37].

37. Trade unions in Nepal germinated along with anti-Rana movement in Nepal. The 1947's Majdur Hartal (Labor Strike) in Biratnagar Jute Mills Ltd is considered as one of the turning point to escalate anti-Rana movement and the future national leaders like Girija Prasad Koirala of NC and Man Mohan Adhikari of CPN-UML debuted in politics with this labor movement. All major political

However, the institutional setup is weak. A culture of settling labor disputes through political interference has made it difficult to achieve fair outcomes (MOICS and UNIDO, 2002). Political parties interfere in labor disputes according to their political interest, with an eye toward achieving popularity. Because they derive benefits by routinely playing a mediating role, the parties have shown a lack of interest in developing strong formal mechanisms for enforcing the minimum wage rate, hiring and firing provisions, and other legal compliance measures (MOICS and UNIDO, 2002 and Acharya and Bhattarai, 2012).

While most political parties have called for enhancing labor skills in their manifestos, they rarely take action in this regard (Rimal et al, 2005). The government has taken only limited initiatives to analyze national skill gaps and design formal and informal education curricula to address them. Only foreign donors have provided significant support in training the labor force (Amatya and Shrestha, 2010). Nepal's education policy has focused on making people literate but not skillful,[38] contributing to the country's low labor productivity in comparison with other South Asian nations (Figure 5.3).

Due to a variety of reasons, including political parties' ambiguous approach to labor management, many Nepali industries hire labor from neighboring countries like India and Bangladesh. A large number of foreign workers are present in all industrial sub-sectors. These workers tend to put in long hours and seldom agitate against their employers because they can be changed whenever necessary. This scenario had been warned against as early as 1983, when a task force was created to analyze internal and international

---

parties have affiliated labor organizations to look after labor issues but the focus of these organization is on advocacy than to resolve real labor issues. Most of industrial issues are resolved by higher political leaders and these organizations are mostly used as entry points for careers in politics. After taking over the power by King Mahendra in 1960, he formed class organization of labor to bring forward their issues but the king got political threat from these organizations so they were not effectively mobilized in later days.

38. Refer to Chapter 7 on Education and Human Resource Development.

Figure 5.3 Per-Worker Labor Productivity in South Asia, 2015*

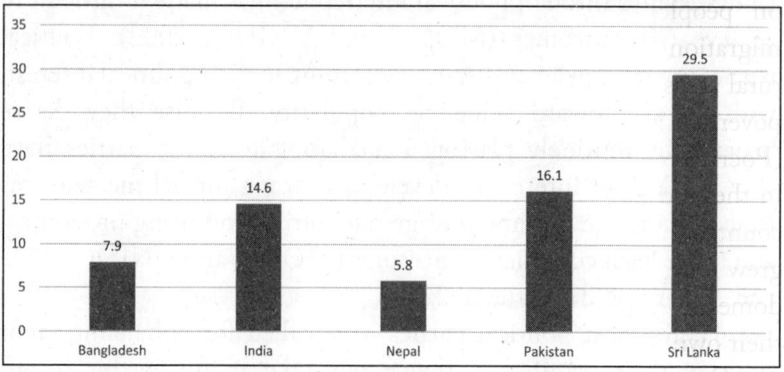

Source: APO (2017; pp 59)
* GDP at constant basic price per worker using 2011 PPP, (in USD thousand with reference year 2015)

migration in Nepal (TFM, 1983).[39] The task force told the government to be attentive to large-scale labor migration from India and out-migration of productive human resource from Nepal, even recommending an entry-permit system to control the flow of Indian migrants. However, its warnings went unheeded.

On the other hand, it should be noted that there is also a long history of Nepali labor migration abroad. Nepali migrants to India in the 19th century were employed in the British Indian Army,[40] on tea estates, as agricultural laborers, as guards, and in other occupations (Seddon, 2005 and Upreti, 2002). Because opportunities to improve occupational proficiency were lacking in Nepal, Nepali migrants were generally unskilled.[41] This trans-border migration

39. The task force was headed by the esteemed geographer Harka Gurung and had eight other expert members from related fields.

40. The British were impressed with the bravery of Nepali soldiers in the 1815-16 war with Nepal. After the Sugauli Treaty between Nepal and British India in 1816, the British created the Gorkha Regiment in its army to recruit Nepali fighters.

41. A few skilled artisans and other workers did leave Nepal for work in neighboring lands. Perhaps the most famous example was the sculptor Arniko, who was sent to China in the 13th century. A monument that he built is still one of the beauties of Beijing. He is the one conferred with taking Pagoda style of temple construction to China, Tibet and beyond.

continued unimpeded in later days because there were no restrictions on people crossing the Nepal-India border.[42] Seasonal labor migration to India remains an important source of livelihood for rural areas in the Mid- and Far-Western Regions of Nepal, where poverty is acute and people have trouble meeting subsistence needs (Poertner et al, 2011). The labor migration pattern began to change in the mid-1990s, as the Gulf and some ASEAN and East Asian countries were opened for Nepali labor. Labor outflow from Nepal grew during the decade-long Maoist armed revolution as the domestic economy faltered and people grew apprehensive about their own security.

Out-migration continued to grow even after the Maoists joined mainstream politics in 2006. Political instability remained unabated until 2015, when the new constitution was promulgated. Ordinary Nepali people continued to fear for their future, often preferring foreign employment over local sources of livelihood. A large number of laborers migrate through formal routes (MOLE, 2016)[43] as well as informal routes (Bhadra, 2007) with the expectation to work in low-skilled jobs (TAF et al, 2013)[44] in countries where there is demand for Nepali workers (CTEVT, 2015).[45] Working conditions abroad are harsh, as labor migrants face physically strenuous jobs and long working hours, and they often have minimal expectations for monthly savings (TAF et al, 2013). In essence, Nepal is exporting cheap unskilled labor and at the same time, it is importing

42. Due to lack of documentation of people crossing Nepal-India border, estimates of the magnitude of labor migration to India vary (World Bank, 2011) but current estimate puts it at two million.

43. MOLE (2016) reports that 219,965 people applied for foreign employment in FY 2008/09, increasing to 499,620 in FY 2014/15.

44. Thirty-nine percent of Nepali aspiring migrants plan to work in low-skill professions like as helpers, cleaners, gardeners, waiters, guards, and salesmen. Likewise, 43.6% of Nepali aspiring migrants plan to work as domestic workers. Only 15% of aspiring migrants plan to take semi-skilled or skilled work (TAF et al, 2013; pp 11).

45. A study on foreign employment advertisements in *Kantipur*, the Nepali national daily newspaper, revealed that 39% of advertisements were for unskilled work, while 24% were for semi-skilled work and 34% were for skilled work (CTEVT, 2015; pp 18).

labor from foreign countries to meet its own labor shortage. Satyal (2019) reports that remittance outflow from Nepal to India is handful of country's remittance inflow which portrays that Indian workers are taking away huge chunk of money from Nepal.

In sum, Nepal lacks a clear vision for labor management at home and skill development for Nepali workers. New Labor Act (2017) has been enacted in the context of federalization of the country but the Act doesn't have clear jurisdiction of federal, province and local government. There is no clarity on role of province and local government on labor management. On the one hand, Constitution 2015 has conferred management of small and cottage industries to local government whereas the new Labor Act (2017) is silent on how local government manage labor problems in small and cottage industries. This, along with other factors discussed in previous sections of this chapter, has hindered the domestic industrialization process. At the same time, due to a lack of training and skills, Nepali workers face difficulties when competing in the international labor market, limiting their ability to earn higher wages. Given these problems, there are doubts that Nepal will be able to attract large-scale investment for industrialization and public infrastructure.

5.5 Investment Climate Despite some visible improvements in recent times, Nepal's investment climate is still poor due to a number of factors. For example, the cost of doing business remains high due to poor infrastructure, unreliable electricity supply, low labor productivity, high cost of labor, politicization of labor relations, political confusion, and unclear messages coming from the government about whether private investment and FDI are really encouraged or not. In the World Bank's cost of doing business ranking, performance of Nepal is poorer than South Asia in paying tax, getting electricity, protecting minority investors, enforcing contract and getting construction permit (Table 5.6). Nepal's ranking isn't also good in other indicators. The institutions designed to oversee and promote the industrial sector are inefficient at best and lack transparency despite policy commitments to fight corruption. Without a smooth-functioning institutional framework, the industrial sector cannot be expected to transform the national economy anytime soon, despite government rhetoric that it will.

Table 5.6: Cost of Doing Business in Nepal*

Details	Nepal	South Asia
Getting Construction Permit	57.99 (148)	61.85 (113)
Starting Business	84.38 (107)	85.44 (101)
Doing Business	59.63 (110)	56.71 (123)
Enforcing Contract	45.26 (154)	43.44 (145)
Resolving Insolvency	47.16 (83)	38.30 (109)
Trading Across Borders	77.17 (82)	62.57 (117)
Paying Tax	52.87 (158)	60.02 (132)
Protecting Minority Investors	58.33(72)	61.67 (64)
Getting Credit	50.00 (99)	47.50 (105)
Registering Property	64.86 (88)	46.91 (144)
Getting Electricity	58.28 (137)	59.36 (122)

Source: World Bank, 2019a

* Score is reflected on a scale from 0 to 100, where 0 represents the lowest and 100 represents the best performance. The value in parenthesis is ranking ranges from 1 to 190 where 1 is best and 190 is worst.

5.6 Conclusion The story of Nepal's industrialization process is one of uncoordinated efforts, grand visions, and limited action. Not surprisingly, industrial output dropped from 21% of GDP in 1994 to 14% in 2018. The industrial and investment climate has yet to be developed, as the policy framework remains confusing and contradictory. Whether the government should incentivize industrial development is an issue of debate without any clear conclusions. The government is focused to maximize revenue while the production related ministries have their own agenda sometimes contradicting for example the supply ministry want to assure adequate supply of essential commodities including food items if necessary by importing while the agriculture ministry is focused on enhancing domestic output and reducing imports. Production initiatives are not adequately linked with market development.

Efforts to reduce costs and make Nepal a competitive investment destination are lacking, meaning that both FDI and domestic private investment are unlikely to be forthcoming. Hence, there is an immediate need to reduce costs, improve quality and enhance overall productivity. Nepal should immediately start working because China and South Asia are soon expected to become the largest market in the world.[46]

46. It is forecasted that China and the South Asia will overtake North America by 2025-30 and Europe by 2035-40.

chapter 6

ECONOMIC SECTORS: MARKET AND SERVICES

6.1 Introduction Trade, commerce, banking, and other service sectors are fundamental to nation building, state modernization, and economic change. This chapter examines how the service sectors have developed in Nepal, beginning with early trade relations.

Nepal has had trade relations with its two neighbors, India and Tibet/ China, and their predecessor states, since ancient times.[1] To facilitate trade, Nepal started minting its own coins in the fifth century. Trade with Nepal's neighbors to the north and south was not only bilateral; Nepal also served as a transit zone across the Himalayas (Sen, 1971).[2] In the 18th and 19th centuries, several wars erupted between Nepal, British India, and Tibet/ China over control of trans-Himalayan trade. Following the Sugauli Treaty between Nepal and the British in 1816, Nepal becamc more dependent on its

1. Sen (1971) quotes the renowned historian Bal Chandra Sharma, who says that Nepal's commercial relations with India and Tibet/ China date to the fifth century BC, referencing Kautilya's *Arthasastra* and the *Mulasarvastivada Vinayasamgraha*.

2. Bajracharya (2016) reports that transit of goods through Nepal flourished in different parts of the country. For example, the Karnali region used to be the center of the gold and silver trade between India and the Western part of China and other adjacent regions. Merchants brought gold from the north in exchange for silver from the south. The trans-Himalayan trade in the Karnali region began to dry up following a decree by King Prithvi Narayan Shah, who closed the route, fearing foreign merchants would loot the country. Bahadur Shah, Prithvi's successor, followed his father's decree.

southern neighbor (Rose, 1971).[3] However, despite many disturbances, the India-Nepal-Tibet/ China transit route persisted, with trade conducted primarily by Nepal's mercantile communities like the Newars and Thakalis. Numerous rudimentary markets developed along trade routes, gradually contributing to urbanization.

At the same time, the Nepali state's main interest was to seek rent, not necessarily to promote meaningful and dynamic commercial activity. This tendency became more pronounced after 1846, when the state was ruled by the Rana family. Regmi (1988) argues that the Ranas' primary interest was to expand the state treasury through large-scale collection of customs and other taxes, which they used for their own benefit. Artisans, craftsmen, and traders who had long played a role in small-scale manufacturing and trade were undermined. Furthermore, as Bista (1991) argues, the socially conservative Ranas took steps to institutionalize the Hindu caste hierarchy, downgrading occupational castes whose skills could have otherwise been harnessed for more manufacturing, trade, and prosperity.

Attempts were made in the 19th and 20th centuries to develop administrative-cum-market centers in various parts of Nepal's hills, many of which grew into small towns populated by Newar merchants who migrated from Kathmandu Valley, as well as other groups of people (Sharma, 2004).[4] Much of Nepal's population remained in villages where connectivity was almost non-existent and the production base was limited to subsistence farming (Regmi, 1984 and 1988). As a result, there was only limited commercial activity between villages, often based on the barter system. Caravan traders connected villages to faraway markets by transporting away local products like grain and bringing back salt, cotton, and other materials using porters or animal power (Regmi, 1984 and 1988).[5]

---

3. Refer footnote 1 of chapter 2 for brief history of Sugauli Treaty and Annex B for a brief history of commercial relations with India and Tibet/China.

4. Major hill towns that developed in the 19th and 20th centuries were Dolkha, Chitlang, Trisuli-Nuwakot, Gorkha, Tanahun, Kaski (Pokhara), Chainpur, Dhankuta, Salyan, Tansen, and Silgurhi.

5. The caravan traders were widespread, particularly in the Himalayan region. Such traders reportedly reached as far as Delhi (Bajracharya, 2016).

6.2 Initial Attempts to Reform the Market At the time of the 1951 political revolution, Nepal's economy remained small, with rudimentary market systems integrated with India (Rajbahak, 1989 and Shrestha, 1981). The country's first Five-Year Plan, for the period 1956-61, committed to improving trade, enhancing domestic markets, and developing services needed for a dynamic economy like transportation, storage, banking, and commerce. The Nepal Agency Act, 1958 was passed to regulate commercial agents, distributors, stockists, and other traders. Likewise, the Export Import (Control) Act, 1957 and the Black Marketing Control Act, 1956 regulated trade and it required permission from the government to operate. There were also some initiatives to develop legal and regulatory frameworks for the transportation, tourism, and civil aviation sectors. Nevertheless, due to the period's political instability, significant attempts to regulate these sectors were not undertaken.

Importantly, Nepal continued its trade relations with newly independent India in the 1950s. Mohan Shumsher, the last Rana Prime Minister, signed the Treaty of Peace and Friendship and the Treaty of Trade and Transit with India in July 1950, just a few months before the fall of his government.[6] The Trade and Transit Treaty committed both countries to enhance their commercial relationship and conferred full and unrestricted rights to Nepal to use Indian territories and ports for commercial transit.[7] Nevertheless, as Panday (1999) notes, "the Letter of Exchange accompanying this treaty provided that if Nepal pursue[d] a policy divergent from that of India, there [would] be mutual consultation so as to ensure that there is no flow into India of goods imported from third countries." The treaty provided duty- and quota-free access for Nepali products in India.

While the two Treaties and the accompanying Letter of Exchange were important, they did not bring significant changes to India-Nepal trade relations. In fact, they marked a continuation of the British-Rana model. In the agreements, India displayed its continued interest in influencing Nepal's trade regime, while the

6. Nepal also signed the Friendship and Commerce Agreement with the USA in April 1947.

7. Ministry of Commerce, 2017; pp 1

Nepali administration demonstrated its rent-seeking mindset, focused on collecting customs and other taxes through large-scale trade with India. Following the agreements, Nepal continued to export primary and intermediary goods and import manufactured and processed items; the volume of trade would grow exponentially over time. The treaties also demonstrated Nepal's geographical dependency on India, which would continue to shape Nepal's economy for decades to come. All succeeding trade and transit treaties between India and Nepal followed the same structure,[8] and the wide industrial gap between the two countries continued. Though some clauses for lowering the administrative hurdles for cross-border trade were later added, they were rarely put into practice.

Both of the 1950 treaties with India were vilified as "antinationalist" by Nepal's leftists, who considered them symbolic of Nepal's subordination to India (Joshi and Rose, 1966). Leftists remained suspicious of succeeding trade and transit treaties with India and other western capitalist countries.[9]

Besides the treaties with India, several other important developments in the 1950s shaped Nepal's international trade. The victory of the Communists in China in 1949 and merger of Tibet with China minimized north-south transit trade and border dispute between India and China halted this transit trade, helping to redefine Nepal's commercial activities and geo-political scenario. Nepali traders in Tibet needed to close their business houses and return back to Nepal[10].

Another important initiative undertaken by the Nepali government during this period was the ending of dual currency

8. The trade treaty of 1997, assisted by the Gujaral doctrine that included consideration of labor in value addition, definitely was a departure. Previously, only local material content was considered while the treaty allowed to consider labor and local material content for being eligible for exporting to India.

9. When the first leftist Prime Minister of Nepal, Man Mohan Adhikari, made his state visit to India in 1995, he raised the issue of revising the treaties. However, nothing was done, although from then onwards both India and Nepal repeatedly talked about revisions without actually following through on them (Baral, 2016). Even in the 2008 Constituent Assembly elections, Nepal's leftists raised the issue of revising the "unfair" treaties with India (Bista, 2014).

10. Refer Annex B for details.

system and legalization of only Nepali currency in the country. At the time, Indian currency was widely used in Nepal and currency arbitrage had made the exchange rate between Indian and Nepali currencies extremely volatile. The government took several measures to institutionalize a unified currency for the country. In April 1956, the Nepal Rastra Bank (NRB)[11] was established as the central bank of Nepal, with the founding objective of increasing Nepali currency transactions throughout the country (NRB, 2016). In the same year, a decree was issued to all line ministries and government offices requiring official transactions to be made only in Nepali currency[12] – a policy that was strongly enforced only after the monarchy's takeover in 1960. Furthermore, the Nepali Rupee was pegged to the Indian Rupee in 1960 to control exchange-rate volatility. The Foreign Exchange Control Act, 1960 also prohibited the use of any foreign currency in internal transactions. The Nepali currency was later pegged to the US Dollar. However, as Maskay (2002) reports, large-scale circulation of Indian currency in Nepal diminished only in the mid-1970s and it is still used freely in areas along the Indian border today.

6.2.1 Trade during the Panchayat Era After King Mahendra's takeover in 1960, trade policy[13] was guided by import substitution, export promotion, and trade diversification in order to maintain foreign currency reserves and make the country self-sufficient (Shrestha, 1981; Rajbahak, 1989, Bajracharya and Sharma, 1996; and Acharya et al, 1998). High tariffs and quota restrictions were

---

11. In 1945, the Sadar Muluki Khana was established as the government treasury. It managed the government's accounts and issued Nepali currency notes with denominations of 1, 5, 10 and 100. From 1959, NRB took over the treasury functions from the Sadar Muluki Khana and started to issue currency on behalf of the Government of Nepal.

12. The Nepali Currency Circulation Act, 1958 was also passed to increase circulation of Nepali currency.

13. To address poverty in Manang, a mountain district that fell on hard times after trans-Himalayan trade diminished, King Mahendra granted people from that area special permission to import extra personal baggage worth NRs 500, laying the foundation for modern trading and trade diversification. Unfortunately, the policy had the unintended effect of increasing smuggling and other undesirable practices.

imposed on imports from countries other than India, although these measures were not as extreme as India's protectionist policies against third countries.

Importers were required to obtain licenses and were restricted by quotas on specified goods from countries other than India. Under law, trade with India was more or less open, and Nepal continued to export primary and intermediary goods to its southern neighbor while importing processed and manufactured items. New Trade and Transit Treaties in 1960, 1971 and 1978 attempted to make this trade freer (Shrestha, 2003).[14]

However, reforms aimed at easing business were rarely put into practice (Panday, 1999). Various types of non-tariff barriers remained, including administrative caveats added in subsequent treaties that made the process for port clearance lengthy. Trade with India needed to be conducted through the banking system, using letters of credit in Indian currency. The NRB, at the recommendation of the Ministry of Finance, would also provide other convertible currency to import items from India. However, Rajbahak (1989), Karmacharya (2002) and Taneja et al (2002) point out that trade with India took place mostly through informal channels outside the banking system. Even today, most trade with India takes place through informal routes, as the government's institutional capacity to control trade along the long, open and porous border remains weak.

Under the Panchayat regime, exports to third countries besides India required licenses and foreign currency proceeds from such exports needed to be surrendered to the NRB within six months of receipt. The government created incentives like the Export Exchange Entitlement Scheme[15] (EEES) to promote export to

14. Beginning in 1971, India granted duty-free access to imports from Nepal on a non-reciprocal basis. Nepali/Indian material content requirement was set at 90 percent meaning only 10 % foreign materials could be used for being eligible for exports, though this was gradually reduced in later years. Likewise, excise duty paid by Nepali importers on Indian goods to the Indian government was refunded to the Nepali Government (Shrestha, 2003) – a provision that continues even today. Furthermore, the 1960 Trade and Transit Treaty designated special sheds in Calcutta Port to provide transit facilities for Nepal.

15. Though exporters needed to surrender foreign currency proceeds to the NRB,

third countries. Furthermore, it signed trade and cooperation treaties with various countries beginning in the mid-1960s in order to diversify trade.[16] Partners included industrial countries like the USA and EU nations, which granted special preference to developing countries like Nepal for specific sectors, such as garments through the Multi-Fiber Agreement (MFA).[17]

Due to these trade measures and other socio-economic changes, Nepal's trade began to be diversified since the early sixties. Nepal began trading with the USA, Germany, Japan, Hong Kong, and Singapore (Table 6.1). Exports to the USA and Germany in particular grew with the emergence of export of manufactured goods like carpets[18], garments[19], and Pashmina[20] produced in Nepal. Exports to

---

they were entitled to use a portion of it for import under EEES. Because profits from imports exceeded profits from exports, this scheme was attractive to traders. However, as trade diversified, export destination countries were not the same as import origin countries, spurring currency arbitration in Nepal.

16. Nepal signed a trade agreement with Great Britain in May, 1965, which was followed by another agreement with Yugoslavia in September, 1965, and then by many other agreements with different countries. A list is available on the Trade and Export Promotion Center's website, available at http://www.tepc.gov.np/pages/trade-agreement.

17. Refer to footnote 11 of chapter 5 on MFA.

18. Carpet weaving was introduced at the Handicraft Training Center, established in 1967 with Swiss support, to provide jobs to Tibetan refugees fleeing the Chinese takeover in 1959. Tourists began to take these products to their countries. The collapse of the Moroccan carpet industry in 1977 helped to create a global niche for Nepali carpets, and Germany became not only a major importer but also the center of a major distribution network for Nepali carpets.

19. The MFA enticed Indian industrialists to come to Nepal to establish industries for export, leading the Nepali industry to grow and garments to become the largest export item in 1999, surpassing carpets, which saw a decline due to end of MFA and ATC agreement. It needs to be pointed out that conservatism persisted in various aspects which continued today, that did not allow to enjoy full benefits from liberalization measures. In the garment industries, FDI was discouraged, though basically it was promoted with Indian investment, due to apprehension of losing employment. On the other hand, Bangladeshi garment industry was developed by Korean investors enabling the sector to emerge as the number one export item to this days. In Nepal, however, garment export have decline severely.

20. Rough pashmina woven on a cotton base was traditionally produced in Nepal. Nepali workers in Kashmir brought back the technology for weaving Pashmina on a silk base, contributing to the industry's phenomenal growth from mid-nineties.

India were dominated by agricultural products, crude inedible materials, and intermediary goods like jute products (Table 6.3), but few manufactured goods.[21] Major imports during the Panchayat era included edible commodities, manufactured goods, machinery, transport equipment, mineral fuels, and lubricants (Table 6.2). Nepal's developing transportation network increased demand for these items. Likewise, chemical fertilizers and drugs, also major imports, were associated with the rise of modern healthcare and initiatives to modernize farming. Likewise, hides and skins were also major commodities of export to overseas countries.

Due to global events like the Vietnam War, the 1970s oil crisis, and the 1980s worldwide balance-of-payments crisis, Nepal's exchange rate system was revised several times in order to maintain the current account balance. The pegging of the Nepali Rupee to the US Dollar was breached four times from 1973 to 1983 meaning the devaluation of Nepali currency (Maskay, 2002) and EEES was replaced by the dual exchange-rate system[22] in September, 1978 (Rajbahak, 1989). However, the dual exchange-rate system led to increase currency arbitration, while the pegging of the Nepali rupee to the dollar further threatened Nepali current accounts. Due to the failure of these policies, the dual exchange-rate system was eliminated in September, 1981, while the Nepali Rupee was de-pegged from the dollar in June, 1983 and allowed to float freely. Foreign reserves reached a record low in FY 1983/84 (Bajracharya and Sharma, 1996 and Acharya et al, 1998) due not only to these Nepali policy changes but also to the global balance-of-payments crisis.

The early 1980s were also marked by a deepening economic crisis due to high inflation, slow growth, a drought that affected agriculture, high government expenditure, increasing national debt, high money supply, and an ongoing trade deficit (Bajracharya and Sharma, 1996). In order to address the crisis, the IMF provided stand-on credit to Nepal in 1985 as part of its Economic Stabilization

21. Refer to the tables in TEPC's regular publication titled "Nepal Oversea Trade Statistics" for commodity-wise details of trade with India.

22. Under this system, the exchange rate for importers of locally available goods and luxurious goods was NRs 15.9 per 1 USD, whereas the exchange rate for importers of raw material and machinery was NRs 11.9 per 1 USD.

Program (ESP). The World Bank initiated the first phase of the Structural Adjustment Program (SAP) for the period 1986-89, followed by a second phase from 1989-92. The IMF and the World Bank programs' key focus was to bring market-oriented reforms and reduce government intervention in the economy; they opened the door to economic liberalization in Nepal (Bajracharya and Sharma, 1996 and Acharya et al, 1998). Under these programs, Nepali currency was devalued against the dollar in November, 1985, while the license scheme for imports was gradually deregulated with the introduction of the Open General Licensing System. Likewise, the Export Duty Drawback System and the Bonded Warehouse Scheme were introduced to promote exports. The latter was particularly helpful for the emerging carpet industry, which needed to import wool as raw material.

The government's efforts to de-regulate and spur exports during the late Panchayat period was only partly successful due to limited quality control mechanisms for locally made products. None of the line ministries relating to edible goods, industrial goods, or service industries had the technical capacity to maintain standards. Beyond carpets and handicrafts, most of Nepal's other exports remained in unprocessed or semi-processed form (Table 6.3). Some attempts were made by the Swiss, USAID, GTZ, The World Bank, UNDP and other donors to develop agricultural processing, value chains, and industrial skill development, but their impact was limited to certain geographical areas and certain sectors (WFP and FAO, 2007; and Bajracharya, 2007). As a result, trade increases and diversification were limited; Nepal remained economically dependent on India. Panday (1999) argues that this dependency allowed India to impose its political interests on Nepal, seen most clearly in the economic blockade of 1989.[23]

23. The 1989 economic blockade was imposed after a Nepal's arms deal with China. Similarly, an economic blockade was imposed in 2015, immediately after the promulgation of Nepal's new federal democratic constitution. India was not happy with this constitution because of its failure to address some issues raised by Nepal's marginalized Madheshi community.

Table 6.1: Direction of Foreign Trade in Panchayat Era (in NRs. Million)

Countries/ Regions	1975/76			1980/81			1985/86			1989/90		
	Export	Import	Balance	Export	Import	Balance	Export	Import	Balance	Export	Import	Balance
Asia	984.10	1,513.96	-529.86	1,281.64	3,883.40	-2,601.75	1,529.39	7,540.29	-6,010.90	1,579.41	12,716.56	-11,137.15
India	893.7	1,227.1	-333.4	992.4	2179	-1,186.6	1,241.1	3,970	-2,728.9	602.5	4,674.5	-4,072
China	29.09	48.01	-18.92	16.45	191.09	-174.65	0.00	301.69	-301.69	16.35	891.57	-875.22
South Asia (Other than India)	0.01	0.65	-0.64	67.11	20.01	47.10	10.58	116.48	-105.90	73.00	478.64	-405.64
ASEAN	44.73	65.96	-21.22	75.14	265.91	-190.77	216.68	236.11	-19.43	32.52	3,495.82	-3,463.29
Japan	5.81	118.89	-113.07	31.53	572.04	-540.51	10.29	1,503.25	-1492.96	24.07	1,628.76	-1604.69
South Korea	0.00	30.04	-30.04	0.00	388.94	-388.94	0.00	463.78	-463.78	27.86	787.40	-759.53
Hong Kong	9.65	20.70	-11.05	93.88	91.77	2.11	49.59	180.26	-130.68	7.50	343.45	-335.95
Other Asia	1.07	2.46	-1.39	4.86	173.36	-168.50	0.91	767.10	-766.19	795.60	416.25	379.35
Europe	96.80	230.93	-134.14	240.79	539.89	-299.09	646.46	986.48	-340.03	2,578.50	2,618.25	-39.74
Germany	20.85	47.79	-26.94	58.28	73.13	-14.85	223.43	282.13	-58.70	1,367.97	565.11	802.86
France	5.16	1.21	3.95	5.51	4.80	0.70	9.25	67.69	-58.44	37.76	595.85	-558.10
UK	16.90	38.50	-21.60	48.18	65.35	-17.18	107.54	100.33	7.20	253.88	145.81	108.07
Others	53.89	143.43	-89.54	128.82	396.61	-267.79	306.24	536.33	-230.09	918.89	1311.48	-392.59
American Continent	55.21	54.08	1.13	38.48	119.56	-81.08	820.14	235.39	584.74	1,482.38	321.55	1,160.84
USA	54.95	48.38	6.58	35.63	94.08	-58.44	806.33	172.77	633.56	1,442.21	193.04	1,249.17
Others	0.26	5.70	-5.44	2.85	25.49	-22.64	13.80	62.62	-48.82	40.17	128.51	-88.34
Africa	21.62	0.53	21.09	30.72	0.47	30.24	0.00	1.38	-1.38	11.46	0.40	11.06
Oceania	2.32	7.40	-5.08	5.70	34.77	-29.07	2.52	49.74	-47.23	6.34	908.44	-902.10
Total	1,160.04	1,806.90	-646.86	1,597.33	4,578.09	-2,980.76	2,998.51	8,813.29	-5,814.79	5,658.10	16,565.20	-10,907.10

(Source: Various Issues of *Nepal Overseas Trade Statistics*, TEPC)

Table 6.2: Import of Nepal by Commodity Groups in Panchayat Era (in NRs. Million)

Major Commodity Goods	1975/76			1985/86			1989/90		
	Total Import	India Import	Oversea Import	Total Import	India Import	Oversea Import	Total Import	India Import	Oversea Import
Food and Live Animal	291.1	258.2	32.9	971.1	738.5	232.6	1,607.7	1,138.3	469.4
Tobacco and Beverages	42.4	31.9	10.5	112.9	112.1	0.8	226.6	202.8	23.8
Crude Materials, Inedible Except Fuels	88.7	31.1	57.6	393.0	99.0	294.0	1,571.1	80.5	1,490.6
Mineral, Fuels and Lubricants	211.7	95.2	116.5	1,054.0	149.3	904.7	1,515.5	36.9	1,478.6
Animal and Vegetable Oil and Fats	7.4	5.5	1.9	101.9	15.8	86.1	476.3	0.6	475.7
Chemicals and Drugs	190.1	114.9	75.2	1170.2	547.1	623.1	2,823.9	934.4	1889.5
Manufactured Goods Classified Mainly by Materials	545.9	409.5	136.4	2,759.5	1,399.2	1,360.3	5,065.0	1,352.4	3,712.6
Machinery and Transport Equipment	413.4	158.1	255.3	2,134.7	693.3	1,441.4	3,790.4	687.9	3,102.5
Miscellaneous Manufactured Articles	168.4	105.4	63.0	637.2	213.2	424.0	1,247.8	240.6	1,007.2
Commodity and Transaction not Classified According to Kind	22.6	17.3	5.3	6.9	3.4	3.3	0.6	0.1	0.5
Total	1,981.7	1,227.1	754.6	9,341.2	3,970.9	5,370.3	18,324.9	4,674.5	13,650.4

(Source: NRB, 2018a)

Table 6.3: Export of Nepal by Commodity Groups in Panchayat Era (in NRs. Million)

Major Commodity Goods	1975/76			1985/86			1989/90		
	Total Export	India Export	Oversea Export	Total Export	India Export	Oversea Export	Total Export	India Export	Oversea Export
Food and Live Animal	804.0	721.6	82.4	835.6	573.0	262.6	616.0	348.8	267.2
Tobacco and Beverages	4.0	3.5	0.5	0.3	0.1	0.1	4.1	1.1	3.0
Crude Materials, Inedible Except Fuels	226.3	136.1	90.2	412.9	364.5	48.4	238.6	179.7	58.9
Mineral, Fuels and Lubricants	1.7	1.0	0.7	0.2	0.2	0.0	0.0	0.0	0.0
Animal and Vegetable Oil and Fats	1.8	1.4	0.4	61.3	56.0	5.3	20.1	11.4	8.7
Chemicals and Drugs	9.3	5.8	3.5	2.5	1.0	1.5	10.9	0.0	10.9
Manufactured Goods Classified Mainly by Materials	104.7	14.5	90.2	899.9	201.7	698.2	2,693.1	53.2	2,639.9
Machinery and Transport Equipment	3.7	1.4	2.3	38.6	37.5	1.1	0.1	0.0	0.1
Miscellaneous Manufactured Articles	23.0	3.1	19.9	826.5	6.8	819.7	1,573.3	8.3	1,565.0
Commodity and Transaction not Classified According to Kind	7.3	5.3	2.0	0.3	0.3	0.0	0.0	0.0	0.0
Total	1,185.8	893.7	292.1	3,078.1	1,241.1	1,836.9	5,156.2	602.5	4,553.7

(Source: NRB, 2018a)

6.2.2: Developing Commercial Markets The establishment of government-managed industrial districts and public enterprises in the Terai helped to develop markets in areas outside of Kathmandu. The Panchayat-era government also created different government offices in the 14 zonal headquarters and 75 district headquarters[24] that aimed to facilitate economic growth in their localities by creating small rudimentary markets. Furthermore, the construction of physical infrastructure like roads, hydropower, and telecommunications also contributed to market development. However, infrastructure development was concentrated in only certain parts of the country; the Mid- and Far-Western Regions remained largely untouched by it.

In order to regulate commercial markets, the Civil Supply Department and the Central Purchase Department were amalgamated to form the Department of Commerce in January, 1960. The Standard Weight and Measurement Act, 1976, the Nepal Standard (Certification Mark) Act, 1975, and the Black Market Controlling Act, 1975 were passed to control quality and to reduce market speculation and other illegal market activities. The National Transport Management Act, 1969 regulated transportation services. Likewise, the Private Firm Registration Act, 1958 and the Partnership Act, 1958 facilitated the opening of retail and wholesale businesses. Supply networks were fed by both private and public firms. Private entrepreneurs were allowed to transact all goods except certain restricted goods. At the same time, public enterprises like the Nepal Food Corporation, the Agriculture Inputs Corporation, the Nepal Timber Corporation, and the National Trading Corporation supplied markets with essential items.[25] Commercial networks of wholesalers, retailers and other supply agents gradually developed, especially in urban areas.

24. Before 1960, the country was divided into 35 districts for administrative purposes.

25. The prime objective of the National Trading Corporation was to channel commodity aid from China and USSR to local markets. It was also entrusted with task of fixing quotas to stabilize domestic prices and to ensure regular supply of construction materials, industrial raw materials, machinery, equipment, and consumer goods.

Table 6.4: Service Sector of Nepal in Selected Years of the Panchayat Period (in NRs Million)*

Fiscal Years	Service Sector GDP (Current Price)	Service Sector GDP (at Constant Price of FY 2000/01)	Share of Service Sector in GDP (%)	Percent of Economically Active Population in Service Sector	Service Sector Growth (%)**
1964/65	1,372	24,140	24.49%		
1970/71	1,930	24,243	21.59%	4.43%	0.07% (1964/65 to 1970/71)
1980/81	6,808	60,848	28.74%	6.43%	9.64% (1970/71 to 1980/81)
1990/91	40,397	108,435	34.79%	14.71%	5.95% (1980/81 to 1990/91)

Source: Various Issues of *Statistical Year Book of Nepal,* Central Bureau of Statistics
* Service Sector also includes basic services, government services, community organization.
** Source: Calculated by Author using CBS Data
**Time period representing the data is mentioned in parenthesis

However, public trading enterprises failed to perform with the same speed and efficiency as the private sector. Interference by high-ranking officials and lack of transparency hindered public enterprises' performance (Bajracharya and Shrestha, 1983). At the same time, there was an expansion of black markets because the government regulators' institutional capacity was weak and because consumer rights were not clearly defined meaning absence of proper acts and regulations and institutions to correct anomalies. The government was mostly unsuccessful in levying taxes; it was able to levy the Sales Tax only at the production point or at customs offices. All other value-addition activities across supply networks were effectively beyond the tax net.

At the same time, donors provided support to develop value-chain networks for rural rudimentary markets (METCON, 1994 and Bajracharya, 2007). However, in rural areas without road access, commercial activities were limited by lack of infrastructure. People often had to travel on foot to visit markets. For example, in the Mid- and Far-Western Regions, some people needed to travel for more than a day. Although the government aimed to reach most rural areas through public supply enterprises, their reach was limited to urban areas.

Despite the limited expansion of markets, the Panchayat era saw significant growth in the service sector, especially in banking, capital markets, tourism, civil aviation, and transportation. As a result, the service sector's contribution to GDP increased from 24.49% in FY 1964/65 to 34.79% in FY 1990/91 (Table 6.4). Service-sector growth was 9.64% in seventies and 5.95% in eighties (Table 6.4). However, the share of the economically active population engaged in the service sector increased only gradually, from 4.43% in 1971 to 14.71% in 1991 (Table 6.4). The vast majority of the population remained engaged in agriculture.

6.3 Liberalization of the Economy Although the liberalization process was initiated during the late Panchayat era at the behest of the IMF and the World Bank, liberalization measures expanded more rapidly under the NC government after 1990. The Eighth Plan, for the period 1992-97, was the foundation for structural change in Nepal's economy (Bajracharya and Sharma, 1996 and Dixit, 1994). Opposition leftists opposed liberalization measures, claiming they would result in large-scale encroachment by Indian and other multi-national corporations seeking to exploit Nepal's resources and people. However, after coming to power in later years, leftists failed to reorient the economy away from the liberalization process initiated by the NC. Leftist governments did announce a few programs that may be contradictory to liberal approaches, but they were never implemented.[26] Rather, it appears that leftists used these issues instrumentally to carry favor among labors, the poor, and farmers who were concerned about injustices in the market economy. Some of their points were certainly valid, and the political discourse between liberal and leftist forces helped strengthen policy outcomes.

26. The FY 1994/95 budget brought by the UML minority government announced the establishment of a new government owned commercial bank because of the lucrative returns in the joint-venture commercial banks. The NC opposed it and the bank never materialized.

6.3.1 Trade Liberalization In the early 1990s, the NC-led government discarded the import-substitution approach in favor of an export-promotion approach by virtually eliminating restrictions on trade and commercial activities (Bajracharya and Sharma, 1996 and Acharya et al, 1998). India was also in the midst of similar reforms to address its own economic crisis, which created pressure on Nepal to act similarly because of the highly integrated nature of the two economies (Dixit, 1994). In 1991, Nepali citizens who conducted foreign currency transactions were allowed to open bank accounts in foreign currency. In March 1992, the government introduced partial convertibility for current accounts. This decision was taken just hours before a similar decision in India, and it effectively released administrative control over imports and abolished the license regime. One of the instigators of the change, the prominent economist Prithvi Raj Ligal, was then a member of the National Planning Commission (NPC). In an article titled "How we Abolished the License Raj," published in the daily *Kantipur*,[27] Ligal stated that the NPC's decision was backed by like-minded officials in the Ministry of Finance and Nepal Rastra Bank (NRB),[28] although some NRB officials argued against the reform, claiming it would deplete foreign reserves. In fact, foreign reserves went up after the decision due to expansion in exports and enhanced mobilization of foreign assistance. A few months later, the convertibility ratio was further raised and, in February 1993, current accounts were made fully convertible.

The budget for FY 1993/94 completely abolished the trading license system, except for a few items listed as "sensitive." Commercial banks were also allowed to provide loans in foreign currency to export-oriented industries beginning in 1993.

27. This article is available online at: http://money2014.ekantipur.com/detail.php?art=5&cat=revisiting-reform.

28. According to Ligal, five people who played instrumental roles in introducing this reform were the erstwhile chairman of the NPC Ram Sharan Mahat, Finance Minister Mahesh Acharya, Finance Secretary Thakur Prasad Pant, Governor of the NRB Hari Shankar Tripathi, and Deputy Governor of the NRB Hiranya Lal Bajracharya. The supporting team consisted of experts, Pushkar Bajracharya, Nirmal Pandey, Champak Pokharel, Roop Bahadur Khadka and Shree Krishna Shrestha.

Furthermore, the Trade Policy of 1992 emphasized the need to diversify trade by establishing a Special Economic Zone (SEZ). With the enactment of IEA, 1992 and FITTA, 1992, Nepal deregulated the manufacturing and commercial sectors, opening most sectors for private and foreign investment without restrictions.

The openness of the economy helped to bring more private and foreign investment in agriculture, manufacturing, and service industries between 1995 and 2000, contributing to economic growth. However, political instability caused by the Maoist movement from 1996-2006 severely affected the market environment. As discussed earlier, mainstream political parties' ambiguous approach to social inclusion and poverty reduction contributed to the escalation of the conflict. In addition to hurting trade and investment, the insurgency contributed to an electricity crisis which resulted in increased energy imports from India, further skewing the trade imbalance (ADB et al, 2009 and IIDS, 2018).

At the same time, corruption hurt trade. Despite a number of policy reforms related to taxes, customs, company affairs, and other state administration, the cost of doing business remained high in Nepal.[29] In many instances, private-sector firms colluded with the state by engaging in bribery to gain advantage and hurt competitors. As a result, a substantial portion of Nepal's trade took place through informal channels (Karmacharya, 2002 and P Bajracharya et al, 2006)[30]. Likewise, the state administration lacked a clear approach for utilizing the labor force, which grew year by year (ILO, 2015). It failed to substantially enhance the skills of the labor force to increase the dynamism of the economy. The Twelfth Plan (2010-2013) made some attempts in this regard, but there was no large-scale change in industrial or agricultural production. As a result, exports failed to diversify beyond a few limited sectors (Table 6.7).

Trade imbalances with India remained skewed according to an age-old pattern whereby Nepal exported primary and intermediary goods and imported processed and manufactured items in even

29. Refer to table 5.6 of Chapter 5 for the cost of doing business in Nepal.

30. It is estimated that informal trade of Nepal was at 41 percent in 2006 (P Bajracharya et al, 2006).

greater quantities. Though Nepal's manufacturing exports increased after FY 1999/2000 (Table 6.7), most of the items under this heading were in fact intermediary goods like textiles, yarn, jute, iron sheet, and zinc and copper wire rods. Nepal continued to heavily rely on India for imports in all major commodity groups (Table 6.5 and 6.6). MNCs began large-scale investments in India after its liberalization in the 1990s, resulting in more and more Indian manufactured items becoming available in Nepal. For instance, before the 1990s, most vehicles and transport machinery in Nepal were imported from third countries. Today, however, Nepal is importing more and more transport equipment from India, as virtually all major manufacturers have started producing there.

The revisions and renewals of the Trade and Transit Treaties with India have enabled the uneven and imbalanced trade relationship to continue unabated. Administrative caveats remain as major non-tariff barriers, and transit through India is still the bottleneck for Nepal's trade with third countries. The average speed of vehicle movement in the India-Nepal corridor is very slow, significantly raising costs (UNESCAP, 2003 and ADB and UNESCAP, 2017). In 2016, a Letter of Exchange between Nepal and Bangladesh established transit through the Kakarbhitta-Phulbari-Banglabandh corridor. In the same year, another Letter of Exchange with India operationalized transit traffic by rail to and from the Vishakhapatnam Port in Andhra Pradesh. The Visakhapatnam Port represents an opportunity for better connectivity because it is a deep-sea port. Otherwise transit through Kolkata/Haldia being provided to Nepal is feeder port so the shipments have to transfer from the mothership to smaller vessels at Singapore port enhancing costs while Vishakhapatnam is directly accessible to motherships. But, the proportion of surface transportation from Vishakhapatnam is much longer that may thwart the advantage of deep sea port. However, the administrative procedures using these new routes through Bangladesh and India remain lengthy. ADB and UNESCAP (2017) have suggested clearer guidelines, automation, a national single-window system, data harmonization, and simplification and reduction of procedures and documents as solutions to mitigate the trade bottleneck. Furthermore, the

Table 6.5: Direction of Foreign Trade in Post 1990 (in NRs. Million)

Countries/ Regions	1995/96			2005/06			2015/16			2016/17		
	Export	Import	Balance	Export	Import	Balance	Export	Import	Balance	Export	Import	Balance
Asia	4,603.80	64,663.16	-60,059.37	43,229.76	140,760.49	-97,530.72	46,508.66	695,737.91	-649,229.25	47,354.80	887,625.07	-840,270.27
India	3,978.60	25,588.10	-21,609.50	41,012.60	109,305.90	-68,293.30	39,095.13	487,597.31	-448,502.17	41,500.84	646,019.02	-604,518.17
China	0.01	3,094.38	-3,094.37	108.17	6,635.51	-6,527.34	2,156.76	117,209.98	-115,053.22	1,809.83	130,241.44	-128,431.61
South Asia (Other than India)	405.73	871.61	-465.88	661.54	475.61	185.92	1,624.00	5,109.90	-3,485.89	1,283.51	5,367.32	-4,083.81
ASEAN	51.12	13,176.12	-13,125.00	451.87	14,571.51	-14,119.63	763.87	40,287.04	-39,523.17	926.10	45,300.98	-44,374.88
Japan	78.98	4,551.15	-4,472.17	572.09	1,935.08	-1,362.99	1,204.03	7,641.42	-6,437.39	1,023.56	6,691.55	-5,667.99
South Korea	28.12	1,099.58	-1,071.47	25.52	1,788.88	-1,763.37	120.41	5,016.04	-4,895.63	160.54	8,938.06	-8,777.52
Hong Kong	28.62	11,706.11	-11,677.49	111.76	930.93	-819.17	345.46	1,048.20	-702.74	227.39	2,946.68	-2,719.29
Other Asia	32.61	4,576.10	-4,543.49	286.22	5,117.07	-4,830.85	1,198.99	31,828.02	-30,629.03	423.03	42,120.03	-41,697.00
Europe	9,021.31	6,512.54	2,508.76	8,057.43	8,884.34	-826.91	13,415.90	41,636.53	-28,220.63	14,972.52	46,387.88	-31,415.36
EU	8,212.27	5,048.06	3,164.22	6,144.96	5,355.78	789.18	7,767.35	19,693.25	-11,925.90	7,618.68	27,252.61	-19,633.93
Germany	6,751.33	2,455.00	4,296.34	2,843.77	2,761.79	81.98	3,157.14	4,347.05	-1,189.91	3,046.90	4,347.21	-1,300.31
France	175.57	513.74	-338.18	1,297.49	909.86	387.63	1,283.75	7,243.80	-5,960.05	1,193.61	13,350.34	-12,156.73
Other EU	1,285.38	2,079.32	-793.94	2,003.69	1,684.13	319.57	3,326.47	8,102.41	-4,775.94	3,378.17	9,555.06	-6,176.89
UK	289.40	1,024.32	-734.92	1,184.08	961.42	222.66	2,851.64	2,210.55	641.09	2,522.77	2,845.15	-322.37
Other European Countries	519.63	440.17	79.46	728.39	2,567.15	-1,838.75	2,796.91	19,732.73	-16,935.82	4,831.07	16,290.12	-11,459.05
American Continent	5,825.26	2,149.75	3,675.52	7,711.44	5,019.89	2,691.55	10,449.48	31,706.88	-21,257.40	9,949.10	36,434.69	-26,485.59
US	5,672.77	765.64	4,907.13	6,993.44	1,677.50	5,315.94	9,340.68	8,703.01	637.67	8,967.11	8,465.22	501.89
Others	152.50	1,384.11	-1,231.61	718.00	3,342.39	-2,624.39	1,108.80	23,003.87	-21,895.07	981.98	27,969.47	-26,987.48
Africa	5.19	31.17	-25.98	108.49	285.97	-177.48	89.84	5,709.29	-5,619.45	121.78	9,122.23	-9,000.45
Oceania	49.52	2,756.14	-2,706.62	183.23	2,442.05	-2,258.81	673.79	6,355.35	-5,681.56	727.16	6,381.46	-5,654.30
Total	19,505.08	76,112.76	-56,607.69	59,290.36	157,392.73	-98,102.37	71,137.66	781,145.96	-710,008.30	731,25.35	985,951.33	-912,825.97

(Source: Various Issues of *Nepal Overseas Trade Statistics*, TEPC)

Table 6.6: Import of Nepal by Commodity Groups in Post 1990 (in NRs. Million)

Major Commodity Goods	1995/96			2005/06			2015/16			2017/18		
	Total Import	India Import	Oversea Import	Total Import	India Import	Oversea Import	Total Import	India Import	Oversea Import	Total Import	India Import	Oversea Import
Food and Live Animal	4,785.80	3,265.70	1,520.10	13,298.70	10,108.80	3,189.90	109,756.50	81,574.90	25,657.10	151,111.70	102,605.40	41,486.80
Tobacco and Beverages	508.60	437.70	70.90	1,161.80	724.50	437.30	6,413.30	3,585.60	2,822.00	8,285.50	3,784.80	4,435.30
Crude Materials, Inedible Except Fuels	4,865.90	889.50	3,976.40	10,562.30	5,437.60	5,124.70	33,391.90	15,071.70	17,173.50	41,983.70	24,098.20	16,769.60
Mineral, Fuels and Lubricants	5,549.30	436.70	5,112.60	36,447.00	35,665.30	781.70	84,088.20	75,530.00	8,234.10	197,835.90	184,875.90	12,821.30
Animal and Vegetable Oil and Fats	2,830.90	51.40	2,779.50	10,196.60	152.60	10,044.00	21,153.30	1744.90	19,406.40	28,611.60	1,471.10	27,137.40
Chemicals and Drugs	8,686.80	3,540.60	5,146.20	24,750.20	13,520.80	11,229.40	103,961.80	53,655.50	29,858.10	125,577.10	74,194.80	36,306.50
Manufactured Goods Classified Mainly by Materials	28,129.70	9,472.60	18,657.10	40,600.50	25,487.40	15,113.10	163,131.60	119,395.20	17,475.40	279,892.40	226,783.00	25,755.50
Machinery and Transport Equipment	15,301.10	5,301.60	9,999.50	26,194.60	11,974.00	14,220.60	189,764.10	109,527.20	34,313.30	314,002.70	169,241.40	62,653.50
Miscellaneous Manufactured Articles	3,794.60	1,001.80	2,792.80	10,417.80	4,072.10	6,345.70	45,864.20	17,127.40	9,678.30	63,322.10	22,759.50	13,806.50
Commodity and Transaction not Classified According to Kind	1.80	1.00	0.80	150.80	0.00	150.80	16,074.20	0.10	16,074.10	32,203.70	0.00	32,203.50
Total	74,454.50	24,398.60	50,055.90	173,780.30	107,143.10	66,637.20	773,599.10	477,212.60	180,692.10	1242,826.80	809,814.20	273,376.00

(Source: NRB, 2018a)

Table 6.7: Export of Nepal by Commodity Groups in Post 1990 (in NRs. Million)

Major Commodity Goods	1995/96			2005/06			2015/16			2017/18		
	Total Export	India Export	Oversea Export	Total Export	India Export	Oversea Export	Total Export	India Export	Oversea Export	Total Export	India Export	Oversea Export
Food and Live Animal	1,946.60	1,267.80	678.80	7,192.00	6,306.70	885.30	1,6421.30	1,3538.90	2,803.30	20,856.90	16,641.90	3,600.80
Tobacco and Beverages	9.70	1.90	7.80	25.00	14.30	10.70	478.30	0.00	476.20	247.80	6.40	240.00
Crude Materials, Inedible Except Fuels	768.70	336.50	432.20	1,223.40	1,163.30	60.10	2,218.30	1,338.30	731.70	3,158.30	2,429.70	607.40
Mineral, Fuels and Lubricants	1.30	1.30	0.00	3.20	0.50	2.70	1.00	0.00	0.90	14.10	13.50	0.50
Animal and Vegetable Oil and Fats	251.30	137.90	113.40	4,284.60	4,145.70	138.90	106.90	102.80	3.10	406.40	358.40	2.80
Chemicals and Drugs	640.40	618.10	22.30	3,686.90	3,564.70	122.20	4,618.10	4,138.50	402.00	4,702.90	3,782.80	420.80
Manufactured Goods Classified Mainly by Materials	10,455.70	1,236.10	9,219.60	28,533.00	21,928.30	6,604.70	32,666.00	17,777.20	13,837.10	37,203.50	20,386.50	15,954.40
Machinery and Transport Equipment	35.20	26.40	8.80	1201.90	111.00	1090.90	399.70	75.60	194.30	1451.70	240.20	905.70
Miscellaneous Manufactured Articles	5,772.20	56.60	5,715.60	1,4081.60	3,477.70	10,603.90	13,204.90	2,522.40	10,491.40	13,592.00	2,745.40	10,416.60
Commodity and Transaction not Classified According to Kind	0.00	0.00	0.00	2.50	2.50	0.00	2.70	0.00	1.80	0.00	0.00	0.00
Total	19,881.10	3,682.60	16,198.50	60,234.10	40,714.70	19,519.40	70,117.20	39,493.70	28,941.90	8,1633.30	46,604.80	32,149.10

(Source: NRB, 2018a)

Government of Nepal is trying to establish dry ports at various border points with China and India to facilitate transit.

Nepal's exports in the past few decades have centered around a few items. Handicrafts and the carpet industry, despite a decline since late nineties, remained major items of export to Europe and the Americas, resulting in "manufactured goods" remaining the top export commodity group through 2017/18 (Table 6.7). Likewise, Nepal exported lentils, primarily to Bangladesh in early nineties. Donor technical support helped enable Nepal to begin exporting other items like pashmina, silver ornaments, wool products, handmade paper, and tea to third countries since early nineties (MOCS, 2010 and MOC 2016). Items like cardamom, ginger, non-timber forest products, medicinal and aromatic plants, fruits, and vegetables[31] continue to be exported in raw form, especially to India, where they are processed and refined for local markets and for re-export (ADB, 2014 and Arenas, 2016).

But aside from these items, Nepal has had little to sell since joining the WTO in 2004 and the regional trade agreements SAFTA and BIMSTEC in 2004. At the same time, it has not followed through on commitments made during WTO accession regarding SPS and TBT, customs reform, and other non-tariff barriers (MOCS, 2010 and MOC 2016)[32]. The Multimodal Transportation of Goods Act was passed in 2006 to regulate trade and transport, but bad road conditions remain a persistent barrier to the free flow of goods. Though the government has harmonized customs tariffs and has tried to simplify the customs clearance process by introducing the Automated System for Customs Data (ASYCUDA) in 1996, the process is still time-consuming (Nepal Chamber of Commerce, 2017). In addition, the government's weak

31. Donors like ADB, World Bank, DIFD, GTZ, SNV, UNDP, NORAD and others have initiated a number of projects to develop value chains for exportable products from Nepal but many items like cardamom, ginger, NTFPs, MAPs, fruits and vegetables are still exported without processing in raw form. Honey export to Norway virtually ended due to SPS clauses.

32. Trade with India was estimated at 28% of total trade in 1994. Ironically, after Nepal joined the WTO, trade concentration with India reached almost to 70% in 2018.

technical capacity has hampered efforts to control quality. As a result, Nepali consignments are often returned to Nepal, although sometimes this is because in Nepal's trade partners impose stringent technical barriers when their own domestic supply is abundance (they are lax at times of low domestic supply).

Studies by the World Bank (2003), MOCS (2010) and MOC (2016) have explored the potential of various products for export by Nepal, but the government has mostly failed to act on their recommendations. While the government has recognized that exportable commodities are a source of growth, it has not taken significant initiatives to address supply-side constraints and challenges. A study by the Nepal Chamber of Commerce (2017) also notes that barriers exist for exporting silver jewelry, ginger, cardamom and other products. The government has stated its intention to promote exports by establishing special economic zones (SEZs), but the necessary legislation was passed only recently, in October, 2016, and significant results have yet to be observed. Likewise, the government failed to seize upon the opportunity provided by special trade preferences given by developed countries in order to develop domestic industries. SAWTEE (2007) argues that Nepal was not able to benefit from its quota for readymade garments provided by the USA under the MFA mainly through limited middlemen, benefitting middlemen rather than domestic industries. In addition, even when products were made in Nepal, much of the labor was migrant from other countries, especially India (Panday, 1989). The export of readymade garments declined after the expiry of the ATC in January 2005, although a few readymade garment industries that achieved operational efficiency have survived (SAWTEE, 2007).

Another opportunity for Nepal came with the 1996 iteration of the India and Nepal Trade and Transit Treaty, which contained a clause for re-export that was favorable for Nepal, helping to increase Nepal's vegetable ghee exports to India. Nepal's vegetable ghee industries relied on palm oil imported from ASEAN countries, which they re-exported to India as vegetable ghee after processing. However, India imposed restrictions again in 2001, leading to closure of most of Nepal's vegetable ghee industries. As in the case of readymade garments, Nepal's state administration failed to capitalize on the special trade preference to develop Nepal's production base and comparative advantage. Instead, the government was overly focused on collecting revenue over the short term.

In sum, despite efforts to liberalize trade in Nepal since the late 1980s/ early 1990s, the country has not been able to develop its export base and expand into foreign markets. At the same time, imports have increased, resulting in a widening trade imbalance with most trade partners. The value of Nepal's exports is equal to a mere seven percent of its imports – a situation that would be untenable but for the inflow of remittances of Nepalis working abroad. Nepal has become increasingly economically dependent on foreign countries, and its lack of electricity generation capacity has made this problem more acute. The government was able to curb load-shedding in 2014 after signing a Power Trading Agreement with India, providing Nepal an extra 500 MW of imported electricity, but this has exacerbated Nepal's trade imbalance with India.

6.3.2 Emergence and Growth of Commercial Markets Amid liberalization in the early 1990s, commercial areas became more vibrant in cities like Kathmandu, Pokhara, Birgunj, Biratnagar, Narayanghat, Butwal, Itahari, and others. More retailers, wholesalers, business complexes, hotels, restaurants, entertainment centers, private hospitals, and educational institutions began to spring up. City life became seen as more desirable with the abundance of newly available products, most of which were imported. In rural areas, infrastructure development also helped to increase the speed of transportation and enhanced rural connectivity. Rudimentary markets began to evolve with road access, even in the Mid- and Far-Western regions that had remained untouched by roads during the Panchayat era.

Amid increasing commercial activity, the government passed the Consumer Protection Act, 1998 to regulate pricing and adulteration of certain products, designating a special council under the Ministry of Commerce and Supplies as the regulating body. Value-Added Tax (VAT) was introduced in 1992 to replace a more complicated taxation system that included the Sales Tax,

Entertainment Tax, Contract Tax, and Hotel Tax, which were subject to different rates. By simplifying the taxation system, VAT was intended to bring all commercial activities into the tax net, reduce tax evasion, and increase government revenue (World Bank, 1994). Likewise, the Motor Vehicles and Transport Management Act, 1993 was passed to regulate transport services. Around the same time, various other restructurings and revisions were made in accordance with market liberalization principles with regard to the education, health and other service sectors (Bajracharya and Sharma, 1996).

However, the initial momentum gained due to liberalization policies after 1990 did not last for long. The decade-long Maoist armed movement did bring notable social changes, but it hit the economy hard. Economic investment and job opportunities almost evaporated in the country, especially in rural areas, resulting in large-scale internal and external migration – a trend that continues even today. This resulted in increased urbanization, and further concentration of markets in cities.

Amidst the political instability, an energy crisis evolved as another factor contributing to Nepal's economic stagnation (ADB et al 2009). Lack of electricity increased the costs of production, further eroding the international competitiveness of Nepali industries. It was only after the Power Trading Agreement was signed between India and Nepal in September, 2014 that regular power-cuts ended.

Furthermore, as the World Bank (2018) and ADB et al (2009) note, a large skill gap emerged as another barrier for developing Nepal's production base. The government has not initiated efforts to assess the country's human resource needs in terms of managerial, entrepreneurial, vocational, and technical skills. Nepal continues to rely on migrant labor from neighboring countries to fill skill shortages. Despite a rise in commercial markets in urban areas, domestic commodities are rare and Nepal continues to import most manufactured goods and commodities. The situation is exacerbated by the government's lack of focus on promoting domestic industry.

Meanwhile, the informal economy has grown unabated. The state administration and the private sector collude in corrupt schemes, rather than establishing free, competitive, and efficient markets. The Competition Promotion and Market Protection Act of 2007 has proven insufficient to address the political-economy of vested interests and make markets more competitive. As a result, commercial services remain of low quality, although the size of the markets have increased. Sub-standard and low-quality goods, delays, and infringement of contracts are routine. Corruption aside, the government also lacks institutional strength to enforce contracts and ensure quality standards. As a result, international bodies have criticized the quality of Nepal's commercial services and in some cases banned Nepali service providers. For example, Nepal's aviation industry currently faces a ban by the European Union and the International Civil Aviation Organization because of a series of safety infringements.

In many rural areas, rudimentary roads have been insufficient to enhance local commercial activities and create rural employment, at least at any significant scale. Although many rural people have useful traditional skills, they often lack marketable skills. Bajracharya (2007) argues that lack of technical knowledge and commercial proficiency among rural populations has prevented the development of rural industries. Road construction has not been sufficiently accompanied by integrated economic development. As a result, markets located along rural roads primarily sell products from urban areas and imports, with few locally manufactured items. Niche agricultural and forest products are generally collected by outsiders in raw form, without local processing, limiting the opportunity for local employment (ADB, 2014). Remittance inflow into rural areas is often spent on consumable items (World Bank, 2011). Nevertheless, some donor projects have helped develop rural value chains, helping enhance commercial activities in some rural areas, although these projects often lack sustainability over the long term. Recently, Department of Commerce is added with portfolio of supply and consumer protection and get new name of Department of Commerce, Supply and Consumer Protection. Likewise, the New Industrial Enterprises Act, passed in 2016, incentivizes the opening of industries in undeveloped areas, but because the act was

Table 6.8: Service Sector of Nepal in Selected Years of Post-1990 (in NRs. Million)*

Fiscal Years	Service Sector GDP (in Current Price)	Service Sector GDP (at Constant Price of FY 2000/01)	Share of Service Sector in GDP (in %)	Percent of Economically Active Population in Service Sector	Service Sector Growth**
1990/91	40,397	10,8435	34.79%	14.71%	5.95% (1980/81 to 1990/91)
2000/01	196,269	19,6269	46.13%	18.27%	6.11% (1990/91 to 2000/01)
2010/11	619,148	30,3319	51.55%	23.90%	4.45% (2000/01 to 2010/11)
2015/16	1,125,779	383,057	54.19%		2.35%
2016/17	1,364,642	414,041	56.56%		8.09%
2017/18	1,557,551	443,689	57.61%		7.16%
2018/19***	1,769,642	476,015			7.29%

Source: Various Issues of *Statistical Year Book of Nepal*, Central Bureau of Statistics
* Service Sector also includes basic services, government services, community organization.
** Source: Calculated by Author using CBS Data
**Time period representing the data is mentioned in parenthesis
*** Preliminary Estimate

Table 6.9: Private Investment and FDI Committed in Nepal's Service Sector (in NRs Million)

Fiscal Year	Total Private Investment Committed		Total FDI Committed	
	Service Industry*	Tourism	Service Industry*	Tourism
1994/95	2,191	4,064	31	22
2000/01	2,243	1,341	343	538
2010/11	11,798	2,750	919	1,184
2013/14	5,062	5,833	4,472	1,302
2014/15	8,073	27,215	5,672	4,333
2015/16	11,850	11,125	7,937	1,891
2016/17	15,879	15,000	5,018	6,008
2017/18	5,882	23,855	2,773	4,123

Source: *Industrial Statistics*, Department of Industry

*Service Industry basically includes wholesaler, traders, retailer, agents, private school, private hospital and others

not drafted according to federal principles there is big apprehension on its implementation.

The service sector's share of GDP has increased significantly, from 34.79% in FY 1990/91 to 46.13% in FY 2000/01 and to 57.61% in FY 2017/18 (Table 6.8). The growth in the service sector was 6.11 percent during the 1990s and 4.45 percent in the 2000s (Table 6.8). However, as mentioned above, the lack of a conducive environment to expand markets, despite liberalization policies, has resulted in relatively slow growth since late nineties. Furthermore, the share of the economically active population engaged in the service sector has increased only marginally, from 14.71% in 1991 to 23.90% in 2011. Much of the labor force remains concentrated in agriculture, as few people have the skills needed to work in the service sector. Private investment and foreign direct investment in the commercial service sector and tourism has fluctuated greatly over the past quarter-century (Table 6.9).

6.4 Development of Banking and the Financial Sector A rudimentary banking system began in Nepal in 1877 with the establishment of the Tejarath Adda to provide credit facilities. In 1937, Nepal Bank Limited (NBL) was established initiating formal banking in Nepal. This bank provided credit only to Nepal's elite particularly in the trade and industry sectors, and remained the sole financial institution for the next two decades including issues of currency notes. A central bank was established with the passage of the Nepal Rastra Bank (NRB) Act, 1958. In 1959 the Nepal Industrial Development Corporation (NIDC) Bank was created, followed by the Agriculture Development Bank Nepal (ADBN) in 1968, and a second commercial bank, the Rastriya Banijya Bank (RBB), in 1966. These financial institutions were all public enterprises and commercial banking remained highly regulated (Shrestha, 2004). Under the Loan and Guarantee Act, 1968 and the Commercial Bank Act, 1974, the NRB played a role in controlling credit, exchange rates and various categories of interest rates. From 1974, the NRB also launched a program for lending to priority sectors requiring commercial banks to lend 12 percent of their resources in these sectors, though this effort generally lacked vision and implementation also suffered as banks preferred to deposit the money with the central bank rather than lending them in the priority sectors.

Despite these developments, the banking sector was still in its infancy during the mid-Panchayat period, with formal banking channels playing a limited role in the economy. Strict government controls repressed the development of private-sector banks, and both of the major government commercial banks, the NBL and RBB, had serious portfolio problems due to a high level of political intervention. Beginning in the late 1970s, the country faced a major economic crisis due to structural rigidity, slow growth, high government expenditure, state-led policy distortions, and a global economic downturn (Bajracharya and Sharma, 1996 and Acharya et al, 1998).

In order to address these problems, major reforms were initiated in the banking sector during the 1980s. In 1984, the Commercial Bank Act was amended to remove barriers for setting up joint-venture banks, allowing for foreign collaboration to operate commercial banking services. In the same year, the Nepal Arab Bank Limited was established as the country's first joint-venture bank; others followed in subsequent years. In June 1983, the government instituted market-determined exchange rates for convertible currencies, and under the IMF's ESP and the World Bank's SAP, Nepal began to partially deregulate interest rates in 1984 and fully deregulated them in 1989 (Bajracharya and Sharma, 1996 and Acharya et al, 1998). ADBN was allowed to carry out commercial functions[33] beginning in 1984, and government securities began to be floated through open market operations in FY 1988/89. In the same year, NRB issued a directive to banks to maintain sufficient capital reserves above a certain threshold, set a loan classification modality, and initiate loan-loss provisioning. The Credit Information Bureau was established in May 1989 to provide information about the clients and their credit worthiness.

33. ADBN initially was established as a development bank providing loans to farmers and the agriculture sector only.

In sum, banking during the Panchayat period was focused on monetizing Nepali currency, institutionalizing banking culture, and liberalizing the financial sector. However, banking services still excluded a large sector of the economy. In FY 1990/91, the year after the fall of the Panchayat regime, the private-sector credit-to-GDP ratio remained low at 11.7%, while the money supply (M2)-to-GDP ratio for the same fiscal year was 31.2% (Figure 6.1). Substantive efforts to reform NBL and RBB were lacking, so their financial condition – and hence the overall financial market – was volatile (Ozaki, 2014).

Figure 6.1 Monetary Sector Scenario of Nepal (in %)

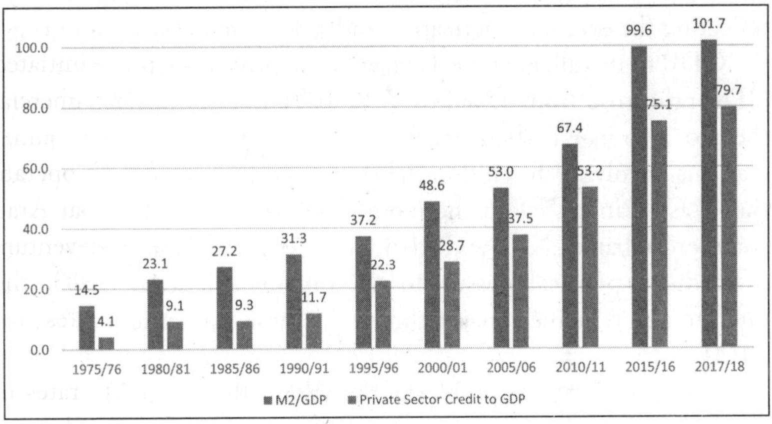

Source: Various Issues of *Economic Survey*, MOF

6.4.1 Banking Sector Reform Financial sector reforms that began in the 1980s accelerated after the 1990 political change under NC governments. The Finance Company Act, originally passed in 1985, was amended in 1992 to encourage the establishment of more finance companies to meet the demand of small borrowers and consumers. New finance companies introduced financial instruments like hire purchase, lease finance, and housing loans. Convertibility in current accounts relaxed administrative control over trade. Likewise, the Development Bank Act, 1999 allowed for the establishment of financial institutions focused on developing specific sectors of the economy. Furthermore, in the second half of 1990s, the NRB introduced a policy to increase the number of commercial banks and encourage all financial institutions to open branches in rural areas. Likewise, micro-credit development banks were introduced to mobilize small deposits. The focus of monetary policies during the 1990s was to maintain forex reserves, control inflation, increase economic activities through banking channels, and supervise and monitor financial institutions so as to institutionalize prudential norms (NRB, 2016 and Paudel, 2009).

As a result of these policies, the decade of the 1990s saw an increase in the number of banking institutions[34], deposit collection, and loan flow. The M2-to-GDP ratio rose from 32% in FY 1990/91 to 37 % in FY 1995/96, then to 49% in FY 2000/01 (Figure 6.1) reflecting the extent monetization and gradual increase in capturing the GDP to its fuller extent. Likewise, the private-sector credit-to-GDP ratio rose from 12% in FY 1990/91 to 22% in FY 1995/96 then to 39% in FY 2000/01. At the same time, there were major scandals involving foreign-exchange misuse, popularly known as the "LC scandal."[35] Furthermore, the two government-owned commercial banks, NBL and RBB, held significant non-performing assets due to political pressure to invest in unviable sectors; political interference remained major threats to these institutions (Ozaki, 2014).[36]

To deal with these problems, the World Bank and ADB came forward with a series of recommended financial reform programs during the 2000s. A New Central Bank Act was passed in 2002, giving more autonomy to the NRB to formulate monetary and

34. NRB (2011) states that the number of commercial banks increased from five in 1990 to 13 in 2000 and then to 27 in 2010. Likewise, development banks have increased from two in 1990 to seven in 2000 and then to 79 in 2010. Furthermore, the number of finance companies increased from 21 in 1995 to 45 in 2000 then to 79 in 2010.

35. In this scandal, some unscrupulous businessmen, along with corrupt officials, had faked letters of credit by creating bogus firms and making false customs declarations to divert USD 36 million to personal accounts.

36. NRB (2005) reports that more than 50 percent of NBL and RBB loans were non-performing in the period FY 2000/01 - FY 2004/05.

foreign exchange policies and to monitor and supervise financial institutions (Shrestha, 2004). Likewise, the Bank and Financial Institution Act was passed in 2006, harmonizing legal provisions for the entire financial sector and simplifying monitoring and supervision procedures.[37] The management of two state-owned banks was handed over to foreign consulting companies in the mid-2000s to improve their financial status. Similarly, the Loan Recovery Act of 2002, the Banking Offence and Punishment Act of 2008, the Money Laundering Prevention Act, 2008 and the creation of a local recovery tribunal in 2002 aim at controlling banking and financial fraud. With the increase in market capitalization, financial institutions also began to give margin lending against securities.

As a result of these reforms, the financial condition of the NBL and RBB improved marginally, but political meddling remains a major threat to these state-owned banks (Ozaki, 2014). Furthermore, due to the increase in the number of financial institutions, the NRB faced serious challenges in monitoring and supervision. As a result, the condition of some financial institutions deteriorated due to misuse of fund. In late 2006, the NRB had to intervene and take control of management of one such institution, Nepal Bangladesh Bank (NBB), which held 19% non-performing loans in 2005. Other banks like the Bank of Kathmandu, Nepal Credit Commerce Bank and a few other institutions also faced financial problems in the late 1990s and 2000s, but, like NBB, they survived by following prudential norms and/ or intervention from the central bank. However, the Nepal Development Bank, which was declared an ailing institution in October, 2007, could not be saved; it became the first financial institution to get liquidated.

The decade of the 2010s saw another financial crisis, as half a dozen financial institutions faced serious challenges due to the partial collapse of the real estate business in the country. Real estate

37. BAFIA, 2006 replaced all previous acts regarding commercial banks, development banks and finance companies. It categorized Nepal's financial institutions into four types: Commercial Banks, or A-Class financial institutions; Development Banks, or B-Class financial institutions; Finance Companies, or C-Class financial institutions; and Micro-Credit Development Banks and Cooperatives, known as D-Class financial institutions.

had become especially lucrative in the 2000s due to fast urbanization, and many banks made loans without prudent assessment of creditors' capacity to repay, often flouting NRB guidelines. As a result, non-performing assets and other bad debt, especially those held by B- and C-Class Banks, increased.[38] To address this problem, the NRB capped the amount of loans financial institutions could make for real estate in early 2011, labelling this sector "unproductive" which brought down real estate prices.[39] Nonetheless, five financial institutions collapsed. A sixth, Vibor Development Bank, got into trouble during the same time period due to the liquidity crisis[40] that engulfed the country for long, but it survived because NRB provided lender of last resort services.

Liquidity crises occurred again and again after 2011 due to rapid expansion of credit to the non-productive sectors (World Bank, 2017b). In response, the central bank has repeatedly revised the caps on unproductive sector lending such as for home loans, real estate, hire purchase loans, and margin lending. These revisions resulted in shifts of the amount of loans falling under these three headings, but as Table 6.10 shows, the total share of loans under these headings did not significantly decline overall, standing at 25.67% in 2011/12, 23.70% in 2015/16, 24.43% in 2016/ 17 and 22.94% in FY 2017/18. Furthermore, due to volatility in the flow of

38. For example, NRB (2011) states that Gorkha Development Bank, which collapsed in 2011, had a capital fund of 2.1%, while its non-performing loans totaled 17.2%. Similarly, Samjhana Finance Ltd, which also collapsed that year, had 49% non-performing loans.

39. Table 6.10 shows that in FY 2011/12, commercial loans like term loans, import loans, demand and working capital loans, deprived sector loans and bill purchase loans made up 13.98%, 4.49%, 23.48%, 3.67% and 1.24% percent of all loans, respectively. Similarly, personal loans like home loans, real estate loans, hire purchase loans and margin loans made up 6.41%, 11.75%, 6.20% and 1.31% respectively.

40. The liquidity crisis was first noted in 2009 during Dashain as the deficiency of new currency notes. Up to June, 2016 the banks have had huge resources which they could not use and the interest rates came down. However, the banks invested these resources into consumer spending and real estate causing credit deposit ratio to go well above the cap of 80%. The paucity of resources with the bank continues despite interference of NRB on occasions. Consequently, the deposit interest rates have come down but the problem of liquidity still persists.

remittances and other externalities, the government adopted the imprudent approach of pumping money out of market and keeping it idle, specifically during FY 2016/17. The NRB also performed poorly in its regulatory supervision role.[41]

The NRB has also taken steps to promote bank mergers. In response to the crisis in early 2011, the NRB required financial institutions to increase their minimum paid-up capital in order to check the increasing number of institutions and bring it down to a manageable number for regulation. The NRB further increased the minimum paid-up capital of commercial banks and development banks by four times and twenty-four times, respectively, in 2015, resulting in more bank mergers.[42] Likewise, a new Bank and Financial Institution Act (BAFIA) was passed in 2017 to strengthen corporate governance in the financial sector and also introduce an infrastructure bank in Nepal's financial market. BAFIA, 2017[43] created strict rules regarding conflicts of interest for bank owners and managers, resulting in the resignation of the chairman of Civil Bank Limited and the resignation of the director of Prabhu Bank from its sister organization – Prabhu Insurance.[44]

Though Nepal's financial market has developed substantially over the past eighty years, it continues to face recurrent problems due to financial irregularities and imprudent lending. Donors like the World Bank and ADB have been providing continuous support for financial sector reforms that have helped to protect the sector from major crises. The economy has become more formalized with

41. As per NRB's regulatory requirement, banks need to maintain an 80% credit-to-core-capital-plus-deposit (CCD) ratio. The World Bank (2017b) argues that the NRB did not readjust the required CCD ratio in a timely fashion to check loans to the unproductive sector.

42. The NRB's Quarterly Report (2018a) reports that the number of development banks decreased from 67 in FY 2015/16 to 33 in FY 2017/18. In the same period, the number of finance companies decreased from 42 to 25 and the number of commercial banks decreased from 32 to 28.

43. BAFIA, 2017 terms D-Class financial institution as "Micro Finance Institutions," replacing the earlier title of "Micro-Credit Development Banks."

44. News of the resignations is available through the online portal "Mero Lagani": https://eng.merolagani.com/NewsDetail.aspx?newsID=33171.

Table 6.10: Product-wise Loans and Advances of Banking and Financial Institutions (in NRs Million)

Details	2011/12		2015/16		2016/17		2017/18	
	Amount	Share in Total (in %)	Amount	Share in Total (in %)	Amount	Share in Total (in %)	Amount	Share in Total (in %)
Term Loan	110,369	13.98%	272,694	16.21%	320,735	16.08%	423,648	17.48%
Overdraft	133,617	16.92%	294,327	17.50%	361,907	18.14%	410,911	16.96%
Trust Receipt Loan/ Import Loan	35,444	4.49%	72,678	4.32%	64,530	3.24%	113,869	4.70%
Demand & Other Working Capital Loan	185,391	23.48%	365,785	21.75%	404,195	20.26%	498,116	20.56%
Residential Personal Home Loan (Up to NRs 15 Million)	50,650	6.41%	142,815	8.49%	168,384	8.44%	201,682	8.32%
Real Estate Loan	92,771	11.75%	108,072	6.43%	127,319	6.38%	142,005	5.86%
Margin Nature Loan	10,334	1.31%	37,681	2.24%	41,170	2.06%	41,129	1.70%
Hire Purchase Loan	48,999	6.20%	110,094	6.55%	150,400	7.54%	171,054	7.06%
Deprived Sector Loan	28,968	3.67%	81,239	4.83%	111,985	5.61%	137,728	5.68%
Bills Purchased	9,791	1.24%	12,531	0.75%	17,354	0.87%	2,859	0.12%
Other Product	83,39	10.56%	183,963	10.94%	226,670	11.36%	279,927	11.55%
Total	789,730	100.00%	1,681,880	100.00%	1,994,649	100.00%	2,422,926	100.00%

(Source: NRB, 2012 and 2018b)

increased use of banks, indicated by the increase in the M2-to-GDP ratio from 49% in 2000/01 to 101% in 2017/18 (Figure 6.1). Similarly, the private-sector credit-to-GDP ratio has increased from 29% in 2000/01 to 80% in 2017/18.

Debates on financial reforms have centered on to what degree the government should channel investment to productive sectors. Proponents argue that investment in productive sectors like agriculture, small and medium enterprises, hydropower, and tourism can check financial-sector volatility. However, critics question where funds can be safely invested, given the absence of growth in such "productive" sectors (World Bank, 2017b). Financial institutions have been reluctant to invest in projects in rural areas, fearing losses, and they have been paying the government penalties for not doing so. Most investment in these priority sectors has come from government projects and initiatives by political parties seeking to bolster their public image.

6.5 Capital Market Development Credit for introducing the "Joint Stock and Limited Liability" principle in Nepal goes to the Rana regime, which passed the Company Act in 1936, but it took much longer to institutionalize a capital market in Nepal. The Securities Exchange Centre (SEC) was established in 1976 to develop, promote, and regulate capital markets.[45] The SEC remained the only capital market institution for one-and-a-half decades, and played a role in enhancing public interest in security investments and regulating brokerage, underwriting, government bonds, and other financial services. It opened the door for secondary trading of government bonds in 1981, and for secondary trading of corporate instruments with the Securities Exchange Act in 1984.

However, investments in capital markets materialized only slowly and were concentrated in urban areas due to lack of knowledge among the general public about how capital markets work. As a result, initial public offerings (IPOs) in the primary market were undersubscribed. Even the first three joint-venture banks – NABIL,

45. Refer to SEBON (2017) for the history of Nepal's capital market.

Nepal Indosuez and Nepal Grindlays – were undersubscribed during their IPOs (Koirala and Bajracharya, 2004).

After the political change of 1990, the government took steps to further strengthen the capital market in order to lay a foundation for faster economic development, in line with liberalization policies initiated at the time. The Eighth Plan – the first five-year plan under multi-party democracy – called for developing merchant banking, setting up a regulator of capital markets, and developing a secondary market for security trading. The Security Exchange Act, 1984 was amended in June, 1993 to create the Securities Board of Nepal (SEBON) as the capital market regulator. [46] A Citizens' Investment Fund was established in March, 1991 as the pioneer merchant banking institution, followed by NIDC Capital Market Ltd in 1993 and other finance companies were also established under the Finance Company Act, 1985.[47] The SEC was replaced by the Nepal Stock Exchange (NEPSE) Ltd in 1993 as the secondary capital market.[48] SEBON instituted various bylaws and guidelines during the 1990s relating to brokers, market makers, securities listings, issue management, and security allotments in order to regulate the capital market. NEPSE opened its trading floor on 7th January 1994 using the Open Outcry System for transactions, and began publishing the NEPSE index the very next day.

The banking sector emerged as the most lucrative sector in the secondary capital market during the 1990s, with high returns on investments. The banking sector probably gained high value due to improvements made through a number of reform programs. As a result, IPOs were oversubscribed (Koirala and Bajracharya, 2004 and

46. SEBON was initially called the Security Board but the Security Exchange Board Act of 2007 changed the name to Security Board of Nepal and made it an autonomous institution. SEBON registers securities, approves public issues, monitors the securities market, provides licenses to stock brokers, and supervises and monitors stock exchange operations.

47. The Finance Company Act, 1985 had conferred merchant banking functions to finance companies.

48. NEPSE, a government-owned company, facilitates transactions of government as well as corporate securities among members and market intermediaries such as brokers.

KC and Pandey, 2009). Market capitalization reached five percent of GDP in FY 1994/95 and increased to 10% of GDP in FY 2004/05. SEBON (2017) reports that there were 27 stock brokers, nine merchant banks and two market makers by the end of FY 2002/03. In other words, the capital market remained small. It was also difficult to develop a market culture during the initial years; only 12% of listed companies submitted their annual financial reports in FY 1996/96 compared to 71% in FY 2002/03 (SEBON, 2017).

In 2007, a new Security Market Act conferred SEBON the status of an autonomous body so that it could fairly regulate the country's capital market. This was complemented by a new Automated Computerized Trading System, replacing the Open Outcry System, along with a Real Time Surveillance System, on 24th August 2017 with technical assistance from the ADB. A circuit breaker was introduced in 2006 and merchant banking entities were required to form institutions separate from their parent banks in 2011.[49] New bylaws also established CDS and Clearing Limited as the central depositary in 2010 and established ICRA Nepal Limited as the credit-rating agency in 2011. Other regulations affected brokers, market makers, government bonds, securities listings, issue management, and securities allotment. The market was dematerialized[50] from February 2016 onward, and SEBON became a member of the International Organization of Securities Commissions in July 2016. Commodities Exchange Market Act, 2017 was enacted to regulate commodities trading.

As a result of these efforts, market capitalization reached 46% of GDP in 2014/15 and further increased to 71% of GDP in 2016/17. The success of the Chilime Hydropower Company, which was listed on the NEPSE in May 2009, was a major breakthrough in Nepal's capital market and helped to diversify it to some extent. Other private power producers have also become attractive to capital market investors.

---

49. Prior to 2011, banks and financial institutions also administered merchant banking but SEBON's 2011 merchant banking bylaw requires these institutions to have subsidiary companies for this purpose.

50. It means the financial security instruments have to be deposited to specific institutions and could not be hold personally.

The NEPSE index hovered between 200 to 400 until FY 2004/05 (Figure 6.2) because of slow growth, partly due to the unstable political scenario prevailing in the country at the time. The market peaked in FY 2005/06, almost reaching the 1000 mark, but it dropped again in 2008/09, dipping below 300 in 2010/11. The market became bullish again in FY 2013/14, but dropped in FY 2016/17. On 27th July 2016, NEPSE index reached its peak at 1888 on daily basis. However, the market decline to 1212 in FY 2017/18 due to poor signal from the government and the central bank. It is contrasting that the market index decline in the period of unprecedented growth meaning that the market has not exactly successful to reflect the real situation.

There are several reasons for the volatility of Nepal's capital market. Shrestha and Subedi (2014) attribute fluctuations of the NEPSE index to the changes in the political scenario and monetary policy. Likewise, Regmi (2012) and Mukit et al (2014) observe fluctuations due to the status of economic growth and political change. Koirala and Bajracharya (2004) argue that capital markets have been slow to grow due to limited industrialization, a fragile environment for investment, opaque corporate governance, and investors who do not play by the rules of the game. Likewise, Regmi (2018) argues that capital markets have been distorted by insider trading.

It is clear that SEBON has not sufficiently regulated the still-immature capital market, which is hobbled by opaque corporate governance. For example, NECON Airway, the first NEPSE-listed private airline in Nepal, was giving investors dividends up to one year before its closure in 2003; the regulator did not take sufficient action and the airline collapsed. Other similar incidents occurred in the years afterward, with some development banks and finance companies failing. The World Bank (2017b) argues that due to weak regulation, Nepal's capital market is connected neither to the real economy of Nepal nor to the other regional markets of South Asia. In other words, it remains a bubble.

Figure 6.2: NEPSE Index

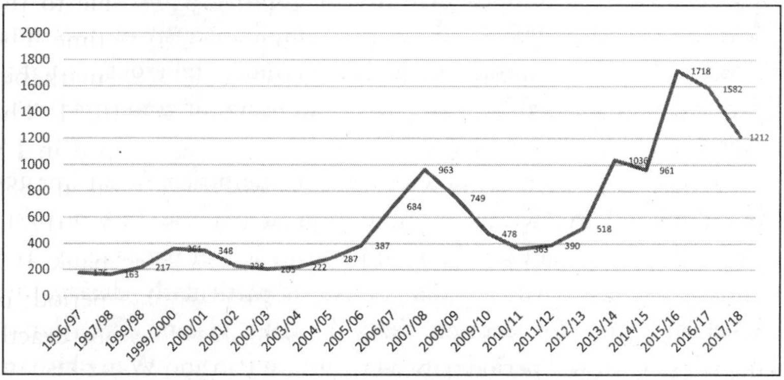

(Source: Various Issues of *Economic Survey*, MOF)

Nonetheless, there is no doubt that the capital market creates an important space for economic activities in Nepal. More regulation is needed, as are efforts to link the market with the realities of the economy. This will require sound corporate governance, proper disclosures, appropriate signals from the government, and strong and efficient supervision by SEBON.

6.6 Tourism and Civil Aviation Nepal is a prime tourist destination due to its unparalleled natural beauty, rich bio-diversity, and captivating array of cultures. The country is endowed with the majestic Himalayan range, including Mount Everest, standing at 8848m, the tallest mountain in the world, and seven other peaks over 8000m. Many urban areas of Nepal, including those in the Kathmandu Valley, are home to UNESCO-designated world heritage sites, while traditional rural settlements are set against dramatic natural scenery. Centuries-old festivals are celebrated throughout the year, the country is blessed with a pleasant climate, and the people are renowned for their hospitality. In 2009, *National Geographic* magazine identified Nepal as "one of the best countries for adventure destination in the world." Likewise, the *Lonely Planet* guidebook has rated Nepal very highly time and again; in 2017, it declared Nepal a best-value destination. As tourism is one of the leading sectors of the national economy, its diversification and growth is indispensable for supporting livelihoods and creating employment opportunities in order to improve living standards. Moving forward, it will be necessary to simultaneously protect and preserve Nepal's natural, biological, ethnic, religious, social, historical, and cultural heritage, and to improve air connectivity in order to build the tourism sector's capacity.

Visitors have been coming to Nepal for centuries. According to Hindu mythology, Rishis (saints) from across the Indian subcontinent visited the Himalayas to perform acts of penance. Many Chinese travelers visited India via Nepal particularly during the Lichchavi period for example Seng Tsai, Fa Hsien, Che Meng, Hiuen Tsang (travel period 626-645) and Lil Pao and Wang Hsuan during the reign of King Narendra Dev (643-690) (Lamsal, 2019). In the Middle Ages, Tibetans traveled to India through Nepal to study Buddhism, and many also studied Bajrayana Buddhism in the Kathmandu Valley, as is reported in Tibetan scriptures.[51] However, following the conquest of Nepal by King Prithvi Narayan Shah in the second half of the eighteenth century, visitors were discouraged from coming, and during Rana regime from 1846-1951, the country was kept in complete isolation from the outside world.[52]

International interest in Nepal was renewed after the French climber Maurice Herzog's conquest of Mt. Annapurna in 1950, the first successful ascent of a peak over 8000 meters. Following the 1951 revolution that reinstated the Shah monarchy and introduced a brief period of multi-party democracy, Nepal flung its doors open for visitors. Tenzing Norgay and Edmund Hillary's ascent of Mt. Everest on May, 29, 1953, further helped to encourage tourism in Nepal. Likewise, the Swiss geographer Toni Hagen, who came to

51. Guru Marpa, one of the legendary gurus of Tibet, is supposed to have lived three years in the Nepal at Kesha Chandra Para Barta Mahavihar. Newars still remember him during the Ghodejatra festival. Guru Padma Sambhavam also went to Tibet from India via Nepal where he spent a long time.

52. Not only were foreigners restricted from entering Nepal, Nepalis were also prohibited from venturing abroad, requiring Rahdanis (passports or letters of permission) even to go beyond Chitlang/Chisapani Garhi. Later on, a few Nepalis went to India to pursue studies. For much of this period, the British regency and the commissary in Kathmandu were the only sources of outside information as well as to the outside world.

Nepal in early fifties, played an important role in introducing Nepal to the world through his landmark 1962 picture book *Nepal: The Kingdom of Himalaya.*

Annual tourist arrivals were recorded for the first time in 1961, at 6127 visitors (MOCTCA, 2019). The government established a Tourism Board in 1959, which was later converted into the Department of Tourism under the line Ministry of Works, Communication and Transport (MOWCT). The Hotel Management and Liquor Sale and Distribution (Control) Act, 1966 and Tourism Act, 1978 regulated different tourism-related industries like hotels, restaurants, travel agencies, and guest houses established by the private as well as the public sector.

To support tourism and other travel related activities, a civil aviation department was formed in 1957 under MOWCT[53] and in the same year the grassy runway of Tribhuvan International Airport (TIA)[54] was paved (CAAN, 2016). In 1959, the government passed the Civil Aviation Act to regulate the sector. The Nepal Airlines Corporation (NAC)[55] was set up as the national carrier in July 1958 with a Douglas DC-3 Dakota aircraft. Nepal took membership in the UN's civil aviation body, the ICAO, in 1960 and, in 1963, it passed the Nepal Airline Corporation Act to administer NAC. In subsequent years, TIA was upgraded, domestic airports were set up in different parts of the country, and the NAC began to serve more national and international destinations. NAC added its first jet aircraft, a Boeing 727/ 100, in 1972. Lufthansa became the first European carrier to serve Nepal, followed by Thai Airways in 1968, and many others in the years since.

53. The first airplane arrived in Nepal in 1949; it was the four-seater single-engine Beechcraft of Indian Ambassador Mr. Surjit Singh Mahathia and it landed on the grassy land of Gaucharan. The first commercial flight took place in 10th October 1950 (Gorkhapatra, 11th August 2019).

54. The airport at Gaucharan of Kathmandu, which served flights to different parts of India and other countries, was named Tribhuvan Airport in 1955 by King Mahendra. It was renamed Tribhuvan International Airport in 1964. King Tribhuvan also landed in 1951 at this grassy land hastening the end of the Rana regime.

55. NAC was originally called Royal Nepal Airlines Cooperation but the word "Royal" was dropped after 2008.

The government had relied on passive publicity brought by mountaineering expeditions in the 1950s and the bottom-up development of the Hippy Trail during the 1960s, but it began to play an active role in tourism promotion from the early 1970s. In 1972, the government developed a Tourism Master Plan, marking the government's first clear vision for tourism development in Nepal. The Plan called for promoting Nepal's natural, cultural and adventure tourism sectors, including specific trekking routes and other tourist sites. It recommended the creation of a Ministry of Tourism, which was set up in 1978; the existing Department of Tourism was brought under it, as was the Department of Civil Aviation at a later date[56]. Also in accordance with the Tourism Master Plan, the National Academy of Tourism and Hotel Management was established in 1972 to develop human resources for the hospitality industry. A Master Plan for tourism development in Lumbini, the birthplace of Lord Buddha, was designed by Kenzo Tange under the aegis of the UN following the 1967 visit of UN Secretary General U Thant to the holy site.

Due to these measures, the number of tourists visiting Nepal steadily increased during the Panchayat era (Figure 6.3). To accommodate tourists, several luxurious hotels[57] were opened in Kathmandu, some of them affiliated to international brands like Oberoi, Sheraton, and Crown Plaza. On top of that, a number of small hotels, guest houses, restaurants, tour operators and travel agencies set up operations in the capital. However, investments in the hospitality industry were not very lucrative; more than 65% of beds at luxury hotels in Kathmandu remained empty during the

56. The Ministry of Tourism was added with portfolio of civil aviation in 1982 so it became the Ministry of Tourism and Civil Aviation and this ministry was added with portfolio of culture in 2000 which give its current name of Ministry of Culture, Tourism and Civil Aviation (MOCTCA).

57. Researchers have not been able to establish the history of the growth of hotels in Nepal. However, the first hotel is estimated to be Paras started by Janak Das Shrestha. Another one is estimated to have been established in Patan followed by Coronation (established during the coronation of King Mahendra) and Valley View hotels. For the sake of the coronation of King Mahendra, Bahadur Bhawan was converted into the first class hotel named Royal Hotel and, for this, Boris Ivanovich was brought to Nepal and entrusted the task of developing and managing it.

Figure 6.3: Number of Tourist Arrivals during the Panchayat Period

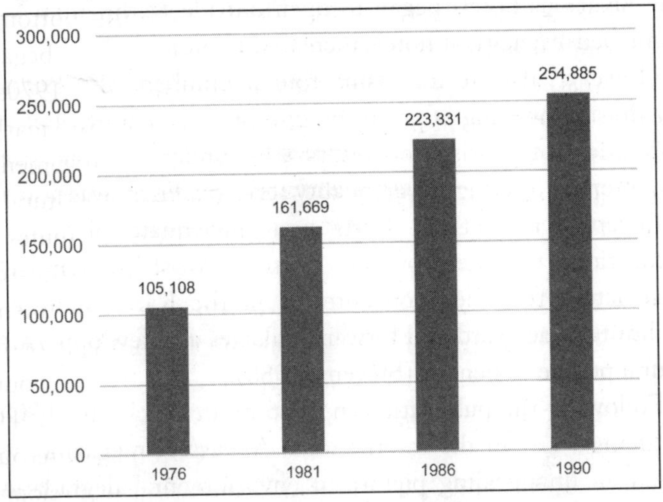

Source: MOCTCA, 2019

period 1981-83, and tourist inflow was dominated by low-spending Indians (Panday, 1989).

6.6.1 Liberalization of Tourism and Civil Aviation Following the establishment of multi-party democracy in 1990, development discourse focused on promoting tourism to earn foreign currency, alleviate poverty, and promote economic development (Shrestha and Shrestha, 2012). The IEA, 1992 allowed greater private sector investment in tourism industries and FITTA, 1992 opened Nepal to foreign direct investment (FDI) in the hotel and hospitality industries. Later, in November 2005, travel agencies and trekking and water rafting businesses were also opened for FDI. The Nepal Tourism Board Act, passed in 1997, established the Nepal Tourism Board (NTB) as an autonomous organization to promote Nepal in the global tourism market.[58] The 1990s saw new trekking routes and mountains opened for expeditions, and the government

58. NTB's focus is to promote Nepal in the international market whereas the existing Department of Tourism remained as the regulating body.

increased its promotion of tourism to religious and cultural sites. Some luxurious hotels began to open outside Kathmandu Valley, and the bed-capacity of hotels increased twofold.

However, despite increasing tourist numbers, the 1990s also saw a drastic lowering of profit margins. This can be attributed to a proliferation of tourism operators who under-cut tour package rates, often by offering lower-quality services. There was also a lack of concerted marketing efforts and inadequate planning and organization of the tourism sector. Most tourism-related infrastructure remained concentrated in the Kathmandu Valley, with limited backward and forward linkages and few opportunities for rural people to benefit (Stevens, 1988).

Following the publication in 1996 of an article titled "Good-Bye Shangri La" in the international *Newsweek* magazine, which painted an unappealing picture of environmental degradation in Kathmandu, Nepal's tourism entrepreneurs clamored for the government to create a counter narrative promoting the country's natural beauty. Partially as a result of this pressure, 1998 was announced as "Visit Nepal Year" in order to improve Nepal's global tourism image. The NTB-led campaign was successful in bringing in more tourists despite the fact that two years earlier, the Maoists had launched their armed revolution. However, as the conflict escalated, the tourism industry went into decline in 2000's. Tourism was also negatively affected by the 1999 hijacking of an Indian Airlines flight from TIA, the 2001 terrorist attacks in the US, and the 2001 Royal Massacre in Kathmandu (Shrestha and Shrestha, 2012). Tourist arrivals declined from 493,000 in 1999 to only 275,466 in 2002 (Figure 6.4). In this sluggish period, tourist entrepreneurs started to promote domestic tourism, which they had previously ignored,[59] thus spreading the culture of traveling in Nepal[60].

59. There were numerous illustrations of Nepali visitors being kicked out of hotels to make room for foreign visitors.

60. Previously, domestic travel was limited due to poverty and lack of interest. Some Nepali were forced to travel, for example to access government judicial offices or educational services that were concentrated in Kathmandu. The establishment of Tribhuvan University in the capital was an early factor bringing unprecedented

With political stability after the Maoists joined mainstream politics, the government in 2006 brought a new tourism policy to promote Nepal's image and encourage rural tourism by introducing the concept of village home stays. Tourist numbers began to increase again, and in 2008 the government launched a campaign for "Nepal Tourism Year 2011," which promoted Nepal as a destination for year-round travel with visitor-friendly activities and initiatives. Encouragingly, tourist arrivals reached 736,215 in 2011 and 803,092 in 2012. However, arrivals plateaued between 2012-2014, and fell drastically to pre-2011 numbers after the devastating earthquakes in 2015. In 2018, 1.2 million visitors came to Nepal, finally surpassing the one-million mark.

To support tourism and other travel related activities, the government brought various reforms to the civil aviation sector in the 1990s. In 1993, a new civil aviation policy committed to liberalize this sector. The Nepal Civil Aviation Authority Act, 1996 converted the Civil Aviation Department into an autonomous regulator in 1998 and renamed it the Civil Aviation Authority Nepal (CAAN). CAAN focuses on developing and regulating civil aviation. Economic reform initiatives of the 1990s that encouraged private investment resulted in the growth of Nepal's airlines industry. NECON Airways became the first domestic private airline operator in September 1992, followed by many others in subsequent years (World Bank, 2003 and MOC, 2016).

However, the government remained a weak regulator, and the increase in domestic aviation services was accompanied by many severe accidents. The Thai Airways crash in July 1992 and the PIA airways crash in September 1992 drew international attention and raised serious questions about the safety of Nepal's skies. Domestic airline accidents have occurred at regular intervals, due in part to the weaknesses of CAAN. The European Union and ICAO have banned Nepal's civil aviation services in Europe.

Nepal's public- and private-sector airlines have also suffered from weak corporate governance and corruption. Extreme political interference in NAC since 1990 has led to a series of scams like

---

migration to the Kathmandu Valley.

Dhamija Scam for leasing Lauda aircraft that has worsened its financial condition. In the mid-2000s', the national flag carrier did not undergo financial audit for three consecutive years. In 2019, there was widely-reported news of a kickback scam involving the purchase of two Airbus jets. Similarly, poor corporate governance of private airlines, coupled with weak institutional capacity of the regulator, resulted in a dozen private airline operators collapsing since 1990.[61]

Nepal's airport infrastructure has also been weak. Travelers using TIA – currently the only international airport of Nepal – complain about the poor quality of services provided there, and domestic airports in other parts of the country are no different. International airlines have increased flights to TIA since the mid-1990s' to serve tourists as well as increasing numbers of labor migrants, further congesting runway traffic and hampering tourism growth. In this context, the ongoing construction of new international airports at Lumbini and Pokhara is expected to help address the problem of air traffic congestion and contribute to tourism development.[62]

Considering the government's overall tourism policies and strategies from 1990 to the present, several significant shortcomings stand out. There has been an over-emphasis on increasing revenue from tourists, without sufficient attention to supporting the tourism sector to improve the quality of services and expand into new arenas (World Bank, 2003 and MOC, 2016). Tourists are charged high fees for trekking and mountaineering expeditions and to enter cultural heritage sites, but are provided with only minimum

61. The collapsed airline operators include: Air Kasthamandup (2009-2016); Agni Air (2005-2012); Cosmic Air (1997-2008); Everest Air (1992-1998); Guna Airways (2009-2013); and many more. The story of NECON Air is especially interesting. This was the first private airline operator of Nepal, the first airline company to be listed on the NEPSE, and the first private airline to start international flights. However, it suddenly shut down operations in 2003. Neither the government nor its promoters gave an explanation for its closure, and its staff were agitating up to 2017 for their unpaid salaries.

62. Another international airport is also in the early stages of construction at Nijgadh, south of Kathmandu, though it has faced long delays.

amenities; hygienic toilets, for example, are frequently lacking (Bajracharya et al, 2007). Besides adventure sports and tours of cultural sites, there are only limited activities on which tourists can spend their money in Nepal. Tourism businesses that fetch more income, such as casinos, discotheques/ clubs, golf clubs, and entertainment businesses are limited to urban areas (Jack and Phipps, 2005). As a result, the expenditure of foreign tourists in Nepal was a mere USD 54 per day in 2017 and USD 44 per day in 2018 (MOCTCA, 2019). [63]

Furthermore, the tourism industry lacks significant backward and forward linkages and so it has done relatively little to address rural poverty (Baskota, 2012). Donors have made some attempts to develop value chains for local commodities along trekking routes, but their impact has been limited. Constraints include rural poor populations' limited access to the tourism market, less commercial viability of their products in terms of quality and price, weak marketing ability, and the lack of a suitable policy framework. Thus, despite strengths and opportunities in the Nepali tourism industry, the country has not been fully successful in tapping the economic benefits for the poor.

Today, Nepal remains highly competitive in the world tourism market from a cost perspective. The declining value of the Nepali currency is an added incentive for visitors to come to Nepal. Tourists are estimated to spend USD 54 per day on average, and USD 544 in total for an average stay of 11.8 days, per person. The three main categories of expenditures are food and beverage (28.9%) gift/ shopping (22.8%) and accommodation (19.3%)[64].

The government has announced a new campaign, "Visit Nepal Year 2020," encouraging the country to dream big: it has set a goal of two million foreign visitors in 2020. This target may not be reached, but it is a worthwhile aspiration. However, this program

63. Panday (2016) states that per day expense of tourist in South Asian countries like Bhutan, India and Sri Lanka are USD 572, USD 90 and USD 156 respectively. Expenditure in Bhutan is higher because the government has defined a minimum spending threshold.

64. SAWTEE (2008) cites Tourism Expenditure Survey (2005) conducted by Nepal Tourism Board.

should focus not only on increasing tourist numbers, but also on improving the quality of services, spreading benefits among the poor, and protecting and preserving Nepal's natural and cultural heritage. Regulations should balance these various interests but also should not unduly burden the tourism and private sector. The government must focus on generating employment opportunities, developing remote regions, and generating a high multiplier effect through the tourism industry.

Figure 6.4: Number of Tourist Arrivals in Nepal from 1991 onward (Thousands)

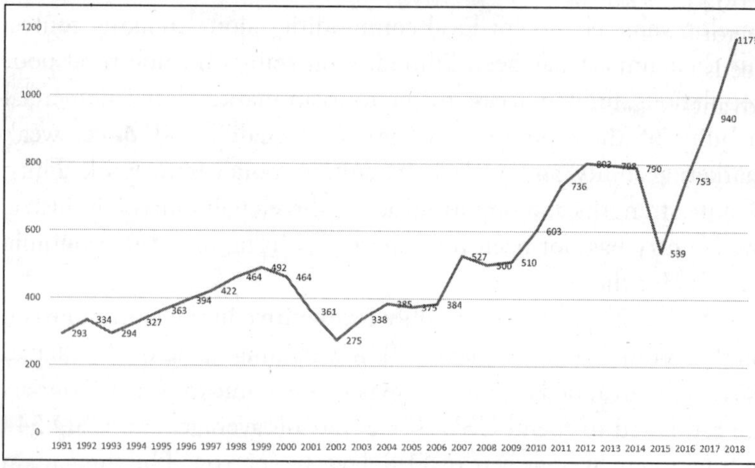

Source: MOCTCA, 2019

6.7 Conclusion Overall, it may be deduced that the services sector, contributing more than 58% of GDP, will continue to grow in the future. There are particularly good opportunities in some of the components of the sector. Despite the traditional theoretical underpinning that economies will gradually transform from the primary to the secondary and then to the tertiary sectors, development in recent times has experienced otherwise indicating service sector has shown greater promise resulting in their steady growth. This is not an exception to Nepal. The secondary sector has proven to be weak and is actually declining due to inability to generate competitiveness and alternatively, the service sector, particularly both domestic and international trade, banking and financial sector, tourism, education, health and other services have shown steady progress explaining the present scenario of almost 60 percent of the economy. However, the clarity of policies, barring in a few components, doesn't exist and, additionally, even in the areas with definite advantage, the real transformation is not as per the expectation. Besides, the reinforcement through steady policies and actions are also not visible. True, we have to give attention to the productive sector but we also must try to capture the full potential of the opportunities emerging in the sector and should not shy away. If the production sector can be integrated with the services sector properly, opportunities will be further enhanced. Nepal needs to be prepared not only to develop on its own but also to take advantage of the fast-growing markets in the neighborhood.

chapter 7

THE FOUNDATION: EDUCATION AND HUMAN RESOURCE DEVELOPMENT

7.1 Introduction The progress of a country depends on the capability of its populace and how it is mobilized. Thus, education and the development of human resources are integral to the development of any economy. This section briefly describes the history of education and human resource development in Nepal while trying to provide an objective evaluation of the efforts initiated.

Although Nepal's current educational system is relatively new, the country has long been a seat of learning and teaching in the region. In Hindu mythology, Nepal is referred to as *Tapo Bhumi*, meaning "land to achieve enlightenment." It is believed that King Janak of Mithila, an ancient kingdom in what is today Nepal's Terai plains, was a great admirer of intellectual discourse. The Lichchavi and Malla dynasties, which ruled from Kathmandu Valley during the medieval period, were also generous patrons of craftsmanship, art, sculpture, and literature. The early Nepali states prioritized skilled human resources to make their societies culturally prosperous (Regmi, 1965). The skills of early Nepali craftsmen were admired not only in Nepal but also in neighboring Tibet and China. In the 13th century, the renowned Nepali architect Arniko traveled first to Tibet, where he built monasteries, and then to China, where he famously constructed the Swet Pagoda (White Temple), still regarded as one of the finest ancient structures in Beijing. Architects from that period are still revered as national symbols for their vision and contributions to the field.

Nepal's early education system was modelled after the great educational institutions of Taxila, Patliputra, and Nalanda in what is today India (Bista, 1991). Buddhist and Hindu academic discourses co-existed in Buddhist monasteries and *vihars* and Hindu *gurukuls* in the early era (Regmi, 1965). However, the advent of *Shankaracharya*[1] marked a turning point, as Buddhist institutions, scientific heritage, and secular literature began to be destroyed and Hindu ritual education, or *gurukuliya shiksha,* became dominant (Bista, 1991).[2] Because *gurukuliya shiksha* focused on religious state-building, it side-lined the transmission and innovation of traditional, indigenous, and practical skills (Bista, 1991). Under King Prithvi Narayan Shah, who united Nepal in mid-eighteenth century, the state continued to emphasize ritual over innovation. Perhaps one reason the state ignored vernacular knowledge systems was that they were mostly inherited by occupational caste groups. These groups passed down knowledge from generation to generation without the use of the written word, but they were ranked lowest in the social hierarchy. Indeed, some of these groups were declared untouchable by law (see Annex A).[3] As a result of the historical suppression and marginalization of skillful people, Nepal has faced continued challenges in spurring innovation and productivity.

7.2 Reforms of the Ranas The Ranas were the first to bring modern reforms to Nepal's traditional education system when they introduced elements of Western education in schools attended

---

1. Shankaracharyas are the highest priests of Hindu religion in India. There are four Shankaracharyas in the four holy Piths of India. The reference here was made to Adi Shankaracharya, supposed to be the first Shankaracharya in eighth century to have demolished Buddhist Monasteries and the heritage.

2. Under *gurukuliya shiksha*, Brahmins learned the Vedas, *niti shastra* (policy study), astrology, geometry and grammar in Sanskrit at *gurukuls*. Education of the Chhetri warrior caste focused on *sastra vidya*, or military and arms lessons, and *rajkul shiksha*, or teachings on governance. With the expansion of the Mughal Sultanate in India, Urdu and Persian became important mediums for communication in the courts, but *gurukuliya shiksha* remained Sanskrit-based.

3. King Jayasthiti Malla, despite being acclaimed as a great reformist, designated all skilled people and craftsmen as untouchables. King Ram Shah of Gorkha, another so-called reformist, followed a similar tune.

by their own children and other elites. Given their conservative mentality and support of the Hindu caste system, which they codified in the Civil Code of 1854, these reforms were somewhat anomalous, but they can be understood from a strategic perspective. The reforms were not intended to benefit the general populace, because the Ranas saw an educated public as one of the greatest threats to their autocratic regime. Instead, the new education system was intended to bolster the administration's human resource capacity, while some measures like establishing a school was done just to show the British.

The first Rana Prime Minister, Janga Bahadur Rana, established Durbar High School, the country's first English-medium educational institution, in 1853, in his palace premise. The school received affiliation from Calcutta University (Sharma, 1990).[4] Janga Bahadur also set up the Department of Education (DOE) in 1858, but it did not play a significant role until the brief reign of Dev Shumsher, the fourth (and most liberal) Rana Prime Minister, in 1901. Shortly after coming to power, Dev Shumsher issued an ordinance to open schools throughout Nepal, but he was ousted within four months by his brother, Chandra Shumsher. Chandra Shumsher scrapped plans to provide the schools with materials like books and writing slates (Wood, 1965). As a result, many of them closed, although some survived with private funding from local business people. Chandra Shumsher restructured the DOE in order to enhance its capacity to inspect the new schools for suspicious activities (Sharma, 1990).

Despite taking steps to limit the public's access to education, Chandra Shumsher nonetheless undertook two important initiatives to enhance Nepal's human resource development.[5] The first came in

4. The school was established on the premises of the Prime Minister's home at Thapathali. Later, Prime Minister Bir Shumsher constructed a new premise at Ranipokhari, laying the foundation for ordinary people's access to education.

5. Chandra Shumsher also established the first civil service school – *Shresthaa Pathsala* (Book and Record Keeping School) – in 1905 to produce clerical personnel. The curriculum focused on Nepali writing, basic arithmetic, laws, and the procedures of government, but not other subjects that were seen as posing a threat to the regime.

1902,[6] when he sent eight Nepali students to Japan for engineering education, although he later halted this practice (Parajuli, 2012). The second was in 1918, when he established Tri Chandra College, the country's first higher education institution, with affiliation to Calcutta University.[7] This decision was taken partly to impress the British[8]. However, Chandra Shumsher remained very suspicious of activities at the college (Sharma, 1990). In 1939-40, Prime Minister Juddha Shumsher issued a decree calling for the promotion of schools and popular education. It is assumed to be visionary in setting the path for educational development. However, rather than being a progressive initiative, the decree was used as a means to exert further control over whatever educational institutions existed at the time.

The DOE introduced the School Leaving Certificate (SLC) Examination under the supervision of Patna University and, in 1946, it began conducting the SLC independently. In 1947, the penultimate Rana Prime Minister Padma Shumsher established the first girls' school. He also initiated a Basic Education System that adopted a Gandhian approach rather than a Western one, aiming to simultaneously please Gandhi and the Indian National Congress (who would shortly be coming to power in India) and to appease dissenters within Nepal who were critical of the Rana regime (Parajuli, 2012). Interestingly, part of the Basic Education System was to recognize practical skills. However, Mohan Shumsher ousted Padma Shumsher within a short period and the Basic Education System could not be implemented.

Despite limited promotion of Western education by Ranas, especially Dev Shumsher's 1901 decision to establish schools and Chandra Shumsher's 1918 decision to establish Tri Chandra College, some non-Rana citizens were able to access education.[9] As

---

6. Bir Shumsher is also reported to have sent few persons to Japan for technical skill training including his son Gehendra Shumsher.

7. Tri Chandra College was later affiliated to Patna University.

8. During inaugural speech of this campus, Chandra Shumsher hoped that the campus won't become a curse to Rana regime.

9. Nepalis returning from the British Army also played an instrumental role in sensitizing people about western education after witnessing the positive effects of education, skill development, and innovation in foreign lands.

per the Rana's apprehensions, these educated people – most of whom came from the elite classes – became one of the major forces that helped topple the regime in 1950-51.[10] Throughout the Rana period, occupational castes continued to transmit their skills to their children outside the formal education system as is being done historically. The government also established the first Western-style technical school in Kathmandu in 1930 to provide a trade course on textile manufacturing. In 1942, an engineering section was added to this school to offer a two-year sub-overseer course for SLC[11] graduates and, in 1945, the school was amalgamated with Tri Chandra College. These institutions produced human resources required for Nepal's fledgling industries.

In sum, the Rana-era educational reforms were not intended to develop human resources for the benefit of the country, but rather to serve the regime and help it maintain its grip on power. Although the reforms envisioned by Dev Shumsher in 1901 were monumental and could have helped transform the nation-state (Aryal, 1970), in actual practice, the education sector remained abysmal, with only two-percent literacy at the dawn of democracy in 1951 (Sharma, 1990).

7.3 Educational Reforms and the National Education System Plan Due to a paucity of trained and capable human resources, the new government after the 1951 political revolution maintained Rana-era bureaucratic staff. Sharma (1989) argues that a major concern of policy makers at the time was to develop an education system suited for the country and to promote Sanskrit education, vocational education, adult education, and teacher training.

In the mid-1950s, the US government provided technical and financial support for education in Nepal (Bista, 1991). Although

10. The Ranas also continued to support ritual Sanskrit schools, which were affiliated to the Varanasi Sanskrit Board. In 1947, the students of one of such school in Kathmandu, Teen Dhara Pathsala, started the first student movement in Nepal – colloquially termed *Jayatu Sanskritam* – demanding the government to improve the curriculum by adding modern subjects. Later, many of the leaders of this movement supported the political revolution against the Ranas.

11. The SLC Exam was completed after class 10. Following SLC, students were introduced to university-level education.

this support was criticized by leftists who saw the US as a neo-colonial power, it played a significant role in strengthening the institutional capacity of the Ministry of Education (MOE). The US also supported the creation of the National Educational Planning Commission (NEPC) under the MOE in March 1954, which identified the country's educational and human resource development needs (NEPC, 1956).[12] The US and India together supported the establishment of Tribhuvan University (TU) in 1956, which began operations in 1959, offering higher education degrees in natural sciences, social sciences, arts, education, law, and commerce.[13] Gradually, new faculties and departments were added and TU began to take over the responsibility of affiliating other colleges in Nepal, ending the country's dependence on foreign universities for accreditation. In 1959, the NEPC also called attention to Nepal's limited skill and capacity development centers. Various efforts to introduce skill-training programs under different ministries and departments were supported by USAID, Swiss-Helvetas[14], the UMN[15], and other donors. Sharma (1989) explains

12. This commission conducted a survey of Nepal's education system with advisory support from American educational expert Hugh B Wood. The survey report, titled "Education in Nepal," was submitted in 1956 and explored, among other things, primary and secondary curriculum, university education, teachers' training levels, and administration and finances of educational institutions (NEPC, 1956). The study remained a key reference for many years in developing Nepal's educational institutional capacity.

13. After much deliberation during 1955-1958, TU was established as a research-cum-residential non-affiliating university and it later became an affiliating university (Shakya, 1984 and Bajracharya, 2011). Higher education had begun earlier at Tri Chandra College, which offered courses in the natural sciences, humanities, and social sciences. Commerce degrees were first offered in 1954. The US helped to establish the College of Education in 1955, and the discipline of law studies began shortly afterward. The NESP later initiated educational programs in management, engineering, medicine, agriculture, forestry, and other subjects.

14. The Swiss began to provide development support to Nepal in early fifties under the leadership of geologist Toni Hagen, who played an important role in technical education as well as promoting tourism in the country. Hagen's trek to Jiri and Lukla was the first of its kind in Nepal, and his path was later developed as a trekking route to Mt. Everest. Hagen played a pivotal role in opening a technical school at Jiri.

15. UMN support to Nepal started in 1954. Odd Hoftun, a Norwegian engineer, came to Nepal with the UMN in 1958 to build a hospital at Tansen. Later, he made

that the focus was to produce sub-overseers, auxiliary health workers, auxiliary nurse midwives, foresters, junior technical assistants for agriculture, and cottage industry workers.

These initiatives were continued after the King's takeover in 1960. USAID initiated technical assistance to offer vocational subjects in secondary school education in the early 1960s, and subjects like secretarial science, trade and industry, and home science were gradually introduced. This was complemented by the establishment, with donor support, of technical schools in various parts of the country.[16] However, Sharma (1989) argues that grants provided to schools before the 1970s were merely enough for poor and rural areas. The colleges established in the 1950s and 1960s were ill-equipped in terms of buildings, library facilities, and competent teachers. There was a lack of policy and planning to supply these institutions with the needed human resource and technical training.

To reform and standardize the educational system, the government introduced the National Education System Plan (NESP) for the period 1971-76, which was complemented by the Education Act, 1971. The prime objective of the NESP was to promote science and technical education in order to produce qualified citizens to meet the manpower requirements for the development of the country (MOE, 1971). It committed support to all levels of schooling and for vocational subjects.[17] At TU, five

---

significant contributions in developing technical capacities in various parts of Nepal, and helped to establish the Butwal Technical Institute in 1963 (Svalheim, 2015).

16. Some of the technical institutes established with donor support included the Swiss-supported Balaju Technical Institute and Jiri Technical School in 1962 and 1982, respectively, as well as the UMN-supported Butwal Technical Institute and the Karnali Technical School in 1963 and 1980, respectively. Likewise, training centers for auxiliary nurses and midwives were established in Hetauda (1958), Bharatpur (1981), Pokhara (1984), Birgunj (1986) and Nepalgunj (1987). Furthermore, the School of Agriculture was established in 1957 along with agro-technical training centers in Lumle, Kaski and in Pakharibas, Dhankuta.

17. After the implementation of NESP, basic schooling took 10 years, with classes one to five referred to as primary, classes six through eight termed lower secondary, and classes nine and 10 called secondary. The SLC examination was given after class 10, upon completion of which the student could join a two years' proficiency-

institutions were created relating to engineering, medicine, agriculture, forestry, and science and technology, as well as four faculties relating to education, management, humanities, and social sciences. Community schools and colleges across the country were nationalized and placed under the monitoring of regional educational directorates and district education offices. Minimum qualifications for teachers were set and provisions to introduce extra-curricular activities were made.

The NESP was followed by the Sixth and the Seventh Five-Year plans, which focused on basic services, including education. A bachelor program in engineering was started in 1978 and further efforts were made in vocational and technical training during the 1980s. The Council for Technical Education and Vocational Training (CTEVT) was established to formulate technical education policies, coordinate technical education providers, and ensure quality of the programs. Likewise, the Higher Education Commission of 1983 set up Mahendra Sanskrit University, which was later renamed Nepal Sanskrit University.

These initiatives helped to improve the literacy rate, which reached 39.6% in 1991, although there was a significant gender gap: male literacy was 54.5% compared to just 25% for females (Khaniya, 2007). School enrollment also increased, as did the number of schools. However, as Sharma (1989) indicates, school-level education faced significant constraints, including a lack of competent teachers to provide instruction in English, Mathematics, Science, and Geography, resulting in disappointing SLC results. The situation in higher education was similar, with a miserably low pass rate of 10% not only at Bachelor but also at Master's level for quite some time.

The Panchayat-era approach to human resource development and mobilization lacked vision because reform measures were hampered by a persistent conservative orientation. The state inherited from the Ranas a culture of *chakari* (sycophancy) and *chaplusy* (flattery), which promoted favoritism and nepotism over

---

certificate level of university education followed by bachelor, masters, and post-graduate degrees.

merit. Innovation, skill development, and quality improvement remained of secondary importance (Bista, 1991). Even competent and well-educated workers needed to appease the egos of their well-established bosses in order to get jobs, promotions, and other discretionary benefits. At the same time, the education system focused on producing certificate-holding graduates at the expense of quality education, and was therefore unable to produce many skilled and able members of the workforce (Bista, 1991 and Sharma, 1989). Furthermore, even as the Civil Code of 1962 outlawed caste-based discrimination, people's job prospects were still largely determined by their caste because of the persistent traditional outlook of the state and society (Bista, 1991). Most higher education graduates came from the high castes, such as the Brahmin and Chhetri groups, and they became dominant in state administrative work and politics. Popular interest in technical education remained weak because of the continued association of technical work with low-caste status (Bista, 1991). Similarly, vocational education programs lacked necessary facilities and did not capitalize on the innovation and knowledge of occupational caste groups (Maden et al, 2009). Vocational and technical graduates found it difficult to get jobs in nascent industries, and TFM (1983) reports that there was large-scale migration of workers from India to undertake technical and skilled works. Thus, educational development during the Panchayat period lacked vision and commensurate effort.

7.4 Human Resources at the Crossroads of Social and Economic Change Following the political change of 1990, political parties made commitments to develop Nepal's human resources in order to achieve large-scale economic growth. The NC's and the leftists' approach to education differed with respect to the role of the state and the private sector. Liberalization measures enacted by the NC during the 1990s chalked a path toward a market-led economy, while the leftists focused on labor issues.

The period saw a shift in the mainstream development agenda, especially as donors and other pressure groups advocated for redressal of historical exclusion of marginalized groups by the state.[18] This agenda was politicized by the Maoists during their armed movement, which helped to break down the conservative orientation of the state and the society, especially in rural areas, but it had a strong detrimental effect on the economy (Karki and Seddon, 2003 and Gellner, 2008). The education sector suffered during the armed revolution, as teachers were targeted and many school-going children were used as arms carriers or were recruited as Maoist cadres or were abused by state forces. Consequently, many schools had to be closed. Hence, the post-1990 period saw immense social and economic change and socio-political conflict. Amidst this socio-political dynamism, the government made a number of efforts to develop the country's human resources, especially focused on basic education but also including measures for higher education and technical and vocational training.[19]

7.4.1 Recent Development in Education Donor support for basic education continued in the decades after 1990. Basic and Primary Education Program was launched in 1992 to improve quality and access in the basic and primary education and to achieve universal primary education (MOE, 1997) and Secondary Education Development Project was brought in 1993 to improve the quality and efficiency of secondary education. Likewise, the multilateral Education for All (EFA) Project was launched in 2004 following a global agreement in Dakar in 2003 to promote basic and primary education (Khaniya, 2007). Another multilateral donor program, the Secondary Education Support Program, began in 2003. The five-year School Sector Reform Program began in 2009, followed

18. Some of the donor-funded development projects focusing on social inclusion were the Enabling Sate Program of DFID, the Social Inclusion Research Fund of Norway, and a number of projects seeking to integrate the principles of ILO 169, to which Nepal became a signatory in 2007.

19. Several notable global commitments for development have been made in recent decades. The United Nations' 2000 Declaration set eight Millennium Development Goals (MDG) to be achieved by 2015, which was followed by the 17 Sustainable Development Goals (SDG) for 2030, seeking to end poverty and hunger. The MDG focused on universal primary education and the SDG focused on quality education and sustainable development.

by another five-year program, the School Sector Development Plan, in 2016 (MOE, 2016).[20] All of these programs set targets to fulfill children's right to an education by improving access, enhancing quality, improving service delivery, enhancing gender parity and strengthening institutional capacities (Bajracharya et al, 2006 and Poyck et al, 2016). Additionally, various scholarship programs were launched to promote basic education for excluded, marginalized, and poor students.

Since 1990, primary and secondary education has received the lion's share of government expenditure on education. Bajracharya et al (2006) states that primary education's share of total education expenditure increased from 53% to 63% in the period between FY 2000/01-FY 2004/05, while the combined share of primary and secondary education increased from 75% to 88% in the same period. Likewise, Poyck et al (2016) state that government expenditure in primary education was 64% in FY 2011/12 and 54% in FY 2014/15, with a need to allocate more resources for technical and higher level education.

Nepal has mostly met the Millennium Development Goals in the education sector, according to NPC's final status report of MDG (NPC, 2016). With increased access to education, Nepal's literacy rate increased from 54% in 2001 to 67.2% in 2012 and to 75% in 2018. Likewise, the Net Primary Enrollment Rate improved from 81% in 2001 to 95.3% in 2013, to 96.6% in 2015. In 2015, 76.6% of students enrolled in grade one were expected to reach grade eight, while the Gross Enrollment Rate in secondary

20. In due course, early childhood education was introduced in public schools and the Education Act, originally passed in 1971, was amended so that all public schools were handed over to communities. Likewise, the higher-secondary level (10+2) was introduced in 1999 with the establishment of the Higher Education Examination Board. As a result, pre-university schooling totaled 12 years, with class one to eight referred to as primary, classes nine and ten as secondary, and classes 11 and 12 as higher secondary. Curricula were also changed many times to encompass revisions in teaching pedagogy and course content. Many vocational subjects were included, and education through the mother tongue was also introduced. The New Education Act, 2017 merged the Secondary and Higher-Secondary Examination Boards to form the Nepal Examination Board, which administers the School Education Examination (SEE), after class ten, replacing the SLC and class eleven and twelve exams.

education was 56.7% and the literacy rate among 15-to-24-year-olds was 88.6%. During the period 1990-2018, the number of schools increased from 23,759 to 64,319 and the number of students increased from 3498 thousands to 7211 thousands (Table 7.1), reflecting the popularity of educating both daughters and sons, despite earlier taboos regarding educating girls (Figure, 7.1). However, the ADB (2017) reports that the average citizen in Nepal has received only 4.23 years of schooling.

The important progress made in increasing public access to primary and secondary education was not matched by improvements in educational quality. ADB(2004), Bajracharya et al (2006) and Poyck et al. (2016), cite poor school facilities (such as libraries and laboratories for practical learning), poor quality of training, limited trained teachers, poor motivation of teachers, delays in book distribution, high dropout rates, and a long school cycle caused by failures as constraints. A significant portion of the education budget was absorbed by teachers' salaries, leaving very limited funds for other educational expenses. Furthermore, the application of new and progressive teaching methods was limited. Despite the introduction of various scholarships for Dalits and other marginalized groups, there were problems in distribution; educational attainment among these groups continued to be low.

The government has also introduced important changes to the higher education sector since 1990. A national education commission was formed in 1992 to identify improvements needed in the sector. The commission recommended decentralizing higher education institutions, all of which the NESP had placed under the umbrella of Tribhuvan University in the 1970s. It also recommended opening multiple universities, establishing an Open University for distance learning, and providing more autonomy to faculties and departments (Joshi, 2007). In line with the recommendations, the University Grants Commission was formed in 1993 to provide grants to universities and monitor them to ensure the quality, efficiency, and relevance of education provided.

TU's monopoly over higher education ended in 1991 with the establishment of Kathmandu University mainly with private sector participation, with more universities and autonomous higher education institutions added in subsequent years. At present, there are 11 universities and three autonomous higher education institutes in Nepal, which have widened the scope of, as well as improved access to, higher education.[21] New faculties and academic programs have been introduced whose curricula, depth, and scope aims to address changes occurring at the global level and meet local needs for various specialties. Private schools and colleges expands especially as a result of the 1990s economic liberalization measures.[22] Some of these private schools and colleges also run programs accredited by foreign education boards and universities, in line with the opening of the higher education sector following Nepal's admission to the WTO.

Access to higher education has improved dramatically since 1990. The number of students enrolled in higher-education programs increased from 123 thousands in 1990 to 487 thousands in 2018 (Table 7.1). Enrollment grew slowly during the conflict years but accelerated after 2005, as the end of the Maoist insurgency created a more conducive environment for higher education. However, only 2.9% of Nepalis aged 15-64 years have completed tertiary-level education (ADB, 2017) meaning there is a long way to go in attaining proper higher education and take it to the masses.

Students' preferences for discipline specialization seem to be guided by job opportunities available in the market. Management, education and social sciences are the most popular subjects at the tertiary level, though science and technology subjects have been

---

21. The 11 universities of Nepal are Tribhuvan University (Kathmandu), Nepal Sanskrit University (Dang), Kathmandu University (Kavrepalanchock), Purbhanchal University (Morang), Far Western University (Kanchanpur), Mid-Western University (Surkhet), Pokhara University (Kaski), Agriculture and Forestry University (Chitwan), Lumbini Buddhist University (Rupandehi), Nepal Open University (Lalitpur), and Rajarshi Janak University (Dhanusha). The three autonomous higher educational institutes are B P Koirala Institute of Health Sciences (Sunsari), Nepal Academy of Medical Sciences (Kathmandu), and Patan Academy of Medical Sciences (Lalitpur). The Constitution of Nepal (2015) has provisioned for central and provincial universities.

22. The MOF's 2014 Economic Survey states that altogether 8,825 schools were operating in Nepal in FY 2013/14, of which 2,814 (31.88%) were private and the remaining 6,011 (68.12%) were government and community schools.

Table 7.1: Number of Schools and Number of Students in School and Higher Education of Nepal

Academic Year	School Education		Number of Students in Higher Education (in Thousands)
	Numbers of Schools	Numbers of Students in Schools (in Thousands)	
1990	23,759	3,498	123
1995	29,168	4,279	101
2000	37,566	4,923	134
2005	41,035	6,464	122
2010	52,182	7,464	244
2015	62,090	7,824	348
2016	62,751	7,346	442
2017	63,795	7,392	453
2018	64,319	7,211	487

Source: Various Issues of *Economic Survey*, MOF.

Figure7.1: Youth Literacy Rate in 15-24 Years Age Group of Nepal (in %)

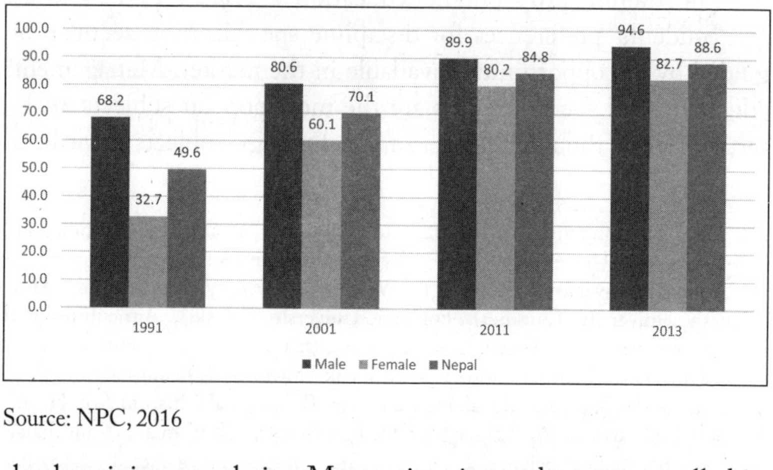

Source: NPC, 2016

slowly gaining popularity. Most university students are enrolled in management or education programs (UGC, 2018). The lack of growth in science and technology subjects at the university level is explained by supply-side constraints as well as students' inability to meet minimum benchmarks for enrollment in these subjects. The worrying aspect is 26% unemployment among graduates (ILO, 2015). This might be due to supply-side problems (i.e. poor quality of education) and demand-side problems, such as poor-quality jobs offering low salaries/wages.

Despite the opening of many new universities as well as public and private colleges, there has been an increased outflow of Nepali students to foreign countries in pursuit of higher education. The number of students pursuing studies abroad gradually rose during the conflict period but started to decline afterwards, probably due to increased hope for the restoration of political stability (Table 7.2). However, the outflow of students rose sharply again after 2012/13, indicating a lack of trust in the Nepali higher education system – a matter of serious worry that the government must attend to with priority and seriousness. In the first eight months of 2018/19, the number of students seeking no-objection letters was estimated to have reached 112,000 – an alarming rise.

While this phenomenon has the potential to develop Nepali human resources at the global level, there are two serious pitfalls to which the government does not seem to have given due attention.

Table 7.2: Number of No-Objection Letters Obtained to Study Abroad

Year	Number of Student
2009/10	26,913
2010/11	11,288
2011/12	9,691
2012/13	15,220
2013/14	27,383
2014/15	28,763
2015/16*	31,000
2016/17	39,307
2017/18	67,226
2018/19**	112,000

Source: MOE
*Estimated, ** Data for 8 months.

First, many Nepali students who study abroad do not return to Nepal, instead seeking work in the countries where they study. Second, there has been a massive outflow of foreign exchange to fund study abroad, which has put pressure on the nation's balance of payments, already unduly affected by high imports.

7.4.2 Technical and Vocational Training There has been a number of efforts, mostly with donor assistance, to develop technical training and vocational education in Nepal since 1990. The ADB has made significant contributions in recent decades to strengthen the technical and institutional capacity of CTEVT and to establish different technical schools. Other donors like DFID, SDC, UMN, KOICA, India, Denmark, and China have also played a significant role to improve CTEVT's capacity.[23] CTEVT programs are focused on SLC graduates. Efforts have also been made to integrate technical and vocational education with secondary school curricula (Sharma, 2010). The Community Support Program funded by DFID and MEDEP and MEDPA of UNDP have supported technical training, while Helvetas, GTZ, SNV and other donors are also active in supporting local communities and the government for vocational trainings.

As a result of these various efforts, the number of technical and vocational training providers has increased dramatically since the end of the Panchayat regime in 1990. Bajracharya (2010) reports that there are around 329 private training service providers under affiliation to CTEVT, while more such entities exist without affiliation.[24] The MOF's Economic Survey of 2019 reports that around 46,000 people were enrolled in technical and vocational training programs during FY 2017/18. There was 22,293 trainees in CTEVT in FY 2014/15 and it increased to 23,098 in 2015/16 and to 31,841 in 2016/17. However, many programs are of questionable quality. Unaffiliated private training centers often lack sufficient mechanisms to control quality (Bajracharya, 2010).

23. CTEVT website available at: http://ctevt.org.np/page.php?page=26

24. In Panchayat era, there were only a few government-run training centers.

A study by the ILO (2015) indicates that 58% of youth aged 15-29 are self-employed (ILO, 2015). Furthermore, 54.7% of young women and 31.4% of young men are associated with family establishments without pay. In other words, a significant portion of youth are not absorbed by the market. There remains a dearth of skilled human resources due to a lack of compatibility between market needs and educational and training programs, poor quality of training programs, and a lack of appropriate attitude of the trainees.

Due to a lack of jobs at home, there has been a large-scale migration of Nepali laborers to the Gulf and other countries over the past few decades. The liberalization measures of the 1990s failed to bring major structural changes to the economy, in part due to the decade-long Maoist conflict and subsequent political instability. Likewise, a large skill gap among Nepali youth, as indicated by studies by the ADB et al (2009) and Shrestha (2017), has hindered growth. APO (2017) reports that Nepal's labor productivity in 2015 was USD 5.8 per worker per day, representing a 1.8% increase from 1990 – a much smaller increase than was experienced by other South Asian countries during the same period.[25]

It should be noted that only two percent of Nepali labor migrants are skilled, while 23% are semi-skilled and 75% are unskilled (ILO, 2015 and Paudyal, 2010). It is unrealistic to assume the country can continue to survive primarily on remittances sent back by unskilled workers. Nepal's domestic skill gap is filled by a large number of workers migrating to Nepal from India. Interestingly, this imported labor take back sizeable amount of country's remittance inflow (Satyal, 2019).

7.5 Unions and Their Implications The history of Nepal's student unions is intertwined with national political movements. Under the Rana regime, a student movement for modernizing curricula at a Sanskrit school in Kathmandu was considered the first of its kind

25. APO, 2017 report that labor productivity of Bangladesh, India, Pakistan and Sri Lanka stand at USD7.9, 14.6, 16.1 and 29.5 per labor respectively for 2015. Growth of labor productivity in Bangladesh, India, Pakistan and Sri Lanka for the time period between 1990 to 2015 stand at 3.3, 4.8, 2.1 and 3.4 percent respectively.

and this movement later became part to topple Rana regime. Likewise, in Indian cities like Banaras, Patna, and Kolkata, Nepali students formed various organizations in opposition to the Rana government (Joshi and Rose, 1966). After taking power in 1960, the king permitted to establish All Nepal National Free Student Union in 1965 which later became affiliated to leftists. In 1970, Nepal Student Union (NSU) was formed. The NSU had ties with the Nepali Congress; the NC leader Krishna Prasad Bhattarai was the chief guest at its inauguration, and its four founding members later became influential NC leaders (among them the current NC President, Sher Bahadur Deuba). The student unions played an influential role in compelling the monarchy to conduct the 1979 referendum on democracy and in bringing about the 1990 pro-democracy movement. The space for student unions opened up more after 1990 political change and they again played an important role in the reinstalling democracy in 2006. Concurrently, teachers, university professors as well as employees created unions that at the earlier period became the major initiator for political changes but are proving to be serious deterrents for objectivity and rational progress.

Despite these important contributions, unions are often criticized for their overt politicization. Hachhethu (2006) and Dhungel (2007) argue that because student unions are considered prime entry points for careers in politics, their leaders are incentivized to follow central party leaders so that they can later obtain high-ranking party posts. Student union elections and National Conventions are held only irregularly, so they are often led by informal committees appointed by party leaders. This has limited the unions' responsiveness to students' needs and demands and quality of education. Snellinger (2007) argues that these unions should focus more on bringing forward the agenda of students and workers in order to pressurize the government and political parties to address relevant issues. Similarly, unions of teachers, professors and employees also need to be responsible oriented towards improving quality of education, access to education and overall teaching- learning environment. The unions have played an important role in the process of democratization but with the culmination of Nepal as a federal republic, their role has become redundant. Hence, their role should be geared toward development and not in 'revolution'.

7.6 Conclusion In summary, Nepal's education system and human resource development institutions began to be modernized according to Western principles during the Rana regime, but early attempts had limited impacts due to the conservativeness of the state and society. Most educational reforms were made according to the rulers' interests in protecting their regime and legitimizing their legacy. It was only after 1990 that the conservative orientation towards human resource development began to change, but it came at the cost of a long period of political instability.

Despite a dramatic increase in overall access to education after 1990, the quality of education has remained low. Unfortunately, the government lacked a concrete vision for improving the quality of educational and human skill development programs. Donors have been responsible for most initiatives in this regard, but the results have not been impressive. The reports on Nepal's education sector have reiterated the same problems again and again, but the government has taken little action, blaming failures on political instability.

As a result, the gap in performance between government educational institutions and private ones – which are often highly expensive – has only grown. There has also been a massive outflow of students pursuing higher education abroad due to the deteriorating quality of education at home, despite the existence of some islands of excellence. There are still reports of discrimination and exclusion in education, highlighted by pressure groups like NFDIN and NNDSWO. Likewise, there is a lack of integration of indigenous knowledge and traditional skills into modern skill development and vocational education programs (Maden et al, 2009). Although the government claims it lacks the resources to sufficiently fund education, it is trying to control more of the sector, raising apprehensions among investors in private educational institutions as well as students so far as the indication coming from the government indicates.

The public's recent realization of the importance of education, reflected in people's willingness to spend their hard-earned money on educating their children, provides reason for hope. Likewise, gender parity has been achieved at all levels of education, with a reluctance to educate girls observed only among some groups, such as Terai Dalits and a few other communities. Besides, the 2015 Constitution has devolved the authorities of education to province and local governments in a confusing manner and New Education Act (2017) also hasn't defined a clear role of these governments. So there is a big apprehension on federalization of education and their possible implications.

chapter 8

THE FOUNDATION: INFRASTRUCTURE

8.1 Introduction Infrastructure is the backbone of economic development because it facilitates service delivery, economic activities and movement of people. It is essential to the development of civilizations and nations. Nepal's infrastructure remains underdeveloped partly as a result of the harsh and difficult terrain. Furthermore, Nepal's geographical location between China and India poses both challenges and opportunities for infrastructure development. The two giant neighbors' priorities in Nepal are guided by their interests in strengthening their influence in the South Asian region. This affects the placement and initiation of roads, hydropower, and other infrastructure development.[1]

8.2 Infrastructure Development in the Rana Period The Ranas made a number of attempts to introduce modern infrastructure in Nepal albeit at rudimentary levels.[2] These attempts were supported

---

1. King Prithvi Narayan Shah defined Nepal as a "yam between two boulders" in his treatise *Divya Upadesh*, specifically alerting people to the vulnerability to Nepal's sovereignty posed by its geographically open southern border with British India, which lacked significant natural barriers. Today, modern infrastructure and technological advancements have reduced the importance of geographical barriers. For example, China is rapidly developing its global connectivity through the OBOR initiative, and has expanded road access to Nepal.

2. The rulers of Nepal – and specifically of the Kathmandu valley – during the medieval period patronized art, craftsmanship, and architecture. Administrative centers were dominated by well-designed palaces and residential settlements

by the British, with whom the Ranas maintained good relations by supporting their colonization of India.[3] Often, the Ranas initiated infrastructure projects at the cost of the state in order to benefit themselves. Dev Shumsher, the most progressive-minded Rana ruler, started the publication of the national newspaper *Gorkhapatra* in 1901. However, he was overthrown by his brother Chandra Shumsher within four months of assuming office, and the newspaper remained highly censored during the Rana period.

In 1908, Chandra Shumsher built Singha Durbar, a palace regarded as one of the finest examples of westernized architecture in Asia. It was used as the official residence of the Rana Prime Minister and still remains the administrative center of the country. Chandra Shumsher built Singha Durbar using state treasury funds, but he later claimed the palace as his personal asset and sold it back to the Government of Nepal.

In 1911, Chandra Shumsher developed a 500 KW hydropower plant at Pharping in Kathmandu Valley, the country's first hydroelectric project and only the second in Asia.[4] Electricity distribution was managed under an act brought in 1921, which stated that hydropower would bring the Nepali people out of darkness and help to industrialize Kathmandu Valley. However, Regmi (1988) argues that infrastructure developed during Rana period was more focused to gain benefit within Rana family than the public.

---

centered around courtyards (Regmi, 1965). Perhaps a rudimentary communication network was also active to serve transit trade between India and Tibet/ China.

3. The visits to Britain by two Rana Prime Ministers – Jang Bahadur Rana in 1850 and Chandra Shumsher SJB Rana in 1908 – provided the regime exposure to modern infrastructure. These two Prime Ministers attempted to copy the British model for infrastructure development in Nepal.

4. Regmi (2002) quotes an 11th February 1910 Gorkhapatra article that states that the equipment used to build the Pharping plant were carried by porters from Bhimphedi to Pharping, which is situated on the southern hills of Kathmandu Valley. Chandra Shumsher issued a decree to households of different parts of the Kathmandu Valley to provide male family members for transporting the equipment; those who disrespected the decree were fined. In 1936, another 600 KW hydropower plant, which was later increased to 900 KW, was installed at Sundarijal, also in Kathmandu Valley. In 1943, a 1600 KW hydropower plant was installed at Letang in Morang District. There were also some privately operated diesel plants in the Terai, particularly in the industrialized areas.

Nepal's connectivity with British India increased when an Indian narrow-gauge railway was built to Nepal's Janakpur in 1925. In 1927, British India built another narrow-gauge railway track connecting Raxaul in India to Amlekhgunj in Nepal. The Ranas' primary interest in the railways was to use them to sell Nepali timber to British India and thereby increase their own treasury holdings (Panday, 1999). Similarly, the development of motorable roads in Nepal was spurred by the Ranas' newfound interest in motorcars. The first motorcar arrived in Nepal in 1921 with Britain's Prince Edward (later King Edward VIII), who came for a hunting expedition in Kasara of Chitwan. Afterwards, the Ranas began to purchase lavish motorcars, many of which were transported to Kathmandu using porters to cross the hills from Bhimphedi to Thankot. In 1928, a ropeway was built from Bhimphedi to Kathmandu and was used for transporting cars as well as other freight to the capital. By the end of the Rana period, a few parts of Kathmandu Valley had access to motorable roads and survey work had begun for a road connecting Kathmandu to Hetauda. Likewise, there was a single-lane, stone-paved road connecting Bhimphedi to Amlekhgunj and another road connecting Amlekhgunj to Raxaul.

Near the end of their reign, the Ranas called for more development activities to benefit the wider public. It is possible that they were simply trying to divert attention from the growing political movement in opposition to their rule (Bajracharya and Agrawal, 1980). In 1936, Prime Minister Juddha Shumsher issued a postal guide to organize the collection and delivery of mail, and he also envisioned the construction of a postal road.[5] The penultimate Rana Prime Minister Padma Shumsher envisioned a postal highway to connect the eastern Terai with the western Terai. Mohan Shumsher, the last Rana prime minister, convened the first planning commission meeting on September 18, 1948 (Bajracharya and Agrawal, 1980). However, all of these initiatives were cut short by the revolution of 1950-51 that overthrew the Rana regime.

5. Nepal's first postal stamp was introduced by the Gorkha kingdom. After unification, King Prithvi Narayan Shah and his successors used the post to transmit official messages. It was opened to the public only from 1879 onward.

The Ranas, who had been rewarded for recognizing British supremacy in India, were weary of Indian independence and an Indian Congress-led government to the south. After gaining independence, India made overtures to Nepal showing that it expected to continue the historical relationship of Nepali dependency. In July 1950, India's ambassador to Nepal, Chandreshwor Narayan Singh, and the last Rana prime-minister, Mohan Shumsher, signed the Treaty of Peace and Friendship, which, along with an accompanying Letter of Exchange, stated that Nepal must not pursue policy changes that would affect India's internal security.[6] Nepal's relations with India would continue to shape the development of its infrastructure and connectivity in the decades to come.

On the other hand, the Ranas did not undertake significant efforts to develop connectivity with Tibet/ China to the north. This was despite a long-standing trading relationship between India, Nepal, and Tibet/ China. Pursuant to British interests, Nepal did not develop roads to link the northern border with Kathmandu. Instead, trade with Tibet shifted to the Nathu La Pass in Sikkim due to policy shift. Many Newar merchants moved their commercial operations from Kathmandu to Darjeeling and Kalimpong in India to continue their trade with Tibet.[7]

8.3 Infrastructure Development under the Panchayat Regime At the end of the Rana regime in 1950, the country had a total of 500 km of road and an electricity generation capacity of 3,650 KW. The newly empowered political parties expressed commitments to develop infrastructure in order to spur growth and expose Nepali people to the outside world. The first Five-Year Plan, for the period 1956-61, prioritized physical infrastructure and connectivity.

6. Khatri (1997) explains that independent India adopted a more retrogressive approach than the colonial power. Kumar (1989) and Panday (1999) claim that India tried to sustain its military power in South Asia and reinforce the British policy of keeping Nepal dependent. By contrast, Indian foreign policy expert SD Muni (2009) argues that India's basic concern in South Asian diplomacy has always been its own security, and that it does not seek to interfere in its neighbors' internal matters.

7. Refer to Annex B for a brief history of Nepal's trade with Tibet/ China.

Successive annual budgets and plans followed and were complemented by the Development Board Act, 1956, which conferred the government the right to form executive committees to carry out development projects for roads, irrigation, hydropower, and other infrastructure. In practice, however, the political instability of the period forced the government to concentrate on general administration and neglect development activities, including infrastructure construction. One notable development was the construction of Tribhuvan Highway (H2) from Kathmandu to Hetauda, designed by Indian army with Indian assistance that linked Kathmandu to Southern border initiating the beginning of connectivity in Nepal. The road was completed in 1956.[8]

After the royal coup of 1960, the King also vowed to enhance infrastructure connectivity to develop rural Nepal (Joshi and Rose, 1966). However, the government lacked resources and qualified human resources to carry out these commitments on its own, consequentially relied on technical and financial assistance from donors. Bilateral donors like India, the USA, China, the USSR, the UK, Norway, and others helped Nepal to initiate infrastructure development in the 1950s and 60s. In the 1970s, multilateral donors like The World Bank and ADB became involved in infrastructure development as well. However, the donors came with their own interests and agendas, creating a challenge for Nepal to address them in a balanced manner.

8.3.1 Initiatives to Develop Connectivity The infrastructural focus of the government after 1950, and especially after 1960, was to enhance connectivity. To improve land connectivity, the government channeled its own and donors' resources into road construction; it also brought repeated proposals to extend the railway system, but to no avail. Improvements in land connectivity

---

8. In 1956 the highway reached Amlekhgunj, from where travelers could take the Nepal Government Railway to reach the Birgunj/ Raxaul border. Later, the road was completed all the way up to the border and so the Nepal Government Railway service was halted in 1965. The Nepal Transport Service, established by two Newari businessmen in 1959, was the first public bus service and provided transportation along the Tribhuvan Highway (H2).

were complemented by efforts to expand the country's air transportation network. Along with developing international air connections, as mentioned in Chapter 6, there were also initiatives to set up domestic air connectivity between different parts of the country, including areas inaccessible by road.

In due course, the Ministry of Works, Communication and Transport was established with a portfolio relating to civil engineering work, tourism, air and land transport, and information and communication.[9] The Department of Roads was set up in 1962 as the prime authority responsible for roads and bridges.[10] In 1974, the Public Road Act was passed to organize road construction and maintenance. The Road Development Board was created to usher in land connectivity. The civil aviation sector was overseen by the Civil Aviation Department, created in 1957; the government established Nepal Airlines Corporation (NAC) in 1958 and passed the Civil Aviation Act in 1959.

Various other road construction projects were initiated to enhance connectivity in the country. One of the most ambitious was the East-West Highway (H1), located in the Terai plains, for which King Mahendra laid the foundation stone in April 1962. The 1,027-kilometer highway crossed through all 17 Terai districts and required large-scale investment.[11] Most sections of the East-West Highway were constructed by the Indian Government, using Indian contractors and laborers. Other sections were built with support from the UK (Butwal-Narayanghat segment), the USSR (Patlaiya-Dhalkebar segment), the US (Narayanghat-Hetauda segment, built as a part of Rapti Valley Development Project) and Hetauda-Patlaiya section that was part of Kathmandu-Raxaul (India) highway built with Indian assistance. India also provided

9. Later restructuring of the state administration led to the creation of separate line ministries for the different sectors.

10. In early fifties, the Public Works Department was set up to carry out all kinds of civil engineering works. As the number of projects under its purview increased, the Department was divided into two in 1962, resulting in the Department of Buildings and the Department of Roads.

11. The East-West highway encompassed and upgraded all major existing tracks in the Terai.

aid to construct the Siddhartha Highway (H10), which connected the Bhairahawa/ Sunauli border with Pokhara.

Just as India sought to increase connectivity between its border and different parts of Nepal, the Chinese constructed the Arniko Highway (H3) in the 1960s to connect the Kodari/ Zhangmu border with Kathmandu.[12] China also constructed the Prithvi Highway (H4), connecting Kathmandu to Pokhara[13], and the Gorkha-Chitwan road. The latter significantly shortened the distance from Kathmandu to Birgunj/ Raxual, rendering large sections of the Indian-built Tribhuvan and Siddhartha Highways redundant. The Chinese later launched more road projects in the middle hills, as well as the Ring Road in the Kathmandu Valley.

As the most powerful foreign power in Nepal, India always sought to maintain influence over Nepal's diplomacy with third countries, including foreign aid and large-scale development programs in Nepal (Panday, 1999 and Khatri, 1997). India had no problem with bilateral assistance from countries like the US, the USSR, the UK, Switzerland, Germany, and others with whom it had good relations. Likewise, India did not oppose Nepal's receipt of aid from multilateral donors like the World Bank and ADB. However, India viewed Chinese aid in Nepal with great suspicion, especially following the Sino-Indian war of 1962 (Riaz and Basu 2007). Because the Chinese-built Arniko Highway (H3) connected to the Tribhuvan Highway (H2), ultimately linking China to India, India feared that the road could be used for an invasion or other military purposes (Panday, 1999). It also feared that greater Nepali connectivity with China would weaken India's influence in Nepal and invite communist infiltration on the Indian periphery. India was also probably concerned about an influx of Chinese goods, which could potentially be dumped on the Indian market. However, such fears proved unjustified, as large-scale dumping did not occur and India remained Nepal's largest trading partner by far (Panday, 1999).

12. The Arniko and Tribhuvan Highways developed north-south connectivity in Nepal for the first time by connecting the Kodari/ Zhangmu border of China with Birgunj/ Raxual border of India.

13. Prithvi Highway (H4), along with Arniko Highway (H3), connected the Kodari/ Zhangmu border of China with western Nepal.

India used its leverage with the Nepali government to prevent Chinese aid from being used to construct roads in the Terai during the Panchayat period (Lama, 2003). For example, in the 1980s, a Chinese contractor was selected as the lowest bidder to construct the Kohalpur-Banbasa section of the East-West Highway in far western Nepal, under World Bank financing. However, India pressured the Nepali Government not to go ahead with the Chinese contractor, promising to build the road itself instead. As a result, the construction was delayed for a decade and Nepal was required to pay a fine to the Chinese contractor for breaching the contract. Such interference by India remained one of the main reasons for slow progress on roads and other large-scale infrastructure work in Nepal.[14] However, Nepal was able to benefit from competition between India and China to provide more aid. And moreover, India built a lot of roads enhancing connectivity in the country, even if it delayed progress on some of them

In the 1970s, Nepal introduced the Strategic Road Network (SRN) initiative with donor support, which was instrumental in initiating connectivity development in Nepal through highway and feeder roads. Donor-funded road projects became incorporated with other aspects of development under the Integrated Rural Development (IRD) approach, popularized in the 1970s. Road standards were issued in 1970 to maintain the quality of the SRN. In the 1980s, donors began to prioritize feeder roads in order to spur rural development. There were also initiatives to link foot-trails in the hills with suspension bridges, supported by funding from the Swiss, UNDP, USAID and the World Bank. The Swiss constructed the Lamosanghu-Jiri highway and the US supported the construction of the Dadeldhura-Dhanagadhi Highway, although this could not be completed and later Government of Nepal built it.

14. The World Bank (1984) reports that only 850 km of the proposed 1040-km East-West Highway (H1) was completed within two decades of its inauguration. The last section to be built was located west of the Karnali River. Until the 1980s, travelers from Kathmandu to the Far-Western Region were required to go via India.

The Kathmandu-Bhimphedi ropeway, which had been built in 1928, was extended up to Hetauda with US support in the early 1960s. This eased the transport of goods to and from Kathmandu. Different donors also supported training programs to develop human resources in engineering by providing scholarships to Nepali students to study abroad. For instance, the Colombo Plan Scholarships were launched in the 1950s for this purpose. Nonetheless, infrastructure construction suffered due to a lack of human resources. There were few construction companies in the country and even the government-owned National Construction Company, established with the technical support from Israel, was plagued by inefficiency (World Bank, 1984). As a result, donor-funded road projects used foreign companies that often employed Indian labor.

While the Nepali Government depended on donors for most road projects, it also launched some road projects on its own. However, these efforts suffered from haphazard strategy. The government made repeated plans for new roads in its annual budgets that ignored constraints in finances and in civil-engineering human resource. Progress was negligible and the country could not fetch returns from the investments made.[15] Likewise, initiatives to construct rural roads through local participation were largely unsuccessful because the government did not provide Village Panchayats sufficient funds for this purpose. Local people were able to perform initial earthworks, but there was no budget for further activities. This resulted in simple earthen roads that were frequently damaged by the monsoon, tying up local human resources in their maintenance. While local road-building efforts may have helped develop a sense of national solidarity, they failed to deliver tangible outcomes. Overall, the length of Nepal's roads increased during the

15. Construction of the Kanti Highway along the shortest route from Kathmandu to Birgunj/ Raxual (via Hetauda) by the Nepal Army in the late 1950s was halted after initial earthwork due to lack of finances and technical expertise (Dhakal, 2002). Similarly, an attempt during the mid-Panchayat period to construct the Karnali Highway (H13) in the Mid-Western Region was delayed significantly and the track could be open only in 2005/06.

Panchayat period[16], although by the mid-1980s only 45% were paved (World Bank, 1984). Furthermore, the Mid- and Far-West Regions remained virtually devoid of roads and other connectivity infrastructure.

The development of railroads fared even more poorly than roads. The Panchayat government made several proposals to donors for projects to extend the railway system, claiming that trains could consume domestically available hydropower and, thus, curtail petroleum imports. However, the government failed to complete the necessary preliminary exercises and miscalculated costs and benefits associated with the projects (World Bank, 1984). The Nepal Railway Act was optimistically passed in 1963, but it remains un-implemented as donors showed little interest in the sector. The two narrow-gauge tracks at Janakpur and Amlekhgunj remained the only railway connectivity with India. These tracks provided only irregular services and were later completely closed while the former continue to operate irregularly till date

Similarly, plans to develop transport along Nepal's waterways failed to bear fruit. In 1971, the government passed the Ship Registration Act and the Nepal Ship (Registration and Logbook) Act in response to requests for licenses to establish private shipping companies. However, only two companies were established and only one ship was chartered for one journey (World Bank, 1984). This was most likely because only short sections of rivers in the Terai are navigable by small watercrafts and the access to sea does not exist in the land locked country.

As discussed in Chapter 6, Nepal saw significant developments in the air transportation sector during the Panchayat era, including the declaration of TIA as an international airport in 1964, membership in ICAO in 1960, arrival of international airlines in 1968, and introduction of jet aircraft to the NAC fleet in 1972. India provided initial support to improve TIA and Israel during the sixties, and later, in the mid-1980s, the ADB came forward to do the same. New domestic airports were constructed in different parts

16. Economic Survey of Ministry of Finance for FY 2000/01 reports that total highway length of Nepal in the end year of Panchayat period was 8328 KM.

of the country, which were served by DC-3s, Twin Otters, and other Short Take-Off and Landing (STOL) aircraft introduced in the early 1970s to serve rural mountainous regions. While international airliners began to fly into TIA, only the national flag carrier served domestic flights, using their limited number of aircrafts. There were only infrequent flights to destinations besides the most popular ones like Pokhara, Birgunj, and Biratnagar. Most airports in the hills and mountains had grassy runways which were used only once or twice per week; the rest of the time, local people used the runways for grazing their animals.

8.3.2 Hydropower Potential and Development Though hydropower development in Nepal began in the Rana era, it took many decades to achieve significant progress in electrifying the country. Hydropower was largely ignored during the 1950s, although the government and private companies installed a few diesel-powered plants in the areas of high electricity demand, such as Kathmandu and the eastern Terai. By the end of the 1950s, electricity supply from diesel plants reached 2,396 KW, exceeding the supply from hydropower, which was 2,077 KW.

The 1950s also saw the signing of two controversial river agreements with India. Both the Koshi River Agreement, signed in April 1954, and the Gandak River Agreement, signed in December 1959, were seen as giving undue benefit to India and remain *bête noire* in Nepali politics even today (Dixit, 2007 and Pun 2009). Leftists strongly opposed the agreements and accused the Congress, which signed them, of being supplicant towards India – a message they had been reiterating since the Delhi Tripartite Agreement of 1951. Because the barrages, electric powerhouses, and irrigation facilities built under the agreements provided greater benefits to India than Nepal, leftists and the press hounded the agreements as "selling the country's sovereignty to India." It is possible that King Mahendra's 1960 coup was partly inspired by these agreements.[17] Due to the mistrust engendered by the Koshi and Gandak agreements

17. The King also accused democracy of encouraging antinationalist elements, implying increasing interference of India during political instability of fifties.

in the 1950s, later Indian proposals for hydropower development projects continued to be viewed with suspicion in Nepal.

Following the 1960 coup, King Mahendra established the Nepal Electricity Corporation in 1962 to manage electricity production and distribution in the Bagmati and Narayani zones. Likewise, a line ministry for hydropower development and the Department of Electricity were formed to oversee generation, transmission and distribution of electricity throughout the country.

Many bilateral donors came forward to support hydropower development after that. In 1966, the USSR commissioned the construction of the 2.4 MW Panauti hydropower plant in Kavre District near Kathmandu. The next year, India supported in the installation of the 21 MW Trishuli plant, followed by the 1 MW Fewa plant in 1969 and the 15 MW Gandak plant in 1979. Likewise, China supported in the construction of the 10.05 MW Sunkoshi plant in 1972. The UMN and Norwegian missionaries helped nurture Nepali talent in the electro-mechanical and hydro-mechanical fields by establishing dozens of institutions like Butwal Training Institute from the 1960s onwards (Svalheim, 2015).[18] Along with other infrastructure like roads and communication facilities, the new hydropower projects of the Panchayat period played an instrumental role in developing the industrial estates of Kathmandu, Patan, and Hetauda by supplying cheap electricity. The Morang-Sunsari industrial corridor, by contrast, was mostly electrified by diesel plants at the time due to confining of electricity production and distribution in the central region.

In the second half of the 1960s, Nepal's policymaking discourse began to focus on the massive potential benefits of hydropower. A senior engineer, Hari M Shrestha, estimated Nepal's theoretical hydropower potential at 83,000 MW in his PhD dissertation in 1965. This was followed by another article by Indian journalist B Verghese, published in 1970, which called attention to the potential of Nepali hydropower to fulfill the energy gap in the Indian states of Uttar Pradesh and Bihar (Dixit, 2007). These and other

18. UMN and Norwegian Missionary also installed 9.4 MW Adhi Khola plant in 1991 and 12 MW Jhimruk plant in 1994.

publications caused the government to view Nepal's water resources with newfound optimism as a potential source of economic growth and foreign currency. Interest in the possibility of using hydroelectricity to power a domestic train network – and thereby reduce petroleum imports – also grew. Later planning documents reiterated the need to develop hydropower.

However, the Nepali government often failed to adequately explore the country's financial and technical constraints to develop hydropower projects. Leaders often presumed the viability of exporting electricity without recognizing associated limits, challenges, and risks. However, it is also true that the country has a massive hydropower potential – recent estimates suggest 105,000 MW (including the summer flush) and a technically and economically feasible potential of 42,000 MW. If properly utilized, this could usher Nepal into a new era of fast and sustained growth and also meet deficits in India and Bangladesh, provided those countries do not switch to other sources of energy (Bajracharya, 2013).

A constraint faced by the hydropower sector during the Panchayat period was that the bilateral grants available were only sufficient for low-capacity plants. As Riaz and Basu (2007) argue, donors sought to use aid to strengthen their footholds in Nepal. However, none were willing to provide grants large enough to install big plants, making it necessary for the country to liaise with multilateral donors like the ADB and the World Bank for loans assistance. Multilateral donors started to emphasize the social and environmental costs of large hydropower construction, which further deterred other actors, including India, regarding hydropower development in Nepal. The problem, in addition, is compounded by lack of conducive vision at the time where the focus was more on meeting immediate needs sans the longer term perspective.

Further challenges in the hydropower sector include among others India objecting development of hydropower plants on Nepal's major rivers by emphasizing the lower riparian state's rights. India showed interest to import hydropower from Nepal, but because it would be the sole buyer[19] of Nepal's electricity, it exerted influence

19. Recently, Bangladesh has also shown interest to import power from Nepal.

over the hydropower sector to stall projects particularly as it appears to wanting to control/supervise the plants as well as ensure security. Panday (1999) argues that India's restrictions on multi-purpose hydropower projects blocked potential benefits for Nepal in terms of irrigation, electricity, and drinking water. For example, donors had been exploring development of a dam along the Karnali since the mid-1960s, but the plan was abandoned due to Indian opposition.[20] Similarly, the Kankai Multipurpose Project in Jhapa District, proposed in the mid-1970s with funding from the ADB, would have generated 38 MW electricity and irrigated 57,459 hectares of land, but the ADB withdrew funding because India opposed it. Development of hydropower on the Seti, another major river, was similarly blocked. India also opposed river-fed irrigation projects, especially in the Terai, and intervened when donors tried to support them. Panday (1999) argues that the World Bank focused on ground water irrigation rather than surface water projects after India objected to its proposed support for the Karnali Chisapani Multipurpose Project and the Rapti Irrigation Project. Similarly, the Water and Energy Commission (WECS), formed in 1975 with Canadian[21] support entrusted the task to plan and manage Nepal's water resources, could not function properly due to alleged objection by India. Thus, Nepal's hydropower development during the Panchayat era suffered due to Indian objection as well as internal constraints like limited finances, a lack of human resources and abilities.

Furthermore, the Panchayat-era government undertook wrong steps in managing its existing electrical capacity. Upon the advice of multilateral donors, electricity companies were nationalized and

20. In 1966, Karnali Chisapani Multipurpose Hydropower Project was the first explored by the Japanese company NIPPON KOI, followed by the Australian company Snowy Mountain in 1968 and the Norwegian firm NOR Consultancy in 1976. India became involved in the Karnali plans in 1978. Under UNDP financial assistance, Nepal trained 250 engineers for the Karnali project in India's renowned Roorkee University in the early 1980s. In 1989, a comprehensive feasibility report prepared with the assistance from the World Bank showed the potential of producing 10,800 MW through the Karnali Chisapani Multipurpose Project. However, it was reported that India pushed against carrying out this project.

21. Interestingly, Canada faces a similar type of problem with the USA as Nepal does with India in river projects.

amalgamated into the Nepal Electricity Corporation in the 1970s, which joined with the Electricity Department to form the Nepal Electricity Authority (NEA) in 1985. Donors hoped to achieve financial sustainability by forming a single agency for power generation, transmission, and supply. However, this created a monopolistic, centralized, and vertically integrated supply chain with no provision for regulating bodies. Gyawali (2001) calls the consolidation "an act of warped socialism which was, ironically, promoted by Western backed donors". Dixit (2007) and Gyawali (2001) argue that the government should have instead encouraged de-concentration of the NEA's functions among multiple organizations. Within a decade, the NEA was partially unbundled again at the recommendation of donors, after they witnessed the deleterious effects of their previous advice. Interestingly, the government neither questioned the donors' multiple position changes nor put forward an alternative approach, perhaps due to human resource constraints and a limited knowledge base. The government's passivity allowed for continued interference by foreign donors, especially India.

By the end of the Panchayat era, total installed capacity of hydropower had reached 230 MW capacity. The major hydropower plants installed were the 60 MW Kulekhani I, the 32 MW Kulekhani II[22], and the 69 MW Marsyangdi and most of them were commissioned under the assistance of the World Bank with consortium financing from Kuwait Fund and Japan. The ADB stepped in to support the Hetauda-Gandak 132 kv transmission line, spanning 154 km. Along with other new roads and communications infrastructure, new hydropower projects played an instrumental role in developing some industries for example cement factories. Electricity and irrigation also brought some improvements in agriculture, although farming remained primarily rain-fed.

However, a large part of Nepal was excluded from infrastructural developments during the Panchayat era. The Mid- and Far-Western Regions remained largely devoid of roads and electricity access, leading to a widespread sentiment that the government had

22. Kulekhani II was commissioned under the support of Japan.

neglected the country's geographical periphery. In areas that were connected to the road network, rudimentary markets developed but they were dominated by inbound goods due to a dearth of locally produced items. The location of such markets frequently shifted as new road heads were established with the development of the road network.

8.4 Infrastructure Development in the Post-1990 Era After 1990, the country introduced the approaches of decentralization, community mobilization, and private sector participation in infrastructure development. The Local Self Governance Act, 1998 conferred responsibility for more development work to local bodies, while the Construction Business Act, 1999 increased the engagement of Nepali private contractors. Broader liberalization measures during the 1990s provided a conducive environment for infrastructure development, and the government's introduction of VAT in 1992/93 increased revenues. Likewise, the country's pool of trained human resources in engineering grew due to scholarship support provided by donors in earlier decades as well as the growing availability of engineering education within the country. As a result, the government did not have to depend on foreign technical support for minor engineering works. The era also saw a gradual rapprochement between India and China, and by 2006, they were ready to re-open the strategic border point of Nathu La, which had remained closed since the 1962 Sino-Indian War. So far not much visible impact is noted from opening of Nathu La and connectivity of Lhasa to Kolkata is still non-existing. The Constitution of 2015 has conferred more power related to infrastructure development to the autonomous provincial and local governments, including responsibilities for preparing development plans and policies.

8.4.1 Enhancing Connectivity After the restoration of democracy in 1990, political parties committed to further improve connectivity. The Strategic Roads Network has contributed to the construction of more highways and feeder roads, most of which were funded by loans from multilateral institutions like the ADB and the World Bank.

A significant accomplishment came in 1994, when the East-West Highway in the Terai was finally completed with the construction of the Karnali Bridge on the border between Bardiya and Kailali districts. In the absence of this bridge prior to 1994, travelers needed to pass through India to reach the other side or cross the river including transport on a ferry. During the tenure of Prime Minister Man Mohan Adhikari, who led the first UML government, the government announced the construction of the Mid-Hill Highway to connect mid-hill districts across the country. Much of this highway – 1,765 km – remains under construction today. When it is completed, travelers will be able to traverse the country from east to west without descending to the Terai.

Progress was also made in improving north-south connectivity, particularly in opening new routes to China. In addition to the Kodari/ Zhangmu border crossing, the Rasuwagadhi/ Gyirong border crossing with China was connected to Nepal's Strategic Road Network in early 2010s'. The road to a third northern border crossing, at Korala/ Lizi, is almost complete except a bridge on river Kali Gandaki. Furthermore, the government is currently extending the Mechi Highway (H7) in the east so that it will connect to the Olangchungola/ Dinggyê border crossing, as well as the Mahakali Highway (H14), the Seti Highway (H15), and the Karnali Corridor in the Far-Western Region to connect to the Hilsa/ Burang border crossing with China.

Since 1990, the government has increasingly relied on private Nepali contractors for road construction.[23] Though contractors are usually only engaged during the construction phase, the government has also encouraged the private sector to build highways and other infrastructure under the build-own-operate-transfer (BOOT) model; the Private Financing in Build and Operation of Infrastructures Act, 2006 was enacted for this purpose. However, the private sector has shown little interest in the BOOT model outside of hydropower sector. Only one company, Nepal Purwadhar Bikash

23. The Federation of Contractors' Associations in Nepal (2018) reported that there are around 12,500 construction enterprises in the country, among which 231 are "A-Class" contractors engaged in large-scale construction works.

Company, came forward to construct the Kathmandu-Hetauda tunnel road, but it failed to deliver. Similar delays were noted in Kathmandu-Nijgadh fast track and recently the task was entrusted to Nepal Army. The BOOT model faces several hurdles: loan financing is still not available for projects under this model, and managing road traffic and collecting road taxes in Nepal remains challenging.

As during the Panchayat era, road construction – especially in border areas – is heavily affected by Nepal's two large neighbors and their geo-political interests.[24] The big question is how relations between India and China will shape Nepal's connectivity, and how Nepal can benefit from it.

The involvement of more Nepali contractors and workers in infrastructure construction has reduced India's domination in the sector, at least in certain aspects. However, India has continued to influence in Nepal's politics and economic development processes, citing geopolitical security threats, such as the 1999 hijacking of an Indian Airlines jet from TIA. India remains cautious of China's support to Nepal, despite a rapprochement following the Doklam border dispute of 2017 (Dahal, 2018 and Jha, 2012).

In the past, China adopted a quiet diplomacy approach, distancing itself from Nepal's internal politics. However, it has become increasingly diplomatically engaged in Nepal over the past decade or so (Bhattarai, 2019). This may be due in part to worries about the protest activities of Tibetan refugees during the 2008 Beijing Olympics. It may also be due to fears about India gaining the diplomatic upper-hand in Nepal after it played an instrumental role in forging the 2006 Comprehensive Peace Agreement between the Maoists and the mainstream political parties, and the subsequent ouster of King Gyanendra, with whom China had cordial relations.

Chinese contractors have also become major competitors in Nepal's infrastructure sector over the past decade, with Chinese

24. Both India and China have emerged as major global powers. China is the largest economy in terms of PPP and the second-largest in cash terms, while India is the third-largest in terms of PPP and the seventh-largest in cash terms. It is expected that China and India will be the largest and the second-largest economies in PPP terms, respectively, by 2050 (Wolf et al, 2011 and IMF, 2017).

FDI commitments in Nepal exceeding India's.[25] Nepal has become a member of China's Belt and Road Initiative (BRI), as well as the China-aligned Asian Infrastructure Investment Bank. During the Nepali Prime Minister's state visit to China in June 2018, China and Nepal issued a joint statement agreeing to intensify cooperation under BRI for enhanced connectivity in terms of ports, roads, railways, aviation, and communications. Similarly, the President of Nepal recently made a state visit to China to participate in the second BRI Summit. Western countries and India have warned Nepal against too much engagement with China, claiming that China seeks to use Nepal as an entry point into South Asia and that Nepal may fall into a debt trap for the sake of better connectivity (Bhattarai, 2019). However, some Nepali commentators have argued that Nepal-China relations are based upon mutual trust and agreement (Dahal, 2018). A Round Table Discussion on Nepal-China Relations organized by the SAWTEE in June 2018 suggested that Nepal should clarify its national interests while advancing its economic cooperation with China (SAWTEE 2018). Many observers have come to the conclusion that, while aid always has geopolitical implications, Nepal should seek to benefit from economic cooperation with both its large neighbors, as well as other countries, whilst minimizing its dependence on any single country.

A number of accomplishments has been made in regard to local infrastructure since 1990. The UML government led by Man Mohan Adhikari announced the "Build Your Village Yourself" program in 1994. Under the program, local bodies and member of parliaments were provided grants to develop local infrastructure, initiating road construction in many rural areas. Though the program suffered from weak administration and lax enforcement of quality standards, it substantially contributed to the expansion of the local road network. Other steps were also taken to devolve infrastructure construction to the local level during the 1990s. The

25. Industrial Statistics of the Department of Industry shows that the 31.07% of FDI commitments over the last nine years came from India, while 35.77% came from China (including Hong Kong).

Department of Local Infrastructure Development and Agricultural Roads (DOLIDAR) was formed under the Ministry of Local Development in 1997 to look after local infrastructure construction work. In 1998, the Local Self Governance Act (LSGA) conferred responsibility for local infrastructure planning and construction to local bodies in collaboration with community organizations. Among the various responsibilities devolved to local bodies through the LSGA, infrastructure construction was perhaps the one that they took up with the most enthusiasm (Sapkota et al, 2009). During the Panchayat era, local Panchayats had faced regular budget shortfalls that rendered local infrastructure efforts ineffective. But the LSGA, DOLIDAR and the "Build your Village Yourself" programs dramatically increased the amount of unconditional grants received at the local level, helping to empower local governments in financing them. This was funded in part by the introduction of VAT in 1993, which substantially increased the government's financial capacity. Local road development was also aided by funding from donors for the Local Road Network, which was conceptualized as an addition to the SRN to further strengthen overall national connectivity. Perhaps local leaders were motivated for local infrastructure development because of election concerns as well.

Economic Survey of 2016 reports that around 39 thousand KM of roads have been constructed by local but around 4 percent of them are blacktopped. There has clearly been large-scale expansion of the local roads network over the last two decades (World Bank and GON, 2013). Local road construction exceeded targets set in the Rural Infrastructure Development Strategic Action Plan of 2007. Although most local roads remain unpaved, the government is currently investing resources to improve earthen and gravel roads. Roads have reduced the time required for citizens to visit government offices to access public services, and they have also promoted economic activities (Table 8.1). However, as during the Panchayat era, road construction is usually not linked with other economic development packages, limiting their impact on livelihoods.

Table 8.1: Percentage of Households Reaching Public Amenities within 30 minutes

Public Amenities	1995/96	2003/04	2010/11
Primary school	88.38	91.4	94.7
Public hospital/PHC			33.6
Bus stop	36.53	53	66.2
Paved road	30.02	37.2	51.4
Local shop/shops		86.2	92
Market center	25.78	34.4	44.7
Agricultural center	24.7	31.9	42.8
Bank	21.27	27.8	39.9
Post office		61	65.4
Telephone booth		53.6	86.3
Internet			43.2

Source: CBS, 2004 and 2011b

Similarly, while the Strategic Road Network has greatly expanded since 1990 (Table 8.2), there remain serious problems regarding quality standards and environmental impacts. The Nepal Road Standards of 1970, which were revised in 1988, 1994 and 1997, and then replaced by the New Road Standards in 2013, set norms for road safety. Likewise, the Environmental Protection Act, 1996 made Environmental Impact Assessments a prerequisite for infrastructure construction. However, frequent political interference and irregularities in contracting resulted in poor quality of roads (World Bank and GON, 2013). At the same time, regulating agencies performed poorly. The Department of Roads failed to sufficiently exercise oversight over politically well-connected private contractors,[26] while the Department of Environment, instituted as a regulator only in July 2012, has failed to properly assess projects' environmental impacts. Due to these lapses, landslides have become an increasingly common threat particularly during monsoon and the government lacks vision to mitigate this problem. Paucity of resources is also responsible for

26. Corruption is rife in construction work, churning out sub-standard infrastructure that neither lasts nor is functional.

the result. There is also a need to strengthen the Land Acquisition Act, 1977 and the Land Acquisition, Compensation and Resettlement Policy to provide a proper regulatory framework for resettlement and providing compensation to victims of those affected by roads and other infrastructure projects. Currently, most resettlement involving large-scale projects is made through *ad-hoc* decisions at the political level.

Table 8.2: Extension of Strategic Road in Nepal (in km)

Fiscal Year	Black-Topped	Graveled	Fair Weathered	Total
1990/91	3083	2181	3064	8328
1995/96	3609	2867	4761	11237
2000/01	4566	3786	7350	15702
2005/06	5048	4727	7658	17433
2010/11	9902	5670	7637	23209
2015/16	12173	6460	9675	28308
2018/19*	14102	7881	9410	31393

(Source: Economic Survey, MOF)
*First Eight Months

Maintenance of roads remains another challenge. For this purpose, the Road Board was formed in 2002, and it has adopted the Annual Road Maintenance Planning model. However, maintenance is neither organized nor effective. A perennial problem is related to financing, as the organizations responsible for road maintenance generally receive funding only in the last quarter of the fiscal year, leading to a hectic spurt of repair work during which proper evaluation and quality-checking cannot be done. Furthermore, the last quarter coincides with the onset of the monsoon, making such initiatives particularly difficult and less effective, because the rains quickly erase the progress made. Local road users' committees created under the LSGA are often influenced by contractors and politicians, resulting in irregularities, poor quality of work and, in many cases, users' committees are observed to be reflections of political and opinionated organizations affecting the development process.

As mentioned in Chapter 6, private airlines have been operating in Nepal since civil aviation policies were liberalized in the 1990s. The Department of Civil Aviation was converted into an independent authority, the CAAN, in 1998. However, the civil aviation sector remains unsafe due to Nepal's rugged topography as well as management abilities and processes. Most private airliners only operate in urban areas like Pokhara, Birgunj, Biratnagar, Nepalgunj and other tourist destinations like Lukla and Jomsom etc. The national carrier, NAC, has not been able to enhance its fleet capacity to reach the remotest areas of the country, and so many airports in rural hill areas remained unused.[27] International air traffic has increased due to tourism and labor migration to the Gulf and Southeast Asia. This has resulted in congestion at TIA, Nepal's only international airport. On top of this, India has provided only one aerial entry point through Simara claiming her security threat making air traffic more crowded and stopping to develop other avenues. There is a confusion regarding whether Nepal's second international airport, Gautam Buddha International Airport in Bhairahawa, will be able to open up for international flights. The issue, here, is whether India will provide avenues or not

The government has made repeated proposals since the 1950s regarding extending railways, but there has been little concrete progress to date. In May 2004, Nepal signed a railway agreement with India allowing transportation of goods from the Haldia/ Kolkata port to the Birgunj/ Raxaul border point by rail. To this end, the route's old narrow-gauge track was replaced with a broad-gauge track[28]. The government introduced the East-West Electrified Railway Project in 2008, with a vision to build a railway

27. Often, improvement in access to roads led to the abandonment of airfields due to the lower cost of road transportation. Some examples of airfields where services have been completely discontinued are: Palungtar, Gorkha; Manang; Patan, Baitadi; Chaurghari, Rukum; Gokule, Darchula; and Manthali, Ramechhap. Other less-used airfields are: Phaplu, Salleri; Suketar, Taplejung; Tumlingtar, Sankhuwasabha; Kolti, Bajura; and Chainpur, Bajhang.

28. In 2006, a feasibility study was carried out for the construction of East West railway along Terai plain and the overall cost estimated by this study was NRs. 635 Billion.

across the Terai region. In 2010, India and Nepal signed a memorandum of understanding to enhance cross-border connectivity. The government formed the Department of Railways in 2011, which endorsed the 20-Year Railway Development Vision to improve north-south and east-west connectivity[29]. The Department is currently carrying out initial work for different proposed railway tracks with support from India and China. A letter of exchange with India in February, 2016 stated Nepal would be able to use Indian railways for transit of items to and from Vishakapatnam port in Andhra Pradesh and for transit of goods to Bangladesh. In practice, however, there has been only negligible use of railways for cargo beyond limited movement along the Birgunj-to-Kolkata route. The old narrow-gauge track from Janakpur to Jayanagar was recently upgraded to a broad-gauge system, which is expected to ease passenger flow. Thus, only minor achievements have been made regarding the various recent plans and agreements for railways.

In recent political manifestos for local and parliamentary elections, parties made a number of commitments on railways[30], water transport[31], and other forms of transportation infrastructure. It is clear that sooner or later, east-west and north-south railway connectivity will link Nepal more closely with China and India. However, the government needs to explore costs and benefits of such initiatives in a more detailed manner. Large investments in

---

29. 20-Years Visions of Department of Railways is available at: http://www.dorw.gov.np/

30. Railways may be costly and should therefore be constructed only after consideration of the following: Is there scope for utilizing resources with quick yield? Secondly, what will be the long-term volume of traffic and what will be the replacement effect on road transport, in which the private sector has made huge investments? Third, what will be the overall Benefit Cost Ratio (BCR) and Economic Internal Rate of Return (EIRR)?

31. Opportunities for water transport are highly limited. Due to dams on the Koshi and Gandaki rivers, river transport is feasible on the Karnali River only, but unfortunately that river lies far from the country's economic centers. For the most part, only small stretches of rivers are navigable.

railways, shipping, metro rails[32], and mono-rails[33] need to be considered according to the national interest and financial and economic implications. The government also set up the Nepal Shipping Office in February 2019 to develop water transport. Development of these agencies without proper assessment will only enhance expenditures in this resource crunch country.

8.4.2 Hydropower Development After 1990, the government and political parties continued to advocate hydropower as a source of economic growth and foreign currency income. To this end, the government undertook hydropower development projects on its own and created new policies to encourage private-sector investment.

The Hydropower Policy, 1992 and the Electricity Act, 1992 opened hydropower generation to the private sector under the BOOT model. As part of the effort to de-bundle the NEA, the Department of Electricity was reinstituted in July 1993 to manage and regulate Private Electricity Producer (PEP). PEPs were allowed licenses for building plants up to 100 MW in size[34], while larger, multi-purpose hydropower plants were reserved for construction by the NEA. The NEA remained the sole organization responsible for electricity transmission and distribution, requiring all PEPs to sell electricity to the NEA according to terms and conditions listed in their Power Purchase Agreement (PPA).

The Electricity Tariff Fixation Commission (ETFC) was created in 1994 to set the NEA's electricity tariff rate, but it was given no role in developing PPAs between the NEA and PEPs. As a result, the ETFC could only fix the NEA's selling rate, but not the rate at which it bought power from private producers. Thus, while the NEA was partially unbundled, it remained the sole buyer

32. Metro-rails are going to be essential in congested cities like Kathmandu. However, construction costs will be enormous and returns low, requiring subsidies from the government.

33. This is not a feasible option for mass passenger traffic and will only act as a showpiece.

34. A task force formed by the government in 1991 identified hydropower projects in the 1-50 MW range for private investment.

of all PEP electricity, giving it *de facto* monopoly control over the country's electricity supply network and negating the possibility of local production for local consumption.

As the government began issuing PEPs licenses to develop projects in the 1990s, a speculative market for the licenses began to grow. This was fueled in part by the long gestation period for hydropower projects as well as due to delays in execution caused by inability to mobilize resources and uncertainty of the market mainly due to delay in power purchase agreements. Some license holders tried to earn lucrative profits simply by applying for licenses and then trading them, without any real intention to construct a hydropower plant. Later, the government introduced tighter controls on licensing in order to minimize this practice.

The NEA also opened up licensing for foreign hydropower companies, but it made some initial poor decisions in the PPA process that had long-term negative repercussions. In the mid-1990s, the Norwegian public utility Statkraft invested in the 60 MW Khimti project, while a US company invested in the 42 MW Bhote Koshi plant. However, with little experience in managing FDI in hydropower, the NEA signed PPAs for both projects in USD without mechanisms to mitigate foreign exchange risk. These agreements resulted in huge losses for the NEA due to sharp depreciation of Nepali currency. Following this mistake, the NEA was reluctant to sign PPAs with foreign investors. Along with Nepal's fragile political situation after the launch of the Maoist movement, this further deterred FDI in Nepal's hydropower sector. In 2016, the government created a Hedge Fund to minimize this foreign exchange risk. Unfortunately, however, conceptual clarity was lacking regarding how this fund will work.

Meanwhile during the 1990s, a proposal for a major hydropower project financed by the World Bank came under heavy criticism. It was expected that half of the production of the 402 MW Arun III would meet domestic electricity demand, while the remaining could be exported to India. The total estimated cost of the project in 1994 was USD 859 million, roughly half of the government budget at the time. The World Bank started initial feasibility work for the project in 1988, but controversies arose relating to the economic costs and environmental effects. Some INGOs and their local partners launched strong campaigns against Arun III domestically and abroad, and in August 1995 the World Bank discontinued the project. The lessons are, low cost projects with least impact on environment should be selected, proper home work should be done before launching and plan B will have to be kept ready in any development initiative. In addition to protests by NGOs and activists, some observers speculated that India also pressured the World Bank against the multi-purpose Arun III project. A road constructed along the Arun River as part of the project would have been the shortest north-south route across Nepal, connecting India with Tibet/ China. China tacitly supported the project, anticipating a new, fast route from Lhasa to the ocean, but India saw the new road as a threat.

As the primary potential buyer of Nepal's electricity, India continued its influence in hydropower development as well as water resource management. A Nepali Congress government signed the Mahakali River Agreement with India in 1996, despite domestic political polarization over the agreement (Dixit, 2007). The CPN-UML, the major leftist opposition, split due to this agreement, while the Maoists launched their armed revolution the day after it.[35] Bhattarai (2009) argues that India also restricted donors from carrying out multi-propose projects on rivers like the Kankai, Kamala, Bagmati, Rapti and others with the assurance that these projects would be carried out with Indian assistance. However, progress on such projects did not move beyond initial feasibility studies meaning that bigger power projects must have strong mutual understanding between India and Nepal for them to really take off.

---

35. Before launching the armed movement, Maoist leader Babu Ram Bhattarai presented a 40-Point Memorandum to the government on 6th February 1996. The second point of this document demanded repealing of the Mahakali Treaty, which was signed on 29th January, 1996, because it gave India an undesired monopoly over Nepal's water resources. However, Prime Minister Sher Bahadur Deuba re-endorsed the treaty on 12th February 1996 during his state visit to India. On 13th February, 1996, the Maoists launched their armed revolution with seven simultaneous attacks in four districts: Gorkha, Rolpa, Rukum and Sindhuli (CPN-Maoist, 2006).

Apprehension grew among the Nepali public about India's ambitions regarding Nepal's water resources, despite the fact that in some cases, India's opposition to third-country foreign investors proved beneficial. For example, in the mid-1990s the American company Enron Corporation showed interest in developing the 10,800 MW Karnali Chisapani project in Nepal. India advised Nepal to delay issuing a surveying license to Enron because it had a poor track record (Pun, 2009). As a result, the Nepali Congress government postponed negotiations with Enron in 1998, despite an uproar in parliament. In 2002, Enron was declared bankrupt and its two main executives were accused of fraud. In this case, Indian advice proved beneficial to Nepal.

The slow development of the hydropower sector after 1990 was also caused by problems within the NEA. The government was not able to control extreme politicization of the institution, hindering its ability for overall electricity planning and implementation. Even in cases where India did not object such as the Kulekhani III, Chameliya, and Upper Tamakoshi projects, the NEA proved ineffective due to its poor administrative and supervisory capacities as well as an unhealthy corporate culture based on political favoritism. In the 2000s, the NEA was able to add only one new plant: the ADB-funded 144 MW Kali-Gandaki (A). The NEA's hydropower generation capacity remained at a standstill at 478 MW from 2010-15, increasing only marginally to 508 MW in 2018 in the public sector with the delayed addition of the 30 MW Chameliya project.[36]

Political pressure also stymied the work of the ETFC in its role as an independent regulator. Despite wide fluctuations in the market price of electricity, the ETFC significantly delayed in reviewing and restructuring tariffs. In addition to the earlier mistakes the NEA made in signing PPAs with foreign investors,

36. The government's Bheri Babai Diversion Multipurpose Project, located in Surkhet, is an exception. Its first phase was recently completed with the support of China, and the project is expected to irrigate 51,000 hectares of land in Banke and Bardiya Districts whilst generating 48 MW electricity. The budget of 2019/20 also proposes to build Sunkoshi Marine project linking Sunkoshi with Bagmati.

this contributed to the deteriorating financial status of the NEA. As a result of these problems and a growing consumer base, the gap between electricity demand and electricity supply widened. Load shedding increased to more than 12 hours per day after 2006. The government had to declare the period 2013-2015 an energy crisis period, with the load shedding reaching up to 17 hours per day.[37]

The government took steps to encourage the private sector in order to meet the energy shortfall, but these were only partly successful. It introduced the Hydropower Development Policy in 2001 in order to enhance production, develop international electricity exports, and enhance technology transfer along with foreign investment. The government also gradually raised the limit of 100 MW for PEPs. However, no provisions were made in the bank policies for loans using hydropower projects as collateral constraining the mobilization of resources for the sector. Furthermore, administrative caveats and the NEA's reluctance to work with foreign investors, as mentioned earlier, compounded the financial constraints.

The Investment Board of Nepal (IBN) was set up in 2011 to facilitate FDI for large hydropower projects of more than 500 MW. The NEA is also supported by subsidiary companies like the Nepal Engineering Company Limited, Power Transmission Company Nepal Limited and Nepal Power Trading Company Limited to enhance hydropower generation and initiate trade.

However, the impact of the IBN and other measures was limited. A few power generation agreements were signed with multinational companies like GMR, CWC and others, but most of them eventually withdrew from these projects. Perhaps these companies were deterred by the fact that the main export market for Nepal's electricity was India, which was already bringing out proposals to use nuclear and other forms of energy. At the same time, Indian multinational companies were anxious about investing in Nepal due to anti-Indian sentiment among the Nepali public. Though Nepal recently signed a power trade agreement with

37. It is alleged that corrupt NEA officials provided energy to industries at a cost of supplying to consumers increasing load shedding hours.

Bangladesh under the paradigm of the South Asian energy nexus,[38] selling to Bangladesh would be more costly and complicated than selling to India. Furthermore, despite the passage of the Electricity Leakage Control Act in 2001, the government has not been able to control unauthorized and prohibited activities by consumers. Many investors remain deterred by the fact that land acquisition for developing power projects and extending transmission lines is done on an *ad-hoc*, political basis, rather than with clearly established guidelines.

As a result of the lack of FDI in hydropower, PEPs have mostly been financed by domestic capital and by Non-Resident Nepalis since 1990. Between FY 2009/10 and FY 2017/18, electricity production from PEPs increased 15% annually, from 167 MW to 512 MW. According to Economic Survey of FY 2017/18, PEPs held 47.67% of the installed capacity of the country. Electricity supply is increasing (Table 8.3) and it is PEPs who is increasing electricity supply (Figure 8.1). PEPs have been responsible for adding most of the generative capacity since 1990 due to the lack of progress by the government and the NEA.

Looking to the future, Nepal must negotiate properly with its neighbors to prepare a comprehensive framework for using its water resources; it is not possible for Nepal to get benefit from shared rivers like the Mahakali, Karnali, Saptakoshi and others by going it alone. Nepal and its neighbors need to agree on rules for water use based on the principle of mutual sharing of costs and benefits. However, deep-rooted anti-Indian sentiment among a section of people who claim Nepal's sole ownership over its water resources – in contravention of international laws and conventions – remains a

38. South Asian energy nexus remains a major agenda between South Asian countries to fulfill each other's energy gap. The agenda drew lot of attention when SAARC meetings were in process. For this purpose, SAARC Framework Agreement for Energy Cooperation was signed between member nations in November 2014 but there was little progress on it. BIMSTEC, of which Nepal is also a member, is also heading in the same line of energy cooperation between its member countries. The important actor to materialize these initiatives is India because all cross border transmission needs to be set up through India. It depends on India's geo-political interest to establish such energy network.

serious barrier. Such mindsets must be changed through continuous education and dissemination of accurate information. Such initiative must benefit Nepal with prior agenda but not at the cost of ill effects to neighbors.

Table 8.3: Hydropower Generation of Nepal (in Million KWH)

Fiscal Year	Hydropower Generation
1990/91	872.5
1995/96	1188.9
2000/01	1641.9
2005/06	2514.68
2010/11	3064.32
2015/16	3294.32
2017/18*	2202.23

Source: Various Issues of *Economic Survey*, MOF
*First Seven Months

Figure 8.1: Installed Capacity of Nepal Electricity Authority and Private Electricity Producers for Selects Years (in MW)

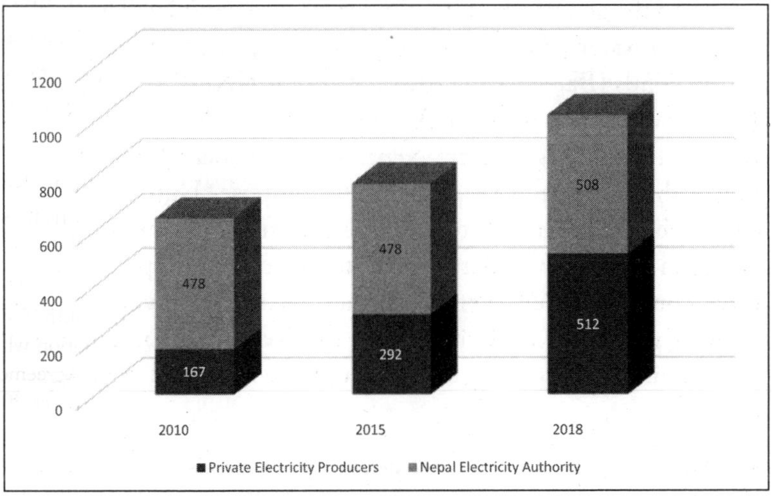

Source: Various Issues of *Economic Survey*, MOF

Besides electricity, water resources are important from two other perspectives as well. First, water is required for agriculture, the primary job creator in the country. Nepal's inability to fully join the Green Revolution is due in part to its lack of attention to irrigation. With its abundant water resources, Nepal should have been able to irrigate all its farmland, prioritizing the plains of the Terai and inner-Terai valleys. However, the government failed to sufficiently develop irrigation, with only about a quarter of farms receiving year-round irrigation facilities. Despite ample irrigation budgets over the past sixty years, misplaced priorities and poor vision meant that Nepal went from being a net food-surplus country to net food-deficit nation since 1989. The Bheri-Babai diversion project, which is still under construction, is a landmark effort to increase irrigation. Similar efforts are required to complete the Sunkoshi-Kamala diversion and to undertake the recently proposed Sunkoshi Marine Project, linking the Sunkoshi with the Bagmati.

Fresh water for drinking and other industrial and household purposes is another area of great importance. However, the fast depletion of fresh water resources will lead to shortages in meeting the needs of a growing population. We speculate that, while the period from the 1970s to the 2030s will be marked by a petroleum crisis and the aftermath of it[39], the succeeding period will be marked by a fresh water crisis, leading to wars to capture water resources[40] by the 2050s (Bajracharya, 2013). A recent UNDP report predicts a severe water crisis in South Asia by 2040 (UN, 2018). As a country with abundant fresh water, Nepal should manage and commercialize the resource with mission and purpose. Unfortunately, to date we have been unable to meet our own requirements and almost all urban areas now suffer from water shortages. Nepal must first meet domestic requirements and then try to create value to meet growing global needs. Besides these, river systems are important for maintaining bio-diversity, environmental security and preservation,

39. War in Iraq may be mainly attributed to petroleum crisis.

40. However, technological developments that make desalination less costly could significantly mitigate the problem. Otherwise, fresh water crisis will engulf most part of the world in the coming era, if not it has already begun.

fishing and water sports that would be affected by hydro power projects.

In sum, hydropower and roads have not fulfilled their potential to contribute to the national economy since the 1990s. Some important initiatives have been taken, such as community electrification[41], which has increased access to electricity in rural areas. New roads and hydropower have provided more opportunities for economic activities among local people. In some cases, new infrastructure has been complemented by donor-funded programs for capacity-building and awareness, helping people capitalize on the new opportunities. However, a large part of the country remains untouched by such economic-package programs. Many local markets remain rudimentary, focused on retailing inbound goods in the absence of locally sustainable economic activities.

8.5 Communications Nepal's postal service was established during the Rana regime and remained the primary means of communication during the Panchayat era. The Postal Act was introduced in 1963 to strengthen the institutional capacity of the General Post Office, and the Domestic Postal Goods (Insurance) Act was introduced in 1962 to regulate insurance of goods dispatched by the post. The government also focused on developing a postal road during the Panchayat era. The government gradually began to allow international as well as domestic courier companies to operate in Nepal. Radio Nepal was established in 1951, soon after the fall of the Rana regime, with support from India. Nepal Television was established close to the end of the Panchayat era, in 1985.

41. Community electrification, an initiative to enhance rural peoples' electricity access, is run under different modalities in Nepal. In many of the rural areas of Nepal, communities are formed to construct local mini hydropower station on cost sharing basis and the generated electricity is distributed among community member households at approved tariff rate. Other modality, generally practiced in the rural areas near urban localities, is to purchase electricity from national grind by community and distribute it among member households at approved rate. The associated body with the name, National Association of Community Electricity Users-Nepal, has been formed which claims Nepal to have around 300 community electrifications. There is substantial role of community electrification in increasing rural peoples' access to electricity.

Telecommunications expanded after the government introduced the Communications Corporation Act in 1971 and subsequently formed the government-owned Nepal Telecommunications Corporation in 1975. With the advancement of technology, this corporation also began providing services like telex and fax. But acquiring a telephone line was big hassle with long delays meaning the capacity was highly limited compared to demand for such services.

The 1980s and 1990s saw some dramatic technical leaps in communications and information technology, coinciding with liberalization of the communications sector in Nepal after 1990. The Telecommunications Act of 1997 opened up the sector for private investment under the regulation of the Nepal Telecommunications Authority. The company Mercantile Communications became the first Internet Service Provider in Nepal in mid-nineties, later followed by many others. Nepal Telecommunications Corporation began to offer mobile services in the late 1990s, and this government-owned cooperation was converted into a public limited company in 2007, under the name Nepal Doorsanchar Company. In the mid-2000s, the government's monopoly over telecommunications ended with the establishment of Mero Mobile (later Ncell), the first privately owned mobile network operator. Mero Mobile was the first company to offer the Global System for Mobile (GSM) service. Many other private telecommunications companies were established in the following years.

Today, the postal service is only used for official government communications; information technology (IT) dominates the communications system in Nepal as is the case elsewhere. The number of persons using telephones, cell phones and internet has increased[42]. However, IT quality standards remain poor. Due to the

42. In the first year of establishment of Nepal Telecom Authority, it had issued telephone license to 2 providers, cellular mobile license to 2 providers and internet license to 31 providers. Economic Survey of 2018/19 states that there are 6 telephone and cellular mobile companies in Nepal along with government owned Nepal Doorsanchar Company. Number of mobile distributed has increased from 15.33 million in FY 2011/12 to 37.55 million in FY 2018/19 and there are 12.29 million internet customers in 2015/16. The increase in communication facilities is primarily due to its extensive use for commercial activities. By FY 2018/19, license

low internet bandwidth available from most internet service providers, the government attempted to set up an IT park with high-speed internet in Kavre district, near Kathmandu, in the 2000s. However, because most IT workers are engaged informally, few showed interest in the IT park which would require them to formalize their work and pay taxes. Today, the IT park is only partially occupied. Perhaps the park would have been more successful had the government provided more incentives for IT operators or linked with optical fiber connectivity when it did not exist in other part of the country. Unfortunately, it is an example of a government initiative undertaken without proper foresight. With the increasing use of IT, government is gradually brining laws and regulations to regulate and control IT crime and cyber cell has also been instituted as an important organ of security agency but technical capacity needs to be enhanced

After the change of 1990, media is legitimized as the fourth organ of democracy by political circuit to ensure freedom of speech so many new media houses and newspapers come up but censorship was imposed time and again during the time of Maoist armed revolution and King's short takeover in 2002 to 2006. Surprisingly, media council bill brought by the recent NCP government has also made people suspicious about the government trying to control media, social media and other contrary to the freedom of expression right strongly enshrined in Nepal's 2015 constitution.

8.6 Conclusion Nepali infrastructure, almost non-existent at the dawn of democracy in early fifties, has made some notable progress with the benevolent support of its development partners and some right initiatives on its own. Connectivity has improved to all district headquarters barring one, Simikot in Humla, contributing to easier movements and opening up of opportunities for economic activities. Despite the improvement in connectivity, the flaws included poor quality of roads, lack of regular maintenance, wild expansion

---

has been issued for 658 FM stations and 47 TV stations operated regularly. Up to FY 2018/19, the government has also issued licenses for 731 daily newspapers published in different languages.

particularly at local level without serious consideration of environmental implications and more importantly development of road infrastructure on the assumption that such connectivity will lead to economic progress. Despite a lot of truth in it and some visible impacts, in many cases the assumption did not prove right and contributed to enhanced imports and external dependency. Lack of integration with economic opportunities[43], has visible implications on inability to promote meaningful initiatives. The needs, hence, in this respect is to have a right vision at least for next 50 years, improve connectivity not only by linkages but by quality of connectivity and the standard of infrastructure, that is one of the major visible indicator of the status of development.

Despite being the second country in Asia to develop a hydropower plant, we entered into dark age – literally – suffering up to 17 years of power outage in a country positioned enviably with its water resource. Proper development has the potential to transform the country with far reaching consequence particularly in availing water to agriculture, the foundation of Nepali economy and supplying drinking water not only for its nationals but also for a large number of regional/ global population. The need, therefore, is to have right envisioning and developing resources both for the nation's populations as well as serving humanity.

Communication sector has developed concurrent to global development but initiatives in speed, technology, early reach and focused development may take the country in a new plateau and prospects with a potential to add value and extend additional competitiveness.

Of course, we can neither ignore the costs nor the environmental implications while ensuring requisite development of infrastructure as a foundation for quick, efficient and humane growth. We may have lost important time but it is never late to lay a proper foundation for meaningful and purposive development.

43. Karnali highway was started in 1979 that included the economic package of apple farming in the Karnali zone with a promise that apple production and road completion will simultaneously contribute for the development of the region. Apples were produced but road reached two decades after the promised date.

chapter 9

THE FINAL WORDS

9.1 The Setting Nepal's history has been shaped by its location at the confluence of the cultural and political spheres of China and the Indian subcontinent. This has come with certain opportunities. For example, the country has long served as a transit point for trade between Tibet/ China and the Indian subcontinent, and as a waypoint for travelers; scholars from China and Tibet visited India to receive Buddhist teachings in various periods particularly during and after the 7th century. But Nepal's proximity to two giant powers has also brought risks. King Prithvi Narayan Shah of Gorkha unified modern Nepal in order to counter the threat of British colonization from the south. Following the formation of the Nepali nation-state in the 18th century, Nepal fought several wars with British India, Tibet, and China. However, due to the physical barrier posed by the Himalayas along Nepal's northern border, it has historically depended on trade with the south more than with the north.

During the middle ages, Nepal's rulers attempted to impose the Hindu caste system on society, beginning a long trend of state oppression of the working castes. Under the Rana regime, the Hindu caste system was codified and imposed even more harshly. Rather than stimulating the economy, the state under the Ranas became narrowly focused on accumulating wealth through taxation, although there were some limited initiatives to establish an education and health system, foster industries, and begin economic planning. The Ranas became dependent on patronage and guidance from the British in India, which remained Nepal's only avenue to the outside world.

Following the fall of the Rana regime, Nepal set out on the path of development during the short democratic interlude of the 1950s. After the King took over power in 1960, the government continued to emphasize the importance of development and carried out state driven programs to this end. However, the vision for real transformation was mostly amiss.

9.2 Democracy, Political Parties and Development With the restoration of democracy in 1990, the political parties attempted to expedite Nepal's development along new pathways. The two forces that contributed most to the 1990 democracy movement – the liberal Nepali Congress (NC) and the leftists – had also fought against the Ranas to bring about the democratic change of 1951, and would topple the monarchy together in 2006, at the helm of a massive popular movement.

While the NC and the leftists held different views about the correct path for development, their political discourse often devolved into name-calling and lacked a hard policy focus. The NC portrayed leftists as a threat to democracy because of their belief in communism, whereas the leftists accused the NC of selling out the country's sovereignty to India. Neither of these forces articulated a clear policy vision to address Nepal's opportunities, challenges, and constraints. Instead, they concentrated on advocating basic fundamental rights – a strategy that was possibly motivated by their interest in gaining easy popularity among the people. The political parties' manifestos and other documents made tall promises, but few of them were feasible and even fewer were acted upon.

There is generally a tradeoff between high economic growth and institutionalization of basic fundamental rights at least among some erudite segments though taking both together is always more desirable. However, the political parties ignored this tradeoff and costs of taking both together by making promises to achieve both. Nepal's leftists have advocated a broad approach guaranteeing basic rights, economic growth, and development. They have learned little from Communist China, which pursued economic dynamism at the expense of individual liberties. Even the NC, which initiated economic liberalization measures during the 1990s, has made intermittent commitments reiterating its socialist foundations.

Nepal has promulgated a series of new constitutions since the mid-20th century, reflecting the frequency of dramatic political changes. The 1951 Interim Constitution – enacted immediately after the 1951 democratic revolution – replaced the 1947 Constitution. This was in turn replaced by a new Constitution in 1959, which was followed by parliamentary elections to institutionalize democracy. After the King took over power in 1960, a new constitution was promulgated in 1962. The 1962 Constitution was amended in 1980 to introduce some democratic features. Another Constitution came following the restoration of multi-party democracy in 1990, which was replaced by the Interim Constitution of 2006, followed shortly by elections to the Constituent Assembly. In 2015, the Constituent Assembly became the first democratically elected body in Nepal to promulgate a new Constitution, which is the current law of the land.

With the exception of the regressive 1962 Constitution, which curtailed fundamental rights, Nepal's constitutions have become increasingly more progressive, prescribing more and more rights as well as broader access to them. The current 2015 constitution has conferred 33 fundamental rights – an encouraging step towards empowering citizens. However, these changes have not been complemented by sustainable economic progress and improvements in the quality of life. For example, while the 2015 Constitution defines education and health as fundamental rights, functional institutional mechanisms to guarantee use of these rights do not exist.

9.3 Planning and Budgeting Despite numerous political changes Nepal has experienced, the development planning process remains essentially the same as it was when it began in the 1950s. The planning framework remains dichotomous, inconsistent, and non-continuous. Most development plans contain wide-ranging visions and goals, but fall short when it comes to focused strategies or priorities. Goals and objectives are repeatedly shifted from one plan to the next, without achieving desired outcomes.

The government has made several attempts to reform the budgeting process, but with little success. Annual budgets brought under the guidance of development plans lack clear vision, often bearing little resemblance to the plans. The introduction of various budgeting strategies to streamline public expenditures, such as performance-based budgeting, program-based budgeting, the mid-term expenditure framework and the result oriented framework have required constant reorientation of government officials, but with few positive results. No new budgeting system has had time to be successfully institutionalized before it is changed again or despite development of the system, we were late to realize and encompass them on time. That too generally due to efforts of the development partners.

Likewise, attempts to reform capital expenditure practices have also been mostly unsuccessful, if not downright counter-productive. The Procurement Act, 2007 attempted to tighten controls on contracting for large-scale construction works to make them more timely and transparent. However, the Act was a gross failure. It did not significantly curb corruption, but it did drastically curtail the government's capacity to spend. Likewise, activism by the Center for Investigation of the Abuse of Authority has not encouraged fairer initiatives. Instead, it has discouraged government officials from undertaking even minimal risk for example tendency of avoiding decisions to the extent possible is emerging. Many other cases can be found where the government has brought about new reforms without properly evaluating their effects. Beyond the introduction of VAT, which has revolutionized revenue mobilization, and some other tax reforms, few initiatives to increase or plan public revenue have been successful.

9.4 Positive Achievements Since 1990, economic liberalization has contributed to market dynamism and economic growth. However, had the government not been preoccupied with settling political instability from the late 1990s onwards, the pace of development would have been much faster.

A leftist-led government introduced the elderly pension scheme in 1994/95, opening the door for the welfare state. Due to the Maoist movement as well as independent activism, the government instituted new policies for social inclusion; proportional representation became an important feature of the new republic after the abolition of the monarchy. The Constitution of 2015 and ensuing political stability has contributed to the achievement of an unprecedented annual growth rate of over 7% during the period FY 2016/17-FY2018/19.

Important achievements have been made regarding infrastructure development. Road connectivity has increased significantly in the last three decades reaching more than 60 thousands km[1] and connecting all but one district headquarter, Humla, where construction is going on, is the only left to be connected, and there is also much greater access to electricity, drinking water, communications, education, and health services. Foreign exchange reserves have also increased due to remittance flow, although labor migration is itself a symptom of political conflict and joblessness in the country. There have also been some improvements in terms of decentralization of development initiatives.

9.5 Shortcomings Despite the progress noted, Nepal's economic development has been slow and unsteady relative to other countries in South Asia. Corruption and a rent-seeking attitude are deeply rooted in politics and the bureaucracy, jeopardizing the development process. The state administrative capacity remains weak and has a conservative orientation, limiting its ability to realize desired outcomes. There is also a lack of coordination between different government organizations both horizontally among different ministries and institutions and vertically among the federal, provincial and local governments.

In agriculture, the country has gone from being a food-surplus nation to a food-deficit one since 1989. Agricultural and land

1. According to the Economic Survey 2018/19, the total road length of Nepal is 31393 km and the road construction by local level is 60,163 km. However, out of the total of over 90 thousands km only about 60 thousands km is motorable.

reform initiatives have failed to deliver. Today, only about a fourth of cultivated land is under year-round irrigation, despite Nepal's ample water resources.

The initial boom observed in the industrial sector during the mid-1990s could not be sustained after the cessation of favorable trade agreements with Western countries like the MFA. Industry has remained stagnant since then, failing to create a significant number of jobs. While cheap electricity could have spurred domestic industry, less than three percent of the country's total hydropower potential has been harnessed and the country remains dependent on imported power from India. The cost of doing business is high due to the government's inefficiency, harsh terrain, poor connectivity and infrastructure and bureaucratic red-tape. Enforcement of quality standards is lax, further catapulting costs for potential entrepreneurs.

Furthermore, political instability has weakened the market environment, contributing fewer jobs and forcing millions of Nepalis to leave the country in search of employment, often under harsh conditions abroad. Likewise, the government has paid little attention to efforts in education and skills training to improve workers' productivity, instead focusing on populist topics like fundamental rights. Given the low domestic production, Nepal's trade deficit with its major trade partners has increased. The current account balance and balance of payment deficit is precarious, and may counteract the positive effects of development initiatives over the long term.

9.6 Conclusion Nepal, thus, has a long but chequered history of development having dawned civilization relatively at an early era and despite efforts of many, however, inconsistent and sporadic development had led to the present situation of poverty, deprivation and underdevelopment with the tag of "Least Developed Country". The biggest challenge has been the lack of a strong and all-encompassing vision without assessing the possible implications thereof that persist even today.

The unification of the country definitely was an act of farsightedness that despite being small in size presented a strong sense of nationhood and withstood foreign aggressions. But some of King Prithvi's strategies acclaimed as the 'holy gospel' have negative implications for example Nepal losing entrepot position and the 'self-sufficiency' approach leading to low level equality. But Nepal could not present similar acumen in the 'soft' war or the diplomatic standing for which numerous illustrations are available of submitting to pressures as is evident from Sugauli Treaty (1817), 1923's treaty with British India, 1950's treaty on Peace and Friendship and treaties on major rivers (Koshi, Gandak and Tanakpur). King Mahendra did show penchant for initiating development, and despite being accorded 'visionary', by many, actually could not think 'big' probably being bogged down by challenges to preserve and protect the undemocratic system and sustain the royal power. King Birendra, hailed as a liberal king, was probably one of the weakest kings of the Shah dynasty and did not provide the requisite leadership for the transformation of the nationhood culminating in pseudo reforms and development initiatives during 30 years of his reign.

After the successful first people's movement in 1990, Ganesh Man Singh, who led the movement, announced that the political revolution had ended and we should march towards economic revolution. Many leaders agreed with it but we have been continuously bogged down by political instability and change. Aspirations and signals of marching towards faster growth with equity has yet to be seen.

The discourse on development during the last two decades or so have been focused on rights and right based approaches at the cost of economic sense as is evident from lack of integrated approaches, very weak coordination (World Bank, 2019b) and high costs of development with the quality of results being poor, unsustainable and lacking tangibility. This preoccupation in politics and political development is manifest in governance, society and the outcomes. The result has been continuation of power struggle despite promulgation of the Constitution2015 and the culmination into political stability. Leadership is emphasized but ownership is ignored meaning current initiatives are founded on the castle of sand.

We have continuously engaged in balancing relations with the neighbors, both in south as well as north, but we have failed to do so, the trust of both appears to be dwindling indicating our inability in governance and diplomacy.

Our policies and efforts do face more ideological struggle than during the actual implementation. Liberalization policies did lay a foundation of growth, explaining growth even when the government has neither shown energy nor ability towards economic transformation. The policies have had to face bumps and barriers and there were reversals in some even breaching international treaties and conventions. The initiators of the policies were also confused with dichotomous discourses due to lack of confined vision and proper analysis.

Lack of economic sense in infrastructure was exhibited by emphasis on connectivity and promoting feeling of nationality with the assumption that connectivity will promote economic development that did not prove to be true in many cases as is also illustrated by impact studies. Desired results could not be consequently harnessed. We try to search answers once the real challenges emerge for example what to do with surplus electricity during the summer particularly at the end of last decade and the beginning of current decade or what activities to promote where. Additional investment in production could have yielded desired results, which, however, was never done. In view of the potential, tourism was promoted everywhere but similar vigour was not exhibited in India and China with far greater potential. On the one hand, we continue to argue about decelerating competitive advantage and, on the other, went on hiking the minimum wages ignoring productivity, probably one of the illustrations of emphasizing rights based approach only.

Similarly, in the education and training, we did not promote economic capacity but rather unknowingly laid a foundation to encourage migration clearly revealing the contrast of what is intended and what are the actual results.

So, even if the words are harsh, it may be deduced that we have not simply initiated development, Whatever, little is done are due to vested interest or because of unintended outcomes generally bogged down by perspective of retaining to power and signaling the Nepali populace with claims of 'bigger development' not supported by investment, activities and initiatives. Finally, the country's recent political transformation to a federal republic has yet to be properly institutionalized. Further, political instability is a possibility, especially given the increasing inequality in wealth and income. This is compounded by the fact that political parties have been unable to address poverty and inequality by proposing and executing feasible development agendas. As a result, the country is moving ahead without a clear direction.

9.7 The Path of Growth with Equity Ensuring Appropriate Quality of Life Our argument is Nepal has chaos and confusion for long not commensurate neither to needs nor to potentials despite suffered from varied political exercises and attempts. The vision, as is rightly enshrined in the constitution, is 'prosperity' with a focus on complete transformation in the quality of life. The quality of life, needs to be defined in clear terms, if needed going beyond the definition of the UN's physical quality of life and the quality of life indicator defined by The Economist (2005), encompassing our own values and aspirations and focusing on the task. The discourse should be taken to political, expertise and people's levels ensuring that the minimum agreements and goals are not changed though strategies to attain them may be different depending on political beliefs and ideologies. The detailed approaches, strategies and way-outs, weaving around – 'Quality of Life' – will be presented in the forthcoming book. The present volume has presented Nepal's economic history and the nature of its development challenges. A forthcoming work will explore policy prescriptions and reform measures to transform the nation regaing paradise and steer it on a clearer course of sustained growth with equity with proper distribution to ensure a sound quality of life to all Nepali populace.

ANNEXES

Annex A:

Social Exclusion Context of Nepal

Nepal is a multi-cultural and multi-lingual society of different caste and ethnic groups inhabited by Indo-Aryans and Mongoloid Tibetan-Burmese people (Bista, 1967, Sharma, 2004 and Gurung, 2006). The rulers of medieval period which included kingdom of Nepal valley[1] and other parts of current Nepal adopted caste hierarchy system adopted in the syncretic society where Buddhism, Vaisnavism, Shaivism and Tantrism coexisted (Bista, 1991 and Sharma, 2004[2]). The caste system in Nepal is basically based on Hindu Caste Hierarchy borrowed from India in which Brahmin (Priests) and Chhetri (Warriors) are highest in level respectively followed by Vaishay[3] and Sudra/Dalits[4]. There is discrimination and social exclusion of last two caste groups, Vaishay and Sudra/Dalit. The kingship of succeeding eras continued the same caste hierarchy system with minimal amendments because it helped to consolidate the state power to king's court and legitimized king's legacy (Bista, 1991 and Sharma, 2004). After taking over the power,

1. Nepal Valley means the territories ruled by the kings of Kathmandu valley.

2. Bista (1991) and Sharma (2004) argued that caste system of Nepal has lineage with Hindu Caste hierarchy system of India but there were some differences in caste classification system.

3. Vaishay includes Traders, Farmers, Occupational Caste (like Halwai-confectioners, Teli-oil pressers and others) and indigenous and ethnic communities following religions other than Hindu. Gurung (2006) reported that though indigenous and ethnic communities were allowed to follow their own culture, the punishments against their religious offences were harsh.

4. Sudra is untouchables that includes occupational caste groups like barber, menial and slump worker, blacksmith, butcher and others.

Ranas further strengthened the institutional structure of Hindu caste hierarchy by codifying it in the country's Civil Code in 1854 to reinforce and tightening of the society by the oligarchic rulers (Sharma, 2004). Brahimins, being of the highest caste hierarchy, were exempted from certain taxes (Caplan, 1970). Punishment for crime also varied on caste basis as Brahmins were exempted from capital punishment. The codification of caste system was also predominantly influenced by the same old politics of persisting power and accumulating the strength of regime. Bista (1991) argued that there were many instances of High Caste Ranas being demoralized and penalized with downgraded punishment for their resistance and low caste loyal Ranas being rewarded with upgradation. Thus, socio-economic structure of Nepal was primitive (Regmi, 1984 and 1988). The caste group of priests and warriors predominated land and state administration which also meant predomination in agriculture and national wealth (Caplan, 1970 and Adhikari, 2010). The occupational caste group and indigenous ethnic communities were ranked lowest in this hierarchy and have limited land and therefore needed to serve landlords (basically priests and warriors) for agro-work besides their occupational work designated by caste (Kisan, 2009).

Rawal (2008) argued that Brahmins and Chhetris, who are most privileged among all caste and ethnic communities, have remained in positions of power since the ancient past thus giving continuity to the feudal society. They used such privileges to shape and reshape the country's governance system and social value in favor of their own communities which consequently diverted the available opportunities and resources away from Vaishay, Dalits and other indigenous ethnic and religious communities. Likewise, Bista (1991) claimed that this type of perception is the metaphor of what has been commonly termed as hegemony. Janajatis (Indigenous Populaces) of Nepal who fall under Vaishay caste category don't have the privilege of state ownership and political decisions due to cultural hegemony of Brahmin/ Chhetri (Bhattachan, 2009). Further, their traditions, which differ significantly from Brahmin/ Chhetri, are gradually pushed into the verge of extinction or were marginalized. Dalits, regarded as untouchable, are ranked lowest in caste group so they are suppressed by all (Kisan, 2009). A social custom of the water being touched by Dalits becomes impure explains the extent of social discriminatory practices prevailed in the country at the time. The dimension of social exclusion can be understood from two angles: impure and enslave-able (Gurung, 2003 and 2006). There is enslavement of religious minority groups and indigenous ethnic groups by majority religious groups. In terms of caste, Dalits are regarded as impure and are enslaved by high caste groups for their manual work (viz. blacksmith, barber, plumber, Haliyas, Kamaiyas, Kamlaris and others). The monthly menstruation of women is symbolized as impure forcing them to live in cow sheds or other such places in some parts of the country particularly the far and middle west and Dalit women faced dual discrimination of gender and caste.

During political revolution against Ranas, amelioration league of Dalits with the name – Dalit Nirbarak Sangh – was formed in Kolkata. After 1950's political change, there were commitments from the leaders to address the issues of social exclusion. King Mahendra, after taking power, amended Civil Code in 1962 which declared untouchability and discrimination as illegal and a punishable act. Likewise, after 1990 change, different measures were taken to address social malpractices and the issue is progressively raised by donor communities like DFID, NORAD, EU and others as well. But, the changes and reforms wasn't gradual and the grievances of marginalized and excluded were banked by Maoists during armed revolution making social exclusion as a political agenda that enabled them to mobilize cadres from ethnic indigenous communities and Dalits. Maoists also pursued the interest of marginalized and excluded by creating ethnic based parallel governments during armed revolution (Gellner, 2008). The Interim Constitution 2006, which was enacted after the Comprehensive Peace Agreement with Maoists, provisioned proportional representation of different caste groups in the house of parliament. The Identity based political parties like Federal Socialist Forum and Rastriya Janata Party emerged with large scale Terai movement. The present Constitution of Nepal (2015) continued proportional representation in the house of federal parliament and provincial parliament and it has provisioned different constitutional commissions to address social exclusion and country's social diversity thus really creating a foundation for inclusion and promoting inclusive society. However, social exclusion still remains an issue in Nepal debated in diverse dimensions and it is important to understand that all reforms after 1950's and 1990's political changes had linchpin of conservative orientation based on traditional social norms and only Maoists put it on a totally different platform and perspective.

Annex B:

History of Nepal's Trade with India and Tibet/ China

Geography has favored Nepal's trade with India much more than it has favored trade with the northern neighbor. Nepal has a long history of relying on India for almost all imported goods, and populous towns along the border have also served as large markets for Nepali products. Indian cities like Patna, Lucknow, Gorakhpur, Nautanawa, Muzaffarpur, Darbhanga, Purnea, and others were the most prominent markets for Nepali traders, beginning in the early eighteenth century (Regmi, 1984).[1] Indian currency was used as the medium of exchange in many parts of Nepal.

On the other hand, Rose (1971) and Regmi (1965) argue that the geographical closeness with India also invited political threats. King Prithvi Narayan Shah's initiative to unify Nepal was partly in response to the threat posed by the expansion of British-controlled territory in India. The Gorkhali war with British India culminated in the signing of the Sugauli Treaty in 1817, in which Nepal gave up many of its territories to British India (Stiller, 1989 and Rose, 1971). This treaty also prevented Nepal from establishing diplomatic ties with third countries without British consent. So while Nepal remained independent, British India held pseudo control over Nepal's large-scale trading and commercial activities.

1. Regmi (1988) reports that there were a number of *golas* (markets) along the east-west Terai belt. For example, Bhangaruwa in Saptari was one of the main trade centers in eastern Nepal, whereas Brahmadeo of Dadeldhura was the main market center for the far-western region. There were also market centers in Birgunj, Butwal, Koilabas, Nepalgunj, Golamadi and other places.

After coming to power in 1846, the Ranas adopted a strategy of strengthening Nepal's relationship with the British in order to secure their regime. Jung Bahadur Rana supported British India during the 1857 Rebellion[2] and other Rana Prime Ministers supported the British in during World Wars I and II. In 1923, Nepal and British India signed a new treaty recognizing Nepal's independence and sovereignty, and for the first time granting transit facilities to Nepal for overseas trade (Panday, 1999).[3] However, the Ranas did not seek to build diplomatic relations beyond the British because of possible threat of doing so that could invite to their own regime (Panday, 1999). This self-imposed isolation suited British interests, as it allowed British India to maintain monopolistic influence in the region. Nepal exported unprocessed goods and commodities to India and imported processed and manufactured goods (Regmi, 1988). The trade relationship was well-illustrated by the construction of a British railways to locations along the Nepali border, such as at Janakpur. The main interest of the British in bringing the railway to Nepal was to buy Nepali timber needed for enhancing Indian railway connectivity (Panday, 1999). The Ranas were happy to sell the timber and thereby increase their treasury. As a result, the Terai was deforested, which also made connectivity between the Hill and Terai regions of Nepal easier. However, the Ranas never considered the environmental impact of deforestation.

Due to Nepal's strong economic integration with India, the dual currency system persisted in Nepal, with both Indian and Nepali currency used for economic transactions. The exchange rate between these two currencies was extremely volatile due to the absence of any regulatory body, and opportunities abounded for currency arbitrage.

On the other hand, the geographical terrain along the border with Tibet/ China is rugged mountains and many areas are not fit for travel during the winter. During the Rana Regime, most trade

2. This rebellion, known as Sepoy Rebellion, was launched by soldiers to free India from the rule of East India Company (British).

3. Refer to Panday, 1999; pp 306-307

routes to Tibet/ China were unpaved, narrow passages fit for only foot or animal traffic (Regmi, 1984). It was difficult even for small wooden carts to pass through these narrow passages, hindering trade flow. Lewis and Shakya (1988) argued that trade with Tibet/ China was via. border point of Humla, Mustang, Kerung, Kuti, Oallngchungola and Kimathangka among which Kathmandu-Kerung and Kathmandu-Kuti were main routes and it is ethnic communities of Newars and Thakalis who dominated the trade with Tibet/ China. Further, Tibet/ China and its major cities like Lhasa, Shigatse, Gyantse and others were not populous and big markets in comparison to neighboring cities of India. So the trade with Tibet/ China was at a low scale compared to India. Despite the fact that trading with Tibet/ China was small in volume, it was lifeline for Tibetan people. So there was wide circulation of Nepali currency in Tibet/ China. This predomination leaded to several invasion of Nepal over Tibet/ China and Tibetans often needed support of Chinese to thrash Nepal's interest. The 1856 Treaty between Ranas and Tibet/ China was result of one such attempt under which Nepal was obliged to support Tibet/ China in the case of a foreign invasion (Rose, 1971). But the benevolence of Rana was always towards British and Cowan (2015) argues that, specifically Chandra Shumsher, was even ready to breach this treaty to support British. After colonization of India, British was more focused on using Nathu La[4] as entrepôt in trade with Tibet and Main Land China so there was gradual decline in Nepal's transit trade with Tibet/ China (Rana and Karmacharya, 2014). So Pant (1962) argues that the traditional Newari traders of Kathmandu needed to make Darjeeling and Kalimpong of India as commercial hub for transit trade with Tibet/ China via Nathu La. There was also major political change in Nepal's northern border during late forties as China became People's Republic in 1949 and it made Tibet its autonomous Region in 1950. The ruler of Tibet, Dalai Lama, fled via Nepal to take political asylum in India. A large number of Tibetans, who were against this Chinese annexation fled

4. Nathu La was border point of Tibet/ China and Kingdom of Sikkim. It becomes border point of India and China after Sikkim was annexed by India in 1975.

to Nepal as refugees and government allowed them to settle in Boudha, Ekantakuna and Pokhara. Immediately after takeover, China also built Peking to Tibet road which also contributed to dwindle Nepal's trade with North (Pant, 1962). The commercial activities of Newari traders in Tibet became standstill as there was border dispute between India and China in 1962 which completely stopped the possibility to use Nathu La as entrepôt to trade with Tibet. Hilker (2005) states that all Newar traders returned to Kathmandu and commercial potential of Darjeeling and Kalimpong dried up. In 1956, Nepal and People's Republic China signed treaty of cooperation and development for first time and it was followed by series of treaties in succeeding years under which many development activities were carried in the areas of transport, industrialization, agriculture, cultural exchange and many others. China is sensitive of Tibetan refugees in Nepal and their anti-China movement. Trade between two countries was at low volume but it increased after mid of 2000's decade reflecting China's increasing ability to meet global requirement.

Annex C: Review of Manifestos of Main Political Parties for Post 1990 Elections

Table C1: Brief Review of Nepali Congress Manifestos

Mission, Goals and Party Ideology	Visions and Strategies	Threats, Constraints and Challenges	Prioritizes		
			1991	2008	2017
• People's Sovereignty and Supremacy • Parliamentary Democracy (dropped Constitutional Monarchy and adopted Federal Democratic Republic since 2008's CA I) • Pluralist Federal Democratic Republic (added from 2008's First CA onward) • Democratic Socialism	• People Centric state to address grievances and problem • Make people aware of basic fundamental rights • Poverty alleviation, employment generation and increase income level through economic liberalization • Rural and regional development • Decentralization • Good governance and accountability	• Kingship and its traditional feudalist and autocratic approach (dropped in 2017 election) • Leftist's inclination toward establishing socialist republic and autocratic regime • Conservative and backward society • Landlocked and difficult geographic terrain	• Progressive agriculture development, land reform and irrigation • Infrastructure development for foundation of economy (transport, communication, hydropower and airways) • Mutual cost and benefit sharing in bilateral water treaty • Industrialization, commercialization, tourism, progressive tax and price control • Utilization of foreign aid for development • Foreign diplomacy (equidistance with neighbors and friendly relations with all)	• Peace and reconciliation • Extensive investment promotion • Infrastructure development (transport, communication, IT, hydropower and airways) • Mutual cost and benefit sharing in bilateral water treaty • Community led development • Cooperative movement • Agriculture Development, agro-tourism and farmers' right • Industrialization, commercialization and promote export potential • Manage and control foreign employment	• Reason of coalition with RPP • "Youth For New Nepal" and youth entrepreneurship development • Effective utilization of water resource, medicinal plants and nature • Tourism to reintroduce Nepal • Foreign diplomacy (equidistance with neighbors and friendly relations with All) • Trade union and good industrial relationship • Assure Social Security • Farmers' right and agriculture modernization • Revitalize industry • Encouragement to women entrepreneurs • Non-Resident Nepali and foreign employment

<table>
<tr>
<td>• To attain economic growth, development and prosperity
• To empower people with fundamental rights and freedom of expression and speech
• Equity and Justice ("Social" was prefixed from 2008's First CA onward onward)
• Strong Nationalism and National Unity
• Constitutional Supremacy and Rule of Law</td>
<td>• Access to Justice
• Social Inclusion (added from 2008's First CA onward)
• Human Resource Development
• Restructuring of State and its Institution (committed in 2017 election)</td>
<td>• Federal demarcation proposed by Maoist and Identity Based Parties (in 2008 and 2013's CA election manifesto)</td>
<td>• Women participation and children development
• Uplift Backward communities and Janajatis and abolish bonded labors (Kamaiya)
• Squatter settlement and population control
• Effective mobilization of labors, teachers, experts, students and youths
• Promote language, literature and culture
• Innovation in science, technology and communication
• Effective utilization of Forest and natural conservation
• Address citizenship problem
• Honor to ex-army (freedom fighters), martyrs and politically affected persons
• Basic service (health, drinking water and education)
• Civil service reform and Security</td>
<td>• Tourism development
• Foreign diplomacy (equidistance with neighbors and friendly relations with all)
• Provide education, health, food security, labor right and social security,
• Effective mobilization of youth and support to senior citizen
• Honor ex-army (freedom fighters)
• Civil service reform and security
• Promote art and literature
• Uplift Indigenous, Madheshi, Backward region, Women, Dalits, Old aged, Disables, Children, Kamaiya, Landless and Third Sex
• Environment conservation and management
• Urbanization and settlement</td>
<td>• Cooperative and Access to Finance
• Infrastructure development (irrigation, transport, communication, IT, hydropower and airways)
• Mutual cost and benefit sharing in bilateral water treaty
• Settlement and urbanization
• Special Infrastructure for Terai Madhesh
• Quality education
• Reliable basic health service
• Protect old-ages and disables
• Women empowerment
• Honor ex-army and revolutionist
• Effective utilization of forestry,
• Disaster management
• Minimize climate change and protect environment
• Institutionalization of federalism
• Industrialization, commercialization and promote export potential
• Railway development</td>
</tr>
</table>

Table C2: Brief Review of Nepal Communist Party (UML) Manifestos*

Mission, Goals and Party Ideology	Visions and Strategies	Threats, Constraints and Challenges	Prioritizes	
			1991	2008
• Peoples' Neo-Democracy and Socialism/ Communism • Economic growth, development and prosperity • Progressive fundamental right • Human right and political freedom • Protect country's sovereignty • Pluralist Federal Democratic Republic (added from 2008's first CA onward) • Social security and welfare • Equity and Justice ("Social" was prefixed from 2008's First CA onward)	• People centric state to address grievances and problems • Make people attentive about semi-feudalism and semi-imperialism threat to Nepal and promote nationalism • Poverty alleviation and employment generation and increase income level through massive mobilization of national capital • Minimize economic dependency of the country by promoting export and national capitalist class and discouraging import	• Semi-feudalist and semi-imperialist Approach of Western Countries and Their Financial Institutions • Geo-political interest of neighbors in making Nepal's dependency • Liberal parties' inclination to foreign forces and western world • Biased international treaties and border problem • Kingship and his interest to hold ultimate state power • Conservative and backward Society	• Agriculture development and assure farmers' right • Reform against feudal land ownership • Industrial development, enhance commercial activities and foreign investment and technology to increase domestic production • Proper supply system and price control • Productive tax policy • Abolish bonded labor (Kamaiya) and uplift other backward and oppressed • Population Control, Squatter Settlement and Urbanization • Security • Prerogative right of Nepali people in its water and other resources • Mutual cost and benefit sharing in bilateral water treaty	• Progressive agriculture development, assure farmers' right and scientific land reform • Industrial development, enhance commercial activities and foreign investment and technology to increase domestic production (with special focus on potential products) • Progressive tax and Access to Finance • Basic service (education and health) • Assure social security • Welfare program to landless and squatter settlement. • Relief and justice to conflict victims • Peace and Reconciliation • Progressive labor relations

• Mixed economy leading forward to Socialism/ Communism • Cooperative and community mobilization • Rural and regional development • Decentralization • Good governance and accountability • Access to Justice • Social Inclusion (Added from 2008's First CA onward onward) • Human resource development	• Landlocked and difficult geographic terrain • Federal demarcation proposed by Maoist and Identity Based Parties (In 2008 and 2013's CA election manifesto)	• Forest management • Environment protection • Tourism development • Basic infrastructure (transport, irrigation and communication) • Basic Services (Education and Health) • Administrative reform • Women Empowerment • Assure labor right • Honor ex-army • Prerogative right of developing countries in foreign aid • Equal preference to all castes, languages and religions • Address citizenship problem • Honor martyrs and politically affected persons • Promote science and technology, knowledge and culture	• Uplift Indigenous, Madheshi Backward regions, Women, Dalits, Old-ages, Disables, Children, Kamaiya and Landless, • Development of Sports • Protect Nature and Environment • Urbanization and settlement • National security • Non Resident Nepali • Promote science and technology, culture and knowledge • Basic infrastructure (transport, irrigation, airway and communication) • Hydropower development, energy trade and mutual cost and benefit sharing in bilateral water treaty • Foreign aid for development

* UML and Maoist party headed by Prachanda joined to formed Nepal Communist Party few days prior to 2017's federal and province parliamentary election

Table C3: Brief Review of Nepal Communist Party (Maoist) Manifestos for Two CA Elections of 2008 and 2013*

Mission, Goals and Party Ideology	Visions and Strategies	Threats, Constraints and Challenges	Priorities
• People's Republic (adopted Multiparty Democracy by signing Comprehensive Peace Aggrement with major mainstream parties in 2005) • Autonomous government of ethnic communities, excluded and discriminated (later to Federalism) • Economic growth, development and prosperity • Human rights, fundamental rights and press freedom • Protect country's sovereignty	• People centric state to address grievances and problems • Restructuring of State and its Institution (Bureaucracy, Administration and Security) • Poverty alleviation and employment generation and increase income level through small industry promotion • Export focused trade • Rural development • Power devolution • Good governance and accountability	• Feudalism and imperialism of western world and their financial institutions • Geo-political interest of neighbors on keeping Nepal dependent • Liberal Parties' inclination to foreign forces and western world • Biased international treaties and border problem • Kingship and its repeated retrogressive steps • Conservative and backward society • Landlocked and difficult geographic terrain	• Peace, reconciliation, readjustment and resettlement of People's Army • Agriculture development and assure farmers' right • Reform against feudal land ownership • Proper supply system and price control • Population control and squatter settlement • Prerogative right of Nepali people in its natural as well as water resource • Hydropower development and mutual cost and benefit sharing in bilateral water treaty • Forest management • Protect nature and environment • Urbanization and Settlement • National Security • Non Resident Nepal • Tourism development • Basic infrastructure (transport, irrigation and communication) • Basic services (education and health) • Assure labor right

• Social equity, social inclusion, social justice and special right	• Access to Justice • Human resource development • Reservation to socially excluded	• Reluctance of other mainstream parties on ethnic based federalism (later dropped during 2nd CA)	• Foreign aid mobilization for national interest of country • Address citizenship problem • Honor martyrs and politically affected persons • Promote science and technology, culture and knowledge • Unemployment benefit and Social Security • Empower social excluded, oppressed, landless, marginalized, geographically backward and other discriminated

* Nepal Communist Party (Maoist) means the one headed by Prachanda but it doesn't include splitter parties. This party fought two CA elections at its own and there is no substantial difference in manifestos for these two elections so we have not prepared comparative tables. This party joined with UML to form Nepal Communist Party a few days prior to 2017's federal and provincial parliamentary elections.

Table C4: Brief Review of Nepal Communist Party Manifestos for 2017 Election*

Mission, Goals and Party Ideology	Visions and Strategies	Threats, Constraints and Challenges	Priorities
• Federal Democratic Republic • Prosperity based on socialism. • Economic growth and development • Human rights, fundamental rights and Press Freedom • Strengthening country's sovereignty and national dignity • Social equity, social inclusion, social justice and special right • Constitutional Supremacy and Rule of Law	• People centric state to address grievances and problems • Restructuring of state and its institutions as per federal principal • Poverty alleviation, employment generation and increase income level through enhancing domestic production • Export focused trade • Rural development • Power devolution • Good governance and accountability • Access to Justice • Human resource development • Unemployment benefit and social security	• Feudalism and Imperialism of western world and their financial institutions • Geo-Political interests of neighbors on keeping Nepal dependent • Liberal parties' inclination to foreign forces and western world • Biased international treaties and border problems • Conservative and backward society • Landlocked and difficult geographic terrain • Threat from Madhesh based parties on surrendering national pride	• Peace • Agriculture development, assure farmers' right and land reform • Proper supply system and price control • Population and squatter settlement • Prerogative right of Nepali people in its natural as well as water resource • Hydropower development and mutual cost and benefit sharing in bilateral water treaty • Forest Management • Protect nature and environment • Urbanization and Settlement • National Security • Non Resident Nepal • Tourism development • Basic infrastructure (transport, irrigation, airways and communication) • Basic services (education, health and drinking water) • Assure labor right

- Foreign aid mobilization for national interest of country
- Honor Martyrs and Politically Affected Persons
- Promote science and technology, culture and knowledge
- Uplift excluded, oppressed, marginalized, landless and other discriminated
- Develop railway and waterway

* Nepal Communist Party means the one formed by unification of UML and Nepal Communist Party (Maoist) headed by Prachanda.

Annex D:

Review of Policies, Programs and Activities Announced in post 1990 Budgets

Year	Proposed Policies, Programs and Activities
1990/91	Formulate Industrial policy in complement to appropriate reforms in Industrial Act and regulations and remove unnecessary control measures and administrative caveats.
	Establish Citizen Investment Fund to mobilize domestic savings
	Establish Revenue Intelligence Division for effective vigilance
	Establish "Rural Self-Reliance Development fund" for growth of agriculture and other sectors to extend concessional loan
	Promote Cottage Industries
1991/92	Bring policy to carryout privatization of public enterprises
	Revise Finance Company Act to attract private sector
	Introduce Partial Convertibility of Current Account
	Reduce basic custom duty on all kinds of raw materials used by indigenous industries
	Establish Agriculture Research Council
	Formulate agriculture policy with focus on innovation in agriculture technology, input, loan, financing and price
	Formulate education policy for expansion of primary and adult education to eradicate illiteracy within next 10 years
	Allocate budget for local and rural development involving local leadership more effectively with the principle of decentralization
	Execute poverty alleviation programmes (Priority Sector Lending, Small Farmers Development Project, Intensive Banking Program, Women Development Programme and Waive Interest of Loan to Poor)
	Subsidy in Bio-Gas Production

	Safeguard children's right Amend existing rules and regulations on bidding and contract Initiate Basic and Primary Education Program (BPEP)
1992/93	Bring Foreign Investment and Technology Transfer Act Bring Industrial Enterprises Act Introduce Full Convertibility of Current Account Provide grant on small tube wells and bio gas plants to farmers. Develop transport to enhance farmers connectivity with market, to improve primary and women literacy education and to establish necessary health posts Execute Food for Work programme Extend communication facilities in all districts' headquarters Establish Udaypur Cement Factory Establish rural development banks to provide small loans to the farmers. Establish new bio-gas plants
1993/94	Establish NEPSE as the secondary security market. Encourage private sector participation in commercial banks, finance companies and insurance companies. Continue privatization of public enterprises Execute package programs on fertilizer distribution, irrigation, rural roads, rural electricity, rural market and development of industrial crops, livestock, fishery and silk farming Provide free education upto class 7, bring women literacy programs and provide free education materials Establish 600 health posts Implement special programs for poverty alleviation and employment generation Promote rural drinking water project
1994/95	Promote export through trade diversification programs including product marketing, quality improvement and R&D activities. Promote commercialize farming system Provide free education up to Grade VIII Initiate preliminary works for establishment of university in eastern development region. Initiate higher education reform Promote tourism in cooperation with private sector.

	Extend economic liberalization in agricultural, forestry and unorganized sectors.
	Amend laws and regulations as per Multilateral Investment Guarantee Agency to promote investor
	Setup health post in each VDC
	Setup area postal office in each VDC
	Initiate necessary Steps to establish dry port in Birgunj
	Construct Mid-Hill Highway (Madhya Pahari Lok Marga)
	Encourage to Establish Development Banks
	Establish government owned commercial bank
1995/96	Announced concrete agriculture policy in order to promote production and agroforestry Industry
	Launch Agriculture Perspective Plan (1996 to 2015)
	Launch "Build Your Village Yourself" in accordance with the principle of decentralization.
	Initiate social protection scheme in selected districts and extend it in all districts
	Form Women and Child Development Council
	Promote cooperative programs and bring bill of Cooperative Savings and Credit Institution
	Establish Small Farmer Development Bank
	Establish Foreign Employment Training Center
	Commission Kulekhani Hydro Power Project
	Initiate the third phase of privatization after completion of the second phase
	Amend Industrial Enterprises Act with extended facilities of One Window System
	Provide incentives to export oriented industries, to bring export push strategy, to initiate Green Channel, to establish cold storage in TIA and to provide concessional foreign exchange loan
1996/97	Amend FITTA to waive investment threshold of NRs. 20 million
	Bring Basic and Primary Education (BPEP) Master Plan (1997 – 2002)
	Form high-level decentralization commission with "Village to Village" initiative under the chairmanship of Prime Minister to study and present necessary recommendations.
	Continue social protection grant and block grant to local bodies

Year	Programme
	Bring policy granting the local bodies to collect land revenue and other local taxes
	Create Kamaiya Loan Relief Fund for income generating opportunities
	Operate Tribhuvan International Airport for 24 hours
	Amend laws and regulations to permit Nepali airline companies to operate in foreign countries
1997/98	Initiate steps for WTO membership
	Develop one VDC of each district as "Model VDC"
	Continue Food For Work program for construction of basic infrastructure
	Launch Kamaiya Elimination Program
	Start construction of inland container depot in Birgunj with commitment to build similar type of depots in Bhairahawa and Biratnagar.
	Initiate Visit Nepal Year 1998 and establish Nepal Tourism Board and Nepal Civil Aviation Authority
1998/99	Form Permanent Revenue Board to revise revenue policies and laws and regulations relating tax
	Publish "Rights of Taxpayers" with clear and transparent information on taxpayer's rights
	Launch "Clean and People Friendly Government, My Right" campaign for friendliness between People and Government
	Enhance tuberculosis drugs distribution throughout the country and launch DOTS(Directly Observed Treatment- Short Course) programme in 50 districts
	Establish Rural Micro Credit Development Center to improve socio-economic condition of the rural women
	Organize International Summit on Buddhism and to prepare Lumbini Master Plan
	Launch "Village to Village Development, Home to Home Employment" to develop rural areas and to generate employment
1999/00	Encourage private sector in infrastructure development
	Form Permanent Revenue Consultative Board
	Introduce crop insurance scheme
	Initiate collection of "Village Education Development Fee" from the private schools operating in the urban areas

Year	Programme
	Initiate necessary steps to establish Eastern Regional University, Pokhara University, University of Agriculture and Forestry and Open University
	Increase social pension amount
	Launch nationwide poverty reduction programme of " Bishweshwar Among the Poor"
	Establish Poverty Alleviation Fund
	Launch "Ganesh Man Singh Peace Campaign" to provide amnesty and financial assistance to surrenders of Maoist conflict
2000/01	Start preparatory arrangement to establish Credit Rating Agency
	Table new securities transactions Act in parliament
	Make income tax base broader by bringing all income generating economic activities
	Prepare and implement long-term export policy and strategy on readymade garments
	Run Karnali Zone Agriculture Development Project
	Launch Education for All Program, provide scholarships to the children belonging to ethnic and tribal groups and make textbooks distribution upto grade five effective and efficient
	Make distribution of vitamin "A" and iodized salt more effective
	Carry out feasibility study of health insurance scheme
	Enhance institutional capacity of the local bodies on management, development plan preparation, information system, training and service delivery through "Gaun Ko Adhikar Gaun Lai" (Villages' right to Villages) programme
	Provide financial resources to local bodies through land revenue and local development fee
	Expand Food for Work program in food scarcity areas.
	Launch programs to improve socio-economic condition of neglected, oppressed, exploited, ethnic tribes, and other native communities
	Launch satellite medium transmission of Nepal Television
	Establish Road Fund
	Promote Build, Operate and Transfer (BOT) model in physical infrastructure development
	Setup Information Technology Park
	Prepare water resources strategy and national water resources plan
	Open new trekking route to promote tourism

	Prepare 20-year industrial perspective plan
	Run youth self-employment program
	Amend labor policy and laws
	Launch "Income to Destitute - Justice to Helpless" programme
	Bring new income tax act
	Form Public Expenditure Review Commission
2001/02	Increase foreign investment threshold in joint venture commercial banks from 50 to 75 percent
	Initiate Export Promotion Year
	Handover management of Nepal Bank Limited and Rastriya Banijya Bank to foreign financial management experts to improve their financial performance
	Continue construction of IT Park
	Form Sick Industry Rehabilitation Committee
2002/03	Declare charter on citizen's right
	Prepare agriculture action plan
	Handover one hundred of primary schools to school management committees and to provide block grant to such schools
	Prepare Decentralization Action Plan
	Extend social security programs related to senior citizens, helpless, widows, blinds and disables
	Institutionalize poverty alleviation monitoring system
	Bring labor policy with flexible hire and fire clause
2003/04	Prepare and enact new bank and financial institution Act
	Prepare and enact laws relating to secured transaction, insolvency, anti-money laundering, asset management company and fiscal transparency
	Bring new company act
	Introduce Contributory Pension System
	Introduce Community Health Insurance Scheme
	Establish Poverty Alleviation Fund (PAF) soon
	Encourage private sector in infrastructure development under Build-Own-Operate-Transfer (BOOT) model
2004/05	Increase VAT rate from 10 to 13 Percent
	Launch Education for All Program 2004–2009
	Organize Second World Buddhist Summit

Year	Policy
2005/06	Register Agricultural Development Bank as public limited company Incorporate all civil service employees in contributory pension scheme Lunch periodic monitoring of priority projects and matters of public concern by Prime Minister's Office and cabinet secretariat Bring public procurement ordinance Provide technical support to develop specific area suited agricultural products. Launch One village One product Carry out feasibility study to integrate school education by changing class 1 to 8 as primary schooling Continue exemption of land registration fee for women Establish Industrial Rehabilitation Fund on the basis of feasibility study Prepare ten year work plan to improve and conserve world heritages of Kathmandu valley Sell 5% and 10% shares of Nepal Telecom Company to employees and public respectively
2006/07	Enact law relating to anti-money laundering, bank fraud control and negotiable instrument Fully exempt customs duty and VAT in Special Economic Zones Formulate foreign investment policy and trade policy Enact competition law Formulate agriculture business promotion policy Operate One-Village-One-Product program under public-private partnership Review and reform higher education policies and to run higher education project Enact law relating to micro finance To establish Industrial Rehabilitation Fund Launch Karnali Employment Program. Revise culture policy and to formulate museum act
2007/08	Promulgate Acts relating to anti-money laundering and banking fraud control Formulate mutual fund law to allow the commercial banks to manage the mutual fund Make arrangement to allow the Non Resident Nepali to invest in secondary securities market

	Enact law relating Special Economic Zone Formulate policy relating to land development and land acquisition Form industrial security force for security of industrial corridor.
2008/09	To establish Money Laundering Control Department Setup Border Security and Revenue Leakage Patrolling Post Provide high priority to minorities, third sex, Dalit and backward Janajatis in services such as education, health, drinking water, social security and all opportunities of socio economic development including employment. Carry out reconstruction of damages due to Maoist conflict with high priority Operate Western Nepal Rural Drinking Water and Sanitation Project Form High Level Scientific Land Reform Commission to abolish feudal land ownership Enact law relating to mutual fund and trust Establish Youth Self-Employment Fund Prepare and implement National Adaptation Plan of Action Enact and enforce Right to Information Rules and Working Journalist Rules
2009/10	Establish Central Deposit System of stock exchange Establish high-level permanent central revenue board Gradually provide free education upto class ten Expand Child Development Centers and provide Child Protection Grant Provide grants to establish and operate the community hospitals Promote 2011 as Nepal Tourism Year
	Launch School Mapping Program to ensure sufficiency in teacher-student ratio Handover management of 5,400 schools to the communities Provide grant to the schools facing teachers' scarcity Provide social security allowances to endangered ethnic group Provide child protection grant to under five years poor-Dalits and to all families in Karnali Zone Make construction of girls' toilets mandatory in each community school

	Continue "People's Housing Program" with extension in Chepang, Raute and Kusunda communities' settlement areas.
	Construct six lane wide roads linking international trade routes, namely: Birgunj-Patlaiya, Belahiya-Butwal, Rani-Itahari and Surya Binayak-Dhulikhel
2010/11	Prioritize construction of bridges linking mid-hill highway (Lok Marga) and district headquarters
	Initiate Nepal Tourism Year 2011
	Launch Karnali Employment Program.
	Construct Tamakoshi Hydropower Project with domestic investments and technical manpower
	Develop the birthplace of Lord Buddha as "International Peace City"
	Execute Presidential Chure Bhawar Area Preservation Program
	Effectively implement laws relating to anti-money laundering to control crimes in economic activities and to take economy into right direction
	Formulate new health policy in order to establish health service as the fundamental right
	To carry out integrated public health campaign by targeting the remote and backward districts having low HDI.
2011/12	Form commission for overall development of far-western region.
	Formulate policy on land use
	Expand Youth Self Employment Program as a national campaign with joint efforts of the government, cooperative and private sector
	Formulate and enact Employment Guarantee Act
	Prepare master plan on hydropower development
	Formulate Act related to disaster risk management
	Create Journalists Insurance Fund
	Operationalize Central Depository System to bring share transaction and commodity market together
	Provide subsidy to export-based industries
	Develop strategy for commercialization, modernization and diversification of agriculture,
	Provide subsidy on rice seed and equipment for seed processing, grading, packaging and storage

	Include vocational education in curriculum of secondary level education,
	Establish universities in each development regions and affiliate the campuses of these regions into those universities
	Provide health insurance program for major 20 diseases such as heart, kidney and cancer to all citizens
2012/13	Formulate laws relating to social security fund
	Adopt Public Private Partnership Policy for the development of physical infrastructure
	Prepare the IT master plan and to encourage the inventions of the talented scientists.
	Develop e-Monitoring System
	Procure two jet planes for Nepal Airlines
	Formulate law in accordance with Land Use Policy
	Enact Special Economic Zone Act to promote export by providing special facility to the export oriented industries
	Launch "Sunaula Hazar Din Program" for awareness on nutrient food and medicine in pregnancy period
	Enact separate law for Social Security Fund
	Establish Single Woman Protection Fund
	Establish Central Emergency Child Rescue Fund
2013/14	Prepare National Master Plan on Child Labor Eradication (2010-20) to eradicate worst form of child labor by 2016 and end all types of child labor by 2020
	Introduce Nano-Technology Policy for development, promotion and upgrading of science technology and environment sector.
	Construct Gautam Buddha Regional Airport and to distribute compensation for acquired land of Pokhara Regional Airport.
	Implement Youth Self Employment Program as a campaign to generate internal employment opportunity.
	Prepare National Action Plan to gradually deliver basic services to the people through information technology
2014/15	Revise Education Act in order to make school education effective, useful and accessible
	Launch Higher Education Reform
	Extend health insurance scheme

	Carry out preliminary work on construction of Inland Container Depot at Chobhar, Kathmandu
	Formulate and implement Vision for Youth Development, 2025
	Develop and implement Greater Janakpur Area Development Master Plan
	Develop master plan for Balmiki Ashram located at Gardi of Chitwan
	Launch national campaign of "One House One Tree, One Village One Forest, One City Multi Park"
	Formulate and implement National Film Policy
2015/16	Organize investment forum to promote investment in the country
	Formulate Single Tax Code by consolidating the provisions of various Acts and Regulations related to tax
	Draft law to establish Central Revenue Board
	Initiate "Police as my Friend" program with mobilization of youth volunteer
	Establish more agriculture processing centers and to conduct agriculture researches on indigenous agriculture products, agriculture productivity enhancement and food security
	Initiate "One Village One Doctor" program
	Provide social security allowance distribution through banking channel in overall Nepal
	Initiate process to procuring additional aircrafts for Nepal Airlines Corporation
	Modernize land management by strengthening institutional capacity in land mapping and record quality
	Prepare master plan to develop a smart city in Kathmandu valley, Lumbini Region and Nijgadh
	Prepare and implement post-earthquake Reconstruction Action Plan.
	Commence preliminary works of Buddhist tourist circuit
	Launch 'Cultural Protection and Promotion Renaissance' campaign
	Establish Krishna Prasad Bhattarai Mass Communication Academy

	Launch "Bank Account for All Nepali" campaign
	Setup fully computerized system of citizenship certificates
	Establish CCTV surveillance and monitoring of the criminal activities in the main cities
	Initiate Social Security Fund for farmers
	Develop Agriculture Development Strategy (2015 to 2035)
2016/17	Establish Madan Bhandari Science and Technology Academy
	Distribute State Security Identity Card to poor of 25 districts
	Initiate Far-Western Uplands Poverty Alleviation Project
	Accelerate Post-earthquake Reconstruction
	Launch private forest development promotion program
	Establish National Zoological Garden at Suryabinayak in Bhakatpur
	Bring new Labor Law
	Make Stock Market transparent and fully automated
	Carry out civil service restructuring and to bring National Civil Service Policy
	Expand agriculture insurance
	Extend National Health Insurance Scheme
2017/18	Launch President Women Entrepreneurs Development Program
	Formulate National Transport Policy and Vehicle and Transport Act
	Formulate Land Use Act
	Restructure disaster management in accordance to federal set up
	Launch National Volunteers Program
	Initiate technical skill development program
	Create Challenge Fund to provide loan to youth
	Establish at least one Health Center in each Ward
	Expand Open University and Alternative Education System
	Formulate Law on Nuclear Energy
2018/19	Establish "Agriculture Knowledge Center" at all local levels
	Protect Public and Guthi land
	Establish Industrial Villages at Local Levels
	Restructure Nepal Food Corporation as National Supply Company
	Launch Visit Nepal 2020

	Initiate construction work on Nijgadh International Airport and Pokhara Regional International Airport
	Complete construction of Ranipokhari, Dharahara and Kasthamandap
	Celebrate FY 2018/19 as the National Sanitation Campaign Year
	Expedite Construction Work on Bheri - Babai diversion, Rani Jamara Kulariya, Sikta and Babai Irrigation projects
	Celebrate the period of 2018 to 2028 as Energy Decade
	Form Electricity Regulatory Commission
	Construct Federal Parliament Building
	Launch Campaign to open bank accounts for all Nepali citizens
	Operate Infrastructure Development Bank
	Formulate an Act regarding operation and management of Public Enterprises
	Implement Ghar Ghar Ma Manab Adhikar
	Establish Cyber and Human Trafficking Bureau
	Establish President Education Improvement Fund
	Prioritize to make Higher Education Vocational and Employment oriented by formulating New Education Programme
	Establish Nuclear Research Centre
	Establish at least one Primary Hospital at Local Level
	Implement No One Will Go Hungry, No One Will Die of Hunger Programme
	Expand Contributory Social Security Programme
	Celebrate Youth Mobilization Year
2019/20	Restructure and expand Prime Minister Agriculture Modernization Programme
	Implement Healthy Food for All campaign
	Enhance capacity of Agriculture Knowledge Centers
	Prioritize development of Multipurpose Water Resources Projects
	Declare current fiscal year as Afforestation Year
	Enact Land Act
	Establish Cooperatives Credit Information Centre and Cooperative Savings and Credit Guarantee Fund
	Emphasise development of Railway Infrastructure

Transform Town Development Fund into Nepal Urban Infrastructure Development Corporation

Carry out Institutional reforms in Nepal Stock Exchange and Security Exchange Board of Nepal

Implement National Single Window for FDI

Strengthen institutional capacity of the National Project Bank

Develop regular monitoring and evaluation of the projects using Information Technology

Formulate Single Tax Code to simplify Tax Laws

Annex E: Reviews of Policies for Selected Sectors Brought in post 1990

Agriculture and Livestock	Forestry	Irrigation
	Policies	
• National Seed Policy (1999) • National Tea Policy (1999) • National Fertilizer Policy (2000) • National Coffee Policy (2002) • National Agriculture Policy (2003 and 2004) • Agriculture Business Promotion Policy (2005) • Organic Technology Policy (2005) • Dairy Development Policy (2006) • Bird Farming Policy (2010) • Poultry Policy (2010) • Agriculture Bio-Diversity Policy (2013) • Agriculture Commercialization Policy (2013)	• Forestry Policy (2000 and 2013) • Herbs and Illegal Wood Security Policy (2003)	• Irrigation Policy (2002 and 2012)
	Objectives	
- Contribute to food security and poverty prevention by achieving high and sustainable economic growth by marketing compétitive agriculture and bird business, contributing to domestic market and export promotion and developing agricultural sector - Conserve and promote rights of farmer's traditional knowledge, skills, search, technology, use and practice	- Meet people's basic needs for fuel wood, timber, fodder, and other forestry products on a sustained basis and contribute to food production through effective interaction between forestry and farming practices - Protect land from degradation by soil erosion, floods, landslides, desertification and other	- Develop and expand irrigation sector by maximum use of water resources, mainly surface and underground

- Arrangement of arbitrary and judicial distribution system of opportunities and benefits from the access and use of agricultural genetic resources and substance - Supply foreign demands by increasing and promoting tea and coffee exports which helps in raising income and employment opportunities, and gradually in poverty reduction - Encourage farmers to safeguard the investment in fish, livestock and agricultural produce - Promote research, programs and development of biological technologies along with organized technology sector, administrative skills, attorneys, qualified researchers and attainment of knowledge to develop internationally competitive and environmentally sustainable natural resources, environment, forest, agriculture and food sectors. - Identification and promotion of women and environment friendly agricultural devices. - Attract investment in private and cooperative sectors in agriculture sector	ecological disturbances, and conserve, use and manage biological diversity and genetic resources in a sustainable way - Develop and promote forest management system based on communities and contribute to growth of local and national economics by creating opportunities for income-generation and employment thereby improving the quality of life of the rural local people managing land and forest resources and developing forest-based industries - Ensure participation of vulnerable groups in natural resource management including collection, reproduction, production and sale of herbs and non-forestry products - Produce herbs and export non-ferrous forest produce abroad as per the sales process in international markets - Increase productivity by upgrading field, and develop and expand rangeland based enterprises - Conservation, distribution, sustainable, scientific and environmentally balanced consumption and use of biological diversity and mines	water, to increase productivity - Provide adequate maintenance service for irrigation infrastructure, effective water management modernization and new irrigation schemes for irrigation structures

Industry	Investment	Trade and Commerce	Tourism
Policies			
• Industrial Policy (1991, 2009 and 2011) • National Minerals Policy (2016)	• Foreign Investment and One Window Policy (1991) • Foreign Investment Policy (2005, 2013)	• Trade Policy (2009, 2014) • Commercial Policy (1991, 2007, 2014) • Supply Policy (2011)	• Tourism Policy (2007)
Objectives			
- Increase the export of industrial products along with growth in national income and employment through enhancement of quality and competitive industrial products and productivity - Increase the contribution of industrial sector in the national and regional development by mobilizing the local resources, raw materials, skills and means - Develop productive human resources, administrative and managerial capacity	- Enhance modern technology and quality management and administrative capacity by attracting foreign investment and increasing geographical investment - Maximize the use of scientific and sustainable resources of local source, skills and instruments as part of foreign investment operations for overall development of the nation. - Increase competitiveness of the country by expanding access to industrial goods and	- Conserving the interest and rights of consumer, develop integrated supply system to poorest consumers and provide necessary food security arrangements - Control non-competitive activity in item and service, and colonies and artificial deficiencies in goods and services - Reduce business and trade-oriented competitive commodity and service clearance and increase access to goods, services and intellectual property in the regional and global market - Promote trade interactions as a competitive and forwarding product, and diversify the business by identifying, developing and producing new products worthy of goods - Expand the private business as well as settle the harmony of this area with other areas	- Develop and promote tourism sector as one of the main basis of national economy of Nepal while also conserving environment and natural resources in a sustainable way. - Develop, expand, promote and improve tourism industry including rural tourism through accessible, secure, reliable and regular air service

required for industrial development thereby establishing Nepal as an attractive place of investment in the South Asia region as well as in the world - Establish industry business as a sustainable and reliable area - Protect industrial intellectual property rights	services in international markets, and by reducing trade deficit and increasing trade balance - Increase productivity and create additional opportunities for income and employment	- Make mineral exploitation simple, effective, and result-oriented, and its institutional structure as the federal structure for preservation, promotion and sustainable use of mineral resources	traffic and by diversification and extension of the sector and creating awareness.

Transport	Civil Aviation	Hydropower and Energy	Communication
Policies			
• National Transportation Policy (2000)	• Civil Aviation Policy (2005)	• Hydropower Development Policy (1992, 2000 and 2001) • Rural Energy policy (2006) • National Energy Strategy (2013) • Renewable Energy Subsidy Policy (2015)	• National Communication Policy (1991) • Telecommunication Policy (2002 and 2004) • Information Technology Policy (2000, 2009 and 2014)
Objectives			
- Contribute to the development of the overall economic, social, cultural, and tourist sector of Nepal by developing sustainable, affordable, less expensive, secure, convenience and self-reliant traffic system, aligning with national traffic policy	- Develop healthy and cost-effective air service by attracting and promoting indigenous and foreign private investors in civil aviation - Expand civil aviation by organizing and promoting development of training institution related to civil aviation, and building airports of nearby areas equipped with state-of-art facilities.	- Develop hydropower resources as reliable and lead energy resource at low cost by utilizing water resources, link up with economic activities and use as exportable commodity. - Ensure sustainable consumption of biomass energy resources and increase employment and productivity through the development of rural energy resources - Reduce dependence on traditional and imported foreign fossil fuel energy by promoting and increasing access to clean and cost effective renewable energy and technologies, especially in rural areas, to minimize detrimental effects on environment.	- Create effective communication by utilizing benefits of democracy based on legal state principles, and maintain the national interest, basic values and beliefs of pluralist democracy to enable communication media to consolidate and strengthen the national unity. - Information and communication technology made affordable and accessible to everyone - Develop government integrated data centers as an infrastructure for information technology development and expand the infrastructure while making government sector lead the announcement of information technology regularly. - Increase employment by establishing knowledge based society and industries through information technology. - In order to bring the access to general public of rural and urban areas of the country to the telecommunication service, arrangement shall be made in a manner that the telecommunication service shall be available within the shouting distance in the inhabited areas - Arrangement shall be made for getting opportunity to use appropriate information and communication technology for poverty alleviation and development of the rural areas.

Labor	Decentralization and Public Private Partnership	Cooperative and Micro Finance	Social Inclusion
Policies			
• Labor and Employment Policy (2004) • Foreign Employment Policy (2010)	• Public-Private Partnership Policy (2002) • Local Infrastructure Development Policy (2003)	• National Micro Finance Policy (2006) • National Cooperative Policy (2011)	• Gender Equality and Social Inclusion Policy (2013) • Inclusive Education Policy for Disabled Persons (2015)
Objectives			
- Create investment-friendly environment and provide sustainable employment opportunities to all people - Develop efficient and competitive knowledge and labor skills as per the demand of international market, and social security system including the informal sector to make labor market safe, healthy, competitive and flexible. - Employ labor practice of decent labor and welfare pattern, while promoting standards of formal labor in the formal and informal areas - Increase employment opportunities and ensure equal access to women, Dalit, tribes and displaced in employment while not employing the child laborers	- Increase access to social services, economic opportunities and resources for the local people through physical and social infrastructure and maximizing private and non-government sector partnership - Attract private sector investment, technology and administrative efficiency in the construction, operation and management of the economic structure and local infrastructure - Develop the services and facilities provided by the State to the local authorities through the local bodies	- Increase access to cooperative and small finance services for poor, marginalized, disabled, landless, backward-class workers and others with weak economic conditions. - Encourage collaboration between government, cooperative, district and development partners to develop, promote and expand cooperative industry making them effective and competitive sector - Enhance institutional capacity development and co-operation of cooperatives through education, training, information, effective management and regulating values and principles. - Prepare micro finance laws and support in the development of micro finance service providers entrepreneurship to be sustainable and self-sufficient	- Promote gender equality and social inclusion process - Inclusive education policy includes ensuring equitable access to quality education, continuous education and skillful employment opportunities

<table>
<tr><th>Human Resource Development</th><th>Land</th></tr>
<tr><td colspan="2">Policies</td></tr>
<tr><td>• National Policy of Education (1997)
• Human Development Education Training Policy(2004)
• Informal Education Policy (2005)
• Private Technical Institution Policy (2005)
• Open and Distance Learning Policy (2005)
• Media Strategy in Education (2005)
• TEVT Skill Development Policy (2006),
• National Youth Policy (2008 and 2014)
• Higher Education Policy (2014)</td><td>• National Policy related to Land Acquisition, Compensation and Rehabilitation in Development Projects (2005),
• Land Use Policy (2015),
• National Geo-Use Policy (2011)</td></tr>
<tr><td colspan="2">Objectives</td></tr>
<tr><td>- Develop viable and skilled manpower by developing, promoting and expanding the competent and beneficial skills of essential knowledge, science and technology for development of the nation.
- Increase access to higher education by making regular, systematic and reputable, establishing, operating, regulation and management of higher education providers
- Develop a highly respected, moral, coordinated, versatile and professionally skilled youth by developing the culture of respect to labor, proper development of the physical, mental, intellectual, moral and social aspects of the youth
- Develop the youth's ability to establish youth as a conductor of national development through meaningful participation based on gender sensitivity in the policy, decision making and implementation process of all levels of the nation's economic, social, political and cultural fields.
- Promote the basic flow of development by empowering youth in groups of special priority through positive discrimination
- Expand the training opportunities and services.</td><td>- Classify/categorize entire land into various Land Use Zones and ensure that land and its resources are used on the basis of Land Use Plans - devised level-wise (federal provincial and local) and based on land use policy - for protection of agricultural land, forest areas, and land with geographical, cultural, religious, historical, tourist, and special areas of importance.
- Protect, administer and utilize the land based on classification
- Determine the minimum rating and landing system based on usage and make arrangement for unused land.
- Assess and apply minimum property valuation and progressive tax system on lands on the basis of specific use after preparing plot based records</td></tr>
</table>

- Make training to all needy citizens accessible and ensure the opportunity of training to all
- Integrate various training modes and training providers into one system.
- Link training contents and outcomes of the training with economic demands.
- Encourage private sector engagement in high-tech education and ensure access to the education for Nepali youth of the backward areas, with women, tribes, Dalit and financial and social issues
- Promote lifelong learning, continuing education and professional development through open and distance learning system by applying mix mode delivery mechanism
- Ensure sustainable funding and provide skill-based and technical education and vocational training through customized courses to cater the needs of labor force seeking employment in the national and international job market
- Creating an avenue for skill certification and accreditation to preserve the traditional skills and customary learning of the tribal and indigenous community
- Open remote education from the modern media mode
- Find a common ground between communication and education sectors and bridge gaps between all concerned stakeholders
- Prepare a permanent citizen for national unity between the caste and community
- Develop the underlying strength and personality of each person.
- Develop and strengthen the national language, culture, literature, beauty and national heritage

- Maintain balance between development and environment including recovery to maintain environmental balance by conserving, promoting and sustainable and scientific biological diversity of the mines
- Mitigate natural and human created-disastrous hazards
- Restoration of displaced large families by providing land based on prevailing market value and other merit giving full compensation, detailed consultation and options with lowest possible displacement, and adequate assistance to meet requirement of their living standard as well as by implementing gender and social equality in the process of implementing land acquisition and rehabilitation plan.
- Complete the transfer of ownership of both landed and voluntary land acquisition and all kinds of compensation.
- Increase local level access for local workers by conducting programs based on savings, credits and income generation.

Annex F:

List of Prevailing Laws and their Regulations Referred in this Book[1]

Acts	Regulations	Post 2015[2]	
		Acts	Regulations
Administration Procedure Regulation Act, 1956			
Amount and Government Contract Management Act, 1963			
Animal Health and Livestock Act 1999	Animal Health and Livestock Services Rules, 2000		
Animal Slaughter House and Meat Inspection Act 1999	Animal Slaughter House and Meat Inspection Rule 2001		
Bank and Financial Institution Act, 2017			
Banking Offence and Punishment Act, 2008			

1. The prevailing acts and regulations are only listed and the acts without regulation are governed by procedures and executive decisions.

2. The country is currently in legal revision process as per federal principle and the new laws and regulations enacted upto end of April 2019 have been included.

Acts	Regulations	Post 2015	
		Acts	Regulations
Black Market Act, 1975			
Private Financing in Build and Operation of Infrastructures Act, 2006	Private Financing in Build and Operation of Infrastructures Rules, 2007		
Civil Service Act, 1993	Civil Service Rule, 1993		
Company Act, 2006			
Competition Promotion and Market Protection Act, 2007	Competition Promotion and Market Protection Rule, 2010		
Construction Business Act, 1999	Construction Business Rule, 2000		
Consumer Protection Act, 1998	Consumer Protection Rule, 1999	Consumer Protection Act, 2018	
Cooperative Act 2017	Cooperative Rule, 2003		
Corporation Act, 1964			
Customs Act, 2007	Customs Rule, 2008		
Development Board Act, 1956			
Domestic Postal Goods (Insurance) Act, 1962	Domestic Postal Goods (Insurance) Rule, 1962		
Education Act, 1971	Education Rule, 2002	Education Act, 2017	
Electricity Act, 1992	Electricity Rule, 1993; Electricity Tariff Fixation Rule, 1994		
Electricity Leakage Control Act, 2001	Electricity Leakage Control Rule, 2002		

Acts	Regulations	Post 2015	
		Acts	Regulations
Environmental Protection Act, 1996	Environment Protection Rule, 1997		
Excise Duty Act, 2002	Excise Duty Rule, 2002		
Export Import (Control) Act, 1957	Export Import (Control) Rule, 1978		
Factory and Factory Workers Act, 1959			
Financial Intermediary Act, 1998			
Financial Procedure Act, 1999	Financial Administration Regulation, 1999 and Financial Procedure Rule, 2006		
Food Act 1966	Food Rule, 1970		
Foreign Exchange Control Act, 1960	Hedging Rule, 2019		
Foreign Investment and Technology Transfer Act, 1992		Foreign Investment and Technology Transfer Act Nepal, 2019	
Good Governance Management and Operation Act,2007	Good Governance Management and Operation Rule, 2009		
Higher Education Act, 1992	Higher Education Rule, 1996		
Hotel Management and Liquor Sale and Distribution (Control) Act, 1966			
Imposition of Tax Act, 1960			

Acts	Regulations	Post 2015	
		Acts	Regulations
Income and Tax Justice Management Act, 1959			
Income Tax Act, 2002	Income Tax Rule, 2002		
Industrial Enterprises Act, 1992		Industrial Enterprises Act, 2016	
Labor Act, 1991	Labor Rule, 1993	Labor Act 2017	Labor Rule, 2018
Land Acquisition Act, 1977			
Land Reform Act 1964	Land Rule, 1964		
Loan and Guarantee Act, 1968			
Loan Recovery Act, 2002	Recovery of Debts of Banks and Financial Institutions Rules, 2002		
Local Self Governance Act, 1998	Local Self Governance Regulation, 1999 and Local Body (Financial Administration) Rules, 1999	Local Government Operation Act, 2017	
Mines and Minerals Act, 1985	Mines and Minerals Rule, 1999		
Money Laundering Prevention Act, 2008	Laundering Prevention Rules, 2009		
Motor Vehicles and Transport Management Act, 1993	Motor Vehicles and Transport Management Rule, 1997		

Acts	Regulations	Post 2015	
		Acts	Regulations
Multimodal Transportation of Good Act, 2006	Multimodal Transport of Goods Rules, 2009		
Nepal Agency Act, 1958	Nepal Agency Rule, 1963		
Nepal Airline Corporation Act, 1963			
Nepal Civil Aviation Authority Act, 1996			
Nepal Electricity Authority Act, 1984			
Nepal Railway Act, 1963			
Nepal Rastra Bank Act, 2002			
Nepal Ship (Registration and Logbook) Act, 1971			
Nepal Standard (Certification Mark) Act, 1980	Nepal Standard (Certification-mark) Rule, (1990)		
Nepal Tourism Board Act, 1997	Nepal Tourism Board Rule, 1999		
Partnership Act, 1958			
Pesticide Act 1994	Pesticide Rule, 1994		
Postal Act, 1963	Postal Rule, 1964		
Private Firm Registration Act, 1958			
Privatization Act, 1994			
Public Procurement Act, 2007	Public Procurement Rule, 2007		
Public Road Act, 1974			

Acts	Regulations	Post 2015	
		Acts	Regulations
Recovery and Settlement of Government Dues Act, 1968			
Road Board Act, 2002			
Securities Exchange Act, 1984	Securities Exchange Rule, 1993		
Security Market Act, 2007			
Ship Registration Act, 1971	Ship Registration Rule, 1972		
Special Economic Zone, 2016		Special Economic Zone Act, 2017	
Standard Weight and Measurement Act, 1976			
Telecommunication Act 1997	Telecommunication Rule, 1997		
Tourism Act, 1978	Hotel, Lodge, Restaurant, Bar and Tourist Guide Rules, 1981 and Travel and Trekking Agency Rule, 2005		
Trade Facilitation and Trade Enforcement Act, 2016			
Trade Union Act 1992	Trade Union Rule, 1993		
Tribhuvan University 1959			
Value Added Tax Act, 1993	Value Added Tax Rule, 1997		

Acts	Regulations	Post 2015	
		Acts	Regulations
		National Dalits Commission, 2017	
		National Natural Resources and Fiscal Commission Act, 2017	
		National Women Commission Act, 2017	
		National Inclusion Commission Act, 2017	
		Electricity Regulatory Commission Act, 2017	
		Contribution Based Social Security Act, 2017	Contribution Based Social Security Rule, 2018
		Civil Servant Adjustment Act, 2017	Civil Servant Adjustment Rule, 2017
		Right to Food and Food Sovereignty Act 2018	
		Language Commission Act, 2017	
		Madheshi Commission Act, 2017	

Acts	Regulations	Post 2015	
		Acts	Regulations
		Muslim Commission Act, 2017	
		Free and Compulsory Education Act, 2018	
		Intergovern-mental Fiscal Arrangement Act, 2017	
		Tharu Commission Act 2017	
		Public-Private Partnership and Investment Bill, 2019	
		Indigenous Nationalities Commission Act, 2017	
		Social Security Act, 2018	

Annex G: List of Government formed after 1990*

Time Period	Prime Minister	Parties
19th April 1990 to 25th May 1991	Krishna Prasad Bhattarai	Interim Government led by NC along with leftist and king's representative
26th May 1991 to 29th November 1994	Girija Prasad Koirala	Majority Government of NC
30th November 1994 to 11th September 1995	Man Mohan Adhikari	Minority Government of CPN-UML
12th September 1995 to 11th March 1997	Sher Bahadur Deuba	Coalition Government led by NC along with Rastriya Prajatantra Party and Nepal Sadbhawana Party
12th March 1997 to 6th October 1997	Lokendra Bahadur Chand	Coalition Government led by Rastriya Prajatantra Party along with CPN-UML and Nepal Sadbhawana Party
7th October 1997 to 14th April 1998	Surya Bahadur Thapa	Coalition Government led by Rastriya Prajatantra Party along with NC and Nepal Sadbhawana Party
15th April 1998 to 30th May 1999	Girija Prasad Koirala	Coalition Government led by NC along with CPN-UML and others
31st May 1999 to 21st March 2000	Krishna Prasad Bhattarai	Majority Government of NC
22nd March 2000 to 25th July 2001	Girija Prasad Koirala	Majority Government of NC
26th July 2001 to 3rd October 2002	Sher Bahadur Deuba	Majority Government of NC
4th to 10th October 2002	King Gyanendra 's Direct Rule	
11th October 2002 to 4th June 2003	Lokendra Bahadur Chand (Rastriya Prajatantra Party)	
5th June 2003 to 2nd June 2004	Surya Bahadur Thapa (Rastriya Prajatantra Party)	Under King Gyanendra's Direct Rule
3rd June 2004 to 31st January 2005	Sher Bahadur Deuba (NC)	
1st February 2005 to 24th April 2006	Tulsi Giri and Kirti Nidi Bista	

25th April 2006 to 17th August 2008	Girija Prasad Koirala	Interim Government led by NC along with CPN-UML, CPN-Maoist and others
18th August 2008 to 24th May 2009	Pushpa Kamal Dahal (Prachanda)	Coalition Government led by CPN-Maoist along with CPN-UML and other identity based parties
25th May 2009 to 5th February 2011	Madhav Kumar Nepal	Coalition Government led by CPN-UML along with NC, Rastriya Prajatantra Party and other identity based parties
6th February 2011 to 28th August 2011	Jhala Nath Khanal	Coalition Government led by CPN-UML along with CPN-Maoist and other identity based parties
29th August 2011 to 13th March 2013	Babu Ram Bhattarai	Coalition Government led by CPN-Maoist along with CPN-UML and other identity based parties
14th March 2013 to 10th February 2014	Khil Raj Regmi	Interim Government under Chief Justice
11th February 2014 to 11th October 2015	Sushil Koirala	Coalition Government led by NC along with CPN-UML, Rastriya Prajatantra Party and other parties
12th October 2015 to 3rd August 2016	K P Sharma Oli	Coalition Government led by CPN-UML along with CPN-Maoist and other parties
4th August 2016 to 6th June 2017	Pushpa Kamal Dahal (Prachanda)	Coalition Government led by CPN-Maoist along with NC and other parties
7th June 2017 to 14th February 2018	Sher Bahadur Deuba	Coalition Government led by NC along with CPN-Maoist and other parties
15th February 2018 to date	K P Sharma Oli	Majority Government of Nepal Communist Party

* CPN-Maoist is regarded as the party headed by Pushpa Kamal Dahal (Prachanda) and the split therein are not included. The splits in NC, UML and Rastriya Prajatantra Party have not been considered because the split away groups returned back to join mother party again. So the names of mother parties have only been used.

BIBLIOGRAPHY

Acharya, Govinda P and Raj K Bhattarai (2012). Insights on Issues of Trade Unions and Industrial Relations: A Perceptual Surveys of Opinion Leaders, in *Administration and Management Review*. Vol 2. No 1. Lalitpur: Nepal Administrative Staff College.

Acharya, Keshav et al (1998). *Economic Liberalization in Nepal: Sequences and Process*. Kathmandu: Nepal Labor Academy.

ADB (1982). *Nepal Agriculture Sector Strategy Study Volume I and II*. Manila: ADB.

ADB (2004). *Project Performance Audit Report: Secondary Education Development Project (Loan 1196-NEP[SF]) in Nepal*. Manila: ADB.

ADB, DFID and ILO (2009). *Nepal Critical Development Constraints*. Manila: ADB.

ADB (2013). *Nepal: Agriculture Development Strategy*. Manila.

ADB (2014). *Agriculture Value Chain Analysis of Nepal*. Kathmandu ADB, Nepal Resident Mission.

ADB (2017). *Human Capital Development in South Asia: Achievements, Prospect and Policy Challenges*. Manila: ADB.

ADB and UNESCAP (2017). *Trade and Transport Facilitation Monitoring Mechanism in Nepal*. Manila: ADB.

Aditya, Anand and Chandra D Bhatta eds. (2016). *The Role of Political Parties in Deeping Democracy in Nepal*. Friedrich Ebert Stiftung.

Adhikari. Jagannath (2010). Access to Land and Social Inclusion in the Context of High Mobility in Nepal, in Kristian Stokke and Mohan D Manandhar eds *State and Society: Social Inclusion and Exclusion in Nepal*. Kathmandu: Mandala Book Point.

Adhikari, Shyam P (1982). *Integrated Rural Development Approach in Nepal*. Kathmandu: Sahayogi Press.

Agri. Business Promotion and Marketing Development Directorate (2010). *Agricultural Marketing Information Bulletin: Special Issue 2010*. Lalitpur: Agri. Business Promotion and Marketing Development Directorate.

Amatya, Shaphalya (2004). *Rana Rule in Nepal*. New Delhi: Nirala Publications.

Amatya Prakash B and Ishwar K Shrestha (2010). *Industrial Relations and Enterprise Economic Survey Nepal- 2010*. Kathmandu: FNCCI.

APO (2017). *APO Productivity Databook 2017*. Tokyo: APO.

APROSC (1981). *Nepal: Trained Manpower for the Agriculture Sector*. Kathmandu.

APROSC (1982). *Nepal Food Grain Marketing and Price Policy*. Kathmandu.

APROSC and John Mellor Associates Inc. (1995). *Nepal Agriculture Perspective Plan*. Kathmandu: National Planning Commission and Asian Development Bank.

Arenas, Guillermo (2016). *Nepal Integration into Value Chains: Stylized Facts and Policy Options*. World Bank Policy Note 2. Washington DC: World Bank. Online Available in the World Bank Website at: http://documents.worldbank.org/curated/en/563961468325392934/pdf/106829-REVISED-WP-P154536-PUBLIC-PN2-GVCs.pdf.

Aryal, Krishna Raj (1970). *Education for the Development of Nepal*. Kathmandu: Shanti Prakashan.

Awasthi Bishnu D and Shrawan K Adhikari (2004). Agreement on Agriculture: Domestic Support Measures, in Ramesh P Sharma et al eds. *The Implication of the WTO Membership on the Nepalese Agriculture*. Nepal: FAO, UNDP and Ministry of Agriculture and Cooperative.

Balassa, Bela (1987). *Public Enterprises in Developing Countries: Issues of Privatization*. World Bank.

Bajracharya, Bhuban B et al (2006). *Technical Review of School Education in Nepal – 2005: A Report*. Kathmandu.

Bajracharya, Bhuban B (2010). Technical Education, Vocational Training and Employment Generation, in *Technical and Vocational Education and Training Development Journal*. Vol 1 No 10. Bhaktapur: CTEVT.

Bajracharya, Pushkar and Jagdish Agrawal (1980). Industrialization during the Rana Regime, in *Public Administration Journal*. 3(2). Kathmandu: Public Administration Campus.

Bajracharya, Pushkar and B K Shrestha (1983). *Problem in Manufacturing Public Enterprises in Nepal*. Kathmandu: Center for Economic Development and Administration.

Bajracharya, Pushkar and Shankar Sharma (1996). *Impact of Economic Liberalization in Nepal:* Kathmandu: IIDS.

Bajracharya, Pushkar and Shilu M Bajracharya (1999). Strategies for Poverty Alleviation: An Integrated Approach, in *Agriculture Credit*. Kathmandu: Agriculture Development Bank, Nepal.

Bajracharya, Pushkar and Shilu M Bajracharya (2002). Total Factor Productivity Growth in Nepal : An Estimate, in *Economic Journal of Development Issues*. 3(1). pp 101-110.

Bajracharya, Pushkar (2007). *Micro Enterprises Development Programme (MEDEP): Scoping Study*. UNDP.

Bajracharya, Pushkar (2011). Higher Education in Nepal: A Historical Perspective, in *Journal of Academia*. 1(1). Kathmandu: Democrat Professors' Association.

Bajracharya, Pushkar (2013). A Vision for Nepalese Development: Need for Breaking the Shackles of Inertia, in Madhavji Shrestha and Anjan Shakya eds *Vision: On Foreign Affairs*. Kathmandu: International Concern Center.

Bajracharya, Pushkar and Clive Grace (2014). *The Nepal Civil Service and Re-structuring of the State*. Kathmandu: Ministry of General Administration.

Bajracharya, Pushkar (2017). *10 Years Karnali Development Plan*. Kathmandu: Karnali Development Commission.

Bajracharya, Rojan et al. (2007). *Tourism a Sustainable Service Sector for South Asian Trade: Lesson from Nepal's Experience*. Islamabad: Sustainable Development Policy Network.

Baral, L S (1972). Opposition Groups in Nepal: 1960-1970, in *India Quarterly*. 28(1). pp 12-45. Reprint in Pratyoush Onta and

Lokranjan Parajuli eds. *Autocratic Monarchy: Politics in Panchayat Nepal.* pp 285-338 (2012). Kathmandu: Martin Chautari.

Baral, L S (1974). "Class Organization" in Nepal: Social Control and Interest Articulation, in *Asia Quarterly*. 3. pp 173-202. Reprint in Pratyoush Onta and Lokranjan Parajuli eds. *Autocratic Monarchy: Politics in Panchayat Nepal.* pp 251-284 (2012). Kathmandu: Martin Chautari.

Baral, Lok R (2004). Unclear Roadmap: Political Parties and the Parliamentary Practice, in Lok R Baral ed. *Political Parties and Parliament*. New Delhi: Adroit Publishers.

Baral, Lok R (2016). A Time for Caution, in *The Kathmandu Post.* Online Available at: https://kathmandupost.ekantipur.com/news/2016-02-08/a-time-for-caution.html.

Baskota, Mahesh (1989). Nepalese Economy and the Five Year Plan, in Kamal P Mall ed. *Nepal: Perspectives of Continuity and Change*. Kathmandu: Center for Nepal and Asian Studies.

Bastoka, Kamal (2012). Impact of Tourism on Local Employment and Incomes in Three Selected Destinations: Case Studies of Sauraha, Nagarkot and Bhaktapur, in *Nepal Tourism and Development Review.* Vol 1 No 2. School of Arts: Kathmandu University.

Bauman, Kurt J (1999). Shifting Family Definitions: The Effect of Cohabitation and Other Nonfamily Household Relationships on Measures of Poverty, in *Demography*. 36(3). pp 315-325.

Bhadra, Chandra (2007). *International Labor Migration of Nepalese Women: The Impact of their Remittances on Poverty Reduction.* ARTNET Working Paper Series 44.

Bhagwati, Jagdish and Arvind Panagariya (2013). *Why Growth Matters: How Economic Growth in India Reduced Poverty and the Lessons for Other Developing Countries*. New York: PublicAffairs.

Bhattachan, Krishna B (2007). Inclusive Restructuring of the State, in Anand Aditya ed *The Inclusive State Reflection on Reinventing Nepal.* Kathmandu: SAP-Nepal.

Bhattachan. Krishna B (2009). Discourse on Social Exclusion and Inclusion in Nepal: Old Wine in New Bottle, in *Identity & Society: Social Exclusion and Exclusion in Nepal.* Kathmandu: Mandala Book Point.

Bhattarai, Babu R (2003). Political Economy of the People's War, in Arjun Karki and David Seddon eds *The People's War in Nepal: Left Perspectives.* New Delhi: Adroit Publishers.

Bhattarai, Damodar (2009). Multi-purpose Projects, in Dwarika N Dhungel and Santa B Pun eds *The Nepal-India Water Relationship: Challenges.* Springer.

Bhattarai, Kamal Dev (2019). *Nepal Inching Toward China.* Online Available at: https://thediplomat.com/2019/05/nepal-inching-toward-china/.

Bista, Dor B (1967). *People of Nepal.* Reprint, Kathmandu: Ratna Pustak Bhandar. (2004).

Bista, Dor B (1991). *Fatalism and Development: Nepal's Struggle for Modernization.* Kolkata: Orient Longman Pvt. Ltd.

Bista, Binod P (2014). Conducting Nepal's Foreign Policy: Present Context, in *Principal and Strategies of Nepal's Foreign Policy and Protocol.* Kathmandu: IFA and Friedrich Ebert Stiftung.

Brown, Archie (2010). *The Rise and Fall of Communism.* London: Vintage Books.

Bruno, Michael, et al (1998). Equity and Growth in Developing Countries: Old and New Perspectives on the Policy Issues, in Vito Jami and Ke Yong Chu eds *Income Distribution and High Growth.* Cambridge, MA: MIT Press.

Burghart, Richard (1996). *The Conditions of Listening: Essays on Religion, History, and Politics in South Asia.* New Delhi: Oxford University Press. pp 226-60.

CAAN (2016). *Civil Aviation Report 2016.* Kathmandu.

Campbell, Duncan (2010). *Employment Targets for Making Employment Central to Growth: A Note on Nepal.* Geneva: ILO.

Caplan, Lonel (1970). *Land and Social Change in East Nepal.* London: Routledge and Kegna Paul.

Central Bureau of Statistics (Various Issues). *Statistical Year Book of Nepal.* Kathmandu: Government of Nepal.

Central Bureau of Statistics (2004). *Nepal Living Standard Survey 2003/04 Vol I and II.* Kathmandu: Government of Nepal.

Central Bureau of Statistics et al (2006). *Resilience Amidst Conflict: An Assessment of Poverty in Nepal, 1995-96 and 2003-04.* Kathmandu: World Bank Nepal Office.

Central Bureau of Statistics (2006). *Agricultural Census Monograph.* Kathmandu: Government of Nepal.

Central Bureau of Statistics (2011a). *Poverty in Nepal.* Kathmandu: Government of Nepal.

Central Bureau of Statistics (2011b). *Nepal Living Standard Survey 2010/11 Vol I and II.* Kathmandu: Government of Nepal.

Central Bureau of Statistics (2013). *National Sample Census of Agriculture Nepal 2011/12.* Kathmandu: Government of Nepal.

Central Bureau of Statistics and UNIDO (2014). *Developing Manufacturing in Nepal: Current Status and Future Challenges.* Kathmandu: Government of Nepal.

Central Bureau of Statistics (2019). *Report on the Nepal Labour Force Survey, 2017/18.* Kathmandu: Government of Nepal.

CESRAN International (2015). *Economic Development Model and Capitalism.* Online Available at: https://cesran.org/economic-development-models-and-capitalism.html.

Chen, Shaohua and Martin Ravallion (1996). Data in Transition: Assessing Rural Living Standards in Southern China, in *China Economic Review.* 7. pp 23-56.

Comte, Auguste (1830). *Cours de Philosophie Positive Vol I and II.* Michel Serres, Francois Dagognet and Allal Sinaceur eds. Paris: Hermaun.

Comte, Auguste (1848). *System of Positive Philosophy.* J H Bridges trans. New York: Burt Franklin.

Cowan, Sam (2015). *The Maharaja and the Monarch.* Online Available at https://www.recordnepal.com/wire/maharaja-and-monarch/.

Cowen, Michael P and Robert W Shenton (1996). *Doctrines of Development.* London: Routledge.

CPN-Maoist (2006). Chronology of Major Political Events and Military Raids during 10 Years' of People's War, in *The Worker: Ten Year Special.* No 10.

CTEVT (2015). *Global Demand Assessment for Nepalese Skilled Workforce: Report Based on Advertisement Analysis.* Bhaktapur: CTEVT.

Dahal (Prachanda), Pushpa K (2003). Inside the Revolution in Nepal, in Arjun Karki and David Seddon eds *The People's War in Nepal: Left Perspectives*. New Delhi: Adroit Publishers.

Dahal, Girdhari. (2018). Foreign Relation of Nepal with China and India, in *Journal of Political Science*. XVIII. pp 46-61.

Dangol, Sanu Bhai (1999). *The Palace in Nepalese Politics*. Kathmandu: Ratna Pustak Bhandar.

Dasgupta, Samir and Jan Nederveen Pieterse eds (2009). *Politics of Globalization*. New Delhi: Sage Publications.

Davis, Kingsley and Wilbert E Moore (1945). Some Principles of Stratification, in *American Sociological Review*. Vol 1 No 10. pp 242-249.

Deininger, Klaus and Lyn Squire (1996). A New Data Set Measuring Income Inequality, in *World Bank Economic Review*. 10(3). pp 565-591.

Demery, Lionel, et al (1995). *Poverty, Inequality and Growth*. ESP Discussion Paper No 70. Washington DC: World Bank.

Department of Industry (Various Issues). *Industrial Statistics*. Kathmandu: Government of Nepal.

Department of Cottage and Small Industries (2017). *Statistical Report of Industries*. Kathmandu: Government of Nepal.

Dhakal, Suresh (2001). Kanti Rajpath Slow Start, in *Spotlight*. 20(45). pp 10-11.

Dhakal, Suresh (2011). *Land Tenure and Agrarian Reforms in Nepal*. Kathmandu: Community Self Reliance Centre.

Dhital, Pankaj R (2017) Agriculture Extension in Nepal: Experience and Issues, in *Journal of Advance in Agriculture*. 7(3). pp 1071-1082. Online Available at https://doi.org/10.24297/jaa.v7i3.6287.

Dhungel, Dwarika N (2004). *Decentralized Governance: A Prospective of Nepal*. Kathmandu: Institute for Integrated Development Studies.

Dhungel, Dwarika N (2007). *Inside Out of Political Parties of Nepal*. Kathmandu: Institute of Integrated Development Studies.

Dhungel, Dwarika N and Santa B Pun eds (2009). *Nepal India Water Relationship: Challenges*. Springer.

Dixit, Praveen M (1994). *Economic Reform in Nepal: A Cursory Assessment.* Kathmandu: Center for Economic Development and Administration.

Dixit, Ajaya. 2007.*Continuing Reasoned Public Debate on Dams and Development: A Summary of National Dialogue on Dams and Development in Nepal.* Nepal: Nepal Water Conservation Foundation and IUCN.

Drèze, Jean and Amartya Sen (2013). *An Uncertain Glory: India and its Contradictions.* London: Penguin Books.

Durkheim, Emile (1893). *The Division of Labor in Society.* George Simpson trans. Reprint, Illinois: Free Press (1960).

Durkheim, Emile (1895). *The Rules of Sociological Method.* W D Halls trans. New York: The Free Press.

Durkheim, Emile (1912). *Elementary Forms of Religious Life.* Carol Cosman trans. Reprint, New York: Oxford University Press (2001).

Economist (2005). *The Economist Intelligence Unit's Quality of Line India.* Online Available at. https://www.economist.com/media/pdf/QUALITY_OF_LIFE.pdf .

Ellingson, Ter (1991). The Nepal Constitution of 1990: Preliminary Consideration, in *Himalayan, the Journal of the Association of Nepal and Himalayan Studies.* Vol 11. No 1. Article 5. Online available at : http://digitalcommons.macalester.edu/himalaya/vol11/iss1/5.

Federation of Contractors' Associations in Nepal (2018). *Nepal Construction Souvenir 2018.* Vol 23 No 26. Kathmandu.

Foster-Carter, Aidan (1973). Neo-Marxist Approaches to Development and Underdevelopment, in *Journal of Contemporary Asia.* Vol 3 Issue 1. pp 7-33.

Gaulee, Uttam (2014). Higher Education in Nepal: Opportunities Obscured by Internal Challenges, in T Karunakaran ed. *English Language Teaching in the Twenty First Century: Issues and Challenges.* Chennai: Kumaran Book House.

Gellner, David N ed (2008). *Resistance and the State: Nepalese Experience.* New Delhi: Social Science Press.

Ghimira, Yubraj (2018). How India and China are keeping the West out in Nepal. Online Available at: https://www.scmp.com/

week-asia/geopolitics/article/2156198/how-india-and-china-are-keeping-west-out-nepal.

Gill, Gerard J et al eds (1990). *Agriculture Statistics in Nepal: A User's Assessment.* Kathmandu: Ministry of Agriculture and Winrock International.

Gill, Peter (2009). The Politics of Land Reform in Nepal: 1951–1964, in *Studies in Nepali History and Society.* Vol14 No 2. pp 217–259.

Ghosh, Biswajit (2012). Understanding Development Theory and Practice, in Biswajit Ghosh ed *Discourses on Development.* Jaipur: Rawat Publication.

Glennerster, Howard et al (2004). *One Hundred Years of Poverty and Policy.* York: Joseph Rowntree Foundation.

Guha, Ramachandra (2007). *India after Gandhi: The History of The World's Largest Democracy.* Picador India.

Gurung, Harka (2003). *Trident and Thunderbolt: Cultural Dynamics in Nepalese Politics.* Kathmandu: Social Science Baha.

Gurung, Harka (2006). *From Exclusion to Inclusion: Socio-Political Agenda for Nepal.* Kathmandu: Social Inclusion Research Fund.

Gyawali, Dipak. 2001. *Water in Nepal.* Kathmandu: Himal Books.

Hachhethu, Krishna (2006). *Political Parties of Nepal.* Baha Occasional Papers 1. Kathmandu: Social Science Baha.

Hagen, Toni (1962). *Nepal: The Kingdom of Himalaya.* Reprint. Kathmandu: Himal Books. (2008).

Hilker, Deb Shova Kansakar (2005). *Syamukapu: The Lhasa Newars of Kalimpong and Kathmandu.* Kathmandu: Vajra Publications.

Hoftun, Martin, et al (1999). *People, Politics and Ideology: Democracy and Social Change in Nepal.* Kathmandu: Mandala Book Point.

Institute for Integrated Development Studies. (2018). *Nepal Economic Outlook 2017-18.* Kathmandu: Institute for Integrated Development Studies.

International Labor Organization (1980). *Poverty and Landless in Rural Asia.* Geneva.

International Labor Organization (2015). *Jobs and Skills for Youth: Review of Policies for Youth in Employment in Nepal.* Geneva ILO.

International Monetary Fund (2017). *World Economic Outlook: Gaining Momentum.* Washington D C: International Monetary Fund.

International Monetary Fund (2018). *South Asia Regional Update.* Washington D C: International Monetary Fund.

Jack, Gavin and Alison Phipps (2005). *Tourism and Intercultural Exchange: Why Tourism Matter.* Clevedon: Channel View Publication.

Jha, Hari Bansa (2012). Nepal's Border Relations with India and China, in *Eurasia Border Review.* Vol. 4 No. 1. Sapporo: Hokkaido University. pp 63-75.

Joshi, Bhuwan L and Leo E Rose (1966). *Democratic Innovation in Nepal: A Case Study of Political Acculturation.* Reprint, Kathmandu: Mandala Book Point. (2004).

Joshi, Durga Lal (2007). *Financing the Higher Education in Nepal.* Kathmandu: Center for Economic Development and Administration.

Joshi, Rajendra Dhoj (2018). *Higher Education in Nepal: Supporting Aspirations for Prosperity.* Submitted to Policy Think Tank, Government of Nepal.

Kansal, Satish (1981) *Data on Income Distribution in Nepal.* World Bank Working Paper 1981-2.

Karki, Arjun. 2004. *Political Process and Challenges for Land Reform and Agrarian Reform in Nepal.* Global University for Sustainability.

Karki, Arjun and David Seddon eds (2003). *The People's War in Nepal: Left Perspectives.* New Delhi: Adroit Publishers.

Karmacharya, Binod K (2002) *Nepal's Informal Trade with India.* South Asia Network Economic Institutes.

KC, Fatta B (2003). Performance of Public Enterprises in Nepal, in *Economic Review*. No 11. Kathmandu: Nepal Rastra Bank.

KC, Surendra (2003). *Nepal ma Communist Andolan ko Itihas- Dosro Bhaaga: 2020-2049 (History of the Communist Movement in Nepal- Volume 2: 1963-1992).* Kathmandu: Vidrathi Pustak Bhandar. (in Nepali).

KC, Surendra (2008). *Nepal ma Communist Andolan ko Itihas- Teshro Bhaaga: 2050-2064 (History of the Communist Movement in*

Nepal-Volume 3: 1993-2008). Kathmandu: Vidrathi Pustak Bhandar. (in Nepali).

KC, Bijaya and Ashok R Pandey (2009). Stock Market and Mutual Fund in Nepal, in *Nepalese Financial System: Growth and Challenges.* Kathmandu: Nepal Rastra Bank.

KC, Bal Kumar et al (2013). *Forced Labour of Adults and Children in the Agriculture Sector of Nepal: Focusing on Haruwa-Charuwa in Eastern Terai and Haliya in Far-Western Hills.* Kathmandu :International Labour Organization. Online Available at: http://www.ilo.org/kathmandu/whatwedo/publications/WCMS_217086/lang--en/index.htm.

Khanal, Dilli R. and Nav R Kanel (2005). *Macroeconomic Policy, Shocks and Poverty Reduction in Nepal.* Kathmandu: Institute for Policy Research and Development.

Khaniya, Tirtha R (2007). *New Horizons in Education in Nepal.* Kathmandu.

Khatri, Shreedhar K (1997). Nepal in the International System: The Limits of Power of a Small State, in Anand Aditya ed. *The Political Economy of Small State.* Kathmandu: Nepal Foundation for Advanced Studies and Friedrich Ebert Stifung.

Kisan. Yam B (2009). A Study of Dalit's Inclusion in Nepali Sate Governance, in *Identity & Society: Social Exclusion and Exclusion in Nepal.* Kathmandu: Mandala Book Point.

Koirala, Parashar and Pushkar Bajracharya (2004). Nepalese Capital Market: Issues and Challenges, in *Economic Review.* No 16. Kathmandu: Nepal Rastra Bank.

Kumar, Dhruba (1989). National Security and Foreign Policy in Nepal, in Kamal P Malla ed. *Nepal: Perspectives on Continuity and Change.* Kathmandu: Center for Nepal and Asian Studies.

Lama, Mahendra P (2003). Strategic Aid. in *Nepali Times. No* 129

Lamsal, Yuba Nath (2019). Diplomacy in Kirat and Lichchhivi Period, in *The Rising Nepal*, 13th July. Kathmandu: Gorkhapatra Corporation.

Lewis, Oscar (1966). The Culture of Poverty, in *Scientific American.* Vol 215 No 4. pp 19–25.

Lewis, Todd Thornton and Daya Ratna Shakya (1988). Contributions to the History of Nepal: Eastern Newar Diaspora

Settlement, in *Contribution Nepalese Studies.* Vol 15 No 1. Kathmandu: CNAS.

Ligal, Prithvi R (2014). *How we Abolished the Licence Raj.* Online version of Ekantipur available at: http://money2014.ekantipur.com/detail.php?art=5&cat=revisiting-reform.

Maden, Kamal et al (2009). Documentation of Indigenous Knowledge, Skill and Practices of Kirat Nationalities with Special Focus on Biological Resource, in *Identity and Society: Social Inclusion and Exclusion in Nepal.* Kathmandu: Mandala book Point.

Mahat, Ram Sharan (2005). *In Defence of Democracy: Dynamics and Fault Lines of Nepal's Political Economy.* New Delhi: Adroit Publishers.

Maskay, Nephil M (2002).*The Exchange rate Policy of Nepal vis-à-vis The Indian Currency.* Kathmandu: Nepal Foundation for Advanced Studies.

METCON Consultant. 1994. *Assessment on Technical Assistance to Nepal's Agriculture and Irrigation between 1950 to 1990.* Kathmandu.

Meyer, Richard L (2011). *Subsidies as an Instrument in Agriculture Finance: A Review.* Washington DC: World Bank.

Mehrotra Santosh and Enrique Delamonica (2007). *Eliminating Human Poverty: Macroeconomic and Social Policies for Equitable Growth.* Hyderabad: Orient Longman.

Mihaly, Eugene B (2002). *Foreign Aid and Politic in Nepal.* Kathmandu: Himal Books.

Ministry of Agriculture Development (2013). *Krisi Sambandhi Niti haru ko Sangalo (Compilation of Agriculture Related Policies).* Kathmandu: Government of Nepal. (in Nepali).

Ministry of Agriculture Development (2015). *Agriculture Development Strategy (ADS) 2015-2035 Part I.* Kathmandu: Government of Nepal.

Ministry of Commerce and Supplies (2010). *Nepal Trade Integration Strategy 2010: Executive Summary.* Kathmandu: Government of Nepal.

Ministry of Commerce (2016). *Nepal Trade Integration Strategy 2016: Executive Summary.* Kathmandu: Government of Nepal.

Ministry of Commerce (2017). *Compendium of Transit Treaties & Agreement of Nepal.* Kathmandu: Government of Nepal.

Ministry of Culture, Tourism and Civil Aviation (2019). *Nepal Tourism Statistics 2018*. Kathmandu: Government of Nepal.

Ministry of Education (1971). *The National Education System Plan for 1971-76*. Kathmandu: His Majesty's Government of Nepal.

Ministry of Education (1997). *The Basic and Primary Education Master Plan for 1997 – 2002*. Kathmandu: His Majesty's Government of Nepal.

Ministry of Education (2016).*School Sector Development Plan 2016-2023*. Kathmandu: Government of Nepal.

Ministry of Finance (Various Issues). *Economic Survey*. Kathmandu: Government of Nepal.

Ministry of Finance (2008a). *Nepal: An Assessment of the Public Finance Management Performance Measurement Framework as of FY 2005/06*. Kathmandu: Government of Nepal.

Ministry of Finance (2008b). *Budget Tarjuma Dighadarsan Choutho Sanskaran* (*Budget Preparation Directive 4th Edition)*. Kathmandu: Government of Nepal. (in Nepali).

Ministry of Finance (2015). *Public Expenditure and Financial Accountability Assessment: Nepal PFM Performance Assessment II as of FY 2013/14*. Kathmandu: Government of Nepal.

Ministry of Finance (2018). *Annual Performance Review of Public Enterprises*. Kathmandu: Government of Nepal.

Ministry of Finance (2019a). *Budget Tarjuma Dighadarsan Aathou Sanskaran* (*Budget Preparation Directive 8th Edition)*. Kathmandu: Government of Nepal. (in Nepali).

Ministry of Finance (2019b). *Budget Speech of Fiscal Year 2019/20*. Kathmandu: Government of Nepal.

MOICS and UNIDO (2002). *Industrial Development Perspective Plan: Vision 2020*. Kathmandu: Government of Nepal.

MOLE (2016). *Labor Migration for Employment (A Status Report for Nepal: 2014/15)*. Kathmandu: Government of Nepal.

Ministry of Law Justice and Parliamentary Affairs (2016). *Identification and Prioritization of Laws Necessary for the Implementation of the Constitution and the Current State of Law Making*. Kathmandu: Government of Nepal.

Moene, Karl O and MichaeI Wallerstein (2006). The Scandinavian Model and Economic Development, in *Development Outreach*. Vol 8 No 1. Washington DC: World Bank.

Mukit, Dewan Muktadir Al et al (2014). Stock Market Development and Economic Growth: An Evidence from SAARC Countries, in *Anveshak International Journal of Management*. Vol 3 No 1. pp 45-60. Pune: Indira Institute of Management.

Muni, S D (2009). *India's Foreign Policy: the Democracy Dimension*. Foundation India.

NARMA Consultancy (2006). *Impact of Fertilizer Deregulation Policy*. Kathmandu: Ministry of Agriculture and Cooperative.

National Education Planning Commission. (1956). *Education in Nepal*. Kathmandu.

National Planning Commission (Various Editions). *Development Plan*. Kathmandu: Government of Nepal.

National Planning Commission (1978). *Employment, Consumption and Income Distribution Survey*. Kathmandu: Government of Nepal.

National Planning Commission (2012): *Assessment of Social Security Allowance Programs in Nepal*. Kathmandu: Government of Nepal.

National Planning Commission (2016). *Nepal and the Millennium Development Goals Final Status Report 2000-2015*. Kathmandu: Government of Nepal.

Nepal, Rosan S (2019). Bhattarai, Yadav Form New Party. in *The Himalayan Time*. May 07. Online available at https://thehimalayantimes.com/nepal/bhattarai-yadav-form-new-party/.

Nepal Chamber of Commerce (2017). *Improving Trade Environment: by Addressing Existing Barrier to Trade*. Kathmandu.

Nepal Rastra Bank (2005). *Banking and Financial Statistics*. Kathmandu.

Nepal Rastra Bank (2011). *Banking and Financial Statistics*. Kathmandu.

Nepal Rastra Bank (2012). *Financial Stability Report*. Kathmandu.

Nepal Rastra Bank (2016). *Nepal Rastra Bank: Then, Now and Ahead*. Kathmandu.

Nepal Rastra Bank (2018b). *Financial Stability Report*. Kathmandu.

Nepal Rastra Bank (2018a). *Quarterly Economic Bulletin*. Kathmandu.

Office of Auditor General (2014). *Mahalekha Paricheka ko Baunnau Pratibedan (Auditor General's 52nd Annual Report)*. Kathmandu: Office of Auditor General. (in Nepali).

Office of Auditor General. (2017). *Mahalekha Paricheka ko Chaunnau Pratibedan (Auditor General's 54th Annual Report)*. Kathmandu: Office of Auditor General. (in Nepali).

Ozaki, Mayumi (2014). *Financial Sector Reform in Nepal – What Works, What Doesn't*. Manila: ADB.

Panagariya, Arvind, 2004. *The Challenges of Subsidies and Trade Barriers*. Copenhagen Consensus.

Panday, Devendra R (1989). The State of Political Economy, in Kamal P Malla ed. *Nepal: Perspectives on Continuity and Change*. Kathmandu: Center for Nepal and Asian Studies.

Panday, Devendra R (1999). *Nepal's Failed Development: Reflection on the Mission and the Maladies*. Kathmandu: Nepal South Asian Center.

Panday, Devendra R (2011). *Looking at Development and Donors: Essays from Nepal*. Seira Tamang ed. Kathmandu: Martin Chautari.

Panday, Rabi Jung (2016). National Images Challenges for South Asian Sub-regional Nations to Sustain Tourism Growth, in *Journal of Tourism and Hospitality*. Vol 6. Lalitpur: AITM School of Hotel Management.

Pant, Yadav P (1956). Budget in Nepal. in *Economic & Political Weekly*. Volume 8. Issue 16.

Pant, Yadav P (1962). Nepal China Trade Relation, in *The Economic Weekly*. Online Available at: https://www.epw.in/system/files/pdf/1962_14/15/nepalchina_trade_relations.pdf.

Pant, Yadav P (1982). *Economic Development of Nepal*. Allahabad: Kitab Mahal.

Pant, Prem R and Pushkar Bajracharya (2019). *Business Environment in Nepal*. Kathmandu: Buddha Academic Publishers and Distributors.

Parajuli, Lokranjan (2012). From Controlling Access to Crafting Minds: Experiment in Education in Late Rana Nepal, in *Studies in Nepali History and Society*. Vol 17 No 2. Kathmandu: Mandala Book Point. pp 297-330.

Parsons, Talcott (1964). *Social Structure Personality*. New York: The Free Press.

Parsons, Talcott (1967). *The Structure of Social Action*. Reprint, New York: The Free Press (2002).

Parliament Secretariat (2013). *Sambhidhan Sabha Darpan (Reflection of Constitutional Assembly)*. Kathmandu: Parliament Secretariat. (in Nepali).

Paudyal, Lokendra P (2010). Push and Pull Factor of Migration: A Challenge of Employing Youths in Nepal, in *Technical and Vocational Education and Training Development Journal*. Vol 1 No 10. Bhaktapur: CTEVT.

Paudel, Dandapani (2009). Central Banking Practices and Evolving Challenges to Nepal Rastra Bank, in *Nepalese Financial System: Growth and Challenges*. Kathmandu: Nepal Rastra Bank.

Picclotto, Robert and Jock R Anderson (1997). Reconsidering Agricultural Extension, in *World Bank Research Observer*. Vol 12 No 2. pp 249-59.

Pieterse, Jan Nederveen (2001). *Development Theory*. New Delhi: Vistaar Publications.

Piketty, Thomas (2017). *Capital in Twenty First Century*. Arthur Goldhammer trans. Cambridge: Harvard University Press.

Piya, Sujan et al (2011). Sources of Agricultural Productivity Growth in South and Southeast Asia, in *Trends in Agricultural Economics*. 4. pp 18-29.

Poertner, Ephraim et al (2011). Migration in far west Nepal: Intergenerational Linkages between Internal and International Migration of Rural-to-Urban migrants, in *Critical Asian Studies*. 43 (1). pp 23-47.

Pokharel, Ramesh and Surya Raj Acharya (2015). Sustainable Transport Development in Nepal: Challenges, Opportunities and Strategies, in *Journal of the Eastern Asia Society for Transportation Studies*. Vol. 11. pp 209-226. Online Available at: https://www.researchgate.net/publication/304734740_Sustainable_Transport_Development_in_Nepal_Challenges_Opportunities_and_Strategies.

Poyck, Maria C et al (2016). *Joint Evaluation of Nepal's School Sector Reform Plan Programme 2009-2016 Final Report*. Hamburg: GFA Consulting Group.

Pun. Santa B (2009). Power Trading, in Dwarika N Dhungel and Santa B Pun eds *The Nepal-India Water Relationship: Challenges*. Springer.

Pyakuryal, Bishwambher (2013). *Nepal's Development Tragedy: Threats and Possibilities*. Kathmandu: Fine Print.

Pyakuryal, Kiran N (1980). *The Concept and Operation of Rural Development in Strategic Elements of Rural Development*. Kathmandu: Center for Economic Development and Administration.

Ra, Sungsup and Chang Yong Rhee (2005). *Nepal Macroeconometirc Model.* Kathmandu: ADB, Nepal Resident Mission.

Ra, Sungsup and Bipul Singh (2005).*Measuring the Economic Costs of Conflict*. Kathmandu: ADB, Nepal Resident Mission.

Rajbahak, Ram P (1989). Nepal's Foreign Trade, in Kamal P Mall ed. *Nepal: Perspectives of Continuity and Change*. Kathmandu: Center for Nepal and Asian Studies.

Rajbhandari, Jasmine (2018). *Social Protection and Jobs in Nepal*. Online Available at: www.iids.org.np/sites/default/files/doc_events/Ms.%20Jasmine%20RajBhandary.pdf.

Rana, Madhukar SJB (2013). China Meets India in Nepal: A Historical and Future Perspective, in *Indian Journal of Asian Affairs*. Vol. 26 No. 1/2. pp 59-73.

Rana, Pradumna B and Binod Karmacharya (2014). *A Connectivity-Driven Development Strategy for Nepal: From a Landlocked to a Land-Linked State*. ADBI Working Paper 498. Tokyo: Asian Development Bank Institute. Online Available at: http://www.adbi.org/workingpaper/2014/09/08/6409.connectivity.dev.strategy.nepal/.

Rapley, John (2007). *Understanding Development: Theory and Practice in the Third World*. Colorado: Lynne Rienner Publisher.

Ravallion, Martin and Shaohua Chen (1996). *What can New Survey Data Tell us about Recent Changes in Distribution and Poverty*. World Bank Paper. Washington DC: World Bank.

Rawal, Navin (2008). Social Inclusion and Exclusion: A Review, in *Dhaulagiri journal of Sociology and Anthropology.* Vol II. pp 161-180.

Regmi, Dilli R (1961). *Modern Nepal: Rise and Growth in the Eighteenth Century (Volume I & II).* Reprint, New Delhi: Rupa & Co. (2007).

Regmi, Dilli R (1965). *Medieval Nepal Volume I and II.* Reprint, Kathmandu: Rupa & Co. (2010).

Regmi, Dwaipayan (2018). Insider Trading, in *The Kathmandu Post.* Vol XXVI No 051. Online Available at https://kathmandupost.ekantipur.com/news/2018-04-10/insider-trading.html.

Regmi, Govinda P (1994). *Industrial Growth in Nepal: A Sectoral Growth and Regional Analysis.* New Delhi: Oxford and IBH Publishing Co. Pvt. Ltd.

Regmi, Mahesh C (1984). *The State and Economic Surplus: Production, Trade and Resource Mobilization in Early 19th Century Nepal.* Varanasi: Nath Publishing House.

Regmi, Mahesh C (1988). *An Economic History of Nepal 1846-1901.* Varanasi: Nath Publishing House.

Regmi, Mahesh C (2002). *Nepal: An Historical Miscellany.* New Delhi: Adroit Publishers.

Regmi, Udaya R (2012). Stock Market Development and Economic Growth: Empirical Evidence from Nepal, in *Administration and Management Review.* Vol 24 No 1. pp 1-28.

Riaz Ali and Subho Basu (2007). *Paradise Lost? State Failure in Nepal.* New Delhi: Adarsh Books.

Rimal, Bishnu et at (2005). *Issues of the World of Work in Nepal.* Kathmandu: GEFONT.

Rose. Leo (1971). *Nepal Strategy for Survival.* Reprint, Kathmandu: Mandala Book Point. (2010).

Sapkota, Krishna P et al (2009). *Nepal ko Saghiye Sanrachana ma Tahagat Sarakar Bicha Karye Jimmebari ra Adhikar ko Nichepan: Bhaga Char (Power Devolution and Function Unbundling in Federal Structure of Nepal: Volume 4).* Lalitpur: Association of District Development Coordination Committees of Nepal. (in Nepali).

Satyal, Vikash (2019). Bidesh Palayan Rokau (Stop Foreign Migration), in *Nagarik.* 2nd April. (in Nepali). Online Available at https://nagariknews.nagariknetwork.com/news/72950/.

Savada, Andrea Matles ed. (1991). *Nepal: A Country Study.* Washington: GPO for the Library of Congress. Online Available at http://countrystudies.us/nepal/.

SAWTEE (2007). *Addressing the Impact of Garment Quota Phase-out on Nepal.* Research Brief No 1. Kathmandu. Online Available at: http://www.sawtee.org/publications/Research-Brief-2.pdf.

SAWTEE (2008). *Nepal's Export Potential in Services: Health, Education and High-end Retail Services.* Submitted to Enhancing Nepal's Trade Related Capacity, Ministry of Industry Commerce and Supplies/UNDP.

SEBON (2017). *Nepal Dhitopatra Board Pachish Barsha 2050-2074 (Nepal Security Board's 25 Years 2050-2074).* Lalitpur. (in Nepali)

Seddon, David (1987). *Nepal A State of Poverty.* New Delhi: Vikas Publishing House.

Seddon, David (2005). *Nepal's Dependence on Exporting Labor.* Washington: Migration Policy Institute. Online Available at https://www.migrationpolicy.org/article/nepals-dependence-exporting-labor.

Sen. Amartya (2000). *Social Exclusion: Concept, Application and Scrutiny.* Social Development Paper No 1. Manila: Asian Development Bank.

Sen, Jahar (1971). India's Trade with Central Asia via Nepal, in *Bulletin of Tibetology*, Vol. 8 No 2. Gangtok: Namgyal Institute of Tibctology. Online Available at: http://himalaya.socanth.cam.ac.uk/collections/journals/bot/pdf/bot_08_02_full.pdf.

Shah, Rishikesh (1990). *Modern Nepal-a Political History: 1769-1955.* New Delhi: Manohar Publishers and Distributors.

Shah, Vivek K (2018). *Witnessing Palace, Power and Politics: Memoir of a Military Secretary.* Fineprint Books.

Shakya, Bijendra (2005). *Sustaining Nepalese Garment Industries after Quota Abolition.* Kathmandu: Garment Association Nepal.

Shakya, Surya Bahadur (1984). *Establishing Tribhuvan University.* Kathmandu: Research Division, Tribhuvan University.

Sharma, Gopi Nath (1990). The Impact of Education during the Rana Period in Nepal, in *Himalayan the Journal of the Association for Nepal and Himalayan Studies.* Vol 10 No 6 Article 6.

Sharma, Om (2013). Impact of Annual Budgets in Economic Development of Nepal: An Econometric Analysis, in *Economic Literature*. Vol. XI.

Sharma, Prayag R (2004). *The State and Society in Nepal: Historical Foundation and Contemporary Trend.* Lalitpur: Himal Books.

Sharma, Ramesh and Jock R Anderson (1985). *Nepal and the CGIAR Centers: A Study of their Collaboration in Agriculture Research.* Washington DC: The World Bank.

Sharma Ramesh, et al eds (2002). *The Implication of the WTO Membership on the Nepalese Agriculture.* Kathmandu: FAO, UNDP and Ministry of Agriculture and Cooperative.

Sharma, Suresh R (1989). Education: Then and Now, in Kamal P Malla ed. *Nepal: Perspectives on Continuity and Change.* Kathmandu: Center for Nepal and Asian Studies.

Sharma, Tanka N (2010). Technical Vocational Education and Training Focused on Soft Skill in Reference to School Sector Reform in Nepal, in *Technical and Vocational Education and Training Development Journal.* Vol 1 No 10. Bhaktapur: CTEVT.

Shrestha, Badri P (1981). *The Economy of Nepal.* Kathmandu: Ratna Pustak Bhandar.

Shrestha, Badri P (1989). Planning and Development in Nepal, in Kamal P Malla ed. *Nepal: Perspectives on Continuity and Change.* Kathmandu: Center for Nepal and Asian Studies.

Shrestha, Ganesh K (2004). Financial Sector Reform in Nepal, in *Economic Review.* No 16. Kathmandu: Nepal Rasta Bank. pp 75-90.

Shrestha, Gyanu R (2003). *Nepal India Bilateral Trade Relations: Problem and Prospect.* New Delhi: Research and Information System.

Shrestha, Hrai P and Prami Shrestha (2012). Tourism in Nepal: a Historical Perspective and Present Trend of Development, in *Himalayan Journal of Sociology & Anthropology*. Vol 5. pp 54-75.

Shrestha, Mangal (1975). *Public Administration in Nepal.* Kathmandu: Educational Enterprises.

Shrestha, Prakash K and Biggyan R Subedi (2014). Determinants of Stock Market Performance in Nepal, in *Economic Review*. Kathmandu: Nepal Rastra Bank.

Shrestha, Prakash K (2017). Economic Liberalization in Nepal: Evaluating the Change in Economic Structure, Employment and Productivity, in *Journal of Development Innovations*. Vol 1 No 1. pp 60-83.

Shrestha, Ram Krishna (2010). Fertilizer Policy Development in Nepal, in *The Journal of Agriculture and Environment*. Vol 11.

Silver, Hilary (1995). Reconceptualizing Social Disadvantage: Three Paradigms of Social Exclusion, in Rodger et al eds *Social Exclusion: Rhetoric, Reality and Response*. Geneva: International Institute of Labor Studies.

Snellinger, Amanda (2005). A Crisis in Nepali Student Politics? Analyzing the Gap between Politically Active and Non-Active Students, in *Peace and Democracy in South Asia*. Vol 1 Issues 1. 18-44.

Spencer, Herbert (1855). *The Study of Sociology*. London: Longman.

Spencer, Herbert (1873). *Principal of Psychology*. London: Henry S King & Co.

Spencer, Herbert (1884). *The Men versus The State*. Reprint, Liberty Classic (1981).

Stevens, Stan (1988). Tourism and Development in Nepal, in *Kroeber Anthropological Society Paper*. No 67/68. University of California. pp 67-80.

Stiglitz, Joesph (2007). *Making Globalization Work*. London: Penguin Books.

Stiller, Ludwig F (1989). Modern Nepal, in Kamal P Mall ed. *Nepal: Perspectives of Continuity and Change*. Kathmandu: Center for Nepal and Asian Studies.

Stokke, Kristian and Mohan D Manandhar eds (2010). *State and Society: Social Inclusion and Exclusion in Nepal*. Kathmandu: Mandala Book Point.

Svalheim, Peter (2015). *Power for Nepal: Odd Hoftun & the History of Hydropower Development*. Katherine M Parent trans. Kathmandu: Martin Chautari.

Taneja, Nisha et. al. (2002). *Informal Trade in the SAARC Region: A Case Study of India, Sri Lanka and Nepal.* South Asia Network of Economic research Institutes.

TAF (2012). *A Guide to Government in Nepal: Structures, Functions and Practices.* Kathmandu: TAF.

TAF et al (2013). *Labor Migration Trends and Patterns Bangladesh, India and Nepal 2013.* Kathmandu: TAF.

Tamang, Sujata, Krishna P. Paudel and Krishna K. Shrestha (2014). Feminization of Agriculture and its Implications for Food Security in Rural Nepal, in *Journal of Forest and Livelihood.* 12(1). pp 20-31.

TEPC (Various Issues). *Nepal Oversea Trade Statistics.* Lalitpur.

TFM (1983). *Internal and International Migration in Nepal: Summary and Recommendations.* National Commission on Population.

Thapa, Bishow Bandhu (2012). BP Sanga Bhet, Gaupharka Bata Chaat (Meeting with BP, Loose Go Back to Village), *in Nepal National Weekly.* Year 13 No 3.

Timilsina, Parthibeswar P (1989). Industrialization Effort in Nepal: Problem and Perspectives, in Kamal P Malla ed. *Nepal: Perspectives on Continuity and Change.* Kathmandu: Center for Nepal and Asian Studies.

Townsend, Peter (1979). *Poverty in the United Kingdom: A Survey of Household Resources and Standards of Living.* London: Allen Lane and Penguin Books.

Transparency International (2018). *Corruption Perception Index 2018.* Berlin: Transparency International.

Tuladhar, Raju, Chandan Sapkota and Naveen Adhikari (2014). *Effects of Migration and Remittance Income on Nepal's Agriculture Yield.* Manila: ADB.

UGC (2018). *Education Management Information System 20161/17.* Kathmandu: UGC.

UNDP (2004). *Nepal Human Development Report: Empowerment and Poverty Reduction.* Kathmandu: UNDP Nepal.

UNDP (2014). *Nepal Human Development Report: Beyond Geography Unlocking Human Potential.* Kathmandu: UNDP Nepal.

United Nations (2018). *6 Clean Water and Sanitation.* New York: United Nations.

United Nations Economic and Social Commission for Asia and the Pacific (2003).*Transit Transport Issues in Landlocked and Transit Developing Countries*. New York: United Nations.

Upreti, B.C (2002). *The Marginal Migrants: A Study of Nepali Emigrants in India*. Delhi: Kalinga Publications.

Weber, Marx (1949). *Methodology of Social Science.* Edward A Shils and Henry A Finch eds and trans. Reprint, New Brunswick: Transaction Publishers (2011).

WFP and FAO (2007). *Food and Agriculture Market in Nepal.* Kathmandu: WFP Nepal Office and FAO Nepal Office.

Wheltop, John (2005). *A History of Nepal.* Cambridge University Press.

Wolf, Charles et al (2011). China and India, 2025: A Comparative Assessment. RAND National Defense Research Institute.

Wood, Hugh B (1965). *The Development of Education in Nepal.* Washington DC: US Department of Health, Education and Welfare.

World Bank (1979). *Nepal Development: Performance and Prospects.* Washington DC: World Bank.

World Bank (1984). *Staff Appraisal Report Nepal: Third Highway Project*. Washington DC.

World Bank (1990). *Agriculture Extension: The Next Step.* Washington DC.

World Bank (1992). *World Development Report 1992: Development and the Environment*. Washington DC.

World Bank (1994). *Nepal Fiscal Restructuring and Public Resource Management in Nineties.* Washington DC: World Bank.

World Bank (2003). *Nepal: Trade and Competitive Study.* 33793. Online Available at: http://documents.worldbank.org/curated/en/817271468290458750/Nepal-Trade-and-competitiveness-study.

World Bank (2005). *Agriculture Investment Sourcebook: Agriculture and Rural Development.* Washington DC: World Bank.

World Bank and DFID (2006). *Unequal Citizen: Gender, Caste and Ethnic Exclusion in Nepal.* Kathmandu: World Bank and DFID.

World Bank (2011). *Large-Scale Migration and Remittance in Nepal: Issues, Challenges and Opportunities.* Washington DC: World Bank.

World Bank and Government of Nepal (2013). *Nepal Road Sector Assessment Study: Main Report*. Kathmandu: Government of Nepal.

World Bank (2017a). *World Development Report: Governance and Law*. Washington DC.

World Bank (2017b). *Nepal Development Update: Strong Rebound, Mounting Risks*. Washington DC.

World Bank (2018). *Nepal Systematic Country Diagnostic*. Washington DC: World Bank.

World Bank (2019a). *Doing Business 2019 - Training for Reform: Economic Profile South Asia*. World Bank Group. Online Available at: http://www.doingbusiness.org/content/dam/doingBusiness/media/Profiles/Regional/DB2019/SA.pdf.

World Bank (2019b). Nepal Development Update. Washington DC: World Bank.

Yadav, Ram P (1989). Agriculture Development Strategies in Nepal, in Kamal P Mall ed. *Nepal: Perspectives of Continuity and Change*. Kathmandu: Center for Nepal and Asian Studies.

Zaman, M A (1973). Evaluation of Land Reform in Nepal. Kathmandu: Ministry of Land Reform.

Websites

Central Bureau of Statistic website available at: https://cbs.gov.np/.

CTEVT website available at: http://ctevt.org.np/page.php?page=26.

Department of Railways, Nepal website available at: http://www.dorw.gov.np/.

FAO Data website available at http://www.fao.org/faostat/en/#data.

Election Manifestos of Political Parties

Nepali Congress: Manifestos for Elections of 1991, 1994, 1999, 2008, 2013 and 2017.

Communist Party of Nepal-Unified Marxist Leninist: Manifestos for Elections of 1991, 1994, 1999, 2008 and 2013.

Communist Party of Nepal, Maoist: Manifestos for Elections of 2008 and 2013.

Nepali Communist Party: Manifesto for election of 2017.

INDEX

ABOUT THE AUTHORS

Pushkar Bajracharya, Professor of management at Tribhuvan University with many scholastic accolades during his studies, retired after teaching more than 43 years and is still teaching, the experience crossing 46 years. To his credit, he has conducted a large number of research works both in Nepal and abroad. He has also authored a number of books and published numerous articles both in Nepal and abroad. He has produced numerous doctoral outputs. He has been a keynote speaker/speaker at numerous national and international forums including universities all over the world. He has specialized in policy formulation, policy analysis, poverty analysis, trade, industry, micro enterprises, strategic management and institution building. He has been involved in policy formulation and planning exercises for Government of Nepal. Besides being a professional teacher, he has served as Member of National Planning Commission, Government of Nepal during 2009-2011; Chairperson of Nepal Trade Promotion Board; Executive Director of CEDA; Member of Board of Directors at Gorkhapatra Corporation and Employees' Provident Fund Corporation and also a member of the team leading to the formation of South Asian University, New Delhi. He has been chairperson or a member of many committees of the Government of Nepal, University systems and other agencies including international agencies. Currently, he is associated with Tribhuvan University, Kathmandu University, Nepal Open University, Mid-Western University and South Asian University. He has received education from Tribhuvan University, Heriot Watt University, Edinburgh and University of Delhi, Delhi. He, at present, is the President of Global College International (GCI), a member of Global College group.

Mohan Das Manandhar is an expert in the politics of development, development management and social inclusion and has more than 30 years of hands-on experience working with government, in development and private sector organizations in Nepal, South Asia, South East Asia, and Africa. Mr Manandhar's work with government has seen him serve as a policy advisor to Nepal's National Inclusion Commission at the Office of the Prime Minister, Government of Nepal; a board member of the Alternative Energy Promotion Development Board, Government of Nepal; and as Senior Advisor at the Social Inclusion Research Fund. He has been Senior Academic Adviser at Nepal Administrative Staff College and Senior Policy Advisor at Nepal Law Society. Currently Mr Manandhar is Chairperson and Executive Director of Niti Foundation and Chairperson of Organisation Development Centre (ODC). He has been a visiting scholar at the Department of Urban Studies and Planning at Massachusetts Institute of Technology (USA). He was Assistant Professor and Interim Dean at School of Management, Kathmandu University, was Head of Institute at the Ace Institute of Management and visiting faculty at Lancaster University (UK). His publications include the co-edited volume, State and Society: Social Exclusion and Inclusion in Nepal (Mandala, 2010) and the co-authored book, Organisation Development in the South (Ekta, 2002). He holds Master of Business Administration from International University of Japan and Bachelor of Civil Engineering from Indian Institute of Technology, Roorkee (India).

Rojan Bajracharya, an Economist associated with Organisation Development Centre (ODC), has been working in development projects of Nepal since last two decades. He has worked as consultant for ADB, SNV-Nepal, UNICEF, Palladium, Agrifood Consulting International and others. He was also engaged for a short time in Economic Policy Research Institute and Institute of Policy Research and Development. He has also edited the book titled "Social Inclusion and Nation Building in Nepal: Abstract for Researches" for Social Inclusion Research Fund in 2009. He was also a team member from PACE Nepal Pvt Ltd to develop "Nepal Trade Integration Strategy 2016" for Ministry of Commerce, GON. He also acted as a consultant of ADB in Nepal Rastra Bank under Technical Assistance of Strengthening Capacity for Macro Economic Analysis. He was also engaged as Project Associate in Ministry of Finance under ADB Technical Assistance of Strengthening Institutional Capacity of Public Debt Management. He is also a founding member of Nepal Energy Foundation.